fifth edition

Race Relations

BB12   00

Harry H. L. Kitano

University of California–Los Angeles

Prentice Hall
Upper Saddle River, New Jersey 07458

Library of Congress Cataloging-in-Publication Data

Kitano, Harry H. L.
   Race relations / Harry H. L. Kitano.—5th ed.
      p.   cm.
   Includes bibliographical references and index.
   ISBN 0-13-011677-7
   1. United States—Race relations.   2. Prejudices—United States.
I. Title.
E184.A1K47 1997
305.8′00973—dc20
                                                                96–14816
                                                                CIP

This volume is dedicated to all who wish to see healthy relationships between racial and ethnic groups. People must be open to ideas, whether they agree with them or not, and racial discrimination and violence have no place in a democratic society. Instead, patience and understanding are two important building blocks toward a healthy society.

Editorial director: Charlyce Jones Owen
Editor in chief: Nancy Roberts
Associate editor: Sharon Chambliss
Editorial/production supervision: Marianne Hutchinson
   (Pine Tree Composition, Inc.)
Cover director: Jayne Conte
Prepress and manufacturing buyer: Mary Ann Gloriande

This book was set in 10/12 New Century Schoolbook by Pine Tree
Composition, Inc., and was printed and bound by Hamilton Printing Company.
The cover was printed by Phoenix Color Corp.

 © 1997, 1991, 1985, 1980, 1974 by Prentice-Hall, Inc.
Simon & Schuster/A Viacom Company
Upper Saddle River, New Jersey 07458

Printed in the United States of America
10   9   8   7   6   5   4   3

ISBN 0-13-011677-7

Prentice-Hall International (UK) Limited, *London*
Prentice-Hall of Australia Pty. Limited, *Sydney*
Prentice-Hall Canada Inc., *Toronto*
Prentice-Hall Hispanoamericana, S.A., *Mexico*
Prentice-Hall of India Private Limited, *New Delhi*
Prentice-Hall of Japan, Inc., *Tokyo*
Simon & Schuster Asia Pte. Ltd., *Singapore*
Editora Prentice-Hall do Brasil, Ltda., *Rio de Janeiro*

Contents

Preface

It is difficult to realize that the first edition of *Race Relations* was published in 1976. The idea that over twenty years have passed leads one to the old cliché that "time goes quickly when you are having a good time." I am not that sure that it has been such a good time, although I can personally say that there have been more good times than bad. But can the same be said for issues of race and ethnicity in American society?

As we approach the end of the twentieth century, many of the developments that appeared to be so promising in the 1970s seem to have been overturned by a pessimism that can lead to discouragement, despair, and the feeling that nothing works—or even more important, that nobody cares. Affirmative action has become a negative code word; terms such as "reverse discrimination" are common, and government-assisted programs for those in need are difficult to defend. Money for prisons seems to have a higher priority than money for education.

A look at some of the events that occurred in 1976 may help to recall the ambience of that time. The *Encyclopedia Britannica* reports that Shirley Temple Black became the Chief of Protocol for the State Department. Jimmy Carter and Walter Mondale defeated Gerald Ford for the presidency. The most acclaimed athlete was the female Rumanian gymnast, Nadia Comenichi; other prominent athletes were Julius Erving (the "Dr. J." of basketball) and Sadaharu Oh (the Japanese slugger, who surpassed Babe Ruth's lifetime home run record of 714). The Boston Celtics beat the Phoenix Suns for the NBA title, while the Oakland Raiders defeated the Minnesota Vikings in the Super Bowl, played in January 1977.

Figures who died included Chairman Mao Tse Tung, Mayor Richard Daly, and the outspoken critic of racial injustice, Paul Robeson. Clarence Kelly, the Director of the FBI, apologized for some of the activities of the Bureau under the 48-year tenure of J. Edgar Hoover, such as the harassment of Martin Luther King, Jr., and the Black Panthers. Earl Butz resigned as the Secretary of Agriculture because of a report that he made obscene remarks about Blacks.

The Dow Jones average passed 1,000, and there were reports of difficulties with Medicaid and food stamps. Alex Haley's *Roots*, the saga of an American family, enjoyed wide popularity, and "One Flew Over the Cuckoo's Nest" won the Academy Award for best picture.

It is sobering to note that many of the readers of the present volume were not even born during the above events and may look upon 1976 as ancient history. However, it is important to recall that during this entire period, if questions concerning how to build better relationships between races were asked, there would be no simple, satisfactory answer. A similar question asked today will also find no simple, satisfactory answer.

The present volume provides data from the 1990 Census, includes a chapter on the Irish and Italians, and introduces the concept of "frame" and "lens" to understand some of the different views of the world held by members of different racial and ethnic groups. It also provides a more thorough coverage of Asian American groups than most books on racial and ethnic minorities.

It is the hope of the present volume to help readers understand some of the problems and complexities involved in the relationship between the many groups that compose our diverse society.

I thank two decades of students who have been exposed to my ideas, and give a special dedication to Lynn and Christine who hopefully will benefit from my writings. A special thanks to Greg Mano for research assistance and Jan DeAmicis, Utica College, and Susan Hoerbelt, University of South Florida, who served as reviewers.

Harry H. L. Kitano
Los Angeles, California

Section I

General Issues and Theories

The first section of this book will present issues of race and racism as major dilemmas in American society. Chapter 2 will discuss major goals of American society, such as assimilation, pluralism, and bi-culturalism. Stratification, including ethnic stratification and inequality, will be covered in Chapter 3 and several theoretical perspectives will be presented in Chapter 4. Prejudice and discrimination will be in Chapter 5 while the adaptations of minority groups will be the focus of Chapter 6. The first section will close with a chapter on Identity.

Chapter 1

Major Issues

It would be nice to wake up one morning and read the following headline:

> RACISM IS DEAD. IT DIED A QUIET DEATH IN THE 1990S SO THAT AS WE FACE THE BEGINNING OF THE TWENTY-FIRST CENTURY, WE NO LONGER HAVE TO DEAL WITH THIS PROBLEM.

Such a headline would certainly be good news, but then an astute reader might ask, "But what about its relatives, such as inequality, stratification, poverty, frustration, prejudice, discrimination, segregation, social class, and ethnicity? Can they also be declared dead? And even more important, how did their deaths come about?

Perhaps the following headline might be more realistic:

> RACISM IS ALIVE AND WELL. THE REPORTS OF ITS DEMISE ARE TOTALLY UNFOUNDED SO THAT AS WE COME TO THE END OF THE TWENTIETH CENTURY, IT REMAINS AS OUR SOCIETY'S MAJOR DILEMMA.

Unfortunately the latter headline is more accurate, and there still remains confusion and the lack of sufficient information to form enlightened public policy. Not that there is a lack of public opinion, differing points of view and models; some see it as related to broader issues such as poverty, social class, stratification, inequality, and ethnicity; others see it as a central issue

Immigrants coming to the land of promise, Ellis Island, 1902.

that supersedes other explanations, while a few continue to argue whether race is a biological rather than a sociological problem.

It is our position that there is *no one, single* explanation for racism, although many adherents argue as if there were such an animal. Much depends on the experiences of the scientist, not only in personal terms but also in terms of his or her group membership and the past history of the category. For example, I see race as a central issue because I was born a Japanese American and, because of that fact, was placed in a concentration camp during World War II. I also knew that my group was singled out, with other Asian groups, for exclusionary policies based on belonging to an "undesirable race," so that race and visibility have always been an important part of my identity. Even today, while lecturing audiences unfamiliar with my background, I hear queries such as, "Where did you learn to speak English?" or, "You people certainly make great cars" and, "Where are you really from?" Today's questioners appear much friendlier and less hostile than those of earlier decades, so that I find it easy to say that I was born in San Francisco, went to school in Berkeley, and never left the United States until I was well into my adult years. Years ago, I would have pretended not to hear the questions or answered, "no speakee English." Either I have changed, or the society has changed, or both of us have changed.

Nevertheless, when issues are framed relating to race and ethnicity, the lens that I use is from a Japanese American perspective. How else can I explain my reactions—from the bombing of Hiroshima, to sympathy for Judge Lance Ito, to outrage at the wartime treatment of Japanese Americans, to sensitivity at the stereotyped role of Asian Americans in the mass media, and rooting for Pitcher Hideo Nomo.

The purpose of this book is to explore the relationship between various racial minorities and the majority group in the United States. We will present a number of different theories, indicate where groups were and where they are now, and close by raising questions about the role of America's racial and ethnic minorities in the future.

HETEROGENEITY

Every nation can claim to be unique, but the United States is unique in a number of areas. First, we are a nation of immigrants so that all groups with the exception of the Native American were brought to this country. Second, even though we are not close to resembling an "ideal" in terms of our treatment of racial minorities, we still appear to be the magnet for much of the world's restless populations. Finally, we are a young country, with a steady flow of new immigrants, so that we remain new even though the descendants of our early pioneers can now trace their ancestors back many generations. Therefore, we have a dynamic mixture of generations, of immigrants from different nations representing different cultural styles, and a variety of expectations, values, and goals.

The heterogeneity provides much of the excitement of living in the United States. Walking along the streets of our urban centers such as New York, Chicago, and Los Angeles can be an international and intercultural experience. All the colors of the human race are represented, as well as a variety of cultures and lifestyles. Perhaps the one common thread is dressing American, that is, if everything from suits and ties to T-shirts and shorts can be considered to be American.

The richness that flows from the various immigrant and native populations represents a diversity and vitality often lacking in more homogeneous societies. But this source of strength can also create harmful schisms; race, nationality, religion, sex, and ethnic group can be used to divide as well as to enrich, and cries of "balkanization" and the demise of the United States can also be heard.

GOALS

Given this diversity, the question of goals is a difficult one. Should we strive for integration, that is, should we try to minimize the differences and to merge and blend along the lines of the melting pot? Terms often associated with this perspective include assimilation, amalgamation, and acculturation. In its most extreme form, this perspective would envisage one language, one culture, and one value system.

An opposing perspective sees the United States in different terms. Pluralists encourage the maintenance of various groupings so that ethnicity, color, culture, and previous nationality provide primary sources of identification. Rather than melting, the pluralist sees the value of various groupings. The society would be likened to a mosaic of coexisting cultures. Metaphors used to describe this model would be a salad bowl and a symphony orchestra, in which there is a richness because of the different ingredients and instruments respectively, all contributing their special tastes and sounds. But it is also important to note that there is a great deal of interaction in an orchestra, so that an appropriate term for this model is *relational pluralism*. Each unit contributes to the whole. There is an imbalance if one section plays so loudly that it drowns out the others. No section sounds good playing by itself.

Then there is separation, where we would be one nation with many languages, diverse cultures, and multiple value systems in which groups live separately, going in whatever way they think is best.

A diverse group of aliens showing new federal ID cards, 1987.

The issues of integration, pluralism, separatism, and points in between are not new. Abramson (1980) indicates that early commentators on American history in the eighteenth and nineteenth centuries were concerned over the issue and generally advocated some type of assimilation over pluralism, although Native Americans and African Americans were excluded. One of the problems with the melting pot was that it was predicated on Anglo conformity: To melt meant becoming white and following Anglo manners, customs, and values. It also included physical appearance, a variable that would preclude the melting of significant numbers of immigrants and their progeny with different skin colors and facial features. It is no accident that the further one is from the Anglo core, the higher the probability of exploring different models.

The issue of goals is not an easy one. Who makes the choice? What process do we use? How do we deal with existing barriers and inequalities? How can the desires of less powerful minorities be included? What if their desires are at variance with the dominant majority group? The current popularity of the English-only movement may be taken as an indication of defining goals by one segment of the society. Conversely, learning foreign languages—such as Chinese, Japanese, Korean, and Spanish—is also popular in an international world of the future. Are these voices being heard?

Although the question of goals is important, perhaps the more important question is survival. Perhaps a society could be successful without addressing abstract goals if it could provide good jobs, an adequate income, decent housing, and food on the table. But racism and inequality can stand in the way of achieving the survival goals.

THE AMERICAN DILEMMA

Gunnar Myrdal (1944) saw the relationship between Whites and Blacks as the fundamental American dilemma. The discrepancy between the "American creed"—high-minded Christian precepts, as opposed to group prejudice against particular persons or types of people—constitutes the dilemma. But if the American choice is between liberty, equality, and fair opportunity (right) for everybody against prejudice, economic advantage, and the force of custom (wrong), then the dilemma is one of political conflict (Sniderman, Tetlock, & Carmines, 1993).

The current dilemma is much more complex. The choice is not between right and wrong, between the values of the American creed and a ragbag full of irrational and self-serving beliefs; the choice now must be made among competing values—compassion, the freedom to achieve, tolerance, the right to be judged on one's individual merits, the reach of the state, and the autonomy of the family—in a word, the very values that make up the American creed (Sniderman et al., 1993:2).

Therefore, the role of the state, respect for individual autonomy and free choice, the level playing field, federal assistance in terms of welfare and affirmative action, the hard work and savings ethic, and family values and taxes all complicate issues related to race and ethnicity.

There is a complex of causality that leads to difficulties in assigning responsibility and courses of action. Issues of race now include the White and Black perspectives, as well as the expectations of other groups—among them Asians, Hispanics, and Native Americans—who are also participants in American society.

Explanations of racism must take into account the history, experiences, attitudes, fears, hopes, and prejudices of all segments of our country. It is no longer just a White problem; and even more important, the solutions, if any, are no longer solely a White solution. Perhaps the wisest saying is, "We are all in this thing together."

DIFFERING PERSPECTIVES

A study of race relations is related to different views of human beings. One perspective emphasizes that humans are conscious, individual agents striving toward goals. From this point of view, concepts such as motivation, desire, and rewards play an important part of any explanation of race relations. Prejudice and discrimination are conscious aspects of the individual, which can be altered and changed under appropriate conditions. Men and women do that they do either because they think that it will bring them closer to what they want or to avoid what they dislike. This perspective focuses on the individual and sees the solution to race relations on an individual level, with the goal of changing the prejudiced individual into a more tolerant human being and accepting the fact that there are different racial and minority groups.

A different perspective emphasizes the role of societal structures, treating individual desires, beliefs, and motives as less important than the organizational and institutional structures of the society. This perspective sees the importance of role, position, status, economic needs, power, and institutional policies in shaping racial behavior more than individual will and desire. Programs to combat racism at this level focus on changing institutions instead of individuals.

Historically, psychiatry, psychology, and social casework have focused more on the individual, while sociology and social psychology have focused more on institutions, but there appears to be a growing rapprochement among the professions toward viewing problems of race in multidimensional terms.

DIRECT AND INDIRECT RACISM

Pettigrew (1973), in discussing racism, distinguished between direct racial discrimination and indirect discrimination. Direct racism occurs when a person is confronted and placed at a disadvantage because of race, whereas in the indirect case, racism is a side effect of other concerns, such as unemployment. It is important to link the explanations of racism to hypothesized cures.

For example, if racism were a phenomenon between people of different colors, then a reasonable solution would entail meeting each other, becoming acquainted, and eventually working together. Confronting the meaning of color, gaining further information, education, counseling, and therapy might be appropriate techniques for bringing about better relationships between racial groups.

However, if racism is perceived as indirect and linked with other concerns, then bringing different racial groups together may be less appropriate. If racism is the outcome of rapid societal change, economic hardship, a competitive society, and urbanization and technological advances, then other efforts may be more relevant in bringing about change. Unfortunately, linkages between broader societal variables and racism are difficult to unravel, and specific suggestions to develop healthier relationships are lacking. The most appropriate generalization may be that there are many causes of racism and that there are no simple, easy solutions.

THE RASHOMON PERSPECTIVE

The relationship between and among various racial and ethnic groups does not fall easily into one valid perspective model. There are a variety of views; a member of the majority might see marvelous progress in race relations, while a member of a minority might perceive little progress. Since there are clearly a number of differing views of reality, we refer to the Rashomon model, named after the classic Japanese film portraying different interpretations of a specific incident. The important point is that views of reality are shaped by position, experiences, emotions, and needs, with variations in time, place, and situation. An explanation from one position may be valid from that point of view, but an observation from a different angle may provide a different perspective. The notion that only one view represents the truth is difficult to defend, unless we assume that one actor has a monopoly on veracity or, more likely, is powerful enough to impose his or her point of view as the truth.

For example, during the famous murder trial of O. J. Simpson in 1995, Whites generally felt that the ex-football star was guilty, while a majority of Blacks felt that he was innocent. Although there is agreement that race plays an important role in society, the picture of Blacks cheering as Whites stood with blank stares indicates that there is still shock when the schism brought about by race surfaces.

FRAME AND LENS

In Chapter 3 we discuss the ramifications of the ethnic stratification system in the United States. When issues are framed in terms of race and ethnicity, the racial and ethnic lens provides the main focus. When issues are framed in terms of gender, another lens may be used. It is difficult to provide a universal, agreed upon lens to view societies and behavior, although in most cases those who own the camera (power) have the most influence.

One way of resolving this dilemma of situational and relative truth is to rely on the scientific method so that observations are systematic and biases are recognized: that the studies are replicable, that the researchers are well trained and that the instruments for measurement are valid and reliable. However, up to the present, the scientific method has not significantly affected our racial problems; in practice, social scientists have probably contributed as much to the confusion and hysteria surrounding the issue as has any other source. For example, studies and opinions on issues such as mandatory busing and affirmative action have seen social scientists lined up on both sides. As a consequence, politicians and decision makers of whatever persuasion can find "scientific studies" and race relations "experts" to back up their respective positions.

Part of the problem is that social scientists themselves are human beings so that their expectations, needs, experiences, racial and ethnic background, sex, personality, training, class position, reference group, status, and ideology shape their research efforts, no matter how faithfully they adhere to scientific methodology. How questions are framed and the variety of lenses that are used have to be taken into account. In the arena of race relations, they are constantly challenged by value references such as good, functional, and desirable. These value judgments are virtually impossible to avoid; for example, from a majority perspective, a good minority might be one that adjusts to its inferior position with a minimum of complaint and disruptive behavior. In contrast, an ungrateful minority might be one that constantly challenges majority group authority. It was not that long ago that a good Indian was a dead Indian; that good slaves were those who dutifully obeyed their masters, or that minorities who "knew their place" in society were praised for their functional adaptation. I still remember a Los Angeles congressman saying that if the Japanese wanted to demonstrate American citizenship during World War II, they would go willingly to the concentration camps.

The issue remains alive today; a successful or model minority from the point of view of those in power would be a group that adapts to less than equal status through passivity, humility, and acceptance; conversely, a bad minority might be a group that refuses to accept less than equal status by indulging in disruptive and deviant behavior.

In race relations, a critical issue is whether one identifies with the majority or the minority. A common complaint in the minority community is that those who identify with the majority tend to blame the victim, that is, to focus on minority group deficits, with only passing reference to the role of the group in power in creating many of the problems. Conversely, those who identify with the minority are often accused of being overly subjective, emotional, and biased. It has only been in the last several decades that a perspective other than that of the dominant group has been presented.

Another major issue facing social scientists is the different uses of the term *race*. One sure way of turning a conference into a state of chaos is to insist that all participants agree upon a definition of race and racism before any discussion can begin. For the terms are emotionally loaded and have a variety of connotations, yet they are used freely.

The Rashomon perspective calls for an analysis that takes into account the various points of view. The principle of triangulation used in surveying and navigation may be appropriate. It stresses the importance of using a number of different sightings in order to gain a fix. Admittedly, gaining several valid perspectives in race relations is extremely complicated. In addition to the previously mentioned problems, there is also the insider-outsider issue mentioned by Merton (1972). The insider feeling that access to the truth can be gained only from the inside derides the effort of the outsider to understand the true feelings and the real issues. The outsider may counter by questioning the objectivity and the biases of the insider.

THE PROBLEM

The reasons behind the problem are not related to science as a technique, methodology, or philosophy. Rather, the problem arises from the social scientists, politicians, and others who write, use, interpret, and act upon the material. In the past, majority group researchers came into minority communities to conduct their scientific studies. Many ethnics felt that they were used and exploited by the researchers—first as subjects, then as objects of the findings. It was analogous to a colonial situation: Ethnics were the raw material from whom data could be extracted. The information was shipped to universities and research institutions to be processed and then returned to the ghettos in the form of policy, advice, and recommendations. The feelings and recommendations of the minority communities were often ignored or rejected; majority group researchers made their reputations on these studies with little benefit to the minority communities.

There were also serious questions about the interpretations and applications of research findings. Minorities have been told that they are deviant, that their family structures lead to pathology, that their personality patterns are neurotic, and that their culture is the reason for their low status in the American social system. They have felt the sting of prejudice through studies that emphasized both their unassimilability and their distance from the mainstream. It is no wonder that many minority communities resist being studied by scientists, no matter how well meaning, which adds another complication to research in race relations.

WHERE ARE WE?

The question of where we are in terms of research on race relations, is a spotty one. The term *racism* as a topic for federal funding virtually disappeared during the Reagan administration; and there is therefore little empirical research to draw upon from the 1980s. Because direct contact with minority community respondents, even for researchers of the same ethnic background, is difficult and expensive, there is a heavy reliance on secondary sources of data, especially the U.S. Bureau of the Census. There are limitations to this source: Because basic information is gathered by decades, near the end of a decade the material becomes out of date, even though the bureau provides periodic updates.

There are complaints about the serious undercounting of minorities. Some minorities are too small in number for statistical analysis, and the variables that are presented are fixed and inflexible. But the advantage of the Census is that the data are available and that there are sufficient numbers for sophisticated statistical analysis.

The question of the insider-outsider perspective becomes relevant as more and more research is conducted using secondary sources. It is possible for a researcher to become an expert on, say, the Vietnamese, for example, without having any personal contact with members of that group. Even though meeting with members of a racial group may be time-consuming, expensive, and difficult, perhaps the effort might prove to be as valuable as spending time in the computer laboratories.

An example of different perspectives was the assessment by various researchers of the effect of the California Alien Law of 1920. The law forbade ownership of agricultural land by Japanese aliens (most of the Japanese in California were aliens, ineligible for citizenship at that time). White scholars, such as Daniels (1962) and Modell (1969), sympathetic to the plight of the Japanese, using hard, secondary sources of data (land ownership figures), wrote that the Japanese in California were not adversely affected by the law.

However, ethnic scholars such as Iwata (1962) and Kitano (1976, 1993) interpreted the effects of the law differently. Having been raised in the ethnic community and having heard stories about this and other anti-Japanese legislation, they felt that it lowered expectations, raised serious questions about the future of the Japanese in California, and heightened feelings of inferiority and difference at a time when the melting pot ethos was a part of the American dream. The ethnic researchers, having grown up in the Japanese community, were sensitive to the moods and feelings of the population in a way that would have been difficult for an outsider. As Petersen (1971) observed, in this case there were clear differences between the ethnic and nonethnic researchers. The outsider, relying on the kind of evidence often thought of as more objective, reliable, and scientific, may have been interpreting from less pertinent data than the insiders with their more subjective orientation.

DEFINITIONS

We will define a few terms; other terms will be defined as they are presented in the chapters.

Race refers to differential concentrations of gene frequencies responsible for traits which, so far as we know, are confined to physical manifestations such as skin color or hair form; race has no intrinsic connection with cultural patterns or institutions (Gordon, 1964:27). There are no pure races, and our use here will coincide with common social usage, which is based primarily on visibility such as skin color. Blauner (1994) adds that race is a political construct and a product of Western colonialism.

Racism is an ideology that considers the unchangeable physical characteristics of groups to be linked in a direct, causal way to their psychological and intellectual functioning and, on this basis, distinguishes between superior and inferior races (Feagin, 1989:5). It means that one group knows that it is superior in every way to another and has the power to reinforce this perspective.

Racists fear interracial marriage or mongrelization because of the mixing of inferior blood and the consequent decline of civilization. White racism would be the perspective that White or European culture is superior to all others; people of color would also be considered racists if they held similar views about the superiority of their own groups and had the power to reinforce their beliefs. Skin color and other visible characteristics that are readily observed form the primary basis for racial classification. The ease of racial identification makes it difficult for an individual to discard his or her racial identity.

Ethnic groups are composed of individuals and families who are members of national, religious, cultural and racial groups who do not belong to the dominant group in a society. They may be differentiated by a combination of their values, expectations, attitudes, customs, lifestyles, rituals, and celebrations (Kitano, 1996).

In addition, ethnicity and sense of peoplehood is recognized by self and others. It may include physical characteristics as well as culture and nationality. It best describes the country of origin, so that an individual of Polish ancestry is a Polish ethnic, whereas an immigrant from China will have a racial identity as an Asian and an ethnic identity as Chinese.

Omi and Winant (1994) indicate that the use of ethnicity deflects from the centrality of race as the major issue. Racial stratification, although similar in many ways, faces issues that are different from ethnic stratification.

The Book

The book is divided into three sections. The first section includes the following chapters:

Chapter 2 will cover goals of society; Chapter 3 will focus on stratification and inequality. Chapter 4 will present selected theoretical persectives, while prejudice and discrimination will be covered in Chapter 5. Chapter 6 will present minority adaptations and the section will close with Chapter 7 on identity.

The second section of the book will present three groupings, based on the racial stratification system in the U.S. The stratification is based on Marger (1991).

At the top of the stratification system are Whites, primarily Anglo-Protestants who hold most of the major wealth and power in society. They will not be covered, although the interaction of all groups will be in the context of the WASP society.

Section 2

The second section will cover the groups at the lower end of the stratification system. Chapter 8 will cover African Americans, and Chapter 9, Mexican Americans. Chapter 10 will focus on Puerto Ricans and Cubans, and Chapter 11 will cover Native Americans. The racial and ethnic lens is important for these groups.

The middle tier is occupied by white Catholics, Jews, and Asian Americans. Ethnicity, religion and race are important and provide an important lens by which they perceive the world. Chapter 12 will focus on the Irish and Italians, Chapter 13 on the Chinese and Chapter 14 on the Japanese. Chapter 15 covers the Koreans and Filipinos and Chapter 16 on the Southeast Asians and Pacific Islanders. Chapter 17 will provide an overview and summary of important points.

The importance of the stratification system cannot be overestimated; the positions shape different perceptions of society. The WASP's advocate an individualistic perspective; individual excellence, merit, and motivation should be rewarded, with little assistance from governmental programs such as welfare and affirmative action. The second tier may be similar to the top tier in many ways but groups there remain conscious of their religious, ethnic, and racial identities. The bottom tier perceives race and culture as important determinants and perceives the importance of governmental programs such as welfare and affirmative action. The stratification is, of course, fluid, and individuals of whatever classification can and do identify with the top of the hierarchy.

SUMMARY

In summary, Chapter 1 presented some of the major issues in society concerning race and racism. There is no simple, single explanation, nor is there any simple solution to the problems associated with racism. Nevertheless, there is the hope that by addressing the issue in the context of the goals of society, we will attempt to understand and develop policy to ameliorate its negative effects.

REFERENCES

ABRAMSON, H. J. (1980). Assimilation and pluralism. In S. Thernstrom, A. Orlov, & O. Handlin (Eds.), *Harvard Encyclopedia of American Ethnic Groups* (pp. 150–160). Cambridge, Mass.: Harvard University Press.

BLAUNER, B. (1994). Talking past each other: Black and white language of race. In F. L. Pincus & H. Ehrlich (Eds.), *Race and Ethnic Conflict* (pp. 18–28). Boulder, Colo.: Westview Press.

DANIELS, R. (1962). *The politics of prejudice: The anti-Japanese movement in California and the struggle for Japanese exclusion*. Berkeley: University of California Press.

FEAGIN, J. (1989). *Racial and ethnic relations*. Englewood Cliffs, N.J.: Prentice-Hall.

GORDON, M. (1964). *Assimilation in American life*. New York: Oxford University Press.

IWATA, M. (1962). The Japanese immigrants in California agriculture. *Agricultural History, 36*, 27–37.

KITANO, H. H. L. (1976). *Japanese Americans: The evolution of a subculture*. Englewood Cliffs, N.J.: Prentice-Hall.

KITANO, H. H. L. (1993). *Generations and identity: The Japanese American*. Needham Heights, Mass.: Ginn Press.

KITANO, H. H. L. (1996). Ethnicity. In *Encyclopedia of Marriage and the Family*. New York: MacMillan.

MARGER, M. (1991). *Race and ethnic relations* (2nd Ed.). Belmont, Calif.: Wadsworth Publishing Co.

MERTON, R. (1972). Insiders and outsiders: A chapter in the sociology of knowledge. *American Journal of Sociology, 72* (2):9–47.

MODELL, J. (1969). The Japanese in Los Angeles: A study in growth and accommodation, 1900–1946. Unpublished doctoral dissertation, Columbia University.

MYRDAL, G. (1944). *An American dilemma*. New York: Harper and Row.

OMI, M., & WINANT, H. (1994). *Racial formulation in the United States*. New York: Routledge.

PETERSEN, W. (1971). *Japanese Americans*. New York: Random House.

PETTIGREW, T. (1973). Racism and the mental health of white Americans: A social psychological view. In C. Wilie, B. Kramer, & B. Brown (Eds.), *Racism and Mental Health*. Pittsburgh: University of Pittsburgh Press.

SNIDERMAN, P. M., TETLOCK, P. E., & CARMINES, E. G. (Eds.). (1993). *Prejudice, politics, and the American dilemma*. Stanford, Calif.: Stanford University Press.

Chapter 2

Who Is an American? Goals of American Society

The question "Who is an American?" is relatively easy to answer. Americans include all who are citizens of the country by birth or naturalization; ancestry, race, ethnic group, social class, and ideology, therefore, do not exclude one from being an American.

A second question—"Who wants to be an American?"—may be a little more difficult to answer. Voluntary immigrants, searching for a new and better life, would surely fit into the category of those who have this desire; but those who were conquered, those who arrived as slaves, and those who feel that they have suffered oppression may give more qualified answers.

Second, third, and succeeding American-born generations may contribute to the diversity of responses. There is unanimity that the United States is a country characterized by freedom, equality, and the Bill of Rights, but then there are discrimination and racism, which result in questions concerning the discrepancy between the real and the ideal.

A third question—"Who decides?"—is probably the most important, since our policy has often excluded people of color. We have even had an un-American Activities Committee to define an American, and politicians constantly refer to "real Americans," in a manner indicating that they have the correct definition. Often, such definitions make minority groups shudder.

A related question asks, "What are the goals of American society?" Is it to make us all Americans, narrowly or broadly defined? Is it to reinforce one culture, one phenotype, one belief, and one value system, or would it include diversity and a more pluralistic outlook? These are some of the issues to be discussed in this chapter.

GOALS

In most of my discussions with nonacademics, the question of the broader goals of U.S. society are seldom mentioned. Rather, goals are thought of in personal terms, so that making a living, finding a good job, and getting a good education are mentioned most often. When talking with newly arrived immigrants, the goals are even more immediate: housing, shopping, transportation, and becoming familiar with everyday norms. Perhaps it is the luxury of academia (and contestants in Miss America pageants) to focus on more distant, abstract goals.

When the question of U.S. goals is raised, one image is that of Mom, the flag, and apple pie. Perhaps there may be a yearning for the good old days when life was simpler, there were no riots or demonstrations, and minorities knew their place in the system. Now sushi, tacos, and pasta have diversified the definition of American cuisine. It is not surprising that given the increasingly individualistic direction of our society and the number of different ethnic, racial, and religious groups in it, that the question of goals leads to a variety of responses.

In a study of majority-group Americans (racial minorities were excluded from the sample), Bellah, Madsen, Sullivan, Swidler, & Tipton (1985) wrote about a high degree of consensus on three individual goals: success, freedom, and justice. Americans tend to believe that the good life is a matter of personal choice, and that the ultimate measure of success is an economic one. In past times, when businesses were small and running a farm or business required a degree of public-spiritedness, success was more closely tied to civic concerns. However, given the present-day economy with its corporations and bureaucracies, current success is measured primarily through promotions, increases in salary, and the acquisition of material goods, with less emphasis on community responsibilities. The question for our society is, can a person reconcile the requirements of personal economic success with concerns of the broader community and with those less fortunate? The current response seems to be toward personal economic success, so that one definition of a "good American" is one who has achieved economic success. Owning a home, a two-car garage, a savings account, and a good job go along with economic independence. Athletic, music, and show business stars who make a lot of money are looked upon as role models, and they achieve a level of recognition that goes beyond race and ethnicity. Shaquille O'Neal and Michael Jordan have a devoted following that transcends color, age, and gender. But their achievements are attributed to individual ability, hard work, and dedication; and their success therefore does little to lift the image of their less talented brethren.

Conversely, Americans who are trapped in the welfare system and those who resort to criminal behavior are "bad Americans," and their image becomes the portrayal of their entire racial group. During World War II, the Japanese, whether in Japan or as Japanese Americans, were considered an "evil race," while it was individual Germans and Italians who were the enemy.

Another common value and goal in American society Bellah mentions is *freedom*. One definition of freedom is being left alone and not having others intrude upon one's values, ideas, or lifestyle. This implies that one is free of arbitrary authority in places of employment, in the family, and in political life. It also includes the notion of being one's own person, of defining oneself, of deciding for oneself what one wants out of life, and of being free, as far as possible, from the constraints of family, friends, and community.

The goal of psychological freedom considers past values and conformity to societal norms less important than discovering what the self really wants. The notions of doing your own thing and living life without hassles are central to this perspective.

Gould (1995) proposes two additional aspects of freedom that are generally ignored. One is freedom as capacity and the second is freedom as the exercise of this capacity for self-development. She also differentiates between enabling, or positive, freedom, and constraining, or negative, freedom. For example, an individual has the freedom to go to college but may not have the necessary resources to achieve this goal.

Freedom as capacity refers to the ability to choose among alternatives. Human actions go beyond mere bodily motions; behaviors are consciously oriented toward some end or goal, or they express some intended meaning.

Freedom as self-development involves more than making choices in isolated actions; it connotes a process of becoming who one chooses to be through actions that express one's own purposes and needs. One is thus free to do what one chooses and able to achieve whatever one has set out to achieve. It would appear that there has been progress toward the elimination of "constraining freedom," but that "enabling freedom," especially for minority groups, has a long way to go.

Bellah notes that the concept of justice in U.S. society means an equal opportunity for each individual to pursue whatever he or she understands by the pursuit of happiness. There is a desire for laws and political procedures to be applied equally and in the same way to everyone. However, this concept of justice does not concern itself with disparities in income and other basic inequalities in our society.

These American goals must come as a shock for those immigrants who come from cultures where norms, the role of the family, and that of society are oriented toward conformity and community responsibility. However, it does not take too long for the newcomers to shape their behaviors toward the American way—if not for themselves, then for their children.

The next section concentrates on the following questions: What happens as different immigrant groups arrive in the United States? Are there predictable patterns? Should our basic direction be toward the melting and merging of the different groups, or should there be an emphasis on retaining the diversity of the different racial, ethnic, and religious groups?

RACE RELATIONS CYCLE

Just as there is a wide range of possible outcomes when two strangers meet, there is also a wide range of interactions when different groups meet. Group size and power, motives, nationality, race, alliances, status, ideology, religion, and history are some of the variables that shape the interaction between groups. Time, place, and situation are also involved, so that predictions and generalizations concerning outcomes are difficult to make.

A number of attempts have been made to analyze the outcomes of different groups that have entered the United States. Sociologist Robert Park (1950) suggested that there were a number of stages—such as contact, competition, adjustment, and accommodation—leading to eventual assimilation and amalgamation. His predictive theory saw the elimination of race problems through the ultimate blending of the diverse groups to a homogeneous peoplehood (Lyman, 1993).

For example, Park studied the case of Hawaii in 1926 and predicted that the native races would disappear as new peoples came into existence, that individual races and cultures would die, but that the majority civilization would live on. The idea of all groups ultimately being absorbed into the American mainstream underscores Park's initial observations of the inevitability of assimilation. Because of his experiences in Hawaii, however, Park modified his original position and saw that the race relations cycle could also result in a caste system or in a majority-minority arrangement.

Bogardus (1930), focusing primarily on the experiences of the Chinese, Japanese, Filipino, and Mexican immigrants in California, saw sufficient recurrences to propose a race relations cycle whose stages were curiosity, economic welcome, then industrial and social antagonism, legislative antagonism, fair-play tendencies, quiescence, and second-generation difficulties.

Shibutani and Kwan (1965:21) wrote that assimilation is a phenomenon found in all cases of interethnic contact in which one group does not exterminate the other. In the United States one need only review the history of various immigrant groups—the Irish, the Poles, the Jews, the Italians, the Chinese, the Mexicans—to see the regularity with which many of them have become incorporated into the mainstream of U.S. life. Shibutani and Kwan defined assimilation as a change of mental perspective in which the immigrant eventually perceives the world from an American point of view, rather than from that of his or her previous national background.

The study of certain cycles of immigration gives a broad picture of the relationship between an immigrant group and the host culture. These progressions should not be mistaken for evolutionary phenomena following natural laws of biological inevitability, but rather as cycles that are influenced by social variables such as welcome, contact, competition, power, discrimination, and prejudice. Therefore, there is no inevitability to the process; individuals and groups will be at different points of contact, although it is probably valid to assume that assimilation will occur if given enough time, and if there are no human barriers to thwart intergroup activity.

Orders of Race Relations

Banton (1967) presented six orders of interracial contact between two groups. Stage one is *peripheral contact*, where there is a minimal amount of contact between two groups. It is often temporary; in the United States, the early interaction between the first settlers and the Native Americans provides an example. Neither group had intimate contact with each other; one familiar image was that of the Indians, concealed in the forest, peering out at the colonists. There was no concerted attempt by either group to learn the language and the culture of the other. The peripheral contact was short-lived, because in time the settlers began to desire the land held by the Indians.

It is difficult to conceive of present-day situations where the model of peripheral contact remains as the primary interaction between racial groups. In some instances, Blacks and Whites may live side by side in sections of a city with a minimum of social, occupational, and voluntary interaction. Peripheral contact changes quickly when there are problems and issues that arise between groups and when there is a pressing need for some type of interaction.

The second stage of intergroup interaction is *institutionalized contact*. Banton indicates that this type of contact is most apt to occur under the following two conditions:

> When one of the two groups has a centralized political structure in which a few leaders control the action of their own members and use their power to dominate the other group. When two societies enter into contact principally through their outlying members and there is no strong competition for resources.

The most common examples of institutionalized contact between relatively equal power groups are those between independent nation states. Embassies and consular offices provide a degree of formal interaction, but this relationship leaves the majority of each group autonomous and independent of each other.

Institutionalized contact between unequal power groups is labelled as paternalism or colonialism (Banton, 1967:72). When subordinates are subjected to some control by a home government (for example, England), there is a high probability that paternalism (colonialism) will become the established order.

Paternalism is a special form of institutionalized contact that maintains the distinctiveness of the interacting societies. Banton observed:

> It is exemplified in some forms of colonial rule, such as those that sanctioned and often reinforced the control tribal chiefs exercised over their peoples. In the pure form of paternalism, the only representatives of the

metropolitan society who have dealings with the indigenous society are approved agents responsible for their action to authorities in their homeland. (1967:72)

Race, career, education, and training are important in determining specific official roles, and the influx of immigrants and new settlers strains the paternalistic order. In paternalistic orders, roles are determined by the desire of the upper group to maintain control over all significant spheres of activity. Van den Berghe (1967) writes that the paternalistic system follows a master-servant model. The master group may be few in number but is able to dominate the subordinates. The subordinates are looked upon as childish, immature, irresponsible, and improvident, but are lovable as long as they remain in their place. Subordinated groups often internalize these inferiority feelings through self-deprecation.

Under paternalism, role and status are sharply defined. Social distance is maintained through etiquette, regulations, and repeated demonstrations of power by the dominant group. There may be high rates of sexual encounters between men of the ruling group with women of the subordinated population, but very few of these relationships end in marriage. Van den Berghe remarked that racial prejudice on the part of the ruling group is present but appears more related to economic and social position rather than to any deep psychodynamic feelings.

Paternalistic societies are rigidly stratified into racial castes. The caste barrier is the most important; although class distinctions do exist, the color line limits mobility between castes. Race remains the major dividing factor, and elaborate ideologies of the inferiority and superiority of races are developed to maintain the system.

Because there are more servants than masters, part of the longevity and stability of this model comes from the acquiescence of the subordinated. Although there have been constant conflicts engendered by rebellious servants, peaceful coexistence is often achieved, especially in the economic area. In addition, sexual relations and other forms of unequal, but often intimate social relations (for example, a black woman mothering white children) may create affective bonds across caste lines.

A form of unequal institutionalized contact called domestic colonialism (Blauner, 1972) will be further discussed in Chapter 4. The third type of interaction, *acculturation*, is familiar to most Americans, especially those of immigrant background. One common definition of acculturation is the process of learning a culture different from the one in which a person was originally raised. The term is generally used to specify movement across different cultures, whereas learning in the original culture is enculturation or socialization.

Acculturation is common to intergroup relations in the United States. It connotes the coming together of different cultures into a common culture. Acculturation occurs when different racial and ethnic groups become similar in their thinking, feeling, and acting. There is a mutuality, so that both groups learn from each other.

Equal-status acculturation most often occurs when societies are small, informal, and noncompetitive. Equal-power acculturation also can be seen in border towns, where individuals from both cultures learn about each other and make appropriate adaptations. Acculturation is only one of many kinds of assimilation.

Gordon (1964) posited differences between cultural, behavioral, structural, and other types. Cultural assimilation (or acculturation) is likely to be the first to occur and consists of a change in the cultural patterns of the two interacting groups. It is not necessary for other types of assimilation to occur, and acculturation by itself can go on indefinitely. It also should be noted that a purely one-way flow of acculturation (one group completely overpowering the other) is rare, and that some mutual learning generally occurs.

The fourth model in Banton's scheme is *integration*. As Banton observed:

> Race is then still used as a social sign, though as a sign indicating an individual's background and probably his claims to deference. It is one sign among many others, being irrelevant in some sectors but of some account in status-sensitive situations of social acceptance or rejection. For nearly all purposes, race has much less significance than the individual's occupation and his other status-conferring roles. Thus, in a racially integrated social order, race is a sign of an independent role, signaling rights and obligations in only a few restricted sets of circumstances. (1967:73)

Multi-racial marriage, 1995.

An integrated order of race relations develops when racial distinctions are disregarded or are given only minor consideration. It means that there is interaction among races on most levels, such as in housing, in schooling, in employment, in interest groups, and in friendship and social relationships. Rigid definitions and rigid, racially prescribed roles are discarded and modified, so that there are more degrees of freedom for voluntary choice and movement across racial lines.

Integration also occurs on a less than equal basis. An integrated army unit may be led by white officers or an integrated company may limit the top echelon to white males, even though the labor force may be a mixture of various races. However, integration does not include intimate social relationships, such as marriage between the groups.

The fifth model is that of *assimilation* or *amalgamation*. By assimilation or amalgamation in race relations, we refer specifically to interracial marriage and its variations, including intimate social interaction and living together. Assimilation can occur without acculturation (for example, war-bride marriages) and is often regarded as an inevitable consequence of integration, which may be one reason why integration is often resisted so vigorously. Once a group can enter freely into the social clubs, cliques, organizations, and institutions of the other group on a peer basis, intermarriage and other levels of assimilation generally will follow (Gordon, 1964; Farley, 1995).

The fear of racial amalgamation has not been the sole province of the dominant group. The simple question "Do you want your daughter to marry one?" was an effective device to warn individuals on both sides of the racial fence not to stray, although there now appears to be a trend among most minorities toward increasing rates of marriage to out-group members.

The sixth model is *pluralism*. In a pluralistic order, racial differences indicate much wider variations in expected behavior than under the model of integration. Pluralism is akin to separate nation states, in which groups live side by side with different languages and cultures, and with a minimum of social interaction, integration, or assimilation.

The cultural pluralist views the necessity of subsocietal separation to guarantee the continuance of the ethnic cultural tradition and the existence of the group, without at the same time interfering with the carrying out of standard responsibilities to the general U.S. civic life (Gordon, 1964:158). Wide-scale intermarriage and extensive primary-group relations across ethnic lines pose the gravest threats to a pluralistic society.

Gordon wrote that the American reality is that of structural pluralism rather than cultural pluralism, although some of the latter remains. The major ethnic and religious groups have separate subsocieties that tend to restrict large-scale, primary-group interaction, but most of them are variants of the U.S. culture.

The important theoretical problem, then, is how ethnic prejudice and discrimination can be eliminated or reduced and value conflict kept within workable limits in a society where the existence of separate subsocieties keeps primary-group relations among persons of different ethnic backgrounds at a minimum (Gordon, 1964:159).

Van den Berghe offered a further perspective on pluralism. Pluralistic societies are segmented into corporate groups and have different cultures or subcultures; their social structure is compartmentalized into analogous, parallel, noncomplementary but distinguishable sets of institutions (1967:34).

Walzer (1980) contrasts the pluralism of Europe with that of America. Old World pluralism had its origins in conquest and dynastic alliance, whereas a large part of American pluralism comes from an immigrant society; the newcomers arrived, settled, and became U.S. citizens. But often they remained tied to their original homeland, so that for a time this was (and still is for some) a country composed of diverse people without a common history or a common culture but sharing residence and citizenship.

Walzer indicated that the primary emotion reinforcing unity was patriotism. He also writes that ethnic self-assertion and pluralism in the United States have been the functional equivalent of national liberation in other parts of the world, serving the following three important functions: (1) to retain cultural communities and provide a collective identity; (2) to provide for the celebration of an identity in a new land with such diversity; and (3) to create institutions, gain control of resources, and provide educational and welfare services.

Pluralism is a matter of degree. South Africa, which is divided into four major castes and several unrelated cultural traditions, is more pluralistic than the United States, with its two major racial castes; but in both countries Whites and nonwhites share the same Western culture and the same language. American pluralism also has to address more than the Black-White issue—there are the Asian, Latino, and Native American groups, the feminists, and the Gays and Lesbians.

Cultural and Structural Pluralism

There are differences between cultural and structural pluralism. Although in practice they both go together, cultural pluralism refers to the maintenance of ethnic subcultures with their traditions, values, and styles. Structural pluralism refers to a society being structurally compartmentalized into analogous and duplicatory but culturally alike sets of institutions.

When power relationships are unequal, pluralism can be seen as domination. The same variations of cultural and structural pluralism are relevant.

Parrillo (1994) indicates that cultural pluralism is not a new concept and that in the colonial period it was quite extensive and in many ways surpassed that of the current era. Through a comparative analysis of immigration rates, foreign-born percentages, and racial composition, he found less diversity today than in past generations. However, it may be that the pluralism of the current era has created much more debate and stress than that of the earlier era.

Biculturalism and multiculturalism are variations of the pluralistic model. "Because it emphasizes the preservation of the distinct cultural characteristics of different racial, ethnic, and religious groups, multiculturalism is similar in meaning to cultural 'pluralism'" (Farley, 1995:167).

A bicultural adaptation is a variant of both acculturation and pluralism and is based on the observation that exposure to several cultures can be additive, so that a person acquires and is comfortable with both the dominant culture and with his or her own ethnic heritage. A bilingual person is one who has acquired one of the skills important to a bicultural adaptation, although language alone is but one factor.

Second-generation (Nisei) children of immigrant Japanese parents generally have had a strong opportunity to retain a bicultural heritage; however, many of them have become so American that a true bicultural orientation may have to wait for other generations.

An individual with a bicultural orientation would have friends in several cultures, enjoy various foods, appreciate various languages, and be able to interact with various groups with an appropriate sensitivity to the different cultures. A bicultural perspective would assume the desirability of a variety of cultural styles. However, such a response is difficult if one culture is thought to be superior or better than the other.

Unequal pluralism can lead to the domination model. Domination based on racial criteria is a two-category system: All members of one category are subordinated to the other and are responded to, not as individuals, but as representatives of their category. As Banton found, this kind of subordination is far harsher, and it provides the most clear-cut illustration of race as a role sign. Whatever their personal qualities, individuals are ascribed to one or the other category, and those in the lower are prevented from claiming the privileges of those in the upper category (1967:71).

Simmel (1955), a German sociologist, felt that all social life was characterized by superordination and subordination. One group or one individual in a social relationship will always dominate, while the other, voluntarily or not, will take the lesser role. Domination is related to power, so that groups with more power become the superordinates of that system. In this model, equality is seldom achieved; rather, groups may be constantly attempting to change their subordinate positions.

The two-category system closely resembles the current stage of race relations in the United States (Kitano & Daniels, 1995). To be white is to belong to the upper half of the system, with its corresponding social-psychological perspectives. Those in power have feelings of superiority, power, and responsibility. They emphasize law and order and gradualism in race relations, and place a high value on rational discussion and scientific studies. They feel that if the "others" would only become more like them, the stratification and the boundaries would disappear.

Obviously, those caught in the subordinate positions view the world differently. They may try to escape their subordinate status by changing their names, undergoing facial operations, or by altering reality. They may over-identify with the dominant group or vent their frustrations on members of other subordinate groups, including their own. They may feel great impatience with the racial status quo and demand immediate action.

In some cases, power, not race alone, determines who plays superordinate and subordinate roles. For example, there are observable differences between West Coast Japanese Americans (subordinate status) and their peers in Hawaii (closer to superordinate status). The less powerful mainland group has acculturated much more rapidly and appears to be more respectful and conscious of race when compared to the Japanese from Hawaii. The domination model will be discussed further in Chapter 4.

ROLE OF POWER

Power is important since it establishes the direction of the interaction between groups. In the real world, especially when discussing racial minorities, there is seldom equal power; thus, the models should be analyzed in terms of the differences in power. It is the more powerful group that determines the direction of the interaction; for example, acculturation will go in the direction of the more powerful dominant group. Therefore, there is a high probability that instead of both groups learning from each other, acculturation in the United States will generally mean the acquisition of the American way, although it does not necessarily mean the discarding of the ancestral heritage. Chapter 5 contains further discussion of power.

DIFFERING GOALS

One example of a conflict involving differing goals is bilingual education programs. From one point of view, the programs are a waste of federal money and effort; from another, they are the best example of federal sensitivity to the needs of certain immigrant populations. It should be recalled that in 1974, the Supreme Court decided in the case of Lau v. Nichols that a group of Chinese-speaking students in San Francisco were being denied educational opportunity because they did not understand the language of instruction. School systems therefore were mandated to rectify the language deficiency by providing suitable instructional programs in languages other than English.

Opponents have attacked the bilingual program as an educational death wish. They ask how teaching children in the language of their native culture would better equip them for the rigors of contemporary life in the United States. European immigrants did not need this crutch to become successful, so that the bilingual program has become an example of bureaucratic waste and fuzzy thinking. Proponents are advocates of a "one America" policy, and the English-only movement has become a code word for those who hold an anti-immigrant, anti-foreigner stance.

But if we view the United States as a pluralistic society, the learning of an ethnic language is an important step in building an ethnic identity. Therefore, a bilingual program could be fully supported and justified from a pluralistic perspective. But even among those who advocate pluralism, there are variations. One group views the main task as bridging; that is, aiding the child in transferring skills from the familiar native tongue of the parents to the English language used in the schools. Programs following this goal see the instruction as temporary until the child can learn in English. The overall goals of the program are still acculturation and integration, although the means for achieving these goals are different from those of the English-only proponents.

Another group views the bilingual program as more permanent, so that a child is continuously educated and eventually acquires fluency in more than one language. Proponents of this goal view the United States in bilingual and bicultural terms. Mastery of the language of a parental culture is viewed as one part of building ethnic identity, heritage, and pride. It would be difficult to argue for the merits of any of these approaches without a prior discussion of the goals of the system.

It is our observation that there is little consensus as to goals in U.S. race relations. We have posed the question to university classes, groups of teachers, and lay audiences, and the general response is generally a blank stare. Yet these audiences are eager and willing to take active stands on issues such as mandatory busing and affirmative action, which are related to societal goals. Perhaps it remains for academics, philosophers, and researchers to talk seriously about goals. We shall here present a brief overview of some of the underlying goals of U.S. society.

U.S. SOCIAL GOALS

Anglo Conformity

Although Anglo conformity was not the overt goal of the early Americans, four out of five of the original settlers were of British Protestant derivation. Therefore, Anglo conformity was an almost inevitable outcome, given the power of the Anglo group and the fact that they had arrived here the earliest and were able to develop their organizations and institutions. But Gleason (1980) notes that it was not a simple White Anglo-Saxon Protestant community model based on country of origin. Rather, there was an idealistic image of America based on universalistic political and social principles in which beliefs and values were viewed as more important than place of birth and country of origin. However, Blacks and Native Americans were excluded from this idealistic image, so that even the beginnings of the country were tinged with racism.

The central assumption behind the Anglo conformity model is the desirability of maintaining the English language and its culture as the standard of U.S. life. This is not to deny that many other influences have also shaped America, but as Gordon remarked:

> As the immigrants and their children have become Americans, their contributions as laborers, farmers, doctors, lawyers, scientists, and artists have been by way of cultural patterns that have taken their major impress from the mold of the overwhelmingly English character of the dominant Anglo-Saxon culture or subculture in America, whose domination dates from colonial times and whose cultural domination in the United States has never been seriously threatened. (1964:73)

From the point of view of the English colonists, the newcomers were a mixed blessing. On the one hand, they were necessary for the growth and development of the country; on the other hand, they were foreigners with alien ways. Nativist organizations often played upon the fear of strangers, and immigrants to America were subject to much scapegoating and hostility (Higham, 1955).

Restrictions against the open immigration policies began to appear in the late 1800s, and in 1882 the first effective federal legislation controlling immigration was passed. Phrases similar to "America, Love It or Leave It" were common, and the immigrants were advised to cast off their old skin, not to look back, to forget the old country, and to adopt the new; if they did not like it, they could always go back.

Adopting the new clearly meant conforming to Anglo standards; the control of the country was securely in the hands of the descendants of the early English settlers. Madison Grant, in *The Passing of the Great Race* (1916), wrote about inferior breeds in differentiating between the southern Europeans and the Anglo-Teutons. The Anglo-Saxon concepts of righteousness, law, and order were clearly those of a superior race; it was necessary to break up inferior groups before they could be assimilated. The height of the Americanization movement occurred during World War I, when foreigners were stripped of their native culture and made into Americans as rapidly as possible. Political loyalty, patriotism, the teaching of American history, and Americanization classes reflected the sentiments of the country and culminated in the restrictions of the Immigration Act of 1924.

Desirable and undesirable races and nationalities were fully differentiated in this law; no immigration for Asians, low quotas for southern Europeans and other less desirable races, and high quotas for those of Anglo-Saxon background.

Americanization was successful among certain European groups. By the second generation, vast numbers had discarded their previous culture, learned English, and become patriotic. They fought and died for the new country (even against their ancestral homelands) and became the new Americans.

Racial ethnic groups have also gone through the same process, and some have successfully acculturated. They have learned English and the American way; they have fought and died for the United States and have subscribed to the tenets of patriotism and love of country. But in one dramatic sense they have not become Anglo—their skin colors and visibility have not allowed for this critical step. Therefore, the separatist techniques of prejudice, discrimination, and segregation have marginalized some minority-group Americans, kept them at a distance, and have raised questions about the validity of Anglo conformity.

Gordon feels that the critical variable in the Anglo-conformity model is not acculturation but structural assimilation. Acculturation often occurs, but structural assimilation does not. Minority-group members have not been allowed to enter into the more intimate circles of the majority:

> The answer lies in the attitudes of both the majority and the minority groups and in the way in which these attitudes have interacted. A folk saying is that, It takes two to tango. To utilize the analogy, there is no good reason to believe that white Protestant America ever extended a firm and cordial invitation to its minorities to dance. Furthermore, the attitudes of the minority-group members themselves on the matter have been divided and ambiguous. (1964:80)

With regard to immigrants, structural assimilation was out of the question. They did not want it, and they had a positive need for the comfort of their own communal institutions. Moreover, Native Americans, whatever the implications of their public pronouncements, had no intention of opening up their primary-group life to entrance by these hordes of alien newcomers. The situation was a functionally complementary standoff (Gordon, 1964:111).

It should be emphasized that because of the power of the dominant society, acculturation and cultural assimilation usually have taken place. Minority groups generally have discarded their native cultures and have acquired the ways of the mainstream. But what Gordon called structural assimilation and its variations—such as fusion, amalgamation, and integration—have been much slower to occur.

It is interesting to note that in the 1960s and 1970s there was a reaction by some majority-group children to the dominant group norms and values. Dropping out, rebelling, running away, and adopting discontinuous lifestyles caused concern among parents of the privileged groups. There is a certain irony to this, since it occurred at the same time that a large number of minority students were going to college and attempting to become part of the mainstream.

The Melting Pot

A much more idealistic goal for American society lay in the theory of the melting pot. The concept proposed that people from all over the world would come to the United States, meet new people and new races, intermix, and come up with a new breed called the American. Integration, amalgamation, intermarriage, and fusion would be desirable outcomes from this perspective.

Part of the support for a relatively open immigration policy was based on the underlying faith in the effectiveness of the melting pot. Rather than Anglo conformity and European influence, the uniquely American character could be explained by the intermingling of different people in this new environment. Frederick Jackson Turner (1963), a historian, was especially influential in presenting the thesis that the dominant influence in U.S. institutions was not the nation's European heritage, but rather the experiences created by the ever-changing frontier. The frontier acted as a solvent for the various nationalities and the separatist tendencies of many groups as they joined the westward trek. Therefore, the new immigrants would amalgamate and produce a new, composite national stock.

The theme of the melting pot was especially strong during the first third of the twentieth century. Israel Zangwill (1909) produced a drama entitled "The Melting Pot," which brought to popular attention the role of the United States as a haven for the poor and oppressed people of Europe. The major theme of the play was the entrance of a myriad of nationalities and races and how their fusion and mixing produced new individuals.

Studies of intermarriage conducted in the 1940s raised questions about the success of the melting pot. Although there was intermarriage across nationality lines, there was also a strong tendency to restrict marriage within the three major religious denominations: Protestant, Catholic, and Jewish. Therefore, instead of a single melting pot, a variant, the triple melting pot, was proposed (Kennedy, 1944).

The concept of the melting pot was perhaps a noble one, but in practice it was difficult to form much more than a vague notion of how it would work. Questions as to proportions, power, and the proper blend and mixture could be raised, although the most logical prescription from this model would be intermarriage and the constant intermixing of races, nationalities, and religions. Such a state could have occurred earlier under more natural circumstances, but prejudice, discrimination, and segregation created barriers to free interaction. People of color, especially, have been denied entrance into any of the white communities, and even the idea of a triple melting pot becomes an exclusivist concept, since it ignores the many individuals who belong to the other world that is not Catholic, Protestant, or Jewish.

Perhaps the most successful example of the melting pot has been the American cuisine. Here one can see the contributions of the various cultures and taste their blending and intermixing. An interesting outcome of this process has been the development of certain foreign dishes (for example, chop suey) that have actually been invented in America.

The melting pot became very similar to the practices of Anglo conformity. The contributions of minorities were often ignored, and the melting process consisted of discarding the ethnic in favor of the American. Many immigrant groups disappeared completely, without leaving a trace of their own cultures.

Entrance by the descendants of these immigrants into the social structures of the existing White Protestant society, and the culmination of this process in intermarriage, has not led to the creation of new structures, new institutional forms, and a new sense of identity that draws impartially from all sources, but rather to immersion in a subsocietal network of groups and institutions that was already fixed in essential outline with a general Anglo-Saxon Protestant stamp. The prior existence of Anglo-Saxon institutional forms as the norm, the pervasiveness of the English language, and the numerical dominance of the Anglo-Saxon population made this outcome inevitable (Gordon, 1964:127).

The basic problem lay in the power differential between the immigrant cultures and the White Anglo society, so that even though the ideal of all groups contributing was an attractive one, the resources of the dominant group made it virtually inevitable that the melting pot would turn out to be another version of Anglo conformity. There remained the problem of the barriers, or as Park (1950) termed it, the doctrine of obstacles, so that cultural assimilation might take place but intimate social interaction would not, except on terms dictated by the majority.

Cultural Pluralism

Both Anglo conformity and the melting pot assumed the absorption and eventual disappearance of the immigrant cultures into an overall American culture. As it has turned out, this was not the desire of many immigrants themselves, and as early as 1818 there were nationality group petitions soliciting for the formation of ethnic communities. These petitions were denied because of the principle that the formal agencies of the U.S. government could not be used to establish territorial ethnic enclaves throughout the nation. Whatever ethnic communality was to be achieved (the special situation of the Native Americans excepted) must be achieved by voluntary action within a legal framework that was formally cognizant only of individuals (Gordon, 1964:133).

Although ethnic communities could not be legally established, ethnic societies developed rapidly. Nationality-group settlements were common; the addition of old friends, relatives, neighbors, and countrymen meant that, in a

A Mexican barrio with stores and people.

strange new land, ethnic ties in the form of a familiar language and culture flourished.

And so came into being the ethnic church, conducting services in the native language, the ethnic school for appropriate indoctrination of the young, the newspaper published in the native tongue, the mutual aid societies, the recreational groups, and beneath the formal structure, the informal network of ethnically enclosed cliques and friendship patterns that guaranteed both comfortable socializing and the confinement of marriage within the ancestral group (Gordon, 1964:134).

Cultural pluralism was therefore a fact in early America, even though its formulation as a plausible theory is of relatively recent origin. The rise of nationalism, patriotism, and Americanism during World War I sorely tested the model of ethnic enclaves and ethnic cultures. Much of what is written about culture conflict, ethnic self-hatred, and identity is a result of these conflicting ideologies.

Social workers, especially those who worked in the settlement houses and slums, were among the first to recognize the role of an ethnic heritage and its institutions in helping immigrants to adjust to the new society. The effects of rapid Americanization were not always beneficial; there were intergenerational conflicts with children turning against their immigrant parents, and symptoms of social and family disorganization such as crime, delinquency, and mental illness.

One of the earliest statements of the pluralist viewpoint was by Kallen (1915), who rejected the melting pot as the correct model for U.S. society. Instead, he was impressed by the ability of ethnic groups to adapt to particular regions and to preserve their own language, religion, communal institutions, and ancestral culture. Yet they also learned the English language, communicated with others readily, and participated in the overall economic and political life of the nation. Kallen argued for culture diversity based on a model of a federation or commonwealth of national cultures. He felt that such a model represented the best of democratic ideals because individuals participated in groups, and therefore democracy for the individual must also mean democracy for the group.

Kallen presented several important themes:

1. Since ethnic membership rests on ancestry and family connections, it is involuntary, but it gives the individual a connection that is of special significance to personality satisfactions and development.
2. The pluralistic position harmonizes with U.S. political and social life. The imposition of Anglo-Saxon conformity is a violation of our ideals. Pluralism encourages the right to be different but equal.
3. The nation as a whole benefits from the existence of ethnic cultures. There is a direct ethnic contribution to enrich and broaden the cultural heritage; and the competition, interaction, and creative relationships among the various cultures will continue to stimulate the nation.

The most important of Kallen's themes, from an ethnic perspective, is that of equality. An unequal pluralism based on the inferiority of ethnic groups is not a good model of cultural pluralism. The stratification system in the United States has prevented many ethnic groups from achieving equality, which in turn has affected their perceptions of the desirability of their own cultures.

Another problem in cultural pluralism is the risk of categorically assigning individuals into groups through birth (although ethnic groups are accustomed to this process). Such roles remain frozen throughout a person's life, severely limiting freedom of choice.

The ultimate goal of cultural pluralism is more difficult to assess, when compared to Anglo conformity and the melting pot. The latter models see their end result as some sort of assimilation, whereas there is disagreement among pluralists as to outcomes. McLemore (1982) writes that one of the problems from a pluralistic perspective is that pluralists advocate varying degrees and types of separation and merger. There exists a range of possible positions, such as:

1. A minority group exhibits and identifies with Americanism, but also retains a large proportion of its ethnic heritage for use within the in-group. The group is bilingual and bicultural and has accepted the realities of living in both the majority and minority world.

2. A minority group exhibits a much higher degree of separation from the American system. There are strong anti-assimilationist sentiments, so that members question the basic values of the dominant society and wish to exert a high degree of independence over their economic, political, social, and educational lives. An extreme form of the separation ideology is that of secession.

McLemore believes that the first type of pluralism is based on the minority group's confidence that the majority group will not use its position of dominance in a malevolent manner; whereas the second model of pluralism, sometimes labelled conflict pluralism (Skolnick, 1975:573; Farley, 1995:167), is less confident about the good will of the majority and sees major flaws in becoming American.

The basic problem with the pluralistic model has been that of unequal power. Ethnic groups often were welcomed in the United States for their labor, but once they outlived their usefulness, they were no longer welcome. The idea of ethnics remaining separate and unequal from the mainstream has a long history. For example, the residual position of ethnics was aptly described in the *San Francisco Chronicle* in 1910:

> Had the Japanese laborer throttled his ambition to progress along the lines of American citizenship and industrial development, he probably would have attracted small attention to the public mind. Japanese ambition is to progress beyond mere servility to the plane of the better class of American workman and to own a home with him. The moment that this position is exercised, the Japanese ceases to be an ideal laborer.

The call for a pluralistic position by America's minorities is difficult to understand if it comes from a dominated position. To be effective in a pluralistic model, the minority subculture must have adequate resources. If large proportions of its population are poor, living in poverty, and dependent on the dominant community for employment and educational opportunities, then pluralism may reinforce already subordinated positions.

If groups are relatively equal, then the concept of a relational pluralism seems appropriate. The concept indicates that the groups are interacting, rather than being separate from one another.

BICULTURAL MODEL

There is considerable appeal among groups such as the Asians and the Mexican Americans for a bicultural model. The picture is that of two cultures living side by side and the individual acquiring familiarity with both of them. Accordingly, Japanese Americans would be acquainted with the Japanese language and culture and also would be comfortable with the American language and culture. The same would be true for the Chinese and the Chicanos; they would have friends, acquaintances, and familiarity with both the ethnic and the dominant culture. The model is similar to that of cultural pluralism, with many of the same problems; both must contend with the power and priority of the Anglo system, so that there remains an unequal biculturalism. Nevertheless, the multiple adaptations are not unusual.

For example, Kitano, in writing about the various styles of Japanese Americans, noted:

> Therefore, within one individual there are often the many personalities, the Uncle Tom to the white man, deferential and humble; the good son to his parents, dutiful and obedient; and the swinger to his peers, wise-cracking, loud, and irreverent. (1976:133)

It has generally been the lot of groups with less power to adapt to changing realities.

A historical force in the development of a pluralistic perspective has been the excesses of the Americanism of previous eras. The abstract and universalistic ideals that lay at the root of being an American, such as loyalty and patriotism, had gone out of fashion by the 1960s, but the issue of what it means to be an American under a pluralistic model is not a simple one. For example, if we paraphrase the old adage that what's good for General Motors is good for America, we would ask the question, Can the good of the country be advanced by competing ethnic claims?

Gleason (1980) indicates that the current writings on pluralism do not provide a theoretical perspective that identifies and deals with problems concerning unity and diversity and how to deal with conflicting claims of the one and the many. Operating under pluralistic models, nations such as Malaysia, Indonesia, and Sri Lanka have had severe racial and ethnic tensions, although the problems were complicated by dominance, inequality, and unresolved historical enmities. Canada is faced with the demands of the French-speaking province of Quebec and its desire for autonomy. Solutions to these problems are probably impossible to resolve; any policy decision will alienate significant sections of the population.

PATTERNS, SUCCESS, AND GOALS

It is difficult to talk about success without clearly stated goals. As we have indicated, there are a variety of patterns that distinguish intergroup relationships. One of the most common models is based on the European experience: voluntary immigration, peripheral contact, integration, and assimilation. This perspective, if viewed as normative, infers that those who are unsuccessful are deviant.

But an exploration of other goals does not imply deviance. Not all groups have experienced the European model; prejudice, discrimination, and racism, as well as historical, ideological, and motivational factors, have led to goals other than assimilation. Pluralism and bicultural models reflect alternative goals.

It should also be noted that the examples of intergroup relationships were based on two groups. There are additional complexities when more groups are added, which is the reality of the American experience. Asians, Blacks, and those of Hispanic descent interact with each other, as well as with the dominant White population, which is also composed of various ethnic and religious groups, so that dyadic models may be limited. Issues regarding the interaction among the various groups will be presented in the second section of the book.

Claiming membership in a racial minority and defining what it is to be successful in the United States is not an easy task. Economic success can be readily measured, but success in terms of identity, acceptance, and feeling comfortable is not simple. Minorities are subjected to powerful contradictions. On the one hand, there are promises of free and equal participation in the American system for all individuals, if not at once, sometime in the future. On the other hand, they also hear messages of ethnic communalism, whereby identity is based on common origin, race, and culture. Further, individuals are perceived as members or representatives of a group and acceptance is often based on the reputation of the group. Finally, most minorities are faced with inequality, as we will discuss in the next chapter.

Thus, goals and success are intimately related. For the assimilationist, a successful minority is one that has learned the American language, acquired its culture, and is on its way to becoming a full participant in the mainstream of U.S. society.

For the pluralist, a successful minority may be one that has maintained an ethnic perspective and network, retained its native language, culture, and values and is independent of the mainstream.

In summary, the following questions are pertinent:

1. What are the goals of U.S. society? Are they Anglo conformity, the melting pot, cultural pluralism, or what? What are some of the preconditions that must be met before these goals can be realistically assessed by the subordinated minorities? Who decides on what goals?
2. How can we empirically demonstrate and evaluate the effectiveness of some of these goals?
3. How do we prevent today's solutions from becoming tomorrow's rigidities and orthodoxies?

REFERENCES

BANTON M. (1967). *Race relations*. London: Tavistock Publications.

BELLAH, R. N., MADSEN, R., SULLIVAN, W. M., SWIDLER, A., & TIPTON, S. M. (1985). *Habits of the heart*. Berkeley: University of California Press.

BLAUNER, R. (1972). *Racial oppression in America*. New York: Harper & Row.

BOGARDUS, E. (1930, January). A race relations cycle. *American Journal of Sociology, 35,* 612–617.

FARLEY, J. E. (1995). *Majority and minority relations* (3rd Ed.). Englewood Cliffs, N.J.: Prentice-Hall.

GLEASON, P. (1980). American identity and Americanization. In S. Thernstrom, A. Orlov, & O. Handlin (Eds.), *Harvard Encyclopedia of American Ethnic Groups* (pp. 31–58). Cambridge, Mass.: Harvard University Press.

GORDON M. (1964). *Assimilation in American life*. New York: Oxford University Press. All excerpts are reprinted by permission of the publisher.

GOULD, C. (1995). "Positive Freedom, Economic Justice, and The Redefinition of Democracy." *Ethical Issues in Contemporary Society*. J. Howe & G. Schedler (Eds). Carbondole: University of Southern Illinois Press.

GRANT, M. (1916). *The passing of the great race*. New York: Scribner and Sons.

HIGHHAM, J. (1955). *Strangers in the land*. New Brunswick, N.J.: Rutgers University Press.

KALLEN, H. (1915). Democracy versus the melting pot. *The Nation*, February 18 and 25.

KENNEDY, R. J. R. (1944). Single or triple melting pot? Intermarriage trends in New Haven, 1870–1940. *American Journal of Sociology, 49* (4), 331–339.

KITANO, H. H. L. (1976). *Japanese Americans: The evolution of a subculture*. Englewood Cliffs, N.J.: Prentice-Hall.

KITANO, H., DANIELS, R. (1995) *Asian Americans*. Englewood Cliffs, N.J.: Prentice-Hall.

LYMAN, S. (1993). Race relations as social process: Sociology's resistance to a civil rights orientation. In H. Hill & J. Jones, Jr. (Eds.), *Race in America* (pp. 370–401). Madison: The University of Wisconsin Press.

McLEMORE, D. S. (1982). *Racial and ethnic relations in America*. Boston: Allyn & Bacon.

PARK, R. E. (1950). *Race and culture*. New York: John Wiley.

PARRILLO, V. N. (1994). Diversity in America: A sociological analysis. *Sociological Forum, 9,* (4), 523–545.

SHIBUTANI, T. & KWAN, K. M. (1965). *Ethnic stratification*. New York: Free Press.

SIMMEL, GEORGE (1955). *Conflict and the web of group affiliations*. New York: Free Press.

SKOLNICK, J. H. (1975). Black militancy. In N. Yetman & C. N. Steele (Eds.), *Majority and Minority* (2nd ed.) (pp. 557–577). Boston: Allyn & Bacon.

TURNER, F. J. (1963). *The frontier in the American history*. New York: Holt, Rinehart & Winston.

VAN DEN BERGHE, P. (1967). *Race and racism*. New York: John Wiley.

WALZER, M. (1980). Pluralism: A political perspective. In S. Thernstrom, A. Orlov, & O. Handlin (Eds.), *Harvard Encyclopedia of American Ethnic Groups* (pp. 781–787). Cambridge, Mass.: Harvard University Press.

ZANGWILL, I. (1909). *The Melting Pot*. New York: Macmillan.

Chapter 3

Racial Stratification and Inequality

As soon as we are able to see the world and to make judgments, we experience hierarchy, status, and power. As youngsters, we use other words and more primitive comparisons—"Bill, the shrimp, owns the baseball so we'd better treat him nice"; "That big dude, Wally, hits you so hard that you'd better obey him"; "Gee, John's house has a swimming pool and they drive a Cadillac"; and "I can't beat Jean in a spelling bee."

We notice that as early as elementary school, children are grouped with innocent-sounding names such as busy bees, flying swallows, and happy turtles. We may wonder why the "smart kids" belong in one group and the slower ones in another. And every day, we are lined up by size and sex; and certain individuals are always chosen to be leaders.

As we grow older, our observations are sharpened. We notice that certain areas and neighborhoods are more run down and are populated by people of color, while the big houses in exclusive neighborhoods belong to Whites. We notice that public buses and streetcars are filled with people of color and that doormen, bus drivers, street cleaners, and gardeners are racially different from those who come to work in business suits and have offices in impressive, big buildings.

We go to the movies and generally see white male heroes, attractive but helpless females, and a host of stereotyped minority groups. Around the family table we notice that our food is often different, and that when we go out to eat it is usually at a fast food outlet such as McDonalds and Burger King, while some of our White peers talk about eating at Spago's or other expensive Los Angeles area restaurants.

It is clear that unless we are totally unaware, we all experience stratification, hierarchy, status, and power. We learn very quickly that although we are told that all Americans are born equal, we also know that some are born more equal than others. There are those who are able to get what they want, and have a life of one opportunity after another, while others live a daily struggle characterized by suffering and the lack of opportunities. And in terms of groups, it appears that people of color are more apt to belong to the latter category.

The purpose of this chapter is to address the following questions: Why is there hierarchy and inequality? Is there a relationship between membership in a minority group and income, education, power, and social status? Are there policies that can lead to change? Is talent and motivation sufficient for minority groups to achieve equality?

We will present views on hierarchy and present the functional and the conflict perspectives as contrasting explanations of inequality. We will discuss power and discrimination in Chapter 5.

INEQUALITY

By inequality, we refer to the distribution of rewards, goods and services, benefits and privileges, honor and esteem, and power and influence available to incumbents of the different social roles and social positions and associated with the different roles and positions. Social inequality based on racial lines means that Whites usually will occupy the more desirable positions, and that people of color will end up with the leftovers. As Rothman (1978) observed, being a Korean, a Black, or a Mexican may be less desirable than being a Canadian or a Swede. It may result in being excluded from certain clubs, occupations, and neighborhoods. The methods and procedures used to assign individuals and groups to different roles and positions is called social stratification (Matras, 1975:6).

Lenski (1966) writes about the relationship between social inequality and social stratification. Inequality is viewed as a condition whereby people have unequal access to the resources, rewards, services, and positions of a society; social stratification occurs when inequality has been institutionalized, so that there is a system of social relationships that determines who gets what and why. In our society, there is presumably equal access to all positions to individuals with proper qualifications; however, an examination of our stratification system reveals the absence of racial minorities in the more desirable roles.

Marger (1991), in his analysis of ethnicity in the United States, indicates that the American ethnic hierarchy can be viewed, very broadly, along the following lines:

1. The top positions are manned primarily by white Protestants of various national origins, for whom ethnicity has little significance except as a means of distinguishing themselves from the remainder of the ethnic hierarchy.

   Dye (1976)—in a book with the intriguing title, *Who's Running America?*—identified 4,000 people considered to be top decision makers in corporate government and public interest sectors. People in these elite positions were generally affluent, White, Anglo-Protestant, and male. There were two Blacks and no Chicanos, Native Americans, or Asian Americans in his list. There were also very few recognizably Irish, Italian, or Jewish names in this list.

   Lind (1995), uses the term the *white overclass* to represent those who have a near monopoly on campaign financing of both the Republican and Democratic parties and control over the majority of judicial and political appointees.

2. The intermediate range includes white Catholics of various national origins, Jews, and Asians for whom ethnicity continues to play a role in the distribution of rewards and influences social life, but in both instances, decreasingly so.

3. The bottom range includes Blacks, Hispanics, and American Indians for whom ethnicity continues to shape the basic aspect of their lives (Marger, 1991:521).

A Hispanic family living in poverty.

A report issued by the American Council of Education, titled *One-Third of a Nation* (1988), shows that although most Americans have progressed economically and educationally, one-third of U.S. citizens have not. For example, in 1988 there was an emergence of one-third of the nation, primarily Blacks, Hispanics, American Indians, and Asian Americans afflicted with the ills of poverty and deprivation. The report indicates that by the year 2000, almost 42 percent of all public school students will be minority children or other children of poverty. They note that although some Asian American groups have achieved a degree of parity with Whites in terms of education and income, there are segments of the Asian American population who have problems similar to other racial minorities.

Importance of Ethnic-Racial Stratification

The ethnic-racial stratification model and its status-power dimension represent one important factor in the disagreements over social policy and implications for understanding behavior. For those who are in, and for those who identify with the elite sector, race, ethnicity, and other group identities are unimportant; rather, the emphasis is on the individual. Merit, achievement, and success are based on individual ability and motivation so that a program such as affirmative action is looked upon unfavorably.

For those in the middle sector, such as white Catholics and Jews, ethnicity and religion provide another lens for viewing the world. For Asians, race is an additional factor.

For those in the bottom strata, race provides the critical lens by which they perceive the world. Experiences of prejudice, discrimination, and segregation have been based on race. The stratification provides the following:

1. The power lies in the elite sector, whose perception—that of individual responsibility—remains the most popular. It follows a functional perspective; those who do not adhere to its norms are at fault. Group explanations of social problems (i.e., poverty, racism, and sexism) obscure the responsibility of the individual. Issues of diversity and policies to compensate for past group injustices are improper.

2. The stratification follows an individual (the elite) to group (ethnicity and race) perspectives.

3. The stratification provides the lens and focus for perceiving the society. The recent O. J. Simpson verdict demonstrated the importance of the differences. The overall white population, using an individual lens based on scientific evidence, felt that he was guilty; the Blacks, viewing society from a racial lens, saw the football star as not guilty.

4. The ethnic-racial stratification follows the overall stratification structure (rich; middle class; working class; and poor) in the United States (see Table 3–1).

Table 3–1   A Model of Stratification Structure in the United States

(1) Class	(2) Approximate Percent of Population	(3) Range of Family Income	(4) Occupational Category	(5) Source of Income
Rich	3%	>$100,000	White collar	Capital, salaries
Middle class	42	$40,000–120,000	White collar	Salaries
Working class	40	$15,000–50,000	Blue collar	Hourly wages
Poor	15	<$18,000	Blue collar	Hourly wages, Public aid

Source: Beeghley, L. (1996). *The Structure of Social Stratification in the United States*, p. 24

There are many individual exceptions to the above hierarchy, but viewed broadly, the categories reflect both the power, role of the individual and over-all stratification as we enter the close of the twentieth century.

Table 3–1 shows the overall stratification in the United States (Beegh-ley, 1996). The rich—primarily the WASP—comprise about 3 percent of the population, with incomes over $100,000 based on capital, investments, and salaries. The middle class comprise 42 percent of the population, with in-comes ranging from $40,000 to $120,000 based on salaries. The working class comprises 40 percent of the population and is characterized by membership in blue-collar occupations and working for hourly wages. The poor, with incomes below $18,000, are also blue-collar, with incomes from hourly wages and pub-lic aid.

It is apparent that the loss of a job hits those whose primary source of in-comes are based on salaries and hourly wages. But the basic generalization is that wealth is concentrated in the top 3 percent and that the stratification clearly demonstrates inequality.

IS SOCIAL INEQUALITY NECESSARY?

Inequality is readily recognizable in all societies. A question then arises con-cerning the inevitability of hierarchical stratification. The unequal distribu-tion of rewards (those factors that increase control over one's own destiny, in-crease material comforts, and make life better), of power (command of resources), of prestige (social honor), of privilege (benefits, opportunities, and exemptions from certain obligations), and of wealth (money and property) is especially evident in complex, urban societies (Burkey, 1978:20). Turner and Starnes (1976:7) found that all societies with economic surpluses have sys-tems of inequality. Rousseau, the French philosopher, wrote in 1754 that the possession of private property was the basis of social inequality and that it was a negative and destructive practice. Ferguson and Miller from Scotland wrote a few decades later, expounding an opposing point of view: They saw the ownership of property and the resulting differences in income and prestige as progressive steps towards a more civilized society (Matras, 1975).

Kerbo (1983:16) lists three kinds of inequalities found in most societies and finds a high correlation among the three factors:

> Inequalities of honor, status or prestige; inequalities of economic influence and material reward; and inequalities based on military, political, or bureaucratic power.

The unequal distribution of rewards has led to the creation of strata or social classes. Social classes are divisions of whole societies or communities within societies that represent divisions of a combination of rewards (Burkey, 1978:29). Burkey discovered that at least three social classes can be identified in almost all complex societies. The greatest amount of rewards, power, prestige, privilege, and wealth is associated with the upper classes; lesser amounts are associated with the middle classes, and the least favored are the lower classes.

The social class system was based partly on the need for a stratification system that would allow for placement based on ability and merit, rather than on the ascriptive criteria of previous stratification systems (Kerbo, 1983).

There are also inequalities such as status, honor, self-esteem, deference, and life styles. Although not all inequalities are based on race, the total picture is relatively consistent; namely, that belonging to the nonwhite group places a person in the lower part of the stratification system.

Oliver and Shapiro (1995) indicate that an unresolved U.S. dilemma deals with the disparity between black and white wealth. Since the early 1970s, the economic status of Blacks relative to Whites has stagnated or deteriorated. Myths held by Whites include the idea that affirmative action has provided equal opportunity for Blacks and that overt discrimination has virtually disappeared. Therefore, there is no need for governmental action. Instead, there is some feeling that Blacks now have an advantage because of affirmative action and that Whites are now the disadvantaged group (reverse discrimination). But, as the authors indicate, the disparity between white and black wealth continues to increase, and that instead of concentrating on black failure, there must be an emphasis on building structural supports. Black college graduates were as likely to live in segregated neighborhoods as black high school dropouts. White America, if left to its own devices, will never finish the task of addressing racial equality without governmental compulsion. It would require leadership at the top and would be a politically unpopular task.

Vobejda (1989), in an article in *The Washington Post*, refers to the report issued by the National Research Council that a third of the black population will continue to be poor and the employment and earnings status of black men relative to white men is likely to deteriorate further. Even if racial discrimination were abolished, serious problems remain for Blacks. The recent economic turndown has affected Blacks the most, and black poverty rates since the 1940s have been two to three times the rate of the Whites.

In 1987, 20 percent of all U.S. children lived in poverty, but among black children, the figure was 45 percent. There was a similar difference in children likely to spend some time in one-parent homes: for white children, 42 percent; for black children, 86 percent. There were a number of other disparities: Residential segregation has remained virtually unchanged since the 1960s and a large proportion of Blacks were not covered by health insurance or Medicaid.

Raspberry (1989), although underscoring the importance of such a report, cites three major limitations. The report covers only Blacks and Whites and does not cover other minority groups; because it cites averages, it does not highlight the growing black elites, as well as the black underclass, and it does not take an advocacy position.

SOCIAL STATUS

Another measure of dominance is social status. Indicators of social status are subjective and often whimsical. But social leaders, the jet set, the beautiful people, the people who are on the covers of *Time* and *Newsweek*, who achieve celebrity and star status, who appear on the society pages, and who set the pace are dominant-group people, with occasional exceptions.

Social-distance scales provide an assessment of the social status of a group. Respondents are asked whether they would admit members of minorities to a variety of situations, ranging from close kinship by marriage, to living close by as neighbors, to exclusion from the country. In Bogardus's measure of social distance (1968), there was very little difference over time in the ranking of minority groups. Native Americans, Japanese, Chinese, Koreans, Mexicans, Blacks, and Indians (from India) clustered on the bottom end of the scale in the 1930s and still held their socially undesirable positions four decades later.

WHY INEQUALITY?

If people on the street were asked why some individuals and groups have acquired more of the goods and services of the American system than others, their answers would include a wide range, including luck, skill, good education, pull, rich parents, brains, knowing the right people, inheritance, personality, winning a lottery, and hard work. Other less socially desirable behavior may also be mentioned—selling drugs, white-collar crime, big business takeovers, bankruptcies, and corporate crimes. These responses cover most of the ideas that social scientists offer in response to the same question.

Although there are variations, social science theories concerning stratification can be divided into two broad overlapping categories: the conservative—also allied with functional and order explanations—and the radical, or conflict, perspectives. Conservative explanations are based on a view of society as a system with various needs that have to be met; they maintain that stratification and inequality are inevitable. Radical explanations are based on a view of society as a system of competing groups; they maintain that stratification and inequality are the result of differential power.

Lenski (1966:22–23) discussed nine major points of disagreement between the conservative and the radical perspectives. Kerbo (1983:89) selected the following three main assumptions that differentiated the two positions.

Functional theorists stress the role of values and norms in holding a society together. Conflict theorists believe that society is held together by competing interests, and that the more powerful groups have the power to impose their values and norms upon less powerful groups. Functional theorists believe the society is a whole and liken it to a biological organism. Conflict theorists tend to focus more on the parts and processes in that system. Functional theorists tend to view society as a social system with specific needs to be met. Conflict theorists perceive societies as providing the setting within which different groups with different norms and values compete.

THEORIES OF INEQUALITY

Functional Theories

The functional school is linked with sociologists such as Talcott Parsons, Kingsley Davis, and Wilber Moore. Durkheim's (1964) early paradigm of social stratification, which likened society to an organism with its need for order and organic solidarity, was important in shaping functional explanations. Inequalities were attributed to differences in ability and talent, and the notion that one group could use its power to dominate another group was never central to Durkheim's analysis (Kerbo, 1983:121).

Parsons (1953) viewed inequality as a consequence of value consensus in societies. Achievement and performance are judged on the basis of the needs, priorities, and goals of the system. Therefore, as Davis (1948) and Davis and Moore (1945) found, in all societies there are different social positions that are differentially valued but have to be filled. It is incumbent upon the abler members of the society to occupy the important and more difficult positions; the other roles also have to be filled and performed. In order to motivate and to allocate all of the positions with a minimum of friction, differential rewards and gratifications must be given, thus leading to social inequality. The relative size of the reward is related to the functional importance of the role or social position for society and the relative scarcity of qualified personnel to fill it. The functional perspective emphasizes that inequality is necessary in order to fill the differential occupational and other positions in a society.

Psychologists also argued for the virtues of inequality. Herrnstein asserted that unequal material awards are needed to attract talented and skillful people to important roles and positions. The notion of intelligent people (as measured by IQ scores) rising to the top and transmitting their mental abilities to their children, with the consequent formation of a group of meritocratic elites, is central to the positions of Herrnstein and Jensen (Anderson, 1974:82). Jensen (1969) further resurrects the view that there is a genetic, racial basis for social and personal inequality.

The much criticized bell curve (Herrnstein and Murray, 1994) resurrects between group differences based on intelligence studies. The implications of this shaky study are sobering; that because of racially inherited differences, a stratification system between "the superior and the inferior" is a natural consequence. It appears that such studies appear regularly from time to time.

Functionalist theory was criticized by Matras (1975:70) on the following grounds:

1. It is imprecise. The meaning of the importance of positions is unclear, and there is no clarification of the extent and direction of inequality. There is little opportunity for empirical testing.
2. It pays little attention to the dysfunctional aspects of institutionalized inequality.
3. It glosses over variations in patterns of inequality and in patterns of allocating rewards, prestige, and power.
4. The assumption of a congruence between the distribution of talent and the inequality of rewards is conservative and can be interpreted to mean that social inequality is in the best interests of society, an assumption that is empirically doubtful.

Possibly the most effective criticism of functional theory is to survey our recent record of leadership and power in places like Washington, D.C. and local city halls, and to question the notion that the cream rises to the top. The blundering, ineptitude, and lack of character and leadership displayed by many in high-salaried positions can lead to the point of view that the facetious Peter Principle (the prediction that people are promoted to their highest levels of incompetence) has as much validity as functionalist predictions (Anderson, 1974:82).

Chomsky observed that wealth and power may not necessarily be reserved for those of noble purpose and character. Instead, it may go to the ruthless, the cunning, the avaricious, the self-seeking, and those who are willing to abandon principle for material gain (Anderson, 1974:87).

It is interesting to note that Lenski (1966), Gordon (1978), and Banton (1977), major theorists in the area of race relations, all assume that the basic selfishness of human beings and their overriding desire to maximize their own gains are central to an understanding of human behavior. If their assumptions are correct, the question then might be how to develop a social system that will deter the most selfish and aggressive from taking over, rather than aiding and rewarding those with such qualities.

Conflict Theories

Conflict theories of inequality are associated with sociologists such as C. Wright Mills (1956), Rolf Dahrendorf (1969), and Melvin Tumin (1953). Karl Marx's writings on class conflict (Marx & Engels, 1965), differing class interests, the ownership and control of the means of production, and the exploitation by one class over another were precursors to the development of conflict theory. Marx saw class and class conflict as the moving forces in history. A dominant class owns the means of production and exploits other classes. It is then in the interests of the dominated classes to overthrow those in positions of dominance and to establish a social order more favorable to their interests. However, Marx did not see a continuous, endless class struggle for power; rather the struggle would end with the proletariat, or workers, in control, with no classes below to exploit (Kerbo, 1983:108).

From the conflict perspective, social inequality arises as a result of the struggle within a society for the goods, amenities, privileges, and rewards, which are in short supply (Matras, 1975:71). The theory emphasizes power and coercion in social life, the exploitation by advantaged groups and individuals to get what they want, and their ability to prevent other groups from getting what they want.

Political parties, labor unions, business groups, religious and racial or ethnic groups are examples of conflict groups. The position of conflict theorists is that the dominant values supposedly held by a society are, in fact, values imposed on it by individuals and groups that are able to hold or to monopolize strategic power positions. Therefore, it is the distribution of power, rather than the needs or values of shared values in a society, that influences how roles, positions, social rewards, and resources are allocated.

One major criticism of conflict theory is the importance it gives to power and authority. It has been accused of relying on power determinism that is difficult to test (Van den Berghe, 1963).

Although the functional and conflict models can be viewed as basically antagonistic, Himes (1980) has shown that they can be viewed as two faces of society. For example, one of the basic problems facing a nonwhite individual in the functional model is that of high alienation and loss of identity. However, racial conflict, with its ideological apparatus and action system, functions to alleviate alienation and to facilitate an ethnic identity. Group solidarity is enhanced, group boundaries are clarified, and the linkage between the individual and the group is strengthened through personal commitment and social action. In time, the group identity can be extended to the larger system through communication; the individual is exposed to larger social networks and to national core values. As a result, in realistic racial conflict, Himes argues, the United States gains some new Americans.

The conflict perspective does not provide the simple role prescriptions and plans of action that are part of the functionalist perspective. The prescriptions of working hard, learning English, and acculturating to the norms and values of the dominant group *are not* central to this position, although one can argue that these paths are important in order to bring about societal changes. The frustration of not being able to find significant ways to effect broad-scale change from low-power positions can lead to disillusionment, alienation, rhetoric, and cynicism, unless there is an ability to organize groups, to achieve an occasional success, and to obtain continued support and reinforcement.

Lenski (1966) found that in every society, those who belong to the dominant social classes have the greatest capacity to explain and to disseminate their views of the existing system of inequality. They are therefore apt to support the social structure and to rationalize their advantage. Thus, functional theory is generally conservative, and inequality is viewed as a natural consequence of value consensus and individual abilities.

The conflict orientation expresses the voices of discontent in the society. It views inequality as a product of coercion, domination, and power. Lenski noted a historical dialectic between these points of view and found that periods of domination are often followed by challenges to the dominance.

It is important to note that there is *no one* explanation for inequality. The purpose of presenting the conservative and radical perspectives was to focus on opposing explanations to facilitate thinking and discussion.

But the importance of the various views of inequality cannot be overestimated, because these perceptions are intimately related to policy, programs, and goals. A true believer in the functional model will view social disorder and unrest as deviant actions, whereas a proponent of a conflict perspective will view disorder and unrest as expected reactions from dominated groups. Each will probably advocate different policies, pursue different kinds of actions, and have different goals in mind.

For example, a counselor operating from a conservative position would feel successful if he or she could counsel a disenchanted individual back into the society, while a counselor operating from a radical perspective might feel successful if the individual would organize and attempt to change the society.

The problem of inequality may be exacerbated in the coming decades as we enter an ever-changing society where education and skills take on additional significance. Automation and competition from foreign economies has diminished the role of unskilled and semi-skilled labor and has divided our economy into two classes, the skilled with their affluence and the unskilled with their poverty. If there is no change in the present distribution of educa-

Chrysler plant using high-tech equipment in the making of automobiles.

tion and skills, high proportions of minority groups will fall into the poverty category.

ROLE OF THE GOVERNMENT

Omi and Winant (1994) emphasize the role of government in defining racial and ethnic equality. The passing of legislation, ranging from immigration to housing to marriage to civil rights and affirmative action, has deeply affected racial and ethnic minorities. In past times, government policy went against racial groups; immigration and naturalization were restricted, as well as civil rights. In the 1960s there was a change in governmental policy; the civil rights agenda achieved a priority, followed by an attempt to redress past discrimination through equal opportunity and affirmative action legislation. However, during the Reagan years, the government no longer played an active role in fighting race discrimination, and Supreme Court rulings by a conservative majority have further eroded some of the past gains by minorities in search of equality.

THE CURRENT AMERICAN DILEMMA

It should be recalled that the original American dilemma (Myrdal, 1944) saw white prejudice and discrimination as the fundamental problem between black and white America. The current American dilemma, if we are to believe survey results, is that although there is a significant decline in anti-black sentiment (Kluegel and Smith, 1986), there is no significant change in our racial stratification system and inequality. It appears that anti-black sentiment has become less direct and now stems from a variety of sources, including a perception that Blacks are receiving favored treatment from the government, and that differences in economic status are not the result of race, but of individual failures. On the basis of telephone interviews with several thousand adult Americans, Kluegel and Smith suggest that there is a dominant ideology concerning social stratification and inequality:

1. The opportunity for economic advancement is available to all Americans who wish to work hard.
2. Individuals are responsible for their own positions in the society. There is a rejection of structural explanations of inequality.
3. Individuals should be rewarded in proportion to their contributions. Respondents felt that our system of economic inequality was equitable and fair.

It is apparent that many members of the dominant group follow the main outlines of the conservative perspective. It may be that many members of minority groups also believe in hard work and individual responsibility, but there are probably many who feel that the conflict perspective is a more accurate explanation of their position. And it is probably true that most individuals, whether majority or minority, indicate that a combination of the perspectives may be closer to their reality.

The current American dilemma is more than the Black-White conflict. There are other major ethnic groups—Asians, Hispanics, Native Americans, as well as European ethnics, females, and Gays and Lesbians. Government policies favoring the wealthy through tax laws and subsidies have also contributed to the inequality dilemma. The ethnic groups will be covered in the second section of the book.

Conflict of Values

Sniderman (1985), in a survey of residents of the San Francisco Bay Area, found that race and inequality were thoroughly entwined with basic American values. Although he found that the general public was remarkably uninformed about a variety of world and national issues, everyone had an opinion of why there was racial inequality. Much of the resistance to equal rights for Blacks did not spring from a failure to learn the value of equality in the U.S. culture; rather it arose from a commitment to the American values of individualism and religiosity. Individualism supports the notion that anybody can make it, whatever the circumstances, if only one would put forth effort. Fundamentalism encourages a belief that the world is divided into sinners and the saved, and a tendency to feel suspicious and judgmental of others. Both of these values represent a deep strain in the popular U.S. culture. Therefore, as Sniderman (1985:117) writes:

> Both individualism and fundamentalism are at odds with the value of racial equality. But the importance of individualism in particular is not limited to shaping people's sense of the way the world should be; at least as important is its impact on people's sense of the way the world is. So the individualists systematically tend to deny or minimize the problem of inequality. Blacks, they say, do not suffer discrimination; nor are women held back; nor is being born poor a handicap. In short, believing in equality of condition, individualists are radical egalitarians.

The dilemma is that we have competing tendencies in the American value system. Individualism, which is central to the American value system, provides a strong source of resistance to the American commitment to racial equality. Moralism divides the world into the deserving and undeserving. Therefore, it is difficult for the country to address racial inequality as a high priority when the reigning philosophy of those in power reflect other values.

Wilson (1987) writes that the most effective way of addressing inequality is to construct programs where the more advantaged groups of all races can also see benefits. Manpower training, child support, and family allowances that are not targeted towards any group are the most likely to gain popular acceptance. As these universal programs draw support, disadvantaged minority groups would gain indirect assistance.

But McGahey and Jeffries (1985) indicate that federal policies for disadvantaged workers sound familiar and have not proved effective. The employment problem of minorities is often seen as a mismatch between inadequate skills and education, so that high training and skills are deemed necessary in the current labor-market structure. The assumption then becomes that economic growth will provide the answer to minority group problems, but even with the growth of the economy in the last several decades, the economic situation of minorities, especially Blacks, has continued to deteriorate.

The one goal that seems the most feasible, but has the least amount of support, is direct income stabilization. Most programs link income stabilization to some type of labor training, but employment in the service and high-tech industries seems to have widened earnings gaps, rather than narrowing them. The authors advocate continued affirmative action programs, public employment, and income distribution. But it seems that any change in the U.S. economy towards a more equitable distribution of economic resources will require active participation of the citizenry in cooperation with the government. But if the government hesitates to take the lead in addressing racial inequality, there is little optimism for those groups who are less than equal.

In summary, we have presented the conflict and the radical perspectives as explanations for inequality. The current American dilemma includes more than the Black-White conflict: It now includes a variety of other groups, competing value perspectives, and the important role of the government.

REFERENCES

AMERICAN COUNCIL OF EDUCATION (1980). *One-Third of a nation*. A Report of the Commission on Minority Participation in Education and American Life. Washington, D.C.: Author.

ANDERSON, C. (1974). *The political economy of social classes*. Englewood Cliffs, N.J.: Prentice-Hall.

BANTON, M. (1977). *Rational choice: A theory of racial and ethnic relations*, Working Paper No. 8. Bristol, England: University of Bristol, SSRC Research Unit on Ethnic Relations.

BEEGHLEY, L. (1996). *The structure of social stratification in the United States*. Boston: Allyn & Bacon.

BOGARDUS, E. (1968). Comparing racial distance in Ethiopia, South Africa and the United States. *Sociology Social Research, 52,*149–156.

BURKEY, R. (1978). *Ethnic and racial groups*. Menlo Park, Calif.: Cummings Publishing Co.

DAHRENDORF, R. (1969). On the origin of inequality among men. In A. Beteille (Ed.), *Social Inequality*. Baltimore: Penguin.

DAVIS, K. (1948). *Human society*. New York: Macmillan.

DAVIS, K., & MOORE, W. E. (1945). Some principles of stratification. *American Sociological Review, 10,* 242–249.

DURKHEIM, E. (1964). *The division of labor in our society*. New York: The Free Press.

DYE, T. R. (1976). *Who's running America?* Englewood Cliffs, N.J.: Prentice-Hall.

GORDON M. (1978). *Human nature, class and ethnicity*. New York: Oxford University Press.

HERRNSTEIN, R., & MURRAY, C. (1994). The bell curve, *Intelligence and class structure in American life*. New York: Free Press.

HIMES, J. (1980). The function of racial conflict. In T. Pettigrew (Ed.), *The sociology of race relations* (pp. 245–255). New York: The Free Press.

JENSEN, A. (1969). How much can we boost IQ and scholastic achievement? *Harvard Educational Review, 39,* 1–123.

KERBO, H. (1983). *Social stratification and inequality*. New York: McGraw-Hill.

KLUEGEL, J., & SMITH, E. R. (1986). *Beliefs about inequality*. Hawthorne, N.Y.: Aldine de Gruyter.

LENSKI, G. (1966). *Power and privilege: A theory of social stratification*. New York: McGraw-Hill.

LIND, M. (1995). *The next American nation*. New York: Free Press.

MARGER, M. N. (1991). *Race and ethnic relations* (2nd Ed.). Belmont, CA: Wadsworth Publishing Co.

MARX, K., & ENGELS, F. (1965). *The German ideology*. New York: International Publisher.

MATRAS, J. (1975). *Social inequality, stratification, and mobility*. Englewood Cliffs, N.J.: Prentice-Hall.

MCGAHEY, R., & JEFFRIES, J. (1985). *Minorities and the labor market: Twenty years of misguided policy*. Washington D.C.: Joint Center for Political Studies.

MILLS, C. W. (1956). *The power elite*. New York: Oxford University Press.

MYRDAL, G. (1944). *An American dilemma*. New York: Harper and Row.

OLIVER, M., & SHAPIRO, T. M. (1995). *Black wealth/white wealth*. New York: Routledge.

OMI, M., & WINANT, H. (1986). *Racial formation in the United States*. New York & London: Routledge & Kegan Paul.

PARSONS, T. (1953). A revised analytical approach to the theory of social stratification. In R. Bendix & S. M. Lipset (Eds.), *Class Status and Power: A Reader in Social Stratification*. New York: Free Press.

RASPBERRY, W. (1989). But where are Blacks going now? *The Washington Post*, July 28, p. A25.

ROTHMAN, R. (1978). *Inequality and stratification in the United States*. Englewood Cliffs, N.J.: Prentice-Hall.

SNIDERMAN, P. M. (1985). *Race and inequality*. Chatham, N.J.: Chatham House Publishers.

TUMIN, M. (1953). On inequality. *American Social Review, 28,* 19–26.

TURNER, J., & STARNES, C. (1976). *Inequality: Privilege and poverty in America*. Santa Monica, Calif.: Goodyear.

VAN DEN BERGHE, P. (1963). Dialectic and functionalism: Toward a theoretic synthesis. *American Sociological Review*, *28*, 695–705.

VOBEJDA, B. (1989). Gains by Blacks said to stagnate in last 20 years. *The Washington Post*, July 28, p. A1.

WILSON, W. J. (1987). *The truly disadvantaged: The inner city, the underclass, and public policy*. Chicago: University of Chicago Press.

Chapter 4

Theoretical Perspectives

In Chapter 2, we discussed some of the problems related to goals, while in Chapter 3, we analyzed inequality and several theories and models were presented. Mills (1962) differentiates between a model and a theory. A model is a systematic inventory of information that helps us to understand what we are studying. It is neither true nor false and is useful to varying degrees. In contrast, a theory is a statement that can be tested to be true or false and may be related to elements of a model.

The purpose of this chapter is to present selected theoretical explanations regarding the interaction between the dominant white group and selected racial minorities in the United States. We acknowledge that there are issues of race, ethnicity, and inequality throughout the world. However, we will concentrate on those theories and models that are especially relevant for Blacks, Native Americans, Hispanics, and Asians in the United States.

Rex (1983) suggests that situations involved in racism have the following three elements:

1. There is exploitation, oppression, and conflict that goes beyond what is considered as normal and peaceful in market situations.
2. The exploitation, oppression, and conflict is between groups rather than individuals.
3. The more dominant group justifies the ongoing system, using some form of deterministic theory, such as genetic or cultural superiority.

RACIAL MINORITIES IN THE UNITED STATES

A cursory analysis of the four major racial minorities indicates a number of significant differences in their interaction with the dominant white group. First, the initial contact and the motivation of coming to America was different. Native Americans were already here when the first colonists arrived; Blacks were brought over as slaves, and initially, Mexicans were conquered in the U.S. Southwest. Early Asians arrived as coolie and contract laborers; in recent times, there have been the refugees. Therefore, motives for migration and initial contact with the majority community may be different from the "European" model of voluntary immigration, acculturation, and integration.

Secondly, all of the groups were desired primarily for their labor. Indians did not work out as laborers; slaves were imported because of the need for cheap labor, as were the early Chinese, Japanese, and Filipinos. The early Mexican residents of the Southwest, including California, owned much of the land, but the bulk of the immigrants from Central and South America were also a source of cheap labor. However, if they desired to move up from their low status positions, there were a number of formidable barriers that hindered upward mobility.

Thirdly, each immigrant group arrived with its own history, language, values, expectations, numbers, family and community structures, and culture, and came (and continue to come) at different epochs in U.S. history.

Italian immigrants on a ferry, 1904.

Therefore, their interaction with the dominant group must take into account the period of their entrance into the U.S. society as well as an understanding of immigration in terms of worldwide social-political-economic conditions. The birth of subsequent American-born generations with changed expectations provides an additional complication.

There are also differences in color and visibility. In a society where physical attractiveness is extremely important, the issue of color, desirability, and racism are intimately connected so that explanations of race relations must also include this element.

Finally, the underlying question to be addressed by our theoretical explanations deals with exclusion or inclusion. The power to include or exclude remains in the hands of the dominant group; whether the racial minority wishes to be included and to become part of the mainstream is secondary to the desires of the group in power. All of our racial minorities were faced with periods of exclusion—when Congress made its first effort to define American citizenship in the Naturalization Law of 1790, only free white immigrants were eligible for naturalized citizenship. Slaves and Indians were excluded; later immigrants from Asia were also denied naturalization. It was only in 1952 with the passage of the Walter-McCarran Act that these exclusion policies were overturned. An explanation of race relations and the persistence of an ethnic identity would have to take this element into account.

EARLY VIEWS

Prior to the development of more humanistic and scientific views of the relationship between the different races of humans, there existed categorical differences such as the division between superiors and the inferiors. The early Greek philosopher Aristotle claimed that inferiors were destined to be slaves and would benefit by living under the rule of their superior masters (Banton, 1967).

There were early attempts to classify the various races of humans. Rose (1974:84) writes that one of the earliest classifications was drawn by Carl Linnaeus, who divided homo sapiens into the following four groups:

1. Africans, who were considered slow, negligent, cunning, and capricious.
2. American Indians, who were tenacious, free, and easily contented.
3. Asians, who were haughty, stern, and opinionated.
4. Europeans, who possessed traits of liveliness and creativity and were considered as superior to the other races.

It was consistent with the thinking at that time, and of that still existing, that the Europeans represented a superior race.

SOCIAL DARWINISM

The publication of Charles Darwin's *The Origin of Species, or The Preservation of Favored Races in the Struggle for Life* in 1859 introduced the notion of evolution, so that the classification of humans through fixed typologies was no longer relevant. His view was that there were no permanent forms in nature; instead, he emphasized natural selection. Banton (1983) indicates that it is difficult to identify any coherent body of theory that could be labelled as Social Darwinism, but finds that it is less confusing to talk about Selectionist Theory, which holds the following:

1. Evolution may be assisted if populations are kept apart so that they can develop their special capacities.
2. Racial prejudice and discrimination keep racial groups apart.
3. Racial categories are influenced by evolutionary processes through inheritance and selection (Banton, 1983:47).

Social Darwinists believe that racial differentiation makes for the improvement of races. Each group develops abilities that will be of most use in their particular environment. There is also the belief that some racial groups are further developed in the evolutionary scale.

Sociobiology represents a current perspective based on selectionist theory. A spokesperson for this perspective is Van den Berghe (1985) who views both race and ethnicity as extensions of kinship and ethnic and racial sentiments. Ethnicity is a special basis of sociality, and it is primordial in the sense that it is irreducible.

Van den Berghe notes that in natural selection, by favoring kin, organisms are contributing to their own inclusive fitness. He suggests that there is an interaction of genes, the physical environment, and culture that results in behavior, and that a phenotype is always the product of the interaction between the genotype and the environment. Nepotism based on the proportion of shared genes serves as the basic mechanism of ethnic solidarity and the commonality of genetic interest is distinct from other interests, such as social class. Ethnicity therefore involves some notion of shared ancestry.

The first U.S. sociologist to provide a systematic analysis of race relations was Park. Starting in the 1920s (Park & Burgess, 1921), he indicated that man was the bearer of a double inheritance. There was a racial inheritance which was transmitted by interbreeding and biological inheritance, and a cultural one, which was transmitted through communication as a member of a social group. We modify Banton's (1983) summary of the main elements of Park's model as follows:

1. Migration brings together, often in unequal relations, people who are racially different.

2. Because of competition, individuals become conscious of their features by which they are assigned different statuses.

3. People who are in the more dominant positions are unwilling to provide equal opportunity for those in less desirable positions. Instead, they tend to look down upon those who are less fortunate as a different category and therefore suited to belong to the inferiors.

4. Prejudice serves the privileged group; it protects their interests and reinforces the superior to the inferior category.

Kitano's model of domination, which will be presented in the latter part of the chapter, explores the boundary maintenance mechanisms of prejudice, discrimination, and segregation that serve to separate the dominant from the dominated minority.

AN EARLY CLASS MODEL

Oliver Cox in *Caste, Class and Race* (1948) introduced a Marxist analysis to American race relations. White capitalists from Europe and North America, in their desire for profits, found people of color as a source of cheap labor. Capitalism viewed labor as an impersonal commodity, similar to rent and interest, rather than as human beings. In order to validate the view of people as commodities, workers were viewed as subhuman and inferior. Banton (1983:87–88) summarizes early class theory as follows:

1. As European capitalism expanded into territories where natural resources were abundant, there were advantages in securing a source of labor power that, being distinctive, could easily be kept in a servile state.

2. Within this unequal relationship, beliefs justifying the inequality were developed. These have been built into the structure of capitalist societies, dividing white workers from black.

3. Racial categories exist in the social life of capitalist societies because (a) they serve the interests of the ruling classes, and (b) the contradictions in these societies have not yet reached the point at which the true nature of the social system is apparent to the workers.

CURRENT PERSPECTIVES

The Split Labor Market

The leading proponent of a split labor market thesis is Bonacich (1972) who recognized that there were differences in power between black and white workers. In order to satisfy the demands of the higher paid white worker, employers have resorted to the dual labor market with a particular set of lower-paying jobs restricted to workers of color. Bonacich, like Cox, sees ethnic conflict as a part of capitalism.

Marxist Perspectives

The Marxist perspective is the view from the nondominant left. Marxists recognize a class-divided society as a result of capitalism. The elimination of inequality means revolutionary changes in the capitalistic system. The basic agreement of the various Marxist perspectives is that there is no race relations problem per se; that the basic structural features of capitalist society are the problem. There are a variety of other approaches, such as the rational choice theory (Banton, 1983; Hechter, 1986), which sees nothing about ethnic and race relations that calls for the development of a special theory. It shares with other rational choice theories in other fields two propositions:

1. Individuals act so as to obtain maximum net advantage
2. Actions at one time influence and restrict the alternatives between which individuals will have to choose on subsequent occasions

It further indicates that individuals utilize physical and cultural differences in order to create categories for inclusion or exclusion. In the process, ethnic and racial groups result from either being included or excluded.

In our analysis of the various perspectives, two models were especially relevant in understanding the major issues faced by the Blacks, Chicanos, Asians, and Native Americans. One was the internal, or domestic colonial model, the other was that of domination.

Domestic Colonialism

The domestic colonial model is a form of unequal institutionalized contact and resembles a master-servant, paternalistic relationship. Blauner (1972) labeled this model internal or domestic colonialism. Rather than limiting the dominant-subordinate relationship to colonized countries, Blauner emphasized the appropriateness of this model to race relations in the United States.

This colonization model has four components. The first concerns the racial group's forced, involuntary entry into the country. Black slaves were in this group. Second, the impact of the interaction is much more dramatic than the slower and perhaps more natural processes of acculturation. The colonizing power carries out a policy that constrains, transforms, or destroys indigenous values, orientations, and ways of life, such as those of the Native Americans and conquered Mexicans. Third, colonization involves a relationship by which members of the colonized group tend to be administered by representatives of the dominant power. There is the experience of being managed and manipulated by outsiders in terms of ethnic status (Blauner, 1972:396). Finally, there is racism.

Since one group is seen as inferior, it is exploited, controlled, and oppressed by the dominating group. It is also important to note that the initial contact of the groups was between inferior and superior.

The colonization concept helps to explain the differences between various immigrant groups. Blauner wrote:

> The crucial difference between the colonized Americans and the ethnic immigrant minorities is that the latter have always been able to operate fairly competitively within that relatively open section of the social and economic order because they came voluntarily in search of a better life, because their movements in society were not administratively controlled, and because they transformed their culture at their own pace giving up ethnic values and institutions when it was seen as a desirable exchange for improvements in social position. (1972:396)

Blauner also underscored the importance of control and ownership of the ghetto by European groups. It was usually less than one generation before these white ethnic groups controlled their own buildings, commercial stores, and other enterprises. The Asian groups also have followed this pattern. The black segregated communities, however, have always been controlled from the outside, and political, economic, and administrative decisions have been taken out of their hands. Outsiders come into the ghetto to work, police, and administer. Teachers, social workers, police officers, and politicians represent the establishment, which governs the ghetto as if it was an overseas colony.

One significant effect of this kind of colonialism is to weaken the will of the colonized in resisting oppression. As Blauner said:

> It has been easier to contain and control black ghettos because communal bonds and group solidarity have been weakened through divisions among leadership, failures of organization, and a general disspiritment that accompanies social oppression. (1971:399)

Blauner also stressed that the cultures of overseas colonies were not destroyed nearly to the extent that the African slave cultures were in the United States. The language, religion, and family structures of these Africans were almost totally obliterated when they were brought into this country.

The internal colonialism model is derived from an analysis of European external colonialism. As Balandier (1966) noted, the recent history of people of color (often referred to as the Third World) has been their subjugation to and dependency on European and American colonialism. The withdrawal of colonial rule after World War II did not end the oppression and dependency of native populations. External colonialism was often replaced by internal colonialism, since in many African and Asian countries power passed on to white colonists and settlers, who now run the show under local control. The exploitation continues; the system produces economic and other advantages for the dominant group and continues to affect the culture and the learning of the colonized (Feagin, 1978:38).

Hechter (1986) used the internal colonialism model to help understand the conflict between the British and the Irish. He discovered that the model seems to provide a more adequate explanation of the persistence of ethnic identities and loyalties than do other explanations.

Criticisms of the theory.   The primary critic of the colonialism perspective is Glazer (1971), who believes that America's racial ethnic groups are not completely trapped and that it is possible for them to move away voluntarily from their pariah status. He cites the increasing number of skilled workers, supervisors, professionals, and white-collar workers among minorities and sees a strong similarity between their situation and that of the European immigrants.

Glazer admits that racial minorities face prejudice and discrimination but states that these barriers are universal and have to be faced by all who are strangers. The level of prejudice and discrimination is determined by what official assistance the minority receives and by the role of the state. Glazer notes that expressed prejudice has steadily declined and that the percentage of minorities has increased on all levels of government employment. Therefore, he believes that the colonial analogy, especially as applied to the U.S. Black, is an invalid one.

THE DOMINATION MODEL: PREJUDICE, DISCRIMINATION, AND SEGREGATION

The model of domination is an example of unequal pluralism and is based on a racial stratification system in which there is a dominant white group and dominated minority groups. Weber (1946) saw societies as divided between those who ruled and those who were ruled, and that status groups tended to draw lines around themselves in order to restrict any type of interaction. There was a tendency toward closed castes and the ranking of people into hierarchies based on class, status, and power.

Immigrants, especially those from Asia, Southern Europe, and Latin America, were generally placed at the bottom of the two-category system. The majority of immigrants did not know the language; they were often unfamiliar with the culture; and all too frequently they lacked the necessary capital or resources to succeed. Furthermore, few had the education and competitive skills necessary for rapid mobility and their phenotypes did not fit into the image of the dominant group. As early as in the colonial period, the wise statesman, Benjamin Franklin, expressed his preference for "purely white people," and excluded Spaniards, Italians, French, Russians, and even

*A wealthy Anglo family with
minority household staff.*

Swedes whom he classified in the "swarthy" complexion category, and instead preferred Germans, the Saxons, and English who made up the principal "White People" on earth (Rischin, 1990:75).

The important point is that some groups achieved a degree of mobility, integration, and assimilation within a short period of time; other groups, mostly those of "swarthy" complexion remained under domination. It is our hypothesis that their mobility and acceptance into the dominant society was hindered, delayed, and deflected by a number of barriers. These barriers included prejudice, discrimination, and segregation, and in extreme cases resulted in individuals being confined in concentration camps, expelled from the country, and even exterminated (Daniels & Kitano, 1970:12).

Figure 4–1 shows the domination model and the barriers that have been used to maintain the system. Unequal stratification is effectuated principally through visibility and racism, based on the premise that dominant group members (D) are superior to dominated group members (d). However, the mere belief in group superiority is not enough—boundary-maintenance mechanisms are erected in order to reinforce the stratification.

The first three interrelated actions to maintain superiority are prejudice, discrimination, and segregation. The primary mechanisms that support these prescriptions include: (1) the use of stereotypes, which leads to avoidance; (2) the use of legal barriers and norms, which leads to a competitive disadvantage; and (3) the isolation of the dominated minority.

Severity of treatment of a dominated group is related to its degree of perceived threat, its unpopularity, and the enforcement power of the dominant group. Generally, a crisis situation (war, revolution) triggers actions such as placing people in concentration camps, expulsion, and extermination. These actions result in exiles, refugees, and genocide. There is a hypothesized interrelationship among all of the variables; the more severe treatments of the minority occur when prejudice, discrimination, and segregation have already ex-

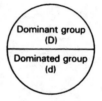

BARRIERS			
	Actions	*Mechanism*	*Effects*
Common actions	1 Prejudice	Stereotypes	Avoidance
	2 Discrimination	Laws, norms	Disadvantage
	3 Segregation	Laws, norms	Isolation
More severe actions	4 Concentration camps	Crisis	Incarceration
	5 Expulsion	Crisis	Exile, refugees
	6 Extermination	Crisis	Genocide

Figure 4–1   Model of Domination.

acted their toll. Therefore, in order to avoid such severe solutions to racial problems as exile and genocide, efforts should be mounted to combat prejudice, discrimination, and segregation.

SUMMARY

In summary, we have presented a number of theoretical perspectives and models that deal with the relationships between groups. Most of the American perspectives concentrate on the black-white issue and range from assimilation to pluralism to separation and a restructuring of society. The domestic colonial and the domination models were presented as being the closest to the problem in the United States. In the next chapter, we will focus on prejudice and discrimination, which will depend much more on psychological models.

REFERENCES

BALANDIER, G. (1966). The colonial situation: A theoretical approach. In I. Wallerstein (Ed.), *Social Change* (p. 35). New York: John Wiley.

BANTON, M. (1967). *Race relations*. London: Tavistock Publications.

BANTON, M. (1983). *Racial and ethnic competition*. Cambridge: Cambridge University Press.

BLAUNER, R. (1972). *Racial oppression in America*. New York: Harper and Row.

BONACICH, E. (1972). A theory of ethnic antagonism: The split labor market. *American Sociology Review, 37*, 547–559.

COX, O. (1948). *Caste, class and race: A study in social dynamics*. New York: Monthly Review Press.

DANIELS, R., & KITANO, H. (1970). *American racism: Exploration of the nature of prejudice*. Englewood Cliffs, N.J.: Prentice-Hall.

DARWIN, C. C. (1859). *The origin of species, or the preservation of favored races in the struggle for life*. New York: Mentor Books.

FEAGIN, J. (1978). *Racial and ethnic relations*. Englewood Cliffs, N.J.: Prentice-Hall.

GLAZER, N. (1971). Blacks and ethnic groups: The difference and the political difference it makes. *Social Problems, 18,* 451.

HECHTER, M. (1986). *International colonialism*. Berkeley and Los Angeles: University of California Press.

REX, J. (1983). *Race relations in sociological theory*. London: Routledge and Kegol, Paul.

RISCHIN, M. (1990). Just call me John: Ethnicity as mentality. In P. Kivisto & D. Blanck (Eds.), *American Immigrations and Their Generations* (pp. 64–84). Urbana: University of Illinois Press.

MILLS, C.W. (1962). *The Marxists*. New York: Dell.

PARK, R. & BURGESS, E. W. (1921). *Introduction to the science of sociology*. Chicago: University of Chicago Press.

ROSE, P. (1974). *They and me*. New York: Random House.

VAN DEN BERGHE, P. L. (1985). Race and ethnicity: A sociobiological perspective. In N. Yetman (Ed.), *Majority and Minority: The Dynamics of Race and Ethnicity in American Life* (4th Ed.) (pp. 54–61). Boston: Allyn and Bacon.

WEBER M. (1946). Class, status, party. In M. Weber, *Essays in sociology* (edited and translated by H. H. Gerth & C. W. Mills). New York: Oxford University Press.

Chapter 5

Prejudice and Discrimination

It is difficult, if not impossible, to live in a society where there is no prejudice. So, one piece of good advice may be to develop a degree of tolerance and minimize prejudgments in relationships with others. Or, in some cases, prejudice may even be beneficial. For example, a prejudice against eating mushrooms, especially if picked in the wild, may be wise.

However, when it comes to *racial prejudice*, especially in terms of prejudging other racial or ethnic groups in negative terms, a greater degree of awareness, more tolerance, and even active attempts to ameliorate the attitude is appropriate. For in the model of dominance presented in the previous chapter, prejudice is the initial step towards exclusion; coupling prejudice with discrimination and segregation may eventually lead to the exile or extermination of a group. Therefore, it is important to understand the role of racial prejudice and discrimination and its effect on the society.

The purpose of this chapter is to discuss prejudice and discrimination, provide possible explanations, and assess their effects on various groups. One problem is that racial prejudice has gone underground; that is, there is now a risk in making overtly racist statements, so that paper and pencil tests or statements derived from interviews and public pronouncements may reflect social desirability, rather than true feelings. It is interesting to note the statements of Detective Mark Fuhrman in the O. J. Simpson trial of 1995; the detective used the N . . . word many times, coupled with overtly racist remarks and behavior. The general negative reaction towards the detective would lead one to believe that prejudice, at least in using certain words, is dead. In reality, however, one can still hear the N . . . word used freely in private conversations.

The Japanese have long recognized the difference between public and socially desirable attitudes and true inner feelings. The term *tatemae* refers to public behavior and what the respondent feels the questioner wishes to hear; *honne* refers to the true feelings of the respondent. We also recognize that social desirability is a strong factor in public attitudes and behavior, especially in areas such as race prejudice and discrimination. Perhaps the one optimistic sign is that overtly hostile attitudes are no longer socially desirable. But the more important question is, Will they also disappear in the private psyche?

PREJUDICE

There are many definitions of prejudice. It is a set of attitudes that causes, supports, justifies discrimination (Rose, 1951:5); an emotionally rigid attitude or predisposition to respond toward a group of people (Simpson & Yinger, 1965:10); and an antipathy based upon a faulty and inflexible generalization (Allport, 1954:7). Prejudice refers to beliefs and attitudes—what people think—and it may or may not be directly related to behavior.

It is generally agreed that race prejudice is an irrationally based negative attitude toward a racial or ethnic group, and it is maintained through stereotypes: They smell bad; they breed like rabbits; they lower property values. According to Allport (1954), a stereotype is an exaggerated belief associated with a category of people, such as a racial, ethnic, or religous group. One adverse effect of race prejudice is that individuals of a target group are avoided because of prejudgments and negative stereotypes.

Prejudice is a difficult phenomenon to study because groups and individuals differ in the direction and amount of prejudice, because racial stereotypes may change, and because the targets of these negative attitudes may also change. Because it is an attitude, it is difficult to measure, especially if an admission of racial prejudice is viewed as socially undesirable.

Pincus and Ehrlich (1994) emphasize that attitudes are composed of an interrelated set of beliefs, feelings, and motivations, so to indicate that a person is prejudiced against a group means that he or she holds a set of beliefs about that group (inferior), has an emotional reaction to the group (feels that they are treacherous), and is motivated to behave in a certain way toward that group (avoidance).

There are many explanations of prejudice. One is its use in exploitation. The dominant group can avoid feelings of sympathy and empathy for the dominated through stereotypes or overexaggerations of negative qualities. One common stereotype in exploitation is to attribute less than human qualities to the subordinates so that they can be compared to and treated like animals.

Ethnocentrism, or the belief that one's own family, racial, religious, or ethnic group is unique and correct, is another explanation of prejudice. As individuals are socialized to the beliefs and behaviors of their own families and societies, they begin to feel that what goes on in their groups is natural, and so begin to judge others from this standpoint. In this sense, ethnocentrism is almost inevitable, since the very standards used to judge others are part of the culture that one has absorbed. Those who deviate are then viewed as unnatural and can become the target of prejudice. The family plays an important part in this process. The way one's family conducts itself is normal. Their food, their conversation, and their lifestyle become part of a familiar standard, and families who differ from it may be judged strange, foreign, or alien.

Ethnocentrism is a part of the identity of an individual and may be linked to other variables, such as pride, belonging, and standards. In this sense it is normal, and some measure of pride in one's own family and culture is a positive strength. It turns into a negative factor when it becomes overly rigid and the individual becomes intolerant of the behavior of others.

Prejudice may also be a product of structural opposition. Prejudice is a part of the we-they phenomenon, in which the existence of one unity in contrast to another leads to certain conditions. As Daniels and Kitano state:

> We prefer an interpretation in which a man is a member of a group of a certain kind by virtue of his nonmembership in other groups. A person belongs to a tribe or its segment, and membership is activated when there is opposition to this tribe. Therefore a man sees himself as a member of a group only in opposition to other groups, and he sees a member of another group as a member of a social unity, however much that unit may be split into opposing segments. (1970:19)

In response to stimuli, people choose to associate with certain persons and not with others. A football team is not really an entity until there is an opponent; once the opposition is present, prejudice between the enemies can be activated.

Frey and Gaertner (1986), in studying prejudice, indicate that racial prejudice among Whites is expressed in subtle and indirect ways, and serves to protect their image as being without prejudice and discrimination. Kimmel (1986) also notes that recent gains by Blacks through political struggles are offset by the persistence of black poverty and new forms of racism that are more subtle, indirect, and ostensibly nonracial. Code words in current use and related to racism and prejudice include affirmative action, mandatory busing, quotas, special admissions, and welfare. For example, "Oh, you're an affirmative action student," or, "You're a special admissions?" may mean that the student is viewed as less qualified than the normal student.

Psychological Explanations

Frustration-aggression theories, psychoanalytic perspectives, and studies of the authoritarian personality view prejudice as transferring internal, personal problems to external objects. Ready objects for externalizing one's problems are racial minorities, who can be stereotyped, blamed, or scapegoated for practically any personal failure.

Dollard (1938), using a Freudian framework, came up with a frustration aggression model as an answer to why people have prejudice. Banton (1983:83) summarizes the four main propositions of the model:

1. Social life causes stress and builds up frustration.
2. Frustration can be eased through the release of aggression.
3. Aggression is more easily displaced on visible minority targets (scapegoating).
4. Direct aggression is accompanied by displaced aggression, adding an irrational element to the prejudice.

The most ambitious study of prejudice was by Theodor Adorno, Else Frenkel-Brunswick and associates with the publication of *The Authoritarian Personality* (1950). They linked prejudice with personality and devised an F, or fascism, scale, which purported to measure the authoritarian personality. Although the study was widely criticized, it provided important information linking a personality type with strong prejudices. The authors were influenced by Freudian theory with an emphasis on repressed impulses and unconscious processes rooted deeply in the personality. Farley (1995:21) summarized four personality types that are linked with prejudice:

1. Those generally unwilling to acknowlege faults in themselves.
2. Those who tend to idealize their parents.
3. Those who would uncritically defend themselves and their parents.
4. Those who would quickly downplay their faults, but very quickly find faults in out-groups, especially Jews and Blacks.

The authoritarian personality also eagerly submits to rigid authority and is hostile towards those who reject authority. They tend to see the world in terms of power and toughness, and to think in very concrete yes-no, good-evil, and strong-weak dichotomies.

Selective experiences and selective learning can also lead to prejudice. A particularly negative experience with a member of an ethnic group or racial groups—such as having lunch money stolen during elementary school by a Black—can be recalled over and over again to justify the negative attitude to all Blacks. The psychiatric term transference is appropriate in this context; feelings toward people and experiences in the past are transferred to people and situations in the present.

There is also the earned reputation approach, in which the justification for prejudice is shifted to the target group (Rose, 1951). It is presumed that prejudice would disappear if the objects of the attitude would mend their ways.

The personal element in any analysis of prejudice should not be underestimated. In discussing the topic with individuals in such diverse areas as Scotland, England, Brazil, Japan, and the fifty states, I have noticed that the answer to the question Is there racial prejudice? is most often answered by a personal reference. Even though there may be rather blatant instances of racism in all of these areas, the individual answer may be no, if the victims are the others and the individual has been spared. Conversely, a negative experience may lead to an indictment of the whole society.

The Stereotype

In our model of domination, there is an interrelationship among prejudice, stereotyping, and avoidance. The negative attitude (prejudice) is reinforced and maintained by the racial stereotype, which is defined as an overgeneralization associated with a racial or ethnic category (ethnocentrism) that goes beyond existing evidence (Feagin & Feagin, 1996:10). The combination of hostile feelings and faulty overgeneralization can lead to avoidance.

Prejudiced feelings may start with, "They all smell bad," "they lower property values," and "What if your daughter married one?" Then the step to segregation: "Keep them on the reservations," and "Don't let them into our neighborhood." It may then lead to even more severe actions, such as concentration camps; "They're treacherous and can't be trusted—put them behind barbed wire;" and "They're animals—the only way to handle them is to get rid of all of them, put them in jails." Then to genocide: "The whole race and tribe should be exiled or eliminated." This sequence is an obvious oversimplification of a complex process, but it is presented here as a sober reminder that these terrible actions have occurred in the past and will no doubt continue to be used in the future to control and to eliminate unwanted groups.

The Mass Media

The effect on prejudice of television and the movies is important, since their portrayal of racial and ethnic groups may be a person's principal source of information. Therefore, if the media deals primarily in stereotypes and the viewer has little opportunity for personal contact with members of that minority, the probability of the stereotype becoming the reality to the viewer is high.

The problem is compounded by the constancy of the stereotype and the paucity of other images. Whites may complain about some of the negative images that are portrayed—greedy, sexual, and materialistic—but there remain other images that show other facets of the dominant group. This balance is lacking in minority group images.

Hollywood movies have thoroughly dehumanized the nonwhite world. The Whites, who are the exploiters, consistently show up as the good guys, as the bearers of civilization and all that is just and humane. Their superiority is taken as the natural order of things, and their justified extermination of the nonwhites provides a happy ending. Hollywood stereotypes have made it almost impossible to explain rationally that the colonized people are also human, and that their resistance to invasion, colonization, exploitation, and mass slaughter can be justified.

Iiyama and Kitano (1982) point to the long history of stereotyped portrayals of Asians in the movies and on television. Since the great majority of Americans have little intimate contact with this group, the stereotyped images of Asian male cooks, servants, and kung fu assassins (the most popular female image is that of the sexy Suzy Wong) become the standard perception.

Reducing Prejudice

Since the hypothesized causes of prejudice vary so widely, there is no simple program that can reduce the phenomenon. There is some agreement that prejudice can be lessened under the following conditions: equal-status contact in a spirit of cooperation, shared goals, working together on a common problem in the face of an external enemy, appropriate education activities, and contact sanctioned by law and by the political authorities (Allport, 1954). It should also be noted that the reduction of prejudice is a goal for those desiring some degree of integration, since the function of prejudice is to keep people apart. As we noted earlier, a totally separatist ideology sees prejudice as desirable since the prejudgments lead to avoidance of other groups.

Although there is a common perception that attitudes are difficult to change, advertising—especially through television—has a strong influence on a variety of attitudes, ranging from avoiding political candidates (negative campaigning) to choosing breakfast cereals. It is important to recognize that the media has a strong influence on attitudes.

In summary, we should note the multiple functions of prejudice. It promotes group unity and identification, supplies cues and scapegoats, serves ethnocentric purposes, and provides needed symbols. In fact, a not-so-facetious statement might be that if we did not have prejudice, we would have to invent it.

The goal of eradicating prejudice (even if we had the necessary technology) thus may not be the highest priority, although any diminution of negative racial feelings would be welcome. Rather, the task may be to prevent the attitude (prejudice) from being acted out (discrimination). As MacIver stated: "Whenever the direct attack is feasible, that is, the attack on discrimination itself, it is more promising than the indirect attack, that is, the attack on prejudice itself. It is more effective to challenge conditions than to challenge attitudes and feelings" (1948:64).

DISCRIMINATION

The second variable in maintaining the dominance of one group over the other is discrimination. Traditional analysis has linked prejudice to discrimination in a causal sequence, so that both our example of prejudice as a step leading to extermination and genocide and our quotation from MacIver are in keeping with this tradition. Allport (1954) saw discrimination as the acting out of prejudice. Myrdal (1944), in his study, *An American Dilemma*, linked valuations and beliefs as being behind discriminatory behavior against blacks. Kinloch (1974) used the term applied prejudice in discussing discrimination in which one stream of thought links prejudice (an intent to harm) and discrimination in a causal fashion.

Another perspective ignored the intent-to-harm motive and instead saw discrimination as motivated primarily by a desire to maintain one's own privileges or territory (Feagin & Feagin, 1996). Antonovsky (1960) saw a difference between gain-motivated discrimination and prejudice-motivated discrimination. Discrimination from this perspective is a result of the struggle over resources. The dominant group practices discrimination to protect its advantage.

Another related type of discrimination that may not necessarily include prejudice is institutional discrimination, a term linked to institutional racism, first introduced by Hamilton and Carmichael (1967). Their book, *Black Power*, pointed out the effects of social and governmental practices in perpetuating inequalities against blacks.

Yetman and Steele (1975) cited two analytically distinct types of institutional discrimination that may not be related to prejudice. Structural discrimination is the result of the normal operation of social structures, so that a business moving out to the suburbs may effectively discriminate against inner-city blacks by becoming inaccessible. Cultural discrimination refers to the ability of the group in power to set standards and criteria that may effectively screen out people with other cultural backgrounds. Bullock and Harrell (1976), in writing about institutional discrimination, offered a threefold typology. The first step is the establishment of prerequisites or preconditions at a point at which a disproportionate number of Blacks cannot qualify. The second step is freezing, in which, after a period of leniency during which many Whites have qualified, all new applicants are placed under newer, more stringent standards and requirements. Finally, there is a strategy called mapping, which consists of drawing geographic lines so as to minimize competition from racial minorities.

Our definition of discrimination is drawn from Feagin and Feagin (1996;19). Discrimination consists of the actions or practices carried out by members of dominant groups, or their representatives, which have a differential and harmful impact on members of subordinate groups. Therefore, discrimination involves actions with the actors discriminating and the victims on the receiving end. The actions may be overt or hidden, direct or indirect, intentional or unintentional. The actors may include individuals, groups, or organizations. The victims may be individuals, groups, or organizations.

Feagin and Feagin (p. 20) suggest four types of discriminatory practices:

Type A: Isolate discrimination
Type B: Small-group discrimination

Type C: Direct institutionalized discrimination

Type D: Indirect institutionalized discrimination

Type A: Isolate discrimination refers to harmful actions intentionally taken by a member of the dominant group against members of the minority. It may still be the most widespread and common type, even though the discriminator is taking the action without the immediate support of norms or standards of conduct in a large group or organizational context. For example, a waitress may serve the minority member last; the salesperson may be rude or indifferent; a police officer may handle the minority suspect much more roughly. Although relatively minor in terms of societal impact, this type of discrimination may prove to be the most irritating to the minority individual because it is so common and is a daily reminder of his or her inferior status.

Type B: Small-group discrimination refers to harmful actions taken intentionally by a small number of dominant-group individuals acting in concert against members of subordinate groups. Church bombings, floggings, vigilante groups, and Ku Klux Klan activities are examples of small-group discriminatory behavior.

Type C: Direct institutionalized discrimination refers to organizationally prescribed or community prescribed actions that are intentional and have been in practice continuously so that they have become institutionalized. Country clubs, social groups, and exclusive schools with restricted membership lists are examples of direct, institutionalized discrimination.

We would add that discriminatory laws have been the most powerful weapon to exclude groups from participation as equals in the society. Immi-

Local Nazi groups hold a "white pride" rally in St. Paul, 1994.

gration, citizenship, housing, education, and marriage have been denied
through legal means in the past so that the level playing field has been tilted
against minority groups.

Type D: Indirect institutionalized discrimination refers to discrimination by organizations that is not directly motivated by prejudice or intent to
harm. Regulations on seniority (last hired, first fired), requisites of education,
training, and graduation from good schools are examples of institutional practices that may not be directly linked to prejudice but are effective in limiting
the mobility and access of subordinated members. It should be noted that only
this category of discrimination is not directly linked to prejudice.

Various combinations of the categories may coexist. From a broader perspective, the picture of the dominant group and its interlocking political, economic, and social organizations; its intentional and unintentional practices;
and a mixture of prejudice and racism is what the Feagins labeled systematic
discrimination. The cumulative effects of systematic discrimination delineate
the oppression that is a part of a subordinate status.

REVERSE DISCRIMINATION

One current charge that comes mainly from white males is that of reverse discrimination. The implication is that heretofore advantaged dominant group individuals are now being deliberately excluded or passed over for positions by less
qualified females and minorities. The issue is not a simple one because it involves definitions of qualifications, standards, and measurement within a political context of shrinking resources and great emotion. Our definition of racism
(from the powerful to the powerless) raises the question of how dominated members can become the discriminators, unless one assumes that current legal decisions are now reflecting minority rather than majority perspectives.

Kahng (1978) took the issue of reverse discrimination further, asking
rhetorically, Can minorities and women do what white males have done to
them? For if reverse discrimination were actually to occur, white males would
have to be brutalized, degraded, and dehumanized to the same extent that
racial minorities and women have been, which is not likely to occur.

Kitano argues that for Whites to understand reverse discrimination in
terms of his own experiences, they would have to go through the following steps:

1. Their parents would be classified as "aliens ineligible for citizenship," so
   that they had no vote, could not own land, were victims of antimiscegenation laws and were banned legal immigration. In addition, they were forced
   to live in segregated ghettoes, with limited occupational opportunities.
2. That their American-born children, although citizens, would face racist
   barriers, and during World War II, the entire population (both citizens
   and aliens) residing along the West Coast would be placed behind

barbed wire, without a hearing and without a trial; their main "crime" was that of Japanese ancestry.

If those citing reverse discrimination had such a historical past, and would be willing to share these steps (admittedly impossible), then there may be some justification for using the term.

Jenks (1983) discusses the complexity of discrimination and its measurement but emphasizes that the effects of discrimination depend on its pervasiveness. Most European groups faced sporadic discrimination that did not seem to harm the victims in the long run, but the universal discrimination faced by the Blacks over many generations has had disastrous effects.

DISCRIMINATION AND POWER

It is important to understand the intimate relationship between discrimination and power. Without power, discrimination is ineffective; with power, discrimination maintains the dominance of one group over the other.

According to Schermerhorn (1978), power is related to numbers, cohesion, and resources. The majority group is characterized by numerical superiority and high cohesion and its control of resources—therefore, it is a group with power. The elite group may lack the size but is characterized as cohesive and in control of resources, and therefore another group with power. The masses may have large numbers but often are disorganized, lack resources, and are therefore a group with low power. The minority group will be deficient in size, in cohesion, and in resources, so it remains a powerless group.

Resources include money, prestige, property, natural and supernatural powers, and such factors as knowledge, competence, deceit, fraud, secrecy, physical strength, voting rights, the ability to bear arms, and membership in organizations. Power is a function of total resources and the degree to which these resources are mobilized (Bierstedt, 1950).

The groups in power are those that can effectively discriminate. They can pass the laws and the rules that help to define who belongs and who remains on the outside.

SOURCES OF POWER

Weber (1946) described three types of power. The rational-legal, the first type, was based on the belief in the legality of norms, rules, and the right of those elevated to authority to issue commands; traditional authority, the second type, was based on historical antecedents; charismatic authority, the third type, relied on the character of an individual.

French and Raven (1959) classified the sources of power into five types:

1. Reward power
2. Coercive, or punishment power
3. Legitimate power
4. Referent power
5. Expert power

The first two types of power depend on the possession of resources that permit the holder either to reward or punish. Legitimate power relates to authority, often based on contracts, promises, elections, or commitments made by one individual to another. Referent power relates to the notion of charisma in which one individual identifies with and likes another and desires to do as the other requests; love and sexuality may be variants of this. Expert power is based on special knowledge.

To this list we would add morality, which may control some of the more naked uses of power by arousing feelings of guilt. Discriminatory behavior, however, can be justified by appealing to moral superiority. Invoking the name of God for one's side has often led to some of the highest levels of discrimination.

Raven (1992), updated the French and Raven model of power by examining its applicability in a number of settings such as hospital infection control, patient compliance with physicians' recommendations, confrontations between political figures, children's influence on their peers, and supervisor/ subordinate relationships. Raven indicates that further research will continue to expand the model.

Many hypotheses are suggested by the French and Raven list. Referent power is one of the historical facts of race relations. Certain charismatic majority (as well as ethnic) group leaders have been regarded as people to trust and to follow, while others, who may be advocating the same programs, are regarded with hostility and suspicion. Legitimate power based on treaties and promises continues to explain our treatment of the American Indian. Appropriately enough, the Indians are also analyzing past treaties in order to exert pressure for more equitable treatment.

Kerbo (1983) suggests that dominant group power and elite power arise from a vast number of decisions made over time. The actions are not always conscious or deliberate, but when added up, they appear as a system of exploitation over less powerful groups.

CAUSES OF DISCRIMINATORY BEHAVIOR

A number of variables are suggested by Schermerhorn (1978) and Blalock (1967) as causes of discrimination. They include group size, social distance, competition, power threat, and status consciousness. All of these variables can be linked to prejudice.

Group Size

Perhaps the simplest explanation for discriminatory behavior among dominant group members is the fear of being overwhelmed by the sheer number of the subordinated masses. The threat and power of numbers may be actual or imagined but the effects are similar. For example, in California, elaborate charts were devised showing the state being overrun by yellow hordes (In reality these hordes almost never exceeded 1 to 2 percent of the population). V. S. McClatchy, the publisher of a major California newspaper chain, believed that the increase of the Japanese population in the United States placed the total in the United States in 1923 at 318,000; in 1933 at 542,000; in 1943 at 870,000; in 1963 at 2,000,000; in 2003 at 10,000,000; and in 2063 at 100,000,000 (Daniels & Kitano, 1970:52). It is interesting to note that the Japanese population in the United States in 1990 was just over 800,000—a figure well below McClatchy's projected 2,000,000. Nevertheless, the specter of hordes of Japanese was one important factor leading to discriminatory legislation against them and other Asians. Racial groups who are perceived to "breed like rabbits" have always been targets for some form of control.

Generally, the smaller the ethnic minority group, the less threatening it is. The one nonwhite family in an all-white community is accepted with friendliness (although it invariably has a low status), and these communities generally congratulate themselves for their racial openness. During the evacuation of World War II, Japanese Americans experienced much less discrimination in the East Coast and Midwest because their groups were small and scattered. Discrimination generally arises only if larger numbers of the minority begin to enter the paradise.

Numbers by themselves are not reliable predictors of discriminatory behavior under most circumstances and may be relevant only when there are actually only one or two visible ethnic minorities in a town or city of some size.

Social Distance

The attempt to maintain a social distance between the dominant and subordinate categories is another cause of discriminatory behavior. Attempts to remain at a distance in schools, jobs, housing, and personal relationships have characterized our past. Numerous empirical examples are available. Early studies by Bogardus (1930) used the concept of social distance to assess the degrees of social intimacy in relation to specific minorities. The degrees of social intimacy ranged from marriage, club membership, friendships, neighbors, employment, citizenship, to exclusion. Overall, there was a predictable pattern: Nonwhite groups were kept at a social distance. The one group that appeared consistently at the bottom was the Turks: Even among American

Blacks, Turks were ranked at the bottom. As we can infer, discrimination against them had little to do with the threat of numbers.

Social distance is maintained through attitudes of liking and disliking. In many instances the object of dislike is unknown or heavily stereotyped. For example, Katz and Braly (1958) asked students to list all the traits they thought typical of a number of ethnic groups. Blacks were regarded to be superstitious, lazy, happy-go-lucky, ignorant, and musical. Jews were seen to be shrewd, mercenary, industrious, grasping, intelligent, and ambitious. A more recent study using the Bogardus scale (1968) indicated that there has been no significant change in the ranking of groups. The important point in this study of stereotypes is how this fantasy about other groups, whether phrased positively or not, becomes the reality of intergroup relations. People feel that they can avoid or discriminate against their fellow citizens because of perceived imaginary traits.

Competition

Competition arises from a simple premise; that when two or more individuals are striving for the same scarce resources, the success of one implies relative failure for the other. Discriminatory behavior, therefore, can limit competition. The intensity of the competition is related to several factors, such as the strength of the goals, the number of satisfactory alternatives, and the number and power of the competitors.

The area of economic competition provides examples of how this belief can be translated into a motive for discrimination. For example, many Californians felt that the Chinese laborers of the early twentieth century were unfair competitors. They worked long hours for low wages, used their family and friends for cheap labor, seldom took holidays, and were therefore a threat to the U.S. standard of living. It was felt that white workers would be the main victims. Their loss of jobs and income lowered their ability to buy goods, which in turn hurt others. Chinese laborers and their unfair competition were among the presumed causes for the high unemployment during the economic depression of the 1870s.

Professional sports provides an interesting example of a competitive situation in which feedback is generally quick and objective (batting averages, pennants won, touchdowns scored), so that racial discrimination may be less likely to occur. It was not always thus: Jackie Robinson entered professional baseball only after World War II. Curiously enough, the field of competitive athletics may be one of the arenas in which functional theory is most likely to be valid, since there is a high probability that those with the talent and motivation are likely to rise to the top.

Blalock (1967) proposed a number of correlations between athletic teams (and by implication, other similar groups) and discrimination. If discriminatory barriers are maintained, an individual, and therefore the team, will not be able to perform to its maximum capabilities. Under these conditions discriminatory barriers will tend to be lowered. This is especially true in professional sports, particularly basketball and baseball. It was not too long ago that both of these sports were all-white. Now there is a preponderance of black athletes on all-star teams.

Power Threat

Perceived minority-group power is related to discrimination; power threat is related to numbers, average resources, and mobilization. The admission of Hawaii to the United States was fought vigorously by those who perceived a threat to white power by a state with a highly visible Asian population. The denial of voting rights to Southern Blacks for many years was in part motivated by the fear of their potential voting power.

Status Consciousness

Status plays an important part in the lives of most Americans, and the treatment of a minority group is strongly influenced by this consideration. As Blalock observed, one of the most pervasive and subtle forms of minority discrimination is that of avoidance, particularly in situations implying social equality or involving potential intimacy (1967:51).

Minority groups generally occupy a low status in American society. Therefore, status-conscious Whites avoid lower-status individuals, especially those of color, and thus strengthen prejudicial perceptions. Even professions are stigmatized if they involve working with low-status groups, the prestige of professions often being related to their client group. For example, professions who work with the poor are generally of lower status; even within a profession, the Beverly Hills doctor has a higher status than his or her colleague who works with the poor.

Although not all avoidance behavior is motivated by status considerations (for example, there may be differences based on values, interests, personalities, or lifestyles), much of the avoidance of minorities is. The mixture of ethnicity and status is often difficult to unravel; the junior executive avoids all close contact with the janitor, both because the janitor is of low status and because he is black.

Equal-status contact between dominant- and subordinate-group members can be threatening and uncomfortable for both sides. The white individual may be irritated at the familiarity of the uppity minority-group member, and the ethnic individual may be sensitive to any sign of condescension from the white peer. Therefore, ritualistic or gaming behaviors are often used to mask the conflict.

Status in the past often resulted in predictable reciprocal behavior. Whereas dominant-group styles encouraged the avoidance of lower-status ethnic groups, lower-status groups prided themselves on their friendships with dominant-group members. Ethnic groups could gauge their rise in status by the number of Whites who could be expected to attend a social gathering. Special favors were granted to them, such as being seated close to the head table, being served first and given special attention. The things that make up status and fashionability, the styles and the people associated with them, however, can shift dramatically, as they have in the past. If interracial gatherings become fashionable, status-oriented individuals may go out of their way to attend them.

Ethnicity, social position, and status are interesting topics for further research. For example, for a white person, does associating with an Asian, a Chicano, or a Black provide more status? What if the Asian were a gardener, the Chicano a lawyer, and the Black a doctor?

SEGREGATION

The third variable in maintaining the dominant-subordinate stratification system is racial segregation. By segregation, we refer to the act of separating and isolating members of a racial group from the main body.

Van den Berghe (1971) discussed three different kinds of segregation, each designed by dominant group members for different situations. The first is *micro-segregation*, referring to separation in washrooms, waiting rooms, post offices, and other public facilities. The Jim Crow laws are examples of this category; their purpose was to segregate racial groups as much as possible in frequent contact situations. The second level is *meso-segregation*, such as in urban housing, in which racial categories are assigned to ghettos. The final level is *macro-segregation*, in which there is a complete geographical separation, such as in reservations and concentration camps.

Housing

Housing is one of the most important areas for racial segregation. Although there are laws to prohibit segregation and discrimination in housing, many methods have been employed to skirt these laws. The method cited by the United States Commission on Civil Rights as the most effective and widely used is simply the refusal to sell. Another method is the racially restrictive covenant made between two parties stipulating that the purchaser of the property will not sell or rent the property to members of specific minority or religious groups. This method is no longer legal. Housing provides one example of the conflict between the right of the individual to sell to whom he or she pleases and the rights of society in specifying nondiscriminatory clauses in the sale.

A more current issue is that of red lining, or the practice of mortgage-lending institutions imposing artificial restrictions on housing loans for particular areas in which minorities have started to buy (Vitarello, 1975). However, Vitarello reported that political pressure has proved to be successful in discouraging this practice. For example, in Chicago all banks and savings and loan associations bidding for deposits of city funds must sign anti-red-lining pledges.

Native Americans on a reservation.

The cost of discrimination in housing has been great. Members of minority groups are not free to obtain housing according to their financial means, and they pay higher prices for lower quality housing than Whites would pay. The effects on morale, ambition, and expectation are destructive. The blight of slum areas spreads, urban renewal lags, and racial tension increases.

Segregation intensifies the visibility of the minority group and demarcates its boundaries, producing problems of conflict and social control. Ethnic riots often occur along the boundaries, and social-control problems within segregated areas are usually quite serious. Police officers, firefighters, and other representatives of the larger community are regarded as intruders and are often treated with hostility.

There is a voluntary element in segregation. The minority-group members may feel more comfortable among their own kind, where food, services, language, and customs are more attuned to ethnic needs. In the ghetto, one can limit contact with the dominant group, and life can continue with old friends who have also chosen to live within the segregated enclave.

The rise of ethnic populations in the cities per se is not a problem, but the general neglect that follows the white exodus is. Jobs, services, and other necessities of city living generally drop as nonwhites take over and there is often a rise in crime and delinquency, as well as an increase in welfare roles. As Sol Linowitz, former ambassador to the Organization of American States, stated: "Tax revenues and better housing are following the migration of affluent whites to the suburbs and leaving the cities in worse shape than before the riots of the mid-1960s" (*Los Angeles Times*, 1972:6).

Kimmel (1986) gives an example of cumulative discrimination based on housing segregation. Most black children in both the North and South (and East and West), attend predominantly black elementary schools. This initial segregation means attendance at largely black high schools, which cumulatively leaves black children less likely to qualify for entrance into colleges and universities. Therefore, children who live in segregated areas are more apt to end up in lower-paying, less skilled jobs in segregated work groups, which in turn means living in segregated areas.

A study by Hallinan and Williams (1989) involving 59,000 students in a high school and beyond survey, found that most friendships were within one's own race and gender and that interracial friendships were rare. Proximity, similarity, and status were important determinants of friendship choices.

On college campuses, there is a strong tendency for ethnic minorities to practice self-segregation so that there are often special areas where minority groups are likely to congregate. For example, we have noticed an Asian corner, a Hispanic area, and several tables reserved primarily for Blacks on various California campuses. Perhaps the major difference between the present and the past is that segregation is more voluntary, since opportunities for social interaction (i.e., fraternities and sororities) are more available.

THE ROLE OF LAW

In our model of domination, the primary mechanism for the support of discrimination and segregation is the law. Burkey (1978) sees law mostly as an instrument of the dominant group and a reflection of its desires, values, and interests. It thus becomes the force of the strong against the weak. The ultimate sanction of the law is power, since without the sanction of force, law becomes legal fiction. The task of eliminating racial discrimination and segregation is made extremely difficult because the primary responsibility for change lies with the perpetrators.

SUMMARY

In summary, we have presented prejudice, discrimination, and segregation as the major elements in maintaining a boundary between the dominant and the dominated group (see model of domination in Chapter 4). Prejudice serves to keep racial groups apart, discrimination limits the ability of the dominated groups to be competitive, and segregation serves to isolate the racial minorities. If we focus on the various goals of the American society, the function of the boundary maintenance mechanisms becomes clear. For those who wish a more integrated and inclusive society, the elimination of prejudice, discrimination and segregation are high priority goals; conversely, for those who desire a separation between racial groups and of exclusion, the maintenance of boundaries is important.

REFERENCES

ADORNO, T., FRENKEL-BRUNSWIK, E., LIVINSON, D. J., & SANFORD, R. N. (1950). *The authoritarian personality*. New York: Harper & Row.

ALLPORT, G. (1954). *The nature of prejudice* (pp. 51–52, 100). Boston: Bacon Press.

ANTONOVSKY, A. (1960). The social meaning of discrimination. *Phylon, 21,* 81.

BANTON, M. (1983). *Racial and ethnic competition*. Cambridge: Cambridge University Press.

BIERSTEDT, R. (1950). An analysis of social power. *American Sociological Review, 15,* 730–738.

BLALOCK, H. M. (1967). *Toward a theory of minority group relations*. New York: John Wiley.

BOGARDUS, E. (1930). A social distance scale. *Sociology and Social Research, 17,* 265–71.

BOGARDUS, E. (1968). Comparing racial distance in Ethiopia, South Africa and the United States. *Sociology and Social Research, 52,* 149–156.

BULLOCK, C., & HARRELL, R. JR. (1976). Institutional racism: Prerequisites, freezing and mapping. *Phylon, 37,* 212–223.

BURKEY, R. (1978). *Ethnic and racial groups*. Menlo Park, CA.: Cumming's Publishing Co.

DANIELS, R., & KITANO, H. H. L. (1970). *American racism*. Englewood Cliffs, N.J.: Prentice-Hall.

DOLLARD, J. (1938). Hostility and Fear in Social Life. *Social forces,* 17: 15–26.

DOLLARD, J. DOOB, L., MILLER, N., et al. (1939). *Frustration and aggression*. New Haven: Yale University Press.

FARLEY, J. E. (1995). *Majority-minority relations*. Englewood Cliffs, N.J.: Prentice-Hall.

FEAGIN, J., & FEAGIN, C. B. (1996). *Racial and ethnic relations*. Englewood Cliffs, N.J.: Prentice-Hall.

FRENCH, J. R., & RAVEN, B. (1959). The bases of social power. In D. Cartwright (Ed.), *Studies in social power*. Ann Arbor: University of Michigan Press.

FREY, D. L., & GAERTNER, S. L. (1986). Helping and the avoidance of inappropriate behavior: A strategy that perpetuates a nonprejudiced self-image. *Journal of Personality and Social Psychology, 50* (6), 1083–1090.

HALLINAN, M., & WILLIAMS, R. (1989). Interracial friendship choices in secondary schools. *American Social Review, 54* (1), 67–78.

HAMILTON, C., & CARMICHAEL, S. (1967). *Black power*. New York: Random House.

IIYAMA, P., & KITANO, H. H. L. (1982). Asian Americans and the media. In G. Berry & C. Mitchell-Kerman (Eds.), *Television and the Socialization of the Minority Child* (pp. 151–186). New York: Academic Press.

JENKS, C. (1983). Discrimination and Thomas Sowell. *New York Review of Books, 30* (3), 33.

KAHNG, A. (1978). EEO in America. *Equal Opportunity Forum, 5,* 23.

KATZ, D., & BRALY, K. W. (1958). Verbal stereotypes and racial prejudice. In E. Maccoby, T. Newcomb, & E. Hartley (Eds.), Readings in Social Psychology (pp. 40–46). New York: Holt, Rinehart & Winston.

KERBO, H. (1983). *Social stratification and inequality*. New York: McGraw-Hill.

KIMMEL, M. S. (1986). A prejudice against prejudice: Growing up in the segregated south convinced this social psychologist that you can't improve race relations without changing society's institutions. *Psychology Today, 20,* 46–52.

KINLOCH, G. (1974). *The dynamics of race relationships*. New York: McGraw-Hill.

LOS ANGELES TIMES (1972). Starting flight of whites to suburbs noted. June 1, part I-B, 6–7.

MACIVER, R. M. (1948). *The more perfect union*. New York: Macmillan.

MYRDAL, G. (1944). *An American dilemma*. New York: Harper & Row.

PINCUS, F. L., & EHRLICH, H. J. (1994). *Race and ethnic conflict*. Boulder, Colo.: Westview Press.

RAVEN, B. H. (1992). A power/interaction model of interpersonal influence: French and Raven thirty years later. *Journal of Social Behavior and Personality, 7* (2), 217–244.

ROSE, A. (1951). *The roots of prejudice*. Paris: UNESCO, Pub. 85.

SCHERMERHORN, R. A. (1978). *Comparative ethnic relations*. Chicago: University of Chicago Press.

SIMPSON, G. E., & YINGER, J. M. (1965). *Racial and cultural minorities*. New York: Harper & Row.

VAN DEN BERGHE, P. (1971). Racial separation in Africa: Degrees and funds. In H. Adams (Ed.), *South Africa: Sociological perspectives*. London: Oxford University Press.

VITARELLO, J. (1975). The red-lining route to urban decay. *Focus, 3* (10), 4–5.

WEBER, M. (1946). Class, status, party. In M. Weber, *Essays in Sociology* (edited and translated by H. H. Gerth & C.W Mills). New York: Oxford University Press.

YETMAN, N., & STEELE, C. H. (1975). *Majority and minority* (2nd ed.). Boston: Allyn & Bacon.

Chapter 6

Minority Adaptations
to Dominated Status

The basic question for those who belong to a racial minority is whether to accept the role, change expectations, or seek some form of change. If one lives in a racist society, it would be difficult to accept all that it means—lack of opportunity, prejudice, discrimination, segregation, a tilted playing field, lack of power, and exclusion from the mainstream. But seeking change is also difficult because it means organizing; expending time, money, and energy; facing frustration and disappointment; and finding that limited inclusion provides only limited satisfaction.

The purpose of this chapter is to present some of the strategies and adaptive mechanisms that racial and ethnic groups have used to cope with their dominated position in U.S. society. It is difficult to justify all minority group behavior as a reaction to their dominated status, but it would also be an error to ignore the role of membership in a racial minority, especially at the bottom end of the stratification system. Variables such as time, place, situation, and personality interact with race to explain behavior.

Since behavior is the interaction between the dominant and the dominated, the overall responses of the dominated are best understood in the context of dominant group thinking and ideology. When the dominant group advocated exclusion, adaptive responses had to deal with this reality; as the dominant group moved slowly into an inclusion mode, adaptive responses had to cope with this changing reality.

The critical factor is that of differential power, and all individuals have faced and have learned to cope with unequal power. Children face more powerful parents, students deal with more powerful teachers, and employees learn to adapt to the idiosyncracies of their employers. The repertoire of coping mechanisms appears to be similar to that of the dominated to the dominator, or as Farley (1995) suggests, the subordinate minority to the superordinate majority, which includes feigned or real acceptance, displaced aggression, avoidance, assimilation.

But, in many cases, the relationships are temporary—the child becomes a parent, the student may become a teacher, and an employee, an employer, whereas membership in a racial minority lasts throughout the life of an individual. Therefore, minority adaptations may be more permanent, so that an individual faced with racism during his or her formative years may still react in a manner of earlier experiences, even though times and conditions may have changed.

The reactions of the more powerful, whether it be parent to child, teacher to student, and employer to employee, are often judgmental—the good child, the good student, and the good employee. Minority adaptations are also judgmental; the dominant group uses terms such as good, healthy, model, problem, and dysfunctional. But what is functional, good, and desirable from positions of dominance may be viewed differently by the dominated. The dominated may use such terms as sell out, oreo, banana, and apple to describe those who have identified with the dominant community.

Wilson (1973) discussed three possibilities for the dominant group in a dominant-subordinate system: acceding to all of the demands made by the minority group, meeting some of the demands through some concessions, or rejecting all demands, often through repressive tactics. In general, the weaker the group, the more safely the dominant group can ignore or reject its proposals.

PAST ACCOMMODATIONS

One of the more dramatic examples of the adaptability of human beings to given conditions and situations has been the past accommodation of many subordinate groups to their less-than-equal status with minimal signs of overt conflict. Racially oppressed groups, whether in the United States or in other parts of the world, have seldom challenged the inequities. As Berry and Tischler stated:

> It is an amazing fact that some human beings have an infinite capacity to endure injustice without retaliation, and apparently without resentment against their oppressors. Instances are numerous, and they come from every part of the world where one group dominates another. Militant leaders of protest movements have been driven to despair by the apathy. Members of dominant groups have often commented on the cheerfulness and loyalty among those who would seem to have no reason for such sentiments. (1978:387)

The ability of the oppressed to mask their resentment and hostility and the inability of the majority to perceive beyond their stereotypes have combined to prolong some of the more common sayings of the past, such as, "Our Negroes are happy," "The Japanese are content behind barbed wire," "Indians enjoy reservation life," and "The Chinese like it in Chinatown." Even under terrible conditions, people have adjusted with relative docility, so that the death ovens at Buchenwald and the World War II concentration camps for Japanese Americans were characterized by a general lack of overt resistance. Perhaps it is the idealism of the oppressed that both sustains and destroys.

But generational and other changes reflect different moods. Williams (1987) reflects on the civil rights years—1954 to 1965—which included a variety of strategies to effect change in Black-White relations. In 1955 there was the Montgomery bus boycott, followed by the Tallahassee bus boycott; the attempt to integrate Little Rock Central High School from 1957 to 1959; and the March on Washington in 1963. In 1995, there was the million black men march on Washington—all attempts to change the relationship between majority and minority.

Other groups have also focused on different strategies. Japanese Americans, once satisified with "forgetting the past," were succesful in challenging the government concerning their forced incarceration in prison camps during World War II, and were able to gain redress in 1988, which included a formal apology and a $20,000 payment to each eligible individual (Kitano, Maki, & Berthold, in press).

This chapter will focus on some of the general adaptations to minority status by dominated groups. Later chapters will analyze some specific minority group responses to the stratification system and changes over time. It should be emphasized that many of the responses presented in this chapter are not exclusively related to racial minority status.

CONFLICT

One important question of intergroup relations concerns whether conflict always follows the meeting of diverse groups. Some type of conflict seems to exist in almost all interethnic contacts, as Berry and Tischler found:

> Even before the dawn of history, primitive bands were moving over the face of the earth, encountering strange peoples, and trespassing upon their lands. Archaeologists suspect that these prehistoric contacts resulted in wars and bloodshed, and in the destruction and displacement of one group by another. Historic evidence supports such guesses, and indicates that conflict of some sort is a common occurrence when unlike peoples meet. (1978:117)

But as we indicated in Chapter 2, various outcomes are possible when different people meet. A conflict-free adaptation seems to be difficult to achieve, although not always, as the following early example shows.

The Tungus and the Cossacks

Lindgren (1938) published a report about two racially and culturally different groups, the Tungus and the Cossacks, who resided as neighbors without any apparent conflict. The Tungus were Mongolian nomads who lived off the reindeer and hunted for their sustenance. The Cossacks were Caucasoid descendants of the Russians who invaded Asia at an earlier time. They were Christian village dwellers who relied primarily on agriculture and stock-raising for their livelihood. Hypothesized reasons for the lack of apparent conflict between these groups included the following:

1. The numbers of both groups were small (less than 1,000) and of approximately equal size.
2. There was little competition for land and resources. There was ample room for both groups to practice their own different ways of making a living.
3. Outside influences drew the groups together. For example, in 1908 the Chinese government imposed taxes upon the fur trade of the Cossacks, which affected the Tungus, too. Therefore, both groups viewed themselves as being oppressed by an outside force.
4. The two cultures established a supplementary and complementary relationship, rather than one based on antagonism and competition.
5. Neither group thought itself racially superior. They respected each other's attitudes, values, and cultural practices, such as marriage, use of land, and property.

If these factors are the key to peaceful intergroup neighborliness, this kind of harmony would be difficult to duplicate in today's world. Size has become virtually uncontrollable, and numerical equality is almost never a reality. Perhaps even more important, power relationships between groups are usually unbalanced. Technology, specialization, and urbanization have created increased competition for space, housing, employment, and shrinking resources. Furthermore, our economic system values competition over cooperation. Race and color are divisive symbols, and the feeling of white superiority and the development of a stratification system built upon color has limited any dreams of racial equality and harmony.

There is a great need for systematic research to explore those variables that affect race relationships. For example, is it possible to predict the consequences of change by using the Tungus and Cossacks as a model? What would be the effect of competition on scarcer resources? How would urbanization and a change in the economic system affect race relations? Would a change in numbers or the balance lead to increased conflict? What would happen if one group began to feel superior? Because social scientists cannot bring large groups into a laboratory to test their hypotheses, they must rely on field studies and sophisticated observations for information.

It would be interesting to study the Tungus and Cossacks at the current time. There seems to be no adequate study to answer questions concerning the current stage of their interaction.

Any analysis of intergroup relations can be misleading if the research covers only a narrow period of time. Even the most stressful relationships—whether in marriage, international relations, or interracial contacts—will have periods of relative tranquility. Therefore, the assumption that the Tungus and Cossacks are a conflict-free example may be erroneous. Finally, some forms of conflict are difficult to assess because they are not obvious. Groups may internalize conflict and give only intangible evidence of it.

Conflict as a Value Question

The idea of a conflict-free adaptation reflects a value orientation and goes back to our discussion in Chapter 4 of the functional and conflict perspectives. Horton (1971) referred to the biases based on one or the other position and asserted that many social scientists are apparently unaware of their own values. For example, Freudian terminology arises from an upper bourgeois patriarchal group with a strong sexual and individualistic orientation; American sociologists' analyses of social problems before 1940 reflect a rural, small town bias; and much current contemporary analysis reflects the researchers' experiences under bureaucratic and administrative organizations. Horton contrasted the two approaches to social problems. Conflict theory focuses on the failure of the system to meet the needs of the individual, whereas the functional theory sees the individual as not adjusted to the system. Since there are at least two viewpoints from which to assess conflict, it is interesting to note which position is chosen. Those who choose the majority perspective often see minority groups as deviant, disorganized, in great conflict, and as examples of social problem behavior. Others, writing from a minority perspective, see the conflict as noble, militant, and having high moral justification.

MEANS-ENDS DILEMMA

Merton (1957) suggested a relationship between societal structures and individual responses. Merton's theory was designed to discover how some social structures exert a definite pressure upon certain persons in the society to engage in nonconforming rather than conforming conduct.

Merton's theory consists of several elements, including culturally defined goals, acceptable modes of reaching those goals, anomie, and types of adaptation. It attempts to demonstrate the importance of sociological variables in producing deviant behavior. For example, success (the goal) in American terms may mean acquiring material wealth. If the pressures toward this goal are exceptionally strong, then considerations of how to attain the goal (the means) may become less important. When the technically most effective procedure takes precedence over culturally approved values or institutionally prescribed conduct, the society becomes unstable, or to use Durkheim's (1951) term, it is in a state of anomie, or normlessness.

Merton's model may be appropriate to ethnic groups. Minorities strive for the same success goals as other groups in American society do, but the barriers of racism limit their access by legitimate means. The resultant strain may lead to high levels of anomic behavior, including retreat, rebellion, and overconformity.

From this perspective, class and ethnic stratification systems are not the critical factors in creating strain; rather, strain results more from the defeat and disappointment of heightened expectations. Presumably, under slavery (exclusion), when an individual did not expect to become successful in general societal terms, there was less stress than under the current conditions (inclusion), which create an obvious incongruence.

In this chapter we shall discuss minority-group responses to prejudice, discrimination, and segregation. These adaptations are the dependent variables to dominant-group actions. The three hypothesized responses are: (1) acceptance of dominated status; (2) aggression, fighting back, and attempts to change the system; and (3) avoidance (Simpson & Yinger, 1965).

ACCEPTANCE

Perhaps the most common adaptive pattern of ethnic minorities has been their seeming acceptance of subordinate status. The power relationships may leave them almost no alternative; and even if many minorities may not really believe in the superiority of the white person, most often they act as if they do.

It is necessary to hypothesize several motivations to explain this pattern. Perhaps the most important is the desire to be like the majority group; conformity to dominant-group role prescriptions is a primary goal. Another important factor is that most minorities prefer the means of the American system—law and order, conformity, conflict-free adaptation, and a don't-rock-the-boat attitude. No matter what the provocation, an ethnic individual's response is primarily acceptance. It would be considered poor form to do otherwise. There may also be a lowering of expectations, and finding a position that creates the least amount of overt stress.

In addition, the reality for many minorities has been socialization and adaptation to vertical family structures with clear superior and inferior positions (typically, father and male sons at the top), so that the racial stratification system is not that unfamiliar. Nevertheless, it must be unnerving to observe the respected head of the household treated as less than equal in the outside community. The unfairness of a racial stratification system in which color determines one's position (and is quite permanent) remains the chief irritant.

Certain subcultural values that lead to acceptance are another factor. The fate orientation, expressed by the Japanese as "shikataganai"—"It can't be helped"—or by Latin Americans and Italians as "que será, será"—"What will be, will be"—encourages this type of adjustment. There is also the belief in some cultures that hardship and suffering are important ingredients of character building, and the stoic, accepting response is a test of inner strength.

Forms of acceptance vary: ritualistic behavior, superpatriotism, and the internalization of stress are three of them.

Ritualistic Adaptation

Ritualistic adaptation is scaling down or abandoning high cultural goals and retaining the moralistic prescriptions of the society. Persons in this situation lower their level of aspiration: He is playing safe, she's not sticking her neck out, and he's not shooting for the stars. They conform to the mandates of the larger society and socialize their children accordingly. Merton hypothesized that ritualism may be most appropriate to the lower-middle class. The person who always goes by the rules and the petty bureaucrat are examples of ritualistic adaptation.

By ritualism, minority groups retain a faith that some of the means and norms in the system will guarantee their acceptability. For example, many ethnics vote faithfully (although even more do not) with the expectation that their participation in this procedure is significant. Voting, however, does not basically change the system, unless the minority has achieved power through political and organizational maneuvers. Then, of course, it is no longer a minority in a political sense.

Superpatriotism

Another means of adapting to the problems of isolation from a system is to overidentify with it. The rituals of belonging, such as learning the anthems and slogans, copying the slang, adopting the dress and the styles are an important part of the adaptation of minority groups. In terms of a lens, the individual begins to perceive the world through a dominant group lens. Generally, the higher the identification with the majority, the higher the probability of discarding the ethnic lens.

The dynamics of ritualism often include incongruous actions. For example, many Japanese who were placed in the wartime relocation centers maintained a strict loyalty to the United States. The Pledge of Allegiance, "The Star-Spangled Banner," and the American flag became extremely important to them, and many purchased war bonds and donated blood. Others even volunteered for the army and eventually gave their lives for democracy, while their parents, brothers, and sisters were still behind barbed wire. They practiced these rituals, believing that such actions would prove to the larger world that they, too, were Americans.

Internalization of Stress

Another form of acceptance is the internalization of the unequal status. To grit one's teeth and accept reality is considered to be mature in some cultures. From a psychoanalytic perspective, internalization and repression may have dysfunctional effects upon the individual. For example, in the Japanese population, there is a high incidence of such internal disorders as stomach ulcers and bowel problems. My father used to relate how, when walking in San Francisco, he would be deliberately shoved off the sidewalk by white bullies. Rather than venting his anger, he would internalize his feelings by gritting his teeth and using the Japanese concept of ga-man, that is, accepting the situation. It was considered more mature to draw in one's breath and not cry, complain, or strike back. However, it may be one explanation for the bad temper that he turned on his family.

Stress is a killer among Blacks. The constant bombardment of racial prejudice and the inability to fight back may take its toll on the body.

The major decisions on acceptance are made by the majority. They can prescribe the conditions by which ethnic members live and react, and they can impose stringent and arbitrary conditions that strain the level of acceptance to the breaking point. History shows how difficult it is for groups in command to understand that intelligent use of power is the most important factor in the survival of their system. Constantly forcing subordinated groups to accept degrading conditions is probably the surest way of creating conditions for militant social change.

The basic dynamic of internalization is the absence of overt cues exhibiting discomfort and hurt. Insensitive dominant-group members often misinterpret this quietness as a reason for maintaining a racial status quo, and even previously quiescent minorities are beginning to perceive that the squeaky-wheel will gain more attention.

AGGRESSION

Aggression generally includes some kind of retaliation. Aggression takes many forms: It may be a direct retaliation to the dominant group; it may mean striking out at more vulnerable groups; or it may be so masked as to be barely detectable. At an earlier time, the lack of overt aggression was often taken as a sign of contentment, especially among slaves. More recent interpretations of slave adjustment have revealed the indirect and hidden ways in which less powerful groups often show their hostility to and resentment of their plight.

For example, Powdermaker (1943) coined the term aggressive meekness to illustrate a style of adaptation that masks the true thoughts and feelings of slaves in their overtly meek and submissive public role.

Aggression can be classified into four kinds: direct, indirect, displaced, and a change of goals.

Direct Aggression

Direct aggression grows out of acute despair. The power arrangements are such that most ethnics see little hope of gaining much through this approach. The resources of the dominant group are truly impressive, especially when compared to those of the minorities. Money, numbers, firepower, legal justification, and institutional resources are so clearly under the control of the majority that only under unusual circumstances will minorities openly direct their aggression at the dominators.

Insurrections.   An insurrection uses armed force against the established order. The main differences among insurrections, rebellions, and revolutions are those of purpose, size, and scope. Racial insurrections have been frequent in the history of the United States. Contrary to some interpretations of U.S. history that emphasize the contentment of the slaves, there were constant plots, though never seriously threatening the institution of slavery, that caused much concern to the white population (Aptheker, 1943; Carroll, 1938; Franklin, 1948).

Denmark Vesey purchased his freedom in 1800. He established himself as a carpenter in Charleston, South Carolina, and for twenty years lived as a respectable free Negro, enjoying a relatively comfortable existence. He was, however, a sensitive person, and he was unhappy over his own freedom and success while others of his race were in slavery. He therefore set about to plot a revolt. His plans were carefully laid, and his associates were chosen with utmost scrutiny. Over a period of years they collected their weapons—daggers, bayonets, and pike heads. The second Sunday in July 1822 was set as the date for the revolt. The Whites, however, were informed, and Vesey hastily moved the date ahead one month. His assistants, scattered as they were for miles around Charleston, did not all get the word, and the insurrection was readily quashed. Estimates of the number of Blacks involved in the plot ran as high as 9,000. About 139 were arrested, 47 of whom were condemned. Four white men were imprisoned and fined for implication in the plot and for encouraging the Blacks (Berry & Tischler, 1978:133).

Nat Turner was a slave who belonged to Virginia planter Joseph Travis. He was a mystic who felt a divine call to free his people. The solar eclipse of February 1831 convinced him that the time had come for him to deliver the slaves from bondage. The date was to be the Fourth of July; but Turner became ill, and he postponed the date until he should see another divine sign. On August 13, 1831, it seemed to him that the sun turned a peculiar greenish blue, and he therefore chose August 21 as the date for the revolt. He and his followers began by killing their master and his family, and then roamed the countryside destroying other Whites. Within twenty-four hours a total of sixty Whites had been killed. State and federal troops were called, and the slaves were speedily overwhelmed. More than a hundred slaves were killed in the encounter, and thirteen slaves and three free blacks were immediately hanged. Turner himself was captured two months later and was promptly executed (Berry & Tischler, 1978:134).

Novelist William Styron's fictionalized account of Nat Turner's rebellion was an immediate success; it was reviewed in major publications and was a Book of the Month Club selection. However, a most dramatic adverse reaction came from members of the black intellectual community. Most felt that Styron's Nat Turner bore little resemblance to the real man and instead saw a racist caricature of a black slave, motivated by lust for white women. Charles Hamilton declared:

> We will not permit Styron's meditation to leave unchallenged an image of Nat Turner as a fanatical black man who dreams of going to bed with white women, who holds nothing but contempt for his fellow blacks, and who understands, somewhat, the basic human desire to be free but still believes in the basic humanity of some slaveholders. We will not permit Styron to picture unchallenged Nat Turner as a leader who did not understand that the military defeat should not be confused with the ideological victory: i.e., a blow for freedom. The rebellion of 1831, led by Nat Turner, is important today for blacks to understand and for whites to accept precisely because its lesson is that there will be leaders who will rise up against all odds to strike blows for freedom against an oppressive, inhumane system. And there can be no refuge in the thought that Turner felt himself divinely inspired or waited for signs from heaven, etc. The important thing is that the desire for human freedom resides in the black breast as well as in any other. No amount of explicating about the harshness of slavery or the gentleness of slavery, about the docility of the masses of slaves, etc. can keep that desire from exploding. Man, black or white or yellow or red, moves to maximize his freedom: That is the lesson of Nat Turner that Styron did not deal with. (Hamilton, 1968:74)

Race riots. Rioting is as old as history. It is a temporary outbreak, mostly spontaneous, of mass disorder. Racial antagonisms are not necessarily the sole occasions for riots. Rioting, often involving more than one side, is mostly an urban phenomenon and is different from insurrections, rebellions, or revolutions in that there is no overt intention of overthrowing the existing political order.

The history of the United States is dotted with race riots. In 1837 over 15,000 Bostonians participated in an Irish riot; Black-White riots have been

Reaction to Rodney King verdict, Los Angeles, 1992.

constant from three decades before the Civil War to the present. Longres, Roberts, and Shinn (1966) analyzed race riots in the twentieth century and included some of the more prominent: Springfield, Illinois, 1908; East St. Louis, 1917; Washington, D.C., 1919; Chicago, 1919; Los Angeles, 1943; Detroit, 1943; Harlem, 1943; New York, 1964; Rochester, 1964; and Los Angeles, 1965. One interesting pattern emerged—the earlier riots were generally characterized by the Whites being the aggressors, with a reversal of roles over time. Currently, it is the minorities who have become the aggressors.

The Watts riot of August 11–17, 1965, probably marked a watershed in recent race relations. As Daniels and Kitano found:

> Watts was not the first riot—there had been serious disturbances in seven Eastern cities the summer before—but it was the first that appeared to have the character of a rebellion. Perhaps the most surprising thing about it was that it happened in Los Angeles, which, only the year previous, had been ranked by the National Urban League as most favorable to Negroes of sixty-eight American cities examined. Although the riots have been widely studied, there is no consensus among its students, but the basic facts are reasonably clear.
>
> On the evening of August 11, 1965, the Negro ghetto of Los Angeles erupted into a flurry of outbreaks of mob violence, at first centered near (but not in) a small area known as Watts; it soon spread over much of the vast ghetto. It was set off by a seemingly routine arrest of a drunken driver; it produced 144 hours of anarchic looting, arson, assault, and homicide. This happened in an area that supposedly had exemplary race relations. More than half the Negro population of the state lived in Los Ange-

les County (461,000 as enumerated by the 1960 Census), most of them in the overcrowded South Los Angeles ghetto that sprawled over some fifty square miles. The housing there was (and remains) substandard. It consists of one- and two-story single and multifamily structures, most of which have at least the hint of a lawn. About half were built before World War II, which is very old for Los Angeles housing. Many of these units, however, are sound and well maintained. These atypical ghetto conditions made it possible for civic leaders (including some Negro leaders) to insist that the city had no real race-relations problem, a kind of dream state peculiarly appropriate to a region that boasts Hollywood and Disneyland. Similar wishful thinking prevailed in the same quarters during much of the Great Depression, when local leaders tried to maintain that Los Angeles was the economic white spot of the nation. Reality finally punctured both illusions; both however, like most illusions, had some basis in reality. As bad as conditions were for the white emigrés of the 1930s—think of Steinbeck's Joads—and are for the Negro newcomers now, they are distinctly better than the conditions they left behind. But in all too many instances these conditions have not lived up to the expectations of the new arrivals, and it is these partially thwarted expectations that have made California, and other Northern and Western promised lands, sociological and political powder kegs, with a markedly lower flash point than the objective conditions within them might suggest.

If the Watts riots seem similar to earlier ethnic violence, that similarity is largely superficial. The most obvious difference is that the earlier violence had been that of a majority directed against a particular minority. The Watts riots (and similar events in other cities) saw a minority, really a small minority within a minority, lash out blindly against the society that, it seemed to them, was oppressing them intolerably. (Historically it would probably be more accurate to suggest that society was not easing its restrictions as fast as expectations were rising.) Another difference is that these riots were largely directed against property, and quite often black-owned and occupied property. The aggressors were almost all Blacks, and so, ironically, were most of the victims.

The ingredients for the Watts and other riots, apart from mimesis after Watts, were simple: an alienated group squeezed into a small ghetto. Within that group there are growing numbers (almost all the estimates are too small) of undereducated, underskilled, and therefore unemployed youths in a nation with the greatest educational system in the world. In Los Angeles the ghetto is not an area of abject poverty—about 60 percent of the population get some kind of welfare, and California standards are relatively high—but of apathy, resentment, and hopelessness. These ingredients were detonated in Los Angeles by a casual incident that resulted in an opportunity for some to lash back at society in general and the police in particular, and gave many, many more a chance for vicarious pleasure in watching them do it.

That this widespread alienation exists so noticeably at a time when Blacks seem to be making such great strides has puzzled and perplexed many, but it should be quite clear that although the social revolution that John Kenneth Galbraith has dubbed affluence has affected the American Black, north and south, not nearly enough of it has trickled down. But within the same society that sees many Blacks achieving upward social mobility and a few grasping political and economic power, there are within most black communities large numbers of socially alienated young men and women, children of the welfare state at its worst, who have neither known extreme economic deprivation nor ever experienced a normal family life. They have not even been able to indulge in the humblest aspect of the American Dream, the reasonable expectation that their children would have a chance to better themselves. It was these people who made and enjoyed the Los Angeles riots, and the many similar incidents that have followed (Daniels & Kitano, 1970:82–84).

Subsequent events in Los Angeles continue to paint a similar, dreary picture. The riots following the Rodney King beating verdict, the Black-Korean conflict, and the differential reactions to the O. J. Simpson verdict in 1995 are indications that racial tensions remain alive.

Strikes and boycotts.   Strikes and boycotts are more often associated with economic conflict and labor disputes than with racial interaction. Nevertheless, these forms have also been used and vary in their effectiveness.

One of the most effective boycotts in recent history was that involving Martin Luther King and the Montgomery, Alabama bus system. The incident started on December 1, 1955, when a black seamstress, Mrs. Rosa Parks, refused to give up her seat and move to the back of the bus when ordered to do so by the bus driver. By the time the blacks called off the boycott approximately one year later, black patronage of the bus lines had dropped as much as 90 percent. Dr. King was found guilty of an illegal boycott and was fined and sentenced to jail. The case was referred to the Supreme Court; on November 13, 1966, the United States Supreme Court declared that the Alabama law requiring the segregation of buses was unconstitutional.

Boycotts and strikes have been used on both sides and in a variety of different ways. Early Californians were urged to boycott "Jap" businesses; often Chinese and Japanese laborers were used as strike breakers, and the Japanese often banded together to boycott certain white establishments known to be anti-oriental.

Highjacking.   A newer form of aggression has been the threat to blow up or to kidnap airplanes in order to effect change. It is based on the old principle of ransom and blackmail, in which one group attempts to extract concessions from another group by holding something of value.

The motivations for highjacking vary—personal profit, the release of political prisoners, the dramatization of the plight of a pariah group, or a change in a dominant group's policy. The tactics are usually a desperate attempt by a powerless group to equalize the power differential, if only temporarily, and its effectiveness in bringing about long-term change is open to question. The precautions instituted by airlines as a response to the threat of bombing and highjacking indicate the vulnerability of more powerful groups to such acts.

Other recently revived forms of showing dissatisfaction include kidnappings, ransom notes, death threats, bomb threats, reprisals, the taking of hostages, and human sacrifice. As with most desperate acts, the lasting effects for bringing about change using these strategies remain questionable.

Indirect Aggression

A more typical method of handling aggressive feelings is through indirect actions. Much indirect aggression must be inferred and therefore suffers the limitations of interpretation. Nevertheless, it is an important adaptation, since it may invite less retaliation than a direct act would.

Fine arts and literature.   Writers, poets, painters, musicians, and actors often deal with oppression and interracial relationships in their own fashion. Black writers such as Richard Wright, LeRoi Jones, and James Baldwin were able to convey their message of conflict and suffering to larger audiences. Utilizing the fine arts as weapons of protest is not limited to the American Black. Perhaps all oppressed peoples do so, even the preliterate peoples.

Ethnic humor.   Ethnic humor is another important way of dealing with conflict. The put-on, the bad-mouth, and the ethnic joke are all attempts to find a more socially acceptable way of handling conflict and aggression. The number and continued popularity of jokes about Jews, Negroes, Italians, Irish, Chinese, Japanese, Poles, Mexicans, and WASPS can be viewed as symptomatic of the use of humor to handle aggression.

There is a hypothesized pattern of ethnic humor that is related to the cohesion, identity, and perceived acceptance of a group. The pattern takes two different forms.

The first form is humor directed against the oppressor. The first stage is so disguised that only in-group members perceive the butt of the jokes. As the group feels more comfortable, the humor becomes much more overt. The disguise is replaced by euphemisms, then eventually by direct references. The final stage occurs when the humor is not limited to ethnic-group audiences but is shared with the oppressor.

The second form is humor by the ethnic group about itself. The first stage is private and confined to the membership; this is followed by a more public display, but still within a localized group. As the group gains acceptance, a fellow ethnic member may feel comfortable enough to carry the humor outside the group. The final stage in this pattern occurs when the ethnic group is able to tolerate a nonethnic member telling ethnic jokes.

This proposed series may help to explain the sensitivities of various ethnic groups to jokes and stereotypes; not all groups are at the same stage, and what is considered appropriate for one group may be offensive to another.

Passive resistance.   Another means of forestalling overt conflict is passive resistance. The origins of passive resistance are probably as old as humans themselves, and phrases such as "Turn the other cheek," or Martin Luther King's exhortation to his followers, "Face violence if necessary, but refuse to return violence," indicate its philosophical underpinnings.

The name most intimately linked to passive resistance is Mohandas K. Gandhi, and more recent followers such as Reverend King acknowledged Gandhi's influence. There is a strong oriental aura in passive resistance, as well as elements of stoicism and internalization.

Job slowdowns, inefficiency, tardiness.   Simpson and Yinger (1965) mention several variations of aggression that are forms of passive resistance. One is the job slowdown, in which ethnic members may work extremely slowly; another is carelessness, in which objects are accidentally dropped and broken. Irresponsibility, shoddy work, and inefficiency also are ways in which minorities react against the dominant system. Dominant-group reactions provide an interesting commentary on the dominant group's perceptions. Instead of identifying some of these actions as aggression, there is a tendency to characterize and stereotype the minority culture as careless, sloppy, or accident prone. Some critics even advance a genetic inferiority explanation.

Other techniques of indirect aggression include high labor turnover, tardiness, and unreliability. Suddenly walking off a job or coming in late and then leaving early fall into this category. A practice that makes producers and coordinators of programs uncontrollably angry occurs when ethnics agree to participate in a program, then cancel at the last minute, or do not show up at all; if they do show up, they may make a number of outrageous demands as the price of their participation.

Role changes.   Another indirect means of handling aggression is either to withdraw or to change the forms of racial roles. For example, ethnic individuals may suddenly change their deferential pattern in a social situation and ask to be served first, or they may publicly challenge the opinions of majority-group members at unusual times, or they may exaggerate their ethnic role in a manner calculated to embarrass a majority-group member. Cohen (1958) gave an example of how a form of military etiquette, the hand salute, can mask aggressive feelings. By overconforming, minority-group soldiers can strain the system; ten enlisted men saluting separately can force ten response salutes from a single passing officer.

Behavioral patterns at variance with expected roles can also be a form of indirect aggression. The stereotype of the welfare mother with a Cadillac and a color TV (if there are such people) is an example of an aggressive response through behavior not normally expected of individuals in this category. The outraged reaction of society to this stereotype indicates the reciprocal feelings held by many against those who do not follow prescribed norms for poor people.

Some ethnic groups handle aggression through high achievement and competitive excellence. Instead of carelessness, indifference, and inefficiency, they handle their aggression by sublimating their drives and outperforming members of the dominant group.

Displaced aggression.   The displacement of aggression is similar to scapegoating. Displacement may occur within a group, making fellow ethnic members targets for much hostility and aggression. Often without realizing that discrimination, segregation, and prejudice are the major problems, minorities consider each other to be the cause of their frustrations. Other minorities can also be targets of displaced aggression, as in squabbles over the funding of poverty programs.

Change of goals.   Perhaps the most revolutionary and rebellious action of the ethnic minorities has been to change their goals. The familiar goal of trying to become white, and its variations—including integration—no longer have the almost universal support that they once had. The unrealistic goal of becoming like the superordinates, with its subsequent strains and anomie, has been replaced by newer goals. Many of these goals are still not clearly articulated, but major variations include pluralism and separatism.

Much of the action has come in the form of organized protests. A wide variety of social movements have developed, from highly emotional, religious,

*Louis Farrakhan speaks at the
"Million Man March,"
Washington, D.C., 1995.*

and nationalistic movements to those that use sophisticated legal, political, and economic weapons. In the black group alone are such diverse groups as the NAACP, the Urban League, CORE, the Black Panthers, and the Black Muslims.

Some movements are dedicated to changing the goals, and others strive to open the American system to include more people of color; most have reacted to the stresses caused by the barriers that limit the participation of ethnics in U.S. democracy.

AVOIDANCE

Because of the difficulty in abolishing racial barriers, as well as the penalties for active aggression, many ethnics adapt by avoiding the problem altogether. Avoidance covers two broad types of adaptation: (1) withdrawing from most forms of interracial contact, and (2) assimilating, denying, or retreating from the intolerable situation.

For example, ethnics may avoid situations in which they may face prejudice in housing by not applying in certain areas; they may walk across the street rather than face even the simplest communication with someone from the majority group. They may use certain lotions or cosmetics that enable them to pass; or they may resort to drugs or withdraw into mental illness.

According to Simpson and Yinger (1965), the most complete form of avoidance is withdrawing entirely from the minority group. Passing, however, is quite difficult for most ethnics because of the color line. By changing their names and accents and by altering their physiological features, some ethnics hope to pass into the larger community. Although there is always the fear of discovery, this is perhaps the most decisive way to avoid the penalties of ethnic status.

Some groups try to seal off contact. Sealing off can occur on different levels: The upper class of an ethnic group might voluntarily seclude itself from both lower-class members of its own ethnic group and members of the dominant group; other ethnic classes might form purposely segregated communities to limit contact with the majority. This type of adaptation is often insufficient because members remain dependent on the majority community for economic and other needs. Finally, some try to insulate themselves by remaining constantly mobile. Mobility may help limit interaction in some ways, but in the long run, it leads to greater exposure and higher intergroup contact. The method of denial or repression means that ethnics avoid racial problems by behaving as if they were no longer there. Some identify completely with the dominant group and behave like them; instances of prejudice and discrimination are repressed; the individual instead focuses on the positives, so that racial realities are glossed over. Like most adaptive mechanisms, the degree of reality distortion remains important to the mental health of the perceiver.

Retreatism and Withdrawal

Retreatism is the rejection of cultural goals and institutional means. People who retreat have dropped out; they may be in the society but are not part of it. They adapt to the problem through defeatism and resignation. Mental patients, pariahs, outcasts, vagabonds, tramps, chronic alcoholics, drug addicts, and hippies are examples of individuals and groups who have adopted a retreatist posture because of continued failure to reach a goal by legitimate or illegitimate means, caused by internalized and societal prohibitions. It is most often a private rather than a group adaptation.

A large percentage of school dropouts, mental patients, and drug addicts are ethnic children. Taking drugs is one of the oldest ways to escape from reality and to avoid conflict. But the ultimate retreat is mental illness—the flight into a world of dreams and fantasy. Schizophrenia and suicide are the most extreme examples of avoidance.

SUMMARY

We have presented a number of ways that minority groups have adapted to their minority status. The basic issue was that of dominant group power: The more powerful rules, and the less powerful adapts. But in analyzing power relationships, the less powerful have developed strategies that attempt to neutralize the power differential.

Not all forms of adaptation and aggression discussed in this chapter are direct results of prejudice, discrimination, and segregation. Hostility, aggressiveness, and conflict are present wherever there is human interaction. Even without racism, these behaviors would continue to exist.

The range of coping behaviors used by individuals and groups is very wide; racism exacts a greater toll in ruined lives and potential than is realized by those who consider it only morally unjustified or economically expensive.

In the final analysis, minority-group behavior is primarily a result of group interaction with the dominant group. Since the majority group is more powerful than the minority, most adjustments in attitudes and behavior are made by the minority. Therefore, if major changes in expectations, attitudes, and behavior are desired, they will have to be a result of changes in the majority, with pressure from the minority community.

But, although there has been an opening up of society for long-suffering minorities, the openings may be insufficient. Many have found that inclusion has meant partial inclusion and marginal status, and that the chances of ever enjoying full participation and equality remain illusory. As one consequence, the pull of pluralism has been strong, even to the point of a voluntary separation from the dominant society. Some have still maintained that integration and assimilation are viable goals, while others have opted for lesser expectations.

REFERENCES

APTHEKER, H. (1943). *American Negro slave revolts*. New York: Columbia University Press.

BERRY, B., & TISCHLER, H. (1978). *Race and ethnic relations* (4th ed.). Boston: Houghton Mifflin.

CARROLL, J. C. (1938). *Slave insurrections in the United States, 1800–1860*. Boston: Chapman and Grimes.

COHEN, J. (1958). Some aspects of ritualized behavior in interpersonal situations. *Human Relations, 2*, 195–215.

DANIEL, R., & KITANO, H. H. L. (1970). *American racism: Exploration of the nature of prejudice*. Englewood Cliffs, N.J.: Prentice-Hall.

DURKHEIM, E. (1951). *Suicide*. New York: Free Press.

FARLEY, J. (1995). *Majority-minority relations*. Englewood Cliffs, N.J.: Prentice-Hall.

FRANKLIN, J. H. (1948). *From slavery to freedom*. New York: Knopf.

HAMILTON, C. (1968). Our Nat Turner and William Styron's Creation. In John H. Clarke (Ed.), *William Styron's Nat Turner: Ten Black Writers Respond* (pp. 73–78). Boston: Beacon Press.

HORTON, J. (1981). Order and Conflict Theories of Social Problems as Competing Ideologies. In N. Yetman & C. H. Steele (Eds.), *Majority and Minority* (pp. 66–75). Boston: Allyn & Bacon.

KITANO, H. H. L., MAKI, M. & BERTHOLD, M. (forthcoming). *The impossible dream; Japanese Americans and redress*. Champagne: University Of Illinois Press.

LINDGREN, E. J. (1938). An example of culture contact without conflict. *American Anthropologist, 40* (4), 605–621.

LONGRES, J., ROBERTS, C., & SHINN, K. (1966). Some similarities and differences in northern urban race riots involving negroes during the 20th century. Unpublished master's thesis, University of California, Los Angeles.

MERTON, R. (1957). *Social theory and social structure* (rev. ed.) (pp. 131–194). New York: Free Press.

POWDERMAKER, H. (1943). The channeling of Negro aggression by the cultural process. *American Journal of Sociology, 5* (48), 750–758.

SIMPSON, G. E., & YINGER, J. M. (1965). *Race and minorities: An analysis of prejudice and discrimination*. New York: Harper & Row.

WILLIAMS, J. (1987). *Eyes on the prize*. New York: Viking.

WILSON, W. J. (1973). *Power, racism and privilege*. New York: Macmillan.

Chapter 7

Identity

Anyone who has filled out a survey questionnaire or a census form is familiar with some of the questions relating to identity. Age, sex, occupation, and income are common items, but interestingly enough, one's name, which is the simplest manifestation of an identity (but also so specific that a person can be readily identified) is often left out. Father, mother, child, student, executive, worker, and religious affiliation are other identities—each person is made up of a number of identities. Some identities are specific and valid only at certain times—the baseball player, the nightclub singer, the cheerleader—although if a person achieves a certain level of fame, the specific identity may remain throughout one's life. For example, Mike Tyson will be known as the heavy-weight champ long after his retirement, just as Joe Louis was so recognized throughout his life. The important point is that an individual has a choice of a number of identities. The rational choice model (Banton, 1983) would predict that an individual would choose among those identities that would best enhance self.

However, there are other identities that are less voluntary. A person's physical appearance is one, and this includes race and visibility. These are permanent identities, meaning that an individual must deal with both his or her physical appearance and membership in a racial minority. Some may change their names or alter physical characteristics (for example, eye operations), others may develop a romanticized view of self in order to escape the stigma of belonging to an unpopular group. It is our perception that those who do not face the issue of identity, no matter how negative the image, will have difficulty in establishing a realistic view of self.

Since identity consists, in a large part, of the way that others view the self, belonging to and looking different from dominant community norms is difficult. A male who was born to a Japanese wife and a black father describes his situation as follows (after growing up in Japan and residing in North Carolina):

> It was awful. We were niggers. Then we were Japs. Then, we were Chinks. I finally got so mad that I went, Make up your minds. So they settled with nigger (Williams, 1986:157).

How the individual perceives and feels about self constitutes the core of an identity. It is the end product of a process of socialization that includes the family, the community, the ethnic group, and the society. For racial minorities, the process includes victimization through prejudice, discrimination, segregation, and racism. The problem of an identity is not limited to groups in the United States, as the following article appearing in the *Washington Evening Star* (1972) indicates:

> Lagos, Nigeria (AP). Thirteen years in Britain, with education at Eton College, has left a Nigerian youth facing a cruel dilemma that many African blacks suffer when they go abroad. It is the problem of lost identity. Who do I really belong to? the youth asked in an article he wrote for a Nigerian newspaper. I am virtually ashamed of my race and color. I have no desire to be white; but my mind is a hundred percent white. As a result, my parents and I do not speak the same language. I cannot picture the day when I will, if ever, return home to settle. When people have amicably asked my name, I have no name. I have often actually replied: My friend, I have no name. My fellow blacks call me Uncle Tom. In America they call me nigger, and in England they call me immigrant.

Johnson (1983), an American Indian, tells a similar story. Dissatisfied with the image of the Indian of the war whoops and war bonnets, Johnson began to research the past. He participated in the long walk to Washington, D.C. in 1978 and started to understand what it meant to be an Indian. But he had no Indian name, did not know the language or the customs, and faced the problem of trying to understand who he was. He was especially sensitive to the plight of his daughter, who would have to face the identity issue, especially when insensitive peers would no doubt bring up some of the stereotypes as their primary image of the Indian.

The concept of an ethnic identity—the Who am I?—is compounded by the essentially negative connotations saddled upon the questioner if he or she happens to have identifiable racial features at variance with what is considered desirable in the United States. The central issue in the United States stems from the identities brought over by its many immigrants and the attempt to create a superidentity from this diversity. The problem is compounded by age and generation.

The problem of an overall identity, not just ethnic identity, is critical in modern society. The issue of identity is minor in more traditional cultures in which populations have remained relatively homogeneous and stable, and family names, villages, and neighborhoods have continued unchanged. But immigrants to the United States have been required to discard their ancestral and national identities and to adopt newer ones based on the image of the self-made individual. In addition, the highly mobile social system, with its heterogeneous populations and ever-changing lifestyles, has made the problem of establishing one's identity very difficult in the United States. Some of the hypothesized correlates of the lack of identity include rootlessness, alienation, anomie, and confused self-concept.

Psychoanalyst Erik Erikson (1950) saw identity as the product of the interaction between self and the social environment. The internal organization of the self provides the framework from which the individual views the world; the environment provides the surrounding, the stimulus, and the input. The self goes through a number of developmental stages (oral, anal, genital), and the successful integration of each stage is important in achieving maturity.

Sociologist Milton Gordon (1964) was also concerned with problems of identity. American identity includes race, religion, and national origin. The term ethnic group is used as the key to social psychological identity, and the individual's ability to come to grips with his or her race, religion, and nationality provides the tools for dealing with this identity.

Isaacs (1975) presented one of the most comprehensive models of identity. He included: (1) body (physical characteristics, genetic structure, skin color, hair texture, facial features); (2) name; (3) language (there are over 4,000 languages, each playing a particular role in the lives of people who speak it); (4) history and origins; and (5) religion and nationality. The search for a basic group identity has led to discarding larger unities. However, Isaacs warned that a tribal type of identity was much too narrow and was to be discouraged.

Newman (1976) analyzed the role strain on members of minority groups when majority-group definitions are unfavorable. Strain occurs when the minority individual perceives the discrepancy between majority-group definitions and his or her own community's definitions of self.

ETHNIC AND RACIAL IDENTITIES

Racial identity is linked to skin color, physical identifiability, and a social definition of race. Because non-Europeans look different from white Americans, they cannot participate fully in the American mainstream, and many attempt to formulate an identity that addresses the problem. One response is the combined identity—the Chinese American or the Japanese American, an acknowledgment that racial attributes cannot be readily discarded or erased. Because of their inescapable features, many realized that developing racial and cultural pride were important, and they tried to understand their own history and culture.

Ethnic identity, a broader term including the racial aspect, is a relatively new term. Glazer (1975) commented that the word ethnicity was not in the Oxford Dictionary of 1933. Patterson (1975) defined ethnicity as a condition in a society in which certain members choose to emphasize a cultural, racial, or national tie as their primary intrafamilial identity. An ethnic group exists only when members consider themselves to belong to such a group. Current views of ethnicity can be divided into the primordial and the structural. The primordial view sees ethnicity as long lasting and permanent; the other sees it as situational and transitory. The primordial view emphasizes ethnicity as basic to group identity and as such, it is passed down from generation to generation. The ethnic identification provides a common outlook that differentiates members from nonmembers.

Greeley (1974) used the term ethnogenesis to explain the persistence of ethnic group identity among Whites. Ties that bind include region, kinship connections, shared religion, language, and social practices. Other bonds include blood, the phenotype, speech, and customs, so that group identity goes beyond personal affection, practical necessity, and common interest. There is a romantic, unaccountable dimension to this view of identity (Stack, 1986).

A group of teenagers in typical outdoor dress, 1994.

Van den Berghe (1981), writing from a sociobiological perspective, indicates that the propensity to favor kin and fellow ethnics is deeply rooted in the genes. Ethnicity is both primordial and situationally instrumental.

Stack criticizes the primordial perspective because of its romanticism, its crude cultural determinism that leads to stereotypes about a national character, and its lack of explanatory power beyond nonrational emotional ties.

The situational approach sees ethnic mobilization as essentially fluid, so that ethnic boundaries are drawn in the context of external stimuli. Bell (1975) explained the resurgence of ethnicity among Whites as a product of the new problems and new alignments brought about by advanced industrial societies. The onset of postindustrial society creates a professional and technical stratum based on credentials and certification. Occupational advancement becomes increasingly difficult because of the need for specialization and extra training: The political route becomes one of few alternatives for individuals and groups who do not have the requisite training for mobility. Ethnic identification then becomes a political unit for power and for obtaining a greater share of the American pie.

Bell gave three reasons for the upsurge of ethnic identification: (1) the greater intermingling of people and the rise and growth of bureaucracy; (2) the breakup of traditional structures and units, such as the nation and social class; and (3) the politicization of decisions. These changes have led people to look for smaller, more relevant units and organizations. Ethnic identity in this explanation is a strategic choice, rather than a primordial phenomenon deeply rooted in a group or individual, and its salience may fade in and out, depending on the circumstances. Therefore, ethnicity is fluid and situationally located; the central assumption is that in the process of modernization, competition between groups is intensified so that ethnicity becomes an important organizational vehicle for advocating group interests.

Patterson (1975) observed that an ethnic identity can be understood only in terms of a dynamic and contextual view of group allegiances. A static descriptive ethnicity that attempts to isolate a set of characteristics or traits, including endless descriptive items of the culture, its festivals, and events, becomes an absurdity; ethnicity must be seen dynamically. Explaining some of the holidays and festivals observed by Puerto Ricans is less relevant than their conscious use of different ethnic identities to serve their own best interests. Ethnicity and blackness may be emphasized in an affirmative-action setting, the Spanish language and culture in another, and a lighter skin color in another. Patterson's view is that people seldom make decisions on the basis of ethnic allegiance, but rather on economic and general class interests.

Hechter (1986) raises the question of whether ethnicity is a stronger means of identification than social class. The relative isolation of racial groups from their counterparts in the mainstream indicates that at least up to the present, ethnic ties appear much stronger, although some authors (Wilson, 1978) write about the diminishing significance of race. But it appears that the upward mobility of ethnic groups is often within their own structures, rather than across ethnic lines. Such changes in identification may take place in the future.

It is interesting to note the rise of ethnic groups throughout the world. Areas and societies as diverse as the former Soviet Union, China, Southeast Asia, Canada, and Ireland, as well as the United States, face ethnic advocacy, ethnic identity, and ethnic self determination as important issues to be addressed. Inflammatory slogans, political instigations, and setting one ethnic group against another provide the seeds for a national disaster.

So the initial question of Who am I?, when merged into a larger group identity, is a double-edged sword. It can contribute to the enhancement of the individual and the group—group pride, group morale, and high self-esteem. But it can also lead to the brutalization of others in the name of identity—our group is better than theirs, and we are more civilized than they.

IDENTITY IN THE AMERICAN PAST

It would have been easy for the early American settlers to conceptualize the national identity in ethnic terms since the great majority of the population was of English background. And to a great extent the English influence prevailed; laws, language, and customs were strongly based upon English models. But the American identity was also drafted in universalistic and idealistic terms. To become an American, it was deemed necessary for individuals to commit themselves to abstractions such as liberty, equality, and a belief in the republic. Therefore, nationality and linguistic, religious, or ethnic background were not deemed necessary. American identity was theoretically open to any person who wished to become an American (Gleason, 1980:32).

But there were fateful exceptions to the idealistic definitions; Indians and blacks were excluded, so that no matter how much these groups might believe in liberty and equality, their racial features placed them outside the definition.

It should be emphasized that individual identity has always been intimately related to group, racial, community, and national identity, and that historical factors have always played an important role. Gleason (1980) indicates that between 1815 and 1850 the major issue was that of religion and its relationship to the American identity. There was a large influx of Catholics during this period into what was heretofore a largely Protestant population, followed by the growth of anti-Catholic sentiment. Catholics were accused of clannishness, of espousing separatism; their dress, language, accent, and manners were considered strange; they were accused of poverty, debauchery, and drunkenness. The Irish were the primary targets of the stereotypes. The Know-Nothing Party was one reaction to the anti-Catholic prejudices. It reached its peak in 1855 when it controlled six states and sent some seventy-five representatives to Congress. But sectional tensions and the issue of slavery soon took precedence over the religious issue. Nevertheless, the influx of Catholic immigrants raised issues that remain familiar today: How will the influx of immigrants affect education, culture, behavioral norms, and the political process?

The years from 1860 to 1924 reflected the entrance of different cultural and racial elements to complicate the American identity (Gleason, 1980:38). The need for labor brought in unprecedented hordes of new immigrants, with resultant complications. The melting-pot ideology was strong, and the prevailing mood was that immigrants must change their ways in order to achieve an American identity. There were clear racial limitations, with the notion that some groups were unmeltable, so that Asians were placed in the pariah category historically reserved for Blacks and Indians. One common complaint was that there were just too many immigrants arriving in too short a period of time to be absorbed into the melting pot, and that some were too different from what was presumed to be the American type.

The 1924 Immigration Act reflected this feeling. Immigrants from presumed assimilable countries (namely, British and northern Europeans) were welcome, while those deemed less assimilable (Asians) were denied entry. So the definition of who is an American seemed to be based more on race and physiological features than on an identity based on belief in the tenets of the system.

The decades after 1924 were punctuated by a great depression, World War II, the civil rights struggles, the 1965 Immigration Law (which eliminated national origins), the Vietnam War, and the 1980s recession. The publication of Myrdal's *American Dilemma* (1944) focused on the treatment of Blacks as a direct contradiction to the American creed. The 1960s saw race riots and the growth of an ethnic consciousness that emphasized ethnic-group membership, ethnic slogans, and ethnic-group interests. This sense of "peoplehood" (Gordon, 1964) provided a set of normative standards based on whether actions strengthened or weakened ethnic solidarity. Ethnics began to question the desirability of the process of Americanization; rather than becoming a part of a bland, homogenized, conformist society, critics looked for regional, local, religious, and ethnic diversity as a better definition of American culture. Cultural pluralism encouraged ethnic studies, ethnic consciousness, ethnic pride, and ethnic dignity. Many members of minorities gave their lives in World War II and the Korean and the Vietnamese Wars in the belief that their attitudes and behavior constituted their American identity, only to find that their racial and ethnic features were more important in the judgment of the dominant society. The realization dawned on racial and other minorities that they could never achieve an American identity based on Anglo conformity, especially if physiological features were to remain a priority, so slogans such as "black is beautiful" became popular.

Stages in an Ethnic Identity for Racial Groups

It is interesting to compare the new white ethnics with the older nonwhite ethnics, since many of the reasons for turning to an ethnic identity appear similar. One difference has been the timing; most nonwhites perceived their

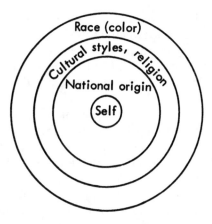

Figure   7–1 Ethnic   identity. (Source: M. Gordon)

inability to become part of the American dream quite early and therefore are much further advanced in the rationale and rhetoric that accompanies a search for identity. But the basic difference is that of physical identifiability and the body, which includes skin color, facial features, and hair texture. The easy identification of the nonwhite ethnic leads to an instant categorization that shapes much of the initial interaction in a color-conscious society. The unsuccessful integration of this variable can lead to repression, denial, avoidance, and gross distortion of identity. Shame for one's self and one's own background are detrimental when dealing with the larger society. Attempts to alter one's image through operations (eye or hair straightening) are desperate attempts to alter the negative view of self.

Other variables making up an ethnic identity—such as cultural styles, national origin, and religion—have been discussed in previous chapters and, although important, are not nearly as critical as race. Figure 7–1 illustrates the components that make up ethnic identity.

The model is informative. The initial lens which others see us through is "race," and the "self" is hidden by cultural styles, religion, and national origin. If we add other factors such as attractiveness and personality, we can appreciate how difficult it is to know the "real self," and the important role played by visibility.

DEVELOPMENT OF A NEGATIVE ETHNIC IDENTITY

One of the constant problems facing nonwhite ethnics is the definition of what is an American that is held by many members of the dominant group, especially the mass media. Race and color are given priority over belief and behavior, so the portrayal of heroes, lovers, or "regular guys and gals" is reserved for "American types" (Whites). How does an ethnic develop an identity when all the role models are impossible to emulate? We hypothesize a number of steps that lead to the development of a negative self identity.

Step 1. Stereotyped minority-group behavior is learned in early childhood. The ability to differentiate between white people (and power) and one's own ethnic people is constantly learned and relearned. Conversely, white people learn about their "superiority" and fulfill the role of validating the "inferiority" of the ethnic. These roles are constantly reinforced by social and organizational interaction.

The ethnic child learns much from urban areas and types of residence; the less desirable areas and shabbier houses are linked to ethnics, while the dominant group lives in the better sections. The mass media, the school system, cultural heroes, and other models reinforce the image of a superior and desirable group distinct from the rest.

If these surroundings were not sufficient, childhood socialization in ethnic families is also geared toward the realities of life. Richard Wright (1937) described how his mother taught him to live under Jim Crow, after he had been severely beaten by some white boys.

> When night fell my mother came from the white folks' kitchen. I raced down the street to meet her. I could just feel in my bones that she would understand. I knew she would tell me exactly what to do next time. I grabbed her hand and babbled out the whole story. She examined my wound, then slapped me.
>
> "How come yuh didn't hide?" she asked me. "How come yuh always fightin'?"
>
> I was outraged, and bawled. Between sobs I told her that I didn't have any trees or hedges to hide behind. There wasn't a thing I could have used as a trench. And you couldn't throw very far when you were behind the brick pillars of a house. She grabbed a barrel stave, dragged me home, whipped me naked, and beat me till I had a fever of one hundred and two. She would smack my rump with the stave and, while the skin was still smarting, impart to me gems of Jim Crow wisdom. I was never to throw cinders any more. I was never to fight any more wars. I was never, never, under any conditions, to fight white folks again. And they were absolutely right in clouting me with the broken milk bottle. Didn't I know she was working hard every day in the hot kitchens of the white folks to make money to take care of me? When was I ever going to learn to be a good boy? She couldn't be bothered with my fights. She finished by telling me that I ought to be thankful to God as long as I lived that they didn't kill me. (Wright, 1937:10)

The realization that the warm, loving parent perceives ethnics and "white folks" differently is often difficult for the ethnic child to handle. But the realities of the power differential are such that most ethnic parents socialize their children to recognize the color and the power differences. In most instances, such a pattern is deemed necessary for survival.

It may be easier to learn the realities of race from early childhood. The jolt of finding out that one is different and therefore less acceptable is always difficult, and this realization at a later age without previous preparation can be a severe trauma. For example, we have met many Asians who had grown up on the East Coast with little overt prejudice and discrimination until they reached the age of serious dating and marriage. They then discovered that they were undesirable, and many of them moved to areas in which there were more ethnics, such as Los Angeles, and thoroughly immersed themselves in the ethnic community, isolating themselves from the white world.

Socialization to the realities of race is much more subtle in the present era. It would still be difficult to find minority parents introducing their children as the future president of the United States. But there has been a rise in expectations, so that ethnics may realistically see their child as a future member of Congress or of the Supreme Court. The elevator may include higher steps, but the top floors remain closed.

Step 2. The stereotype of one's ethnic group is continually reaffirmed, especially in schools and on the job. As was pointed out earlier, stereotypes often become the reality. Concepts such as the self-fulfilling prophecy, operant conditioning, and other precepts of learning theory all are applicable. What minorities do and do not do in school, on the job, in their homes, and in their social interaction is shaped by the expectations and reinforcements of the more powerful group. The mass media play an extremely important part in the process. Labeling and stereotyping are reinforced by discriminatory laws, prejudices, habits, and customs; individuals and institutions shape the behavior of both the minority and majority according to the stereotype.

Step 3. Minority-group socialization has another dimension—socialization into one's own ethnic group. Very little research evidence is available in this area, but the duality of the socialization—behaving in one way in white society, and in another way with one's own group—is a part of growing up for all minorities. Perhaps the freer, more exploratory type of self that develops with one's peers becomes part of the buffer that enables many minority-group individuals to grow up with an adequate view of self. Most members of the majority group never see this side of the minority group.

For example, the stereotype of the quiet, conforming, hard-working, highly motivated Japanese American student is quite widespread. If one limits one's observations to the public schools, the observation appears valid. However, the behavior of many Japanese American students in ethnic language schools cancels this image. The Japanese language school that the author attended after the regular school day was often pure chaos. Shouting, profanity, book-throwing, cheating, rowdiness, and disorder were all widespread. The students often bragged about how many Japanese teachers they had been able to drive out of the profession. Interviews with current Japanese American students indicate that some of this behavior still persists in ethnic schools. Kingston (1976) made a similar observation concerning Chinese American students attending Chinese schools.

Ethnics are forced to employ multiple identities and roles. Not only do they have to adjust to the normal societal roles in their families and in their jobs, but they also have to come to terms with their subordinate ethnic status. Ethnics must be careful about going to certain places, filling certain positions, performing out of the generally prescribed roles; they must remain wary in social situations. For example, a cross-country automobile journey may call for much more careful planning by ethnics in order to avoid embarassing situations. Ethnics often choose first class hotels and restaurants (despite the additional expense) to forestall possible stressful incidents.

Conversely, majority-group members are more able to develop a single, universal identity. Dominant-group members do not have to be as careful since their position allows them to perform in a consistent manner. Others generally have to adapt to them. They define the situation and are in control of the interaction. They can travel throughout the world secure in their status and can interact with others on a fairly predictable basis. The picture of domineering, aggressive Americans ("ugly Americans") who "come on strong" no matter where they are is an example of individuals who generally are used to having their way. Clues to feelings about ethnicity, self, and the treatment accorded to majority-group members can be deduced from the following interview with an articulate Japanese woman:

> The way my family treats my white husband as something special really stands out. The rest of my sisters are married to Nisei (Japanese) men; they are all good citizens and nobody makes a fuss. But the special niche given to the white man—bowing, scraping, deferring, and the attempts to please him—should give you some idea of the role differences, even today.

This stage of the ethnic identity is confirmed when the individual begins to accept the roles prescribed by the majority society. Roles become stabilized under the following hypothesized conditions.

Step 4. The labeled minority is rewarded for playing the stereotyped role. For example, an Asian American worker is praised for being prompt, quiet, neat, and reliable, and may be used as a model for other workers. The pressures to conform to the stereotype may come from both the outside community and from the ethnic community and family.

Step 5. The labeled minority is punished if it attempts to play a less conventional role. This applies to the great majority of ethnics. An Asian American who talks back or performs less stereotypically is viewed with suspicion. There are individual exceptions—the talented few—but it is more comfortable for most to play the role. Some of the roles may even be well paid and include a rise in status. Nevertheless, they are stereotypes, and the irony is that selected ethnics are often used to demonstrate the openness of the system. Once a person is placed in such a status, he or she is rewarded for conformity and is punished for deviant behavior.

Overt punishment is not the only barrier. There are few opportunities to play other roles (for example, ethnics are restricted to a few roles in movies and television); thus, the range of choices is narrowed, and the ethnic stereotype is reinforced.

Step 6. In times of crisis for the minority group, options are greatly reduced, and the stereotyped role may be the only feasible alternative. Ethnic-group individuals are constantly reminded of their vulnerability. During World War II, the Japanese American survived by playing the role of a patriot. During race riots in Watts, the normal activities of those ethnics not even remotely involved were also restricted; Blacks reported that many white colleagues were constantly suspicious ("Are you one of them?").

Step 7. The final stage of the ethnic identity is achieved when ethnic individuals internalize the stereotyped roles preferred by the majority. They may even believe that their role is the best of all possible roles and that those who wish to change the ethnic stratification system are crackpots, "commies," or worse. They may even believe that they are not ethnics at all and overidentify with the majority group.

ACHIEVING A POSITIVE IDENTITY

The process of achieving a healthy identity for those who do not have the requisite or desired physiological attributes or for those who are in subordinate positions has generally been ignored. We hear terms such as "losers," "second best," and the like, with the implication that working hard and becoming more desirable are the solutions. Yet powerless positions are the reality for

Ethnic festival day at a grade school.

many. Can individuals and groups assigned to subordinated positions on the basis of race ever achieve a positive self-image?

There is no easy answer to this question, but one of the interesting developments among racial minorities is that of an instant ethnic identity. Previous negative color prescriptions are reversed, so that "black is beautiful," and "yellow is mellow." The turnabout reverses the "white is right" mentality and is accompanied by a new vocabulary of metaphors, such as "oreo," "banana," "coconut," and "apple"—each used as pejorative terms for ethnics who are, respectively, black, yellow, brown, and red on the outside, but white on the inside.

The pride in blackness, yellowness, redness, and brownness has served a useful function. It has made possible an alternative and perhaps a healthier self-identity, since becoming White seldom could be achieved, or achieved only at a high cost (repression, alterations) to the nonwhite individual.

Ethnic identity also raises questions about child development and personality theories that emphasize "normal" stages of development. Most people of dominated status are seldom afforded such normal stages; they are constantly reminded of their secondary positions in the society. Yet a generalization concerning their deficiencies and lack of normality is inappropriate since most function well, with positive self-identities. It appears that we have just barely scratched the surface on how self and identity develop.

Another form of identity is what Gans (1985) calls a symbolic identity. It may be a generational phenomenon; third and fourth generation ethnics may no longer need the kinds of organizations and structures of their parents and grandparents. But, they may retain a symbolic ethnicity (that is, attending an ethnic movie; participating in a yearly festival). Although symbolic ethnicity may last many generations, Gans does not see it as a permanent identity.

SUMMARY

Ethnic and racial identity can be divided into a primordial and a structural view. The former sees ethnicity as permanent; the latter as temporary. It is our interpretation that both operate at different times and at different levels, but that ethnic identity based on a phenotype is apt to be more permanent, unless there is a dramatic change in the inclusion-exclusion process.

Historically, the treatment of northern Europeans and the English differed from people of color. Indians, Blacks, "swarthy" Europeans, and later, Asians were not included in the American dream. Therefore, even though there has been a change towards inclusion, rather than exclusion, the racial minorities may not follow "straight line" theory. As Gans (1986) writes, the history of European ethnics follows a straight line from their own immigrant cultures to the "American way," which means that eventually, by generation, their identity will bear only the minutest trace of their national origin. Such a development will be altered or delayed for Third World immigrants as long as race is used as an exclusionary device. And the strength of an ethnic identity shapes the lens used to explain the world.

REFERENCES

BANTON, M. (1983). *Racial and ethnic competition*. Cambridge: Cambridge University Press.

BELL, D. (1975). "Ethnicity and social change." In N. Glazer & D. Moynihan (Eds.), *Ethnicity* (pp. 141–174). Cambridge, Mass.: Harvard University Press.

ERIKSON, E. (1950). *Childhood and society*. New York: W. W. Norton.

GANS, H. J. (1985). Symbolic ethnicity: The future of ethnic groups and cultures in America. In N. Yetman (Ed.), *Majority and minority*. Boston: Allyn & Bacon.

GLAZER, N. (1975). Introduction to Ethnicity. In N. Glazer & D. Moynihan (Eds.), *Ethnicity*. Cambridge, Mass.: Harvard University Press.

GLEASON, P. (1980). American identity and Americanization. In S. Therstrom, A. Orlov, & O. Handlin (Eds.), *Harvard Encyclopedia of American Ethnic Groups* (pp. 31–58). Cambridge, Mass.: Harvard University Press.

GORDON, M. (1964). *Assimilation in American life*. New York: Oxford University Press.

GREELEY, A. (1974). *Ethnicity in the United States*. New York: John Wiley.

HECHTER, M. (1986). Theories of ethnic relations. In S. F. Stack, Jr. (Ed.), *The primordial challenge* (pp. 13–23). New York: Greenwood Press.

ISAACS, H. (1975). *Idols of the tribes*. New York: Harper & Row.

JOHNSON, L. P. (1983). For my Indian daughter. *Newsweek*, September 5, p. 8.

KINGSTON, M. H. (1976). *The woman warrior*. New York: Vintage Books.

MYRDAL, G. (1944). *An American dilemma*. New York: Harper and Row.

NEWMAN, W. (1976). Multiple realities: The effects of social pluralism on Identity. In A. Dashefesky (Ed.), *Ethnic identity in society* (pp. 39–47). Chicago: Rand McNally.

PATTERSON, O. (1975). Context and choice in ethnic allegiance. In N. Glazer & D. Moynihan (Eds.), *Ethnicity* (pp. 305–345). Cambridge, Mass.: Harvard University Press.

STACK, J. F. (1986). Ethnic mobilization in world politics: The primordial perspective. In J.F. Stack, Jr. (Ed.), *The primordial challenge* (pp. 1–9). New York: Greenwood Press.

VAN DEN BERGHE, P. (1981). *The ethnic phenomenon*. New York: Elsevier.

WASHINGTON EVENING STAR. (1972). January 12, p. B-11.

WILLIAMS, T. (1986). International Amerasian Identity: The Case of Third Culture Eurasian and Afroasian Americans in Japan. University of California, Los Angeles, Master's Thesis, Asian American Study Center, September.

WILSON, W. J. (1978). *The declining significance of race*. Chicago: University of Chicago Press.

WRIGHT, R. (1937). The ethics of living under Jim Crow. *Uncle Tom's children*. New York: Harper & Row.

Section II

Groups in the Third Tier of the Stratification System

Section II presents groups divided along the model suggested by Marger (1991) as covered in Chapter 3. The following three tiers were identified:

> The **top elite**—primarily WASPS. Part of the group will be covered in the final chapter, although not as formally as for the minority groups.
> The **second tier**—white Catholics, Jews, and selected Asian Americans.
> The **third tier**—African Americans, Mexican Americans, Cubans, Puerto Ricans, and Native Americans.

This section will cover groups in the third tier of the stratification system, including Chapter 8 on African Americans, Chapter 9 on Mexican Americans, Chapter 10 on Puerto Ricans and Cuban Americans, and Chapter 11 on Native Americans.

Chapter 8

African Americans

The year 1995 was a prominent one for African Americans. There was the O. J. Simpson trial, which was likened to a soap opera, since it appeared on television daily and had all of the ingredients that made for popular viewing. The climax was the acquittal, with Blacks cheering and Whites stunned to silence. Racism, wealth, jury selection, role of legal counsel, poor police work, and a myriad of other variables were analyzed as reasons behind the acquittal. But the basic generalization was that the trial had exacerbated black-white relations.

Then, in October, there was the million man march on Washington. It had its share of controversy, ranging from the role of Louis Farrakhan, to the lack of females, and to the undercount (400,000 to 800,000). But it also showed a sense of unity, of the fact that Blacks pay taxes, raise children, and want a better life. As one participant, Ben White, said, he had found new friends and a new resolve:

> to watch my mouth, treat my brothers and sisters with respect, get my life together, and carry the message back to my community (*Newsweek*, Oct. 30, 1995).

Among the many questions that were raised, the most important related to goals: Was it self-help and participation in the mainstream, or was it separatism, with its emphasis on developing their own community apart from the dominant society? But these questions are not new; they were always a part of the black experience. But what might have been new was the show of strength and solidarity among African American males, often referred to as an endangered species, since such a large number end up in the justice system.

There was also the rise of African American conservatives, a process that started earlier with the elevation of Judge Clarence Thomas to the Supreme Court, and writers such as Shelby Steele, Thomas Sowell, and Dinesh D'Souza. D'Souza's (1995) main theme, supported by African American conservatives, is that racism is dead, so African Americans should ignore race and concentrate on individual responsibility and mobility.

But there were also other voices. Mike Kelly (1995) saw an increasing polarization of color and race, while bell hooks (1995) saw race as well as sexism as central issues.

All of these views are relevant because among all of our racial minorities, African Americans (or Blacks, or Americans of African ancestry) have suffered the longest. They have been and continue to be the principal victims of racism: the primary objects of prejudice, discrimination, and segregation. They are also the most "American" of our groups; the conditions of their forced immigration and the length of time in the country means that there is little remembrance of a country of origin.

The process of incorporating American ideals and the high expectations that go with them has created what Festinger (1957) labeled a cognitive discrepancy that appears to have been resolved through a push for social change. The discrepancy refers to a gap between what is expected and what can be realistically achieved. In the process, African Americans have raised the fundamental question, "Can people of color truly share in the American dream?" Some immigrant groups have not had to face the question as directly as the African Americans because of a nationality or religious identity that could serve as a feasible alternative.

Even though African Americans have been in the United States from its very beginnings, they still do not possess the economic, educational, or political resources to exert the necessary leverage for an independent existence. Rather, the dependency relationship with the dominant group and the position at the bottom of the racial stratification system have continued. Their power lies in their numbers, although for a long period the strength of these masses could not be translated into action such as voting because of discriminatory and other barriers.

One of the most divisive issues for African Americans, ever since their forced arrival, has been the question of whether to establish a separatist existence or to integrate into the dominant culture. This question, which has been constantly debated, has created bitter enmities and divisions, and has strained efforts toward a workable coalition.

The most eloquent spokespersons for these positions were Malcolm X (1925–1965) and Martin Luther King (1929–1968). Both were known as leaders, heroes, traitors, or fools depending on one's point of view; both died prematurely at the hands of assassins.

Malcolm X challenged a Harlem audience in 1963 by asking whether they wanted to integrate into the wicked white society or to separate themselves from the group that had enslaved them. He recognized that Whites considered themselves far superior to Blacks and that integration was meant only for Blacks who thought like Whites, and on their terms. Therefore, the only intelligent and lasting solution was for Blacks to separate themselves completely from that world (Blair, 1977:34).

Malcolm X articulated nine essential components of a black nationalist movement (Blair, 1977:58–59):

1. Unity among all Blacks throughout the world.
2. Black self-determination: The right to control their own lives, their history, and their future.
3. Community control: Strong, all-black communities and organizations to fight injustice (high rents, high prices, lack of jobs).
4. Education: Black-led institutions raising people to levels of excellence and self-respect.
5. Economic security: Black control of the economy for the benefit of Blacks.
6. Armed self-defense: The ability to fight back when unlawfully attacked.
7. Social and moral uplift: The need to get rid of the effects of years of exploitation, neglect, and apathy, and to fight against police brutality, organized crime, and drug addiction.
8. Rediscovery of the African heritage: Opening up communications with Africa; a study of African history, culture, and philosophy.
9. Internationalization of the black struggle.

Malcolm X summarized many of the dreams and expectations voiced by black leaders of the past and charted a course for future action. He rejected the model of black working people being led by the black middle class, which was allied with and dominated by the white power structure. Instead, he placed the interests of all Blacks against all Whites, and later the interests of all revolutionary forces, whether black or white, against all regressive forces, black or white.

Martin Luther King saw a different goal for Blacks. He saw the breakdown of barriers, the fight for civil rights, and the achievement of equality as the highest priorities. In his famous "I have a dream" speech, he spoke of the time when little black boys and black girls will be able to join hands with little white boys and white girls as sisters and brothers. He envisaged the day when "we will be able to work together, pray together, to struggle together and all of God's children, black men and white men, Jews and Gentiles, Protestants and Catholics will be able to join hands and sing" (Schulke, 1976:218).

*Reverend Martin Luther King
answering questions on desegrega-
tion, 1963.*

These two leaders defined the goals of the American system, with Malcolm X advocating pluralism and separatism, and Reverend King, integration. Both men were also in agreement about the current state of the black community, whether it be one of domination, colonialism, or some other variation.

EARLY HISTORY

The first African arrivals in the United States were twenty slaves sold to Virginia settlers in 1619, one year before the Mayflower arrived. Studies by Donnan (1935) and Herskovits (1941) indicate that many of the slaves imported to the American colonies came from an area not more than 200 miles inland from the coast of West Africa. The black migrants represented many different African cultures, ranging from sophisticated empires to isolated groups; once in America, however, they all were mistreated alike. Slaves were sold and dispersed throughout the country, and systematic efforts were made to stamp out their native cultures. Although some of the African culture has survived in language, folk tales, and music, it was generally impossible for slaves to maintain their old ways.

Therefore, although there were many slaves, they were powerless. They were scattered, family units were destroyed, their cultures were dismantled, and they were permanently assigned to the lowest rung of the stratification system.

Several conditions were responsible for this state. First, slaves were generally young. They came from a social system composed of clans and kinship groups (parents, aunts, uncles, grandparents, and cousins) and were unprepared for life in a competitive, individualistic society (Holt, 1980). Upon arrival, they were thrown in with Africans from all different groups; finally, their socialization was geared toward the slave system. The two categories—white/nonwhite, superior/inferior—were beginning to form.

The transformation from laborer to slave was a complicated process, and it can never be accurately traced, according to Jordan (1968). It must have occurred partly in accordance with the English view of the black person's blackness, religion, different style of life, animality, and sexuality. Further, slaves became social and economic necessities because conditions in America required a permanent, subservient, and controllable labor force.

The greatest problem in race relations has been the variable of color as an almost impenetrable barrier, thus, there has been a clustering of nonwhites at the bottom half of the stratification system. For example, there are currently no white indentured servants identified as such; they were absorbed and integrated into the mainstream centuries ago, and, no doubt, many of their descendants refer proudly to their early pioneer stock. But the African Americans, who arrived at the same time, could neither advance nor be absorbed, and many of their descendants remain at the bottom of the U.S. system.

SLAVERY

The single most important experience for the African American in the United States has been living under the conditions of slavery. It has stamped both slave and slave-owner with an indelible mark that has been difficult to erase, even though the Emancipation Proclamation is well over 100 years old, and today no one can claim to have lived under slavery. Yet the system that classifies people into human/subhuman, master/servant, adult/child, owner/owned, and the techniques for maintaining this disparity have survived in both overt and subtle forms.

The notion that slaves were property was central to their treatment. Since they were defined as subhuman, they could be completely dominated by their master and used in whatever way he or she chose. They could be bought, sold, given away, or eliminated. The master provided room and board, medical care, and any other treatment he or she saw fit.

Slavery was also a permanent state: once a slave, always a slave. There was no reasonable hope of passing on higher expectations to a new generation.

The adverse conditions of slavery included high morbidity and mortality rates, illness, filth, disorder, and disruptive life conditions. Equal social interaction with Whites was nonexistent, and education and other means of self-advancement and upward mobility were restricted.

Patterson (1980) compared slavery in various places throughout the world and emphasized that the basic stratification system was based on human domination. Life and death were dependent on the master's whim. In addition, the slave was a genealogical isolate, a nonperson formally alienated from ancestors, kin, or descendants. The slave could not exercise such rights as protecting kin, achieving family security, laying legitimate claim to children, aspiring to a better status, or defending honor. Slavery was a state of social death, of being a nonperson in most matters that counted.

THE CIVIL WAR

The problem of slavery was one of the critical factors leading to the Civil War. Neither side really conceived of the African American as an equal. For example, the Northern armies rejected early African American enlistees for a variety of reasons, most of them overtly racist and pertaining to black inferiority and cowardice.

As the war developed, army commanders were permitted to use their own discretion about utilizing "Negroes." Some commanders insisted on returning runaway slaves to their owners, and others permitted them to fight. When they were finally permitted to enlist, African Americans did so enthusiastically. By the end of the Civil War, approximately 186,000 African American troops had been enrolled. These troops took part in 198 battles and suffered 68,000 casualties. (Pinkney, 1975:19).

Even more took part in the overall war effort as servants, laborers, and spies. But a familiar racist pattern was in evidence; African Americans served in segregated units under white officers. The Confederate armies were less successful in enlisting African American soldiers. The South was limited by one basic fear—that armed African Americans might turn against their former masters. Late in the war, the Confederates drafted a conscription bill, but most African Americans fled rather than be drafted into the Southern army.

THE POSTWAR PERIOD

The Emancipation Proclamation, signed on January 1, 1863, while the war was still in progress, brought a formal end to the institution of slavery. In retrospect, although the bill was a dramatic political gesture, it created many problems for most slaves. There had been very little planning for active black citizen participation, a necessary step since African Americans had lived under the bonds of slavery, illiteracy, and dependence for so many years. The President also made it clear that the primary purpose of the Proclamation was to preserve the Union, rather than to abolish slavery.

The South was a defeated and devastated region at the end of the Civil War. Reconstruction of the area seemed far more important than the civil rights and living conditions of the newly emancipated. Moreover, the defeated Southerners still maintained their feelings about the inferiority of their former slaves, and violence, both legal and illegal, was a common solution to racial problems.

For example, DuBois (1935) found that Southerners tried to reinstitute slavery through a series of legalisms that would recreate the institution in everything but name. The Black Codes specified conditions of work, property rights, rights to public assembly, ownership of firearms, and other aspects of black life. Blacks could be arrested by any white man, suggesting apartheid: "Every Negro freedman who shall be found on the streets after ten o'clock at night without a written pass or permit shall be imprisoned or pay a fine" (DuBois, 1935:177). Although the Black Codes were suspended by the Freedman's Bureau before they became fully effective, most Southerners actively opposed granting equality to their former slaves. Rather, a return to the two-category system, whether called slavery or another name, was their choice.

RECONSTRUCTION

For a short time after the Civil War, African Americans participated actively in the political arenas in the South. A series of reconstruction acts and the passage of the Fifteenth Amendment (1870) guaranteed African Americans the right to vote. The Civil Rights Act of 1866 gave African Americans the rights of American citizenship, and the Fourteenth Amendment prohibited states from depriving any person of life, liberty, or property without due process of law and also guaranteed equal protection. According to Pinkney:

> During the period of Radical Reconstruction black people participated in politics to a greater extent than in any other period in American history. They often held important offices, but there was never a Negro governor. There were two lieutenant-governors, and several Negroes represented their states in the United States Congress. (1975:25)

However, violence against Blacks was a constant problem. The disputed election of Republican President Rutherford Hayes, which resulted in the Compromise of 1877, was a turning point for the freed slaves. Rather than advancing toward equality, they were moved back to the pre-Civil War era. Federal troops were withdrawn from the South, and the old Southern leadership rapidly returned. The years from 1877 to World War I were difficult for African Americans in the United States. The Civil War had been fought and won; the Emancipation Proclamation had abolished formal slavery; the opportunity for a new relationship existed, but the clock did not move forward.

In 1896 the Supreme Court decision on the Plessy v. Ferguson case strengthened the Jim Crow laws, and separate but equal (which in reality was separate but unequal, or the model of domination) became the law of the land. One critical factor affecting the power position of the African Americans in the South during this era (and lasting much beyond this time) was their inability to purchase the land on which they lived. Many were in debt and found that putting in long hours, working hard, and following American values were not translated into upward mobility and economic independence.

For example, throughout the nineteenth century, African Americans were the majority of the labor force in the rural South, yet they never owned more than 6 percent of the land, and these were typically small operations on marginal land. The situation in the Southern cities was similar. African American labor was at the mercy of the dominant group, which was content to retain a racial caste system (Hraba, 1979:275).

The conditions under which African Americans were forced to live belied any free status. The boundary mechanisms of the two-category stratification system—prejudice, discrimination, and segregation—became stronger than ever. African Americans were, for all intents and purposes, relegated to a caste position based on color, and no black person could expect equal treatment. Informal, spontaneous methods of maintaining the boundaries and keeping the African Americans in their place were frequently used. Lynchings were one of the most popular.

It was also one of the more drastic means of asserting the power of the Whites. As Berry writes:

> Finally, the period of the Civil War and the Reconstruction saw the pattern of lynching firmly established: Courts of law, though in full operation, are circumvented; no effort is made to determine the guilt of the accused; punishment is invariably death, often accompanied by torture; and the victim is usually a Negro. (1951:125)

One source estimates the number of lynchings since 1882 to have been more than 5,000 (Shay, 1938:7). Lynching declined in popularity over time. It reached its height in 1892, when there were 235 recorded lynchings; by the 1920s the average number had dropped to 31.2 per year, and since the 1920s, there have been only scattered reports.

Although lynching served mainly as a symbolic device to keep the Blacks in their place, it was symptomatic of the racial barriers. Any form of behavior that threatened the ego of the white Southerner could be punished violently.

As could be expected under these negative conditions, there was an exodus of African Americans from the South to the northern urban areas. They were attracted by the promise of more jobs and better social opportunities. But the African Americans discovered that racism was not confined to the South, and that northern white behavior was less than Christian. Laws, customs, standards, and rationalizations established barriers and created segregated areas often as stringent as those in the South. A newer feature—mob violence in the form of race riots—was added to the already impressive list of techniques to maintain white superiority.

THE TWENTIETH CENTURY

Booker T. Washington (1856–1915), W. E. DuBois (1868–1963), and Marcus Garvey (1880–1940) were prominent during the early part of the century. Washington advocated a drive toward self-sufficiency and self-determination through training in vocational pursuits and business. He felt that proficiency in specific skills was far superior to liberal arts training and that investing dollars for profit made more sense than to spend a dollar for an opera (Hall, 1977). Washington's model was that of acculturation and adaptation to existing realities. It was based on a functional model of society in which hard work, education, and the learning of a trade were deemed as priorities in becoming a part of the mainstream.

DuBois, whose name is linked with Pan-Africanism, the Niagara movement, and the National Association for the Advancement of Colored People (NAACP), opposed Washington's programs. He criticized Washington for abandoning the fight for political and civil rights, although he agreed on the need for racial pride and improved economic conditions.

DuBois (1935) perceived the basis of Southern white power as a combination of high social prestige, ownership of property, and ability to disenfranchise the Blacks. The gentleman Southerner was able to use power and prestige in the context of economic interests and gain to establish and maintain the two-category system. Henderson (1976) wrote that DuBois was one of the first Blacks to show the relationship among the Southern economic structure, racial discrimination, segregation, brutality, and the exploitation of black labor.

Garvey, originally from Jamaica, established the Universal Negro Improvement Association (UNIA) in Harlem around 1919 (Hall, 1977:6). Garvey saw Africa as the national homeland and envisaged Blacks from all over the world marching to the continent and taking it back from its colonial oppressors. Both DuBois and Garvey saw the black problem in conflict terms, so that organization and power were important in obtaining concessions from the dominant group. All of these approaches had their adherents, but they all failed because of the lack of power in the local community. There was never the combination of unity, cohesion, numbers, and resources necessary to put these plans into operation. Nevertheless, the dream of black liberation and escape from white domination, which was the common motivating factor behind these plans, continues as the main theme for black leaders to the present day.

As early as 1900, African Americans instituted a boycott against Jim Crow streetcars in the deep South (Meier & Rudwick, 1969a). The protest was remarkable in several respects. It occurred in an era when separate but equal was the law of the land; it took place in the heart of the deep South in such cities as Atlanta, Memphis, Montgomery, Natchez, Richmond, and Savannah;

and it occurred at a time when most African Americans were disenfranchised. Although the boycott was unsuccessful, it was a symptom of protest and unrest.

Hall (1977) saw the 1930s, the depression years, and the New Deal as changing the emphasis of black movements. Most of the black organizations could not deliver viable economic programs, whereas the New Deal sponsored by the federal government could, and people opted for "meat to eat" plans rather than "pie in the sky" programs. Therefore, in the mid-1930s, there was increased concern among African Americans for getting a piece of the pie, no matter how small, rather than concentrating on separatist, ideological movements.

Possibly the most important document in this era was the publication of Myrdal's *American Dilemma* in 1944, which concluded that it was to the advantage of American Blacks to work toward assimilation into the dominant white system. But it also pointed out that a resolution of the black-white dilemma was critical to America's future.

The 1940s brought World War II, and the main African American activity was focused on the NAACP and its legal battles for obtaining fair and equal employment. President Franklin D. Roosevelt issued an executive order banning discrimination in industries with federal contracts. But Garfinkel (1959) questioned the effectiveness of that order.

THE AFRICAN AMERICAN REVOLT

The year 1955 saw the beginning of a changed social movement among blacks (Gerschwender, 1971:3). Previously there had been revolts, insurrections, runaways, the Niagara movement, and Marcus Garvey's Back-to-Africa drive that signaled the desire for social change among many Blacks. But generally, these acts were isolated, uncoordinated, and lacked continuity, although the last two were more ambitious. There had also been organizations—the Underground Railroad, the abolitionist movement, the NAACP, and the Urban League—that aimed at amelioration and change, but they all were under white control.

Several important factors underlie the historical development of these social movements. World Wars I and II provided a major impetus for social change: (1) They opened up job opportunities previously unavailable to many African Americans; (2) they provided new experiences and new exposure, especially to those who were sent overseas; and (3) they raised the level of black expectations and standards of living, so that during the postwar readjustment period many African Americans were unwilling to settle for less.

African Americans began to feel acutely deprived and dissatisfied when they compared their situation to the rapid progress of the Whites. Whites had made impressive gains in jobs, income, and education, but Blacks lagged far behind. Even so, between 1940 and 1960 African Americans began to enter the universities at an accelerated rate. Rather than feeling alienated from their background, these educated African Americans felt a responsibility toward their communities and re-established ties with them. Thus arose a collective sense of deprivation, an awareness of common grievances, a view of the White as the maintainer of the barriers, and the beginning of black solidarity.

The civil rights movement in the early 1950s was dominated by middle-class African Americans and college students. As late as 1962, the middle-class African American was at the forefront (Orbell, 1967), but by 1964 differences in class background began to diminish (Orum & Orum, 1968). As the movement shifted from black middle-class domination, its tactics also became more militant. Leaders changed rapidly as the moods and responses of the movement evolved and strategies shifted. Newer organizations came into being and a wider spectrum of tactics replaced the accommodationist strategies of the previous era. Terms such as direct action, confrontation, and nonnegotiable demands reflected this newer response.

SUPREME COURT DECISION OF 1954

The 1954 Supreme Court decision prohibiting racial segregation in public education was an important milestone in race relations. But, as with most landmarks, it was not an isolated, accidental occurrence. Rather, the decision itself was both the culmination and the beginning of a series of actions affecting the two most important features of boundary maintenance—legal discrimination and legal segregation.

There was a corresponding change in the black community. Many no longer accepted the status quo of the two-category stratification system. The past had given way to a new series of strategies. Whiteness and white role prescriptions were no longer the desired norms; blackness in the form of black militancy, black power, black identity, and black autonomy had come to the fore. Similar movements in former colonized African areas added an impetus and led some Whites to suspect a worldwide conspiracy.

Other members of the dominant majority were now aware that their ideas of democracy and the melting pot were based on ethnocentric and racist assumptions. They recognized that adaptation, adjustment, and acculturation had been a one-way flow, from people of color to people of one color—white.

But the stresses created by newer goals, strategies, and techniques led to conflict, often of a tragic nature. Violence had been used to maintain the boundaries, and violence was used to change them. The rhetoric flowed as newer leaders replaced new leaders.

INCREASING VIOLENCE AND URBAN RIOTS

One of the results of the changes in tactics and strategies has been the increase in violent interaction. The period from 1964 to 1968 was characterized by urban riots and slogans such as "Burn, baby, burn," and "Kill the pigs." Expectations had risen through a series of advances in civil rights. For example, the Civil Rights Acts of 1964 and 1965 desegregated public facilities, ensured voting rights, and addressed the problem of job discrimination. But the effect of these changes on black lives was very slow; there were numerous instances of white intransigence and violence—bombings, intimidation, and the ever-present charges of police brutality (Lieberson & Silverman, 1965). It did not help when most of these charges went unheeded.

Only a small percentage of the total black population actually participated in outbursts in any given city; most of the urban riots were spontaneous (Meier & Rudwick, 1969b) and loosely organized, if at all (Downes, 1968). The participants tended to be younger African Americans between the ages of fifteen and twenty-four, better educated, and with incomes comparable to nonparticipants, although the African Americans had a slightly higher rate of unemployment. They were motivated by a sense of relative deprivation, which gave the groups a feeling of solidarity. White-owned property was the primary target of violence (Downes, 1968; Meier & Rudwick, 1969b).

Government and industry responded to the outbursts with jobs and promises of better conditions. But as the riots of 1967 continued into 1968, many African Americans began to question the cost in black lives in cities such as Los Angeles, Newark, and Detroit. The riots were seen to be counterproductive, and potentially violent outbursts were defused. Ghetto riots diminished and virtually disappeared in the early 1970s but were replaced by a series of shoot-outs between black militants and police (Knopf, 1969).

But the 1990s saw the Rodney King beating, which was caught on camera and shown on television, indicating that overt violence had not disappeared. The subsequent verdict favoring the police officers led to an eruption in Los Angeles and exacerbated tensions between the black and Korean communities.

BLACK POWER

The Black Power slogan emerged during a nonviolent march through Mississippi led by William Meredith in 1966. A shot fired by a White hit Meredith and turned a relatively small demonstration into a major one. Stokely Carmichael became the chief advocate of Black Power, defining it as the ability of black people to politically get together and organize themselves so that they can speak from a position of strength rather than a position of weakness (Ladner, 1967:202). Since that time there have been so many definitions and applications of this phrase that its original meaning has been misunderstood (Franklin, 1969).

Generally, the Black Power movement has sought to redistribute the power in society by any means possible. The Black Power ideology is mainly socialistic and sees capitalism as the major problem because it is exploitative. The overthrow of capitalism would eradicate the exploitation; black autonomy, community control of the ghettos, and economic self-sufficiency are viewed as means by which power can be established to oppose all forms of capitalism.

Another branch of its ideology sees power in the hands of a few Whites. Blacks, as well as poor Whites, are exploited by this select few. Black Power contains the possibility of an alliance between Blacks and exploited Whites.

One goal of black separatism was to create an independent black nation. This may be a temporary goal in order to integrate the Blacks and build a power base from which they can attain full equality. Though the advocates of Black Power and black separatism may differ in rhetoric and tactics, their goals were essentially the same (Gerschwender, 1971).

The two major variations within the black separatist movement were tactical separatism and ultimate separatism (Gerschwender, 1971:434). Tactical separatism views separation as a means of gaining control over one's own destiny and achieving self-determination by driving out the white colonists who own or control the ghetto industries and schools. Ultimate separatism sees separation as an end in itself, rather than as a means to gain power, and desires a strictly black state.

Among the first avowedly separatist movements after World War II was the Nation of Islam (Black Muslim), which espoused ultimate separatism (Howard, 1966). It preached that white people were devils created by a black scientist named Yakub. The Whites were considered mentally, physically, and morally inferior to the Blacks, who were the first to populate the earth. Yakub's work was met with anger by Allah, who ordained that the white race shall rule for a fixed amount of time over the Blacks. In the process the Blacks will suffer, but they will gain a greater appreciation of their spiritual worth by comparing themselves to the Whites. The Black Muslims desired to free Blacks from all white influence and secure land for themselves within the continental United States. Furthermore, their goal was to make black people aware of their special role and future destiny and to educate them in their past history. Though the Black Muslim movement has split since its inception, its actual membership has never been fully ascertained; it proved to be a threat to the white establishment. The Muslims became the targets of police harassment and negative publicity.

All these changes in strategies threatened white domination. Predictably, in some instances Whites mounted a counterreaction out of fear and hostility (Franklin & Starr, 1967), which in turn triggered the formation of black protective and defense organizations.

BLACK PANTHERS

In 1966 Huey Newton and Bobby Seale founded the Black Panther Party, which became one of the leading revolutionary black nationalist groups in the country. Originally organized as a self-defense group, it soon developed a radical ideology, which included goals of overthrowing capitalism (Foner, 1970). The program appealed to large numbers of unemployed, poor African Americans.

Because of the Panthers' policy of maintaining arms for self-defense and their radical ideology, they soon became targets of police throughout the country. Between 1968 and 1970, dozens of Panthers were killed; thousands of others were arrested, and the group was constantly under police surveillance and harassment. By 1971 the party was divided internally, and Eldredge Cleaver went to Algiers to head the international section, in opposition to Newton and the national organization. In 1972 the national organization redirected its efforts toward providing services for the black community. Although the history of the Black Panthers is brief, it has had a powerful influence on other racially oppressed groups in the United States, such as the Chinese Americans, Chicanos, and Puerto Ricans (Pinkney, 1975:216).

THE 1970s

Fueled by nationalist movements, civil rights struggles, and radical ideology, the momentum of the 1960s cooled down in the early 1970s. The halt came about partly because of the politics of President Richard Nixon, who impounded congressional funds to aid the poor, appointed racial conservatives to the Supreme Court, and endorsed a policy of benign neglect for African Americans. Nixon was able to consolidate white support for his policies, so that in the 1972 election, two-thirds of white America voted for him while at least 87 percent of African Americans voted against him (Pinkney, 1975:219).

The affirmative action program, aimed at increasing employment and education opportunities for minorities and women, began in the mid-1970s. The program was a recognition by the federal government that employers (including the federal government) could play a more active role in searching for qualified minorities in hiring. Affirmative action is essentially a process-centered approach to discrimination in that it emphasizes open competition for positions, while discouraging the old boy network of friends and acquaintances as the mechanism for filling slots. Affirmative action programs are built on a functionalist model of society; fully qualified minorities and women constitute the pool for upward mobility. The main problem of the program is institutional discrimination built on past racist policies, so that definitions of who can qualify and who possesses the relevant credentials result in intense competition and in very slow overall progress in changing the basic ethnic makeup of the institutions.

Ethnic studies and black studies programs also began in this era. By 1978 questions concerning both affirmative action and black studies were raised by Middleton (1978). Despite progress, evidence of a white backlash, ghettoization, and isolation were felt by African American professors and students. Some professors indicated that they were not real members of the club and instead found that they formed friendships with African American faculty members in other universities. Declining student interest in black studies was another problem. An interview with an African American chairman of a sociology department at a major midwestern university revealed that some students and faculty were faced with feelings that they were there only because of affirmative action and a lowering of standards.

Black athletes have been able to rise to the level of their ability without overt discriminatory barriers. Medoff (1975) compared the salaries of white and black baseball players for the 1967–1968 season and saw no differences. Mogull (1975), studying the 1971 baseball season, also saw no salary discrimination.

There was a feeling of pessimism concerning the future of blacks by the end of the decade. For example, O'Gorman (1978), a white teacher in Harlem, saw the forces of evil continuing to destroy "his" children through lack of proper food, proper rest, medical attention, generally filthy conditions—an intolerable situation that continues to cry for curative psychiatric, spiritual, and parental care. He looked with disfavor on some black intellectuals who romanticized the plight of a deteriorating Harlem. James Baldwin, the novelist (1974), in *If Beale Street Could Talk*, painted a bleak picture in which institutional racism was powerful and in which Blacks had been left alone in their struggle. Yette (1971) maintained that Blacks had been allowed to become obsolete, so that the very survival of a residual population was at stake. He cited the nation's priorities to illustrate his thesis. For example, when the Southern Christian Leadership Council asked for $1 billion to feed the country's poor, they were turned down; on the other hand, over $30 billion were spent to destroy Vietnam.

THE 1980s

The 1980s began with some changes in emphasis in the black community. The push for civil rights, although still important, was muted in order to accommodate economic and employment issues. For example, at a Black Alternatives Conference held in San Francisco in 1980, one of the keynote speakers was conservative Chicago economist Milton Friedman, and discussions centered on economic rights, market incentives, tax credits, youth employment, free-enterprise zones, urban homesteading, and private sector programs. Rivera (1983) wrote about the NAACP shift in emphasis from schools and housing to economic issues.

Wilson (1981) noted three developments that have changed black perspectives:

1. The growing economic disparity within the black class structure
2. The chronic problems of unemployment and labor-force participation of poor blacks, especially teenagers and young adults

3. The rise of black female-headed families and the resulting negative effect on black family income

The reduction of racial barriers through antidiscrimination and affirmative action programs has been welcomed, but the paradox has been the growth of a black underclass with limited occupational opportunities and mobility. Wilson contends that equal opportunity and affirmative action programs have not addressed the fundamental causes of black poverty. Well-educated and well-trained minorities and women were the primary beneficiaries of affirmative action, but such issues as the dislocation of the poor and black working class, the technological advances that have replaced unskilled workers, and labor surpluses have been ignored.

As a consequence, there appears to be an increased differentiation within the African American social structure, and the writings of African American social scientists reflect these differences. Sowell (1981), writing from a functionalist perspective, contends that government programs have had a negative impact on African American communities. Wilson (1978) concludes that race is no longer an inhibiting factor in occupational mobility. This perspective contends that governmental programs, which were aimed at bettering the lot of all minorities, have had a deleterious effect on the majority of African Americans.

For example, affirmative action has probably benefitted the highly trained and skilled African American, but the large numbers in the untrained and unskilled categories have remained untouched. Sowell (1978) advocates a functionalist, assimilationist strategy for blacks, patterned after the more successful minorities (Asians) and questions governmental programs as patronizing and demeaning.

Oliver and colleagues (Oliver & Glick, 1982; Oliver & Shapiro, 1995) offer a contrasting view. Their analysis of occupational data from the U.S. Census comparing black males to white males showed that gains were meager and that race remained an important factor in restricting mobility. Therefore, contrary to Wilson's thesis of the declining significance of race, their conclusion affirms the enduring significance of race. Instead of eliminating programs, these authors support government policy aimed at fostering economic equality. The National Urban League (Williams, 1980), concerned about high unemployment and poverty, also overwhelmingly supports the idea of federal programs to combat social welfare problems.

Fisher (1982) indicates possible new directions for Blacks and other Third World people. With the demise of European colonialism, there will be a need for nonwhites to work with formerly oppressed colonial people. Bonds of friendship based on a common background of racist oppression can aid in the newly developing areas and provide links between Blacks and Third World development.

Possibly the most visible gains for Blacks occurred in the area of athletics. Littwin (1983) points out that the first black athlete to receive a scholarship in the Southeast Conference was Vanderbilt's Percy Wallace in 1966. The idea of blacks playing basketball (one of the most visible sports) at major Southern universities was revolutionary at that time, but now it is not un- usual to see a team composed of all black starters playing at universities in the deep South. Wallace recalled that he had to play a polite game, similar to what baseball player Jackie Robinson had to go through: no pushing, not even pushing back, no playing out of control, only playing a cautious, conservative game. Although he was successful and became the team captain in his senior year, he was treated as an invisible man on the campus.

Sociologist Harry Edwards (1973), himself a former black athlete, de- cried the overemphasis on athletics as a way of becoming successful, citing the victimization of young Blacks in the collegiate athletic structure. Instead of getting a decent education, many are steered into easy courses and easy colleges and universities. Their athletic abilities are developed and show- cased, but the odds against their becoming professional athletes are so astro- nomical that academic studies and the college degrees should be their highest priority.

But it is also interesting to note that professional football, baseball, and basketball, activities that once were closed to Blacks for any number of racist reasons, are now dominated by them. The remarkable progress in these areas could serve as a model for those occupations and professions that still hesitate to open their doors for full and equal participation.

THE 1990s

The 1990s saw mixed signs for Blacks. The picture depends on the position of the observer, as indicated in the Rashomon perspective. There are successful individuals who hold significant positions, such as Justice Mitchell on the Supreme Court, Mayor Willie Brown of San Francisco, and General Powell, mentioned as a future President. Famous black athletes are so familiar that they are known as "Shaq," "Michael," "Magic," and "Penny," and have appeal beyond the black community. William Wilson was elected to head the Ameri- can Sociological Association, and the number of Blacks on television and in the movies is looked upon with envy by other minority groups. One can cite these individual examples as evidence that race is no longer a handicap. From this perspective, occupation and a social class lens may supercede a racial lens.

But, as we have written in the chapter on inequality, Blacks are also the most unequal. As a group, they are low in income, educational achievement, and occupational advancement; high in poverty, unemployment, and crime. And the mood of the country has also changed—the "three strikes law," the shift from rehabilitation to punishment in the prison system and an impa- tience with understanding the "roots" behind criminal behavior. The Republican takeover in Congress has meant a more punitive stance towards welfare, immigration, and the poor.

Crime is related to the expression of frustration and alienation, especially among the black youth who belong to the underclass. Their chances for meaningful employment are slim. Employment is a form of social control; it encourages responsibility and discipline, and supports family life. Jobless youth are more likely to be free of these restraints, and they are unlikely to be deterred by the threat of imprisonment. The underclass does not think in terms of cost-benefit analysis or rational payoffs, and the punitive threats are not taken seriously. Most important, they have very few alternatives. The reality of facing society with low education, with minimal skills, without strong family support, and with the wrong skin color does not predict for high success. Illegal activities—including pushing drugs for sizable sums—offer alternatives.

A number of independent events that occurred toward the end of the decade served as a reminder that racial tensions between Blacks and Whites had not been resolved. In 1987, three African American men were gang-attacked at Howard Beach, New York by a group of Whites. In the melée, one of the African Americans was killed while attempting to escape across a highway. In 1989, a 28-year-old white female jogger was attacked by a group of adolescent African Americans who allegedly raped, sodomized, and beat the victim in New York City's Central Park. Then later in the same year, a gang of white youths surrounded a group of African American teenagers who had entered a predominantly white Brooklyn neighborhood. One of the black youths, Yusef Hawkins, was shot to death.

Clegg, the chief deputy city attorney for the city of Compton, California, points out that seemingly senseless crimes have long been a part of U.S. history, but noted that press reactions to the above incidents were different. Blacks, when they are the perpetrators, are pictured as a pack of wolves, and there is a national outcry for blood and the death penalty. Conversely, there is little national outrage, nor pictures of white juveniles as animals, when the situation is reversed (Los Angeles Times, 1989). As a footnote to the 1980s, Huey Newton was shot to death in Oakland in 1989; his death presumably related to drugs.

THE POPULATION

In 1990, African Americans numbered close to 30 million, or 12.1 percent of the total United States population (U.S. Bureau of the Census, 1991a). In 1980, they constituted 11.8 percent of the population. Pinkney (1975) indicates that at the time of the U.S. Census in 1720, the 750,000 blacks represented 19.3 percent of the total population.

What was initially a rural population has become highly urbanized. In 1990, 87 percent of blacks lived in urban areas. African Americans are concentrated in the large industrial cities of the Great Lakes and Northeast regions as well as in the South. O'Hare (1992) indicates that they are less likely to live in the suburbs, although the percentages are rising.

It is a young population. In 1990, about 33 percent were under the age of eighteen, compared to 25 percent of whites. The median age of African Americans was 28.1, compared to the white median age of 34.4 (U.S. Bureau of the Census, 1992b, p. 23).

Numbers are most readily translated into political power. The rise of African Americans to elected positions is one indication of their rise in political power. The number of African Americans in government, from county officials and mayors to members of Congress, is increasing steadily: Their numbers leaped from 100 in 1965 to 1,185 in 1969, and had nearly tripled by 1975, when there were 3,503 African American elected officials in forty-five states and the District of Columbia (Blair, 1977:192). The major gains were in the South, which accounted for 55 percent of all African American elected officials.

The increased concentration of African Americans in urban areas means that the probability of electing African Americans as mayors and other elected officials will remain high, given any kind of organizational unity. But it would not be too difficult to predict that the divisions inherent in most groups will surface, so that the internal struggles for power may at times be decisive in allowing other, more organized groups to gain power, even when there may be a high population of African Americans.

STRATIFICATION

Most of the status distinctions within the ethnic community parallel those of the white community. Variables such as income, occupation, education, and family background are common measures of status in most cultures. Other indications of social status include property ownership, organizational affiliation, leadership ability, charisma, and lifestyle. Lifestyle is an especially interesting variable and will be discussed more fully later.

Certain distinctions in social status—such as white ancestry, skin color, speech accent, and cultural similarities to the whites—used to be important to the black subculture. The growth of black identity and changed views of color and white ancestry have led to a reevaluation of these variables.

The Upper Classes

A relatively visible class structure has appeared in the black community. An early study by Drake and Cayton (1945) described a small upper class made up of persons with the most money, education, political power, and the best family backgrounds. Most of them were doctors, lawyers, newspaper editors,

Poet Maya Angelou at the Presidential Inauguration, 1993.

civic leaders, and politicians. More stress was placed on education, professional status, and lifestyle than on income.

Billingsley (1968) commented on the differences between the old and
new upper classes. The group described by Drake and Cayton was primarily
the old upper class. They were men and women whose parents belonged to the
upper or middle classes. Their privileged status extended back to the slave
days, when they were given inheritances and more education. Many have
done remarkably well; men such as former Senator Edward Brooke and Justice Thurgood Marshall are exceptional by any standard. But Billingsley
added that it would be an error to think that these men pulled themselves up
by the bootstraps. They came from families who had already given them a
head start, and they were able to build upon the many opportunities available
to upper-class people.

The most common characteristic of the new upper class is that their mobility has been achieved in one generation. The principal attributes have been
talent and luck. Many gained wealth and prestige by becoming athletic and
show-business celebrities. Another small group received an upper-class in-

come by means of the shadier occupations—gambling, racketeering, and hustling; through their own abilities they have been able to wield a considerable amount of influence in the black community (Billingsley, 1968).

Freeman, in writing about the black elite (1976), attributed the success of the new group to education and the emergence of black professionals. Comer (1972), a black psychiatrist at Yale, described his personal experiences on the way to professional status. The stereotyping of blacks by white colleagues and their overall insensitivity were common grievances.

The black upper class as a group generally supports civil rights activities through the NAACP or the Urban League; they are usually Protestants and are active in social clubs such as fraternities and sororities (Pinkney, 1975). They usually entertain at home, and their guests are of equal status. Tate (1976) studied 350 traditional black elites and 350 new elites in Oakland, California. He found few ideological differences between the groups and discovered that both were evenly divided as to the concept of internal colonization of their community. All respondents saw an increasing stratification by economic class in the black community.

The Middle Classes

There is a growing black middle class. The occupational categories cover a wide range—professionals, independent business persons, clerical and service workers, and laborers. There are many civil service workers, public school teachers, ministers, and social workers.

Like the white middle class, black middle-class families are small, stable, and planned; they want to own their own homes and are concerned about the quality of public schools. They usually belong to a number of organizations and social clubs and have perceptions and values similar to those of their white counterparts.

But there are several important differences. Billingsley (1968) referred to the precarious economic situation of most blacks; they do not enjoy the same measure of financial security as do whites. They tend to make up for this insecurity by highly visible spending and consumption patterns—the familiar stereotypes of Cadillacs, sharp clothes, and traveling first class that have nothing to do with income. Lifestyle becomes extremely important.

Frazier (1957) used the term black bourgeoisie for members of the middle class. He saw many living in a fantasy world and emulating white values and culture. The world of fraternities and sororities is a way of escaping the stigma of color and traditional black culture; the establishment of an American lifestyle without the corresponding economic basis is at the root of the fantasy. They are concerned about respectability and want to maintain certain standards of living, often without adequate economic means, and this creates great stress.

The Lower Classes

The lower-class Blacks are at the bottom of the community class structure. Most Blacks fall into this category. Pinkney (1975) estimated that as many as two-thirds of the urban Blacks belong to the lower class. But they do not belong to the simple, stereotyped group of welfare recipients. According to Billingsley:

> Most Negro families are composed of ordinary people. They do not get their names in the paper as outstanding representatives of the Negro race, and they do not show up on the welfare rolls or in the crime statistics. They are headed by men and women who work and support their families, manage to keep their families together and out of trouble most of the time. They are now what might be generally conceived of as achieving families. They are likely to be overlooked when the white community goes looking for a Negro to sit on an interracial committee, or take a job where Negroes have not been hired before. For they have not gone to college and they are not part of that middle- and upper-class group most likely to come into intimate, daily contact with the white world. At the same time, they are likely to be overlooked by the poverty program and other efforts to uplift the poor and disadvantaged. They often do not qualify to take part in these programs because they are not on welfare. They are, in a word, just folks. And yet, these ordinary Negro families are often the backbone of the Negro community. They are virtually unknown to white people, particularly white people who depend on books and other mass media for their knowledge of life in the most important ethnic subsociety in America today. (1968:137)

Billingsley divided the lower class into three distinct groupings: the working nonpoor, the working poor, and the nonworking poor. The working nonpoor are semiskilled but often well-paid men in industrial jobs: truck drivers, construction workers, and auto mechanics. If it were not for the color of their skin, they would comprise a majority of some labor unions and possess modest homes in the suburbs. But only a relatively small elite group constitutes the hard-hat lower class among the Blacks.

The working poor are the majority of poor blacks. They live in nuclear families headed by men who work hard every day, and are still unable to earn enough to pull their families out of poverty (Billingsley, 1968:139). These families are self-supporting and include the unskilled laborers, service workers, domestics, janitors, and porters. Many of the values that are associated with working-class people—hard work, frugality, a college education, and wanting a better life for their children—are part of their culture. But this group remains invisible and is likely to be ignored when individuals representing the black community are selected.

The bottom rung of the lower-class ladder holds the nonworking poor, sometimes referred to as the underclass. Pinkney (1975) estimated that as many as two-thirds of the urban Blacks fall into this category. They include the chronically unemployed, the welfare recipient, and the newcomer from the South. Family disorganization is great and is brought to the attention of the larger public only through violent acts or political slogans. These individuals become the stereotype of the urban, disorganized Black; they are readily available scapegoats for absorbing some of the frustrations of the taxpayer. Their interaction with the larger society consists mostly of being clients to social workers, teachers, and other professionals, or of being problems to the police. Needless to say they are "nothings" to the majority, who ignore and forget their existence.

The overriding characteristic of lower-class Blacks is alienation. They are powerless; they have very little hope for a better future; and they lack the education and organization to help alleviate their despair and suffering. They tend to belong to fundamentalist churches and are rejected by Blacks of higher status. One of the more damaging factors affecting the status of all Blacks is that the lower-class black man serves as the stereotype for those who want to maintain the boundaries between races.

THE FAMILY

It is impossible to talk about the black family without discussing the influence of the surrounding communities, both black and white. It is shortsighted to assume that the family exists in isolation and is therefore the independent variable that causes problems. From this perspective family disorganization becomes the cause, and social problems such as crime, delinquency, and mental illness become the effects of the family pattern. But the family itself can be thought of as a response or adaptation to the pressures of survival, and its structure and function is a reflection of a host of other variables.

The distortions are even more pronounced when the white family is used as the standard of excellence. For many members of ethnic groups, there is nothing magical about the white family structure, with its ever-increasing rates of separation and divorce. But a report by Moynihan, then assistant secretary of labor, entitled *The Negro Family: The Case for National Action* (1965), saw the deterioration of the black family as the fundamental source of weakness in the black community. The author cited the number of dissolved marriages (one-quarter), illegitimate births (one-quarter), female-headed households (one-quarter), and the startling increase in welfare dependency (no figures given).

Black writers like Billingsley have questioned the Moynihan report's emphasis—nearly one-quarter—which leaves over three-quarters of black families with a normal structure. Bernard observed:

> Many readers will be surprised to learn that the typical (in the sense of commonest) type of family among Negroes is one in which both husband and wife are living together in their first marriage. (1966: preface)

Staples (1988) writes that the past thirty years have been extremely difficult for the black family. Many of the changes reflect changes in all American families—an increase in the number of single adults, out-of-wedlock births, divorces, and single-parent households. But the institutional decimation of the black male is the most serious, for there is an insufficient number of men who have the ability to provide support for women and children in a family setting (Williams, 1984). As a result, many black women are denied a choice of a monogamous marriage.

Therefore, Staples indicates that the crisis of the black family is the crisis of the black male, who because of the restrictions of racism, is unable to carry out the normative responsibilities of husband and father in a nuclear family. Although many children are able to overcome the handicap of growing up in poor, one-parent households, large numbers of them, especially the males, will follow their biological fathers to an early grave, prison, and the ranks of the unemployed (Staples, 1988:321).

Disorganization in many black communities extends far beyond the family itself. Racism, boundary-maintenance mechanisms, and pariah-group status are but a few of the variables that have created pressures on all black institutions, including the family. For example, adequate income alone would help greatly in making black families independent. The lack of income forces an interdependence with the surrounding community. If jobs are scarce and the black father is unemployed, the nuclear family will break down (as would any family), especially when the presence of a male in the home makes the family ineligible for public welfare. Conversely, as job security and income are assured, stable middle-class family patterns will no doubt emerge. Billingsley (1968) showed that the black family in Africa was strong and central to African civilization. Generally, it was male-dominated and had various patterns of marriage, lineage, kinship ties, rights, and obligations. Slavery broke up these patterns and did not permit black families to assimilate into American culture.

BLACK CHURCHES

The best known and the earliest community organization in the black community has been the church. There are a number of reasons for its importance. First, religious gatherings were the first forms of association permitted under slavery, so that religious activity reaches far back into black history in the United States (Simpson & Yinger, 1965). Second, the strong interest in religion and ritualistic practice reflects ancient African traditions, so that the church builds on a cultural continuity (Herskovits, 1941). Finally, the church satisfies a wide variety of needs, in addition to its religious function.

For example, the church made life bearable for the masses and gave meaning to a harsh and often cruel life. It allowed self-expression, provided entertainment and recreation, helped individuals adjust to life crises, and met economic and welfare needs. It offered opportunities for developing leadership skills and helped individuals achieve recognition and status. It served as a community center and was especially helpful in aiding rural inhabitants adapt to urban life. It is no surprise that black leaders such as Martin Luther King Jr. and Jesse Jackson came from ministerial backgrounds.

However, the very large number of black churches with their different leaders, ideologies, forms of worship, and congregations may be an indication of the divisions in the community. Some church goals include an acceptance of the status quo, no matter how dreadful, but others provide models for social change.

DOMINATION AND PATERNALISM

The two models that most closely approximate the black position in society are domination and paternalism (also called domestic colonialism and neo-colonialism). Data on social indicators of inequality demonstrate black inequality in comparison to white male norms on all levels, including education, occupation, income, housing, power, and status.

The lack of power was aptly demonstrated by Pinkney:

> Chief among the characteristics of the urban black community are its powerlessness and its dependence on the frequently hostile white community which surrounds it. These enclaves are kept powerless by powerful individuals and institutions in the white community. The dwellings of the urban black community are usually owned by absentee white landlords and institutions, and no attempt is made to maintain the buildings or to provide the customary services to their inhabitants. Residential buildings, for which the occupants are charged high rents, frequently do not provide safe and adequate shelter. Often they are owned by wealthy and politically prominent suburban residents. (1975:62)

The analogy to a colonial possession seems appropriate. Blacks are there to serve the larger community with a supply of cheap labor. Major decisions are made for them from the outside. During periods of disorder, the ethnic ghetto can be sealed off, and specially trained police and military forces can be rushed in to meet the enemy. Ghetto residents themselves often see the police, social workers, and teachers as the enemy or as representatives of an alien force.

But domination has not been complete. There are numerous exceptions in which talent and ability, as well as luck, have fostered a breakthrough. The most obvious exception to a totally colonized model is the growing number of blacks who have become successful. Or as Raybon (1989) says in a national newsmagazine, the constant message that black America is dysfunctional should be challenged. Most black Americans are not poor; most black teenagers are not on crack, and most black mothers are not on welfare. Perhaps one of the best kept secrets is that blacks are a strong, capable people.

SUMMARY

It is important to reiterate three variables that, when taken together, distinguish the black experience from other immigrant experiences.

1. Blacks came from a continent where norms and values were dissimilar to the American way of life; they were from different tribes, each with their own language, traditions, and culture, and they arrived in chains.

2. In the beginning they came without women and most importantly, they came as slaves. Once in the United States, their past cultures were systematically dismantled; their family systems destroyed, and they faced the almost insurmountable barrier of racism. Programs such as affirmative action should be judged with this background in mind. Likewise, cries of reverse racism seem shallow when placed in historical context. It is also remarkable that many Blacks have done well, considering their historical circumstances.

3. The basic question is the same question that has always been a part of the black experience—Integration? Assimilation? Pluralism? Separation? Can Blacks ever be accepted as equals?

The same questions have to be addressed by the dominant community. Do they wish to exclude or include the Blacks as equals? Have years of exclusion been so long and so effective that attempts at inclusion may be too little and too late?

The past and present experiences of Blacks indicate that the primary lens for perceiving the world is the black one. The view is reinforced by the dominant society; blackness is seen first—other qualities develop later.

Since their earliest arrival in the United States, Blacks have faced racism, and although there is no longer slavery, the black lens remains as the frame for perceiving society. Although individual Blacks may have modified their perceptions, prejudice, discrimination, and segregation have affected the majority. Therefore, it should come as no surprise that most Blacks, framing the O. J. Simpson trial in racial terms, saw the football star "not guilty," whereas those using a different lens felt the man was guilty.

REFERENCES

BALDWIN, J. (1974). *If Beale Street could talk.* New York: Dial Press.

BERNARD, J. (1966*). Marriage and family among Negroes.* Englewood Cliffs, N.J.: Prentice-Hall.

BERRY, B. (1951). *Race relations.* Cambridge, Mass.: Riverside Press.

BILLINGSLEY, A. (1968). *Black families in white America.* Englewood Cliffs, N.J.: Prentice-Hall.

BLAIR, T. (1977). *Retreat to the ghetto*. New York: Hall.

COMER, J. (1972). *Beyond black and white*. New York: Quadrangle Books.

DONNAN, E. (1935). Documents illustrative of the history of the slave trade to America. *Carnegie Institute Publications, 4* (409).

DOWNES, B. T. (1968). Social and political characteristics of riot cities: A comparative study. *Social Science Quarterly, 49,* 504–520.

DRAKE, S., & CAYTON, H. (1945). *Black metropolis*. New York: Harcourt Brace Jovanovich.

D'SOUZA, D. (1995). *The end of racism*. New York: Free Press.

DUBOIS, W. E. B. (1935). *Black reconstruction*. New York: Harcourt Brace Jovanovich.

EDWARDS, H. (1973). *Sociology of sport*. Homewood, Ill.: Dorsey Press.

FESTINGER, L. (1957). *A theory of cognitive dissonance*. New York: Harper & Row.

FISHER, S. (1982). *From margin to mainstream*. New York: Prager.

FONER, P. (Ed.). (1970). *The Black Panthers speak*. Philadelphia: Lippincott.

FRANKLIN, J. H., & STARR, I. (Eds.). (1967). *The Negro in 20th century America* (pp. 185–258). New York: Random House.

FRANKLIN, R. S. (1969). The political economy of Black Power. *Social Problems, 16,* 286–301.

FRAZIER, E. F. (1957). *Black bourgeoisie*. New York: Free Press.

FREEMAN, R. B. (1976). *Black elite*. New York: McGraw-Hill.

GARFINKEL, H. (1959). *When Negroes march: The march on Washington movement in the organizational politics for FEPC*. New York: Free Press.

GERSCHWENDER, J. A. (Ed.). (1971). *The black revolt*. Englewood Cliffs, N.J.: Prentice-Hall.

HALL, R. L. (1977). *Black separatism and social reality: Rhetoric and reason*. Elmsford, N.Y.: Pergamon Press.

HENDERSON, V. (1976). Race, economics and public policy with reflections on W. E. B. DuBois. *Phylon, 37,* 1–11.

HERSKOVITS, M. J. (1941). *The myth of the Negro past*. New York: Harper & Row.

HOLT, T. (1980). Afro-Americans. In S. Thernstrom, A. Orlov, & O. Handlin (Eds.), *Harvard encyclopedia of American ethnic groups* (pp. 5–23). Cambridge, Mass.: Harvard University Press.

HOOKS, B. (1995). *Killing rage*. New York: Henry Holt.

HOWARD, J. R. (1966). The making of a Black Muslim. *Trans-Action, 4,* 15–21.

HRABA, J. (1979). *American ethnicity*. Itasca, Ill.: F. E. Peacock.

JORDAN, W. D. (1968). *White over black*. Baltimore: Penguin.

KELLY, M. (1995). *Color lines*. New York: William Morrow.

KNOPF, T. A. (1969). Sniping: A new pattern of violence? *Trans-Action, 47,* 22–29.

LADNER, J. (1967). What "Black Power" means to Negroes in Mississippi. *Trans-Action, 5,* 7–15.

LIEBERSON, S., & SILVERMAN, A. R. (1965). The precipitants and underlying conditions of race riots. *American Sociology Review, 30,* 887–898.

LITTWIN, M. (1983). Playing in pain in the deep south. *Los Angeles Times,* March 13, part III, p.1.

LOS ANGELES TIMES. (1989). Blacks rejected more often than whites for home loans, survey shows. January 23, part IV, p. 2.

MEDOFF, M. (1975). A reappraisal discrimination against blacks in professional baseball. *Review of Black Political Economy, 5* (3), 259–268.

MEIER, A., & RUDWICK, E. (1969a). The boycott movement against Jim Crow streetcars in the south, 1900–1906. *Journal of American History, 55* (4), 756–775.

MEIER, A., & RUDWICK, E. (1969b). Black violence in the 20th Century: A study in rhetoric and retaliation. In H. Graham & T. Gurr (Eds.), *Violence in America: Historical and Comparative Perspectives.* A Report to the National Commission on the Causes and Prevention of Violence.

MIDDLETON, L. (1978). Black professors on white campuses. *The Chronicle of Higher Education, 17,* 1.

MOGULL, R. (1975). Salary discrimination in major league baseball. *Review of Black Political Economy, 5* (3), 269–279.

MOYNIHAN, D. (1965). *The Negro family: The case for national action.* Washington, D.C.: U.S. Department of Labor, Government Printing Office.

MYRDAL, G. (1944). *An American dilemma.* New York: Harper & Row.

NEWSWEEK. (1995). October 30, p. 30.

O'GORMAN, N. (1978). *The children are dying.* New York: Signet Classics.

OLIVER, M., & GLICK, B. (1982). An analysis of the new orthodoxy on black mobility. *Social Problems, 29* (5), 511–523.

OLIVER, M., & SHAPIRO, T. (1995). *Black wealth/white wealth.* New York: Routledge.

ORBELL, J. M. (1967). Protest participation among Southern Negro college students. *The American Political Science Review, 61,* 446–456.

ORUM, A. M., & ORUM, A. M. (1968). The class and status bases of Negro student protest. *Social Science Quarterly, 49,* 521–533.

PATTERSON, O. (1980). *Slavery and social death: A comparative study.* Cambridge, Mass.: Harvard University Press.

PINKNEY, A. (1975). *Black Americans.* Englewood Cliffs, N.J.: Prentice-Hall.

RAYBON, P. (1989). A case of "Severe bias," *Newsweek,* October 2, p. 11.

RIVERA, N. (1983). NAACP shifts its spotlight from schools, housing to economic issues. *Los Angeles Times,* September 11, Part V, p. 3.

SCHULKE, F. (1976). *Martin Luther King, Jr.* New York: W. W. Norton & Co.

SHAY F. (1938). *Judge Lynch: His first hundred years.* New York: Ives Washburn.

SIMPSON, G., & YINGER, J. M. (1965). *Racial and cultural minorities* (3rd ed.). New York: Harper & Row.

SOWELL, T. (1981). *Markets and minorities.* New York: Basic Books.

SOWELL, T. (1978). *Essay and data on American ethnic groups.* Washington, D.C.: The Urban Institute.

STAPLES, R. (1988). The black American family. In C. H. Mindel, R. W. Haberstein, & R. Wright (Eds.), *Ethnic families in America* (pp. 303–324). New York: Elsevier.

TATE, W. D. (1976). *The New York black urban elites.* Palo Alto, Calif.: R and E Research Associates.

U.S. BUREAU OF THE CENSUS. 1992a. Current Population Reports. Series P-60, No. 175. Poverty in the United States, 1990. Washington, D.C.: U.S. Government Printing Office.

U.S. BUREAU OF THE CENSUS. 1992b. 1990 Census of the Population. General Population Characteristics, United States. Report No. 1990CP-1-1. Washington, D.C.: U.S. Government Printing Office.

UNITED STATES DEPARTMENT OF COMMERCE, BUREAU OF THE CENSUS. (1970). *Special Studies: The Social Economic Status of Negroes in the United States.* Washington D.C.: Bureau of Labor and Statistics Report, U.S. Government Printing Office.

WILLIAMS, J. D. (1980). *The State of Black America, 1980.* New York: National Urban League.

WILSON, W. J. (1981). The black community in the 1980s: Questions of race, class, and public policy. *Annals of the American Academy of Political and Social Science, 454* (March), 26–41.

WILSON, W. J. (1978). *Power, racism, and privilege.* New York: Macmillan.

YETTE, S. (1971). *The choice: The issue of black survival in America.* New York: Putnam's.

Chapter 9

Mexican Americans

This chapter and the next will cover the Mexicans, the Puerto Ricans, and the Cubans. Although there are disparities between and within the categories, group comparisons place the three Hispanic groups at the low end of the ethnic racial stratification system. For example, Table 9–1, based on 1992 data, shows the disparity in family income and poverty rates between Puerto Ricans, Mexicans, and Cubans in the United States and families of European origin (Feagin & Feagin, 1996).

The group with the lowest median family income was the Puerto Ricans ($20,301); Mexicans were next ($23,714), and the Cubans had the highest income ($31,015). However, all are lower than the median family income of those of European origin ($40,420).

In terms of poverty, there is a reverse order: The Puerto Ricans have the highest rate of poverty (52.1%), followed by the Mexicans (39.5%), the Cubans (22.3%), and the Europeans (13.2%).

Table 9–2 shows the disparities between the groups in educational achievement. On all levels, the figures are unfavorable to the Hispanic groups, and favorable to those of European origin. For example, in terms of less than five years of school completed, the Mexican rate was 15.4 percent, followed by the Puerto Ricans with 8.2 percent, the Cubans with 5.3 percent, and the Europeans at 0.8%.

In terms of high school graduate or more, the Mexican rate was 46.2 percent, the Puerto Rican's, 59.8 percent, the Cuban's, 62.1 percent and the European's, at 84.1%. In terms of bachelor's degree or more, the Mexicans were

Table 9–1   Family Income and Poverty Rates

	Puerto Rican Origin	Mexican Origin	Cuban Origin	European Origin
Median family income	$20,301	$23,714	$31,015	$40,420
Families with incomes of $50,000 or more	14.6%	14.9%	27.0%	37.5%
Percentage of families below poverty level	32.5%	26.4%	15.4%	7.3%
Percentage of children less than 18 years old below poverty line	52.1%	39.5%	22.3%	13.2%

Source: Joe Feagin and Clairece Feagin (1996). *Racial and ethnic relations.* Englewood Cliffs, N.J.: Prentice-Hall, p. 306.

the lowest, 5.9 percent, followed by the Puerto Ricans, 8.0 percent, the Cubans, 16.5 percent and the Europeans at 23.8 percent.

Unemployment rates and occupational categories also reflect inequality (Feagin & Feagin, 1996), and the dark, "Native American-looking" Mexican Americans earned substantially less that their lighter, "more European-looking" counterparts (p. 35). It is clear that the Hispanic groups are at the bottom of the stratification system.

Although there is a wide disparity within the Mexican American population, the popular image is portrayed most often in negative terms. As a consequence, when all Mexican Americans are lumped together, they fall into the lower part of the racial-ethnic stratification system where racial, ethnic, and cultural concerns provide the focus for dealing with the dominant society. In addition, there is nationality, since Mexico is so close geographically and there is constant movement, both in and out.

One of the common problems in writing about Mexican Americans is that the diversity cannot be described by a single ethnic name. For example, there are a variety of terms used to refer to persons of Mexican descent. Cortes (1980:697) writes about various regional terms: Hispano and Spanish

Table 9–2   Educational Achievement

	Mexican Origin	Puerto Rican Origin	Cuban Origin	European Origin
Less than 5 years of school completed	15.4%	8.2%	5.3%	0.8%
High school graduate or more	46.2%	59.8%	62.1%	84.1%
Bachelor's degree or more	5.9%	8.0%	16.5%	23.8%

Source: Joe Feagin and Clairece Feagin (1996). *Racial and ethnic relations.* Englewood Cliffs, N.J.: Prentice-Hall, p. 318.

American in northern New Mexico and southern Colorado; Tejano, Latino, and Latin American in Texas; Mexican in Arizona. A broader term, Hispanic, was used by the Census Bureau in 1970 as a convenient word to cover all people of Latin American extraction, but del Omo (1989) writes that the term casts Chicanos in an erroneous light. He notes that Mexican Americans are a unique group and that their historical experiences are different from Cubans and Puerto Ricans on the east coast, and that the process of self-definition should not be sidetracked by the nomenclature used by outsiders. He acknowledges that there will be many Mexican Americans who would disagree with his position.

The most commonly used term is Chicano, which refers to a multiracial group with Spanish and Indian roots. There are a number of explanations concerning the derivation of the term Chicano, such as a short form of Mexicano or an obsolete pronunciation of "x" as "ch" (Marden & Meyer, 1978:255), but the social definition is more important. Aguirre (1973:122) defined the Chicano as a Mexican American with a non-Anglo definition of self, which ties in with the process of self-definition other racial minorities are also experiencing.

The Chicanos began as young urban militants, emphasizing their Indian heritage, who felt that they represented the poorer stratum of Mexican Americans (Marden & Meyer 1978:254). Today the terms Chicano and Chicanismo reflect an eclectic ideology that sees Mexican Americans as a conquered and dominated people who have lost their land, history, and culture to the Anglos. Central to their ideology is rejection of materialistic standards and individual self-achievement for collective orientations and group advancement (Moore & Pachon, 1976:152).

The Mexican Americans are a diverse ethnic group. On one hand, they are an indigenous people who were overpowered by white settlers and are therefore similar to the Native Americans. On the other hand, their continuing immigration from Mexico to the United States also makes them one of the newest and largest immigrant groups. Their immigration has included the temporary worker, or *bracero,* the legal immigrant, and an unknown number of illegals, or the undocumented. Some have a European complexion and can pass as white, while others are of pure Indian descent and are darker. Some are fully integrated and assimilated into the United States and have a high rate of intermarriage, and some live almost exclusively within their ethnic enclaves. Some are aristocrats and millionaires, but most are desperately poor. Some retain strong ties to Mexico and return there frequently, while others prefer a more acculturated posture and remain in the United States. There are also those who partially integrate without assimilating, but whose lives do not center exclusively on the ethnic enclave.

There also are differences in the area of settlement. The California experience is different from that of New Mexico and Texas, which in turn is different from that of the Midwest. Developing one model to explain this diversity is clearly an impossible task.

Yet in the minds of the majority, there remains a stereotype of a lazy, stoic peasant, or its opposite, a ruthless, cruel bandito. An everyday image in Los Angeles includes young males, standing on street corners, waiting to be hired, while the image of the Latin lover may be more favorable, but still a stereotype.

EARLY HISTORY

The interaction of Mexican natives with the Europeans started with the Spanish invasion of Mexico during the sixteenth century. The translated chronicles of Diaz (1963) illustrate several factors that are relevant not only for an understanding of Mexico, but also for an insight into race relations. First, the Mexicans were extremely active in defending their lands, and the natives would probably not have been overwhelmed so easily, except for the infighting among themselves. The use of dissident tribes as allies was a critical factor in the Spanish success. Second, the natives thought that Cortés was a god, with his white face and those strange creatures he brought with him—horses. The superiority of European technology and weaponry proved decisive in combat. Finally, the Spanish were strongly motivated by their religious and imperialistic zeal.

The United States became involved with Mexico several centuries later. The Battle of San Jacinto and the fall of the Alamo occurred in 1836. The Gadsden Purchase enabled the United States to acquire Texas, New Mexico, and parts of Colorado, Arizona, Utah, Nevada, and California in 1853. The actual number of Mexicans in these new territories was relatively small, and they were quickly engulfed by the more restless and ambitious white settlers. All Mexicans, whether they were land-owning and racially "pure" Spanish, or mixed breeds, or laborers, were perceived by the Whites as inferior. By 1900 they were already a subordinated population, having lost title to their lands because they could not supply proof of ownership. The white settler made no distinction between the original Mexican inhabitants—the old-timers, and the immigrant newcomers—they all were consigned to the same low status. Only in New Mexico, where the Mexicans retained numerical superiority, did they retain any degree of political power.

The basic conflict was over land, and the story is now a familiar one; the more powerful Anglo settlers coming into contact with the established but weaker Hispanic community and eventually acquiring the land. Hraba (1979:237) indicated that until they lost their lands, the fate of the Mexicans and Indians was similar, but instead of being herded into reservations, the Mexicans were incorporated into the economy of the Southwest.

There were many reasons why the Mexicans were included in the southwestern economy, albeit at the lower part of the structure, whereas the Indians were not. The Mexicans were experienced in farming, ranching, and mining; most Indian tribes were not. The Mexicans lived near the fertile river valleys in sufficient numbers to constitute a readily available labor pool, while the Indians were scattered and less accessible. Mexican labor was also easier to organize into work gangs because of their *padrone-peon* (master-servant) system; thus, the Anglo employer had an efficient way of dealing with the labor force. It should also be noted that the Mexicans had few competitors; black laborers did not move into the Southwest in significant numbers, Asian field workers remained in the Pacific area, and European laborers generally secured better employment positions (Hraba, 1979:244–245).

Large-scale Mexican migration took place in the 1900s. Factors leading to the move (pushes) included a revolution and the unsettled economic conditions in Mexico. The attraction (pull) was the rapid expansion of the southwestern economy through a number of actions occurring at that time. One was the National Reclamation Act of 1902, which ensured an adequate water supply for the arid region; another was the acquisition of large private and public holdings of land by business interests with the assistance of the United States government. There also was a need for labor, especially in cotton farming and other forms of agriculture, and in labor gangs on the railroads (McWilliams, 1968).

This pattern of employment meant that most Mexicans were kept isolated and segregated. They were hired in groups, primarily in rural and migratory jobs, and were kept apart from workers of other backgrounds. During the 1920s and 1930s, attempts were made to unionize the Mexican laborers, but their hopes for recognition and a more equitable share of the American pie were constantly frustrated by repression and discrimination (Meier & Rivera, 1972:184). As a consequence, the pre-World War II era saw the Mexicans shunted aside from the American mainstream—not as isolated as the Indians, but also not participating in the dominant society as easily as immigrants of European background did.

It was not until the 1940s and World War II that the mechanisms for keeping the Mexican laborer on the periphery of the American economy began to change. The increasing mechanization of agriculture and the need for urban labor to meet the wartime economy began to break down the old pattern of Mexican agricultural employment. Thus, the Mexican American entered America's urban economy a generation later than even the most recent of European immigrants (Hraba, 1979:245). This delay meant that other groups had gained a head start in establishing occupational niches in the cities, where they had organized and become a part of the unions, taken advantage of urban schools, and oriented themselves to compete in the American economic system.

Discrimination remained a major problem for Mexicans during World War II. For example, in Texas there was a pattern of discrimination in employment, management, and the labor unions; continuing exploitation in agriculture, including competition from illegal aliens; refusal of service in some public and private places; denial of access to real estate and housing; exclusion from jury duty; and terrorism by police officers (Marden & Meyer,

1978:248). The following two incidents are dramatic case histories of the treatment of Mexicans in California.

Sleepy Lagoon

Although Mexicans generally shared in the increased opportunities of the World War II years, two incidents revealed the extent of white prejudice: the Sleepy Lagoon murder case and the zoot-suit riots in Los Angeles in 1942 and 1943.

The Sleepy Lagoon murder (the press invented the romantic title—the scene of the crime was actually an abandoned gravel pit) took place on the night of August 1–2, 1942 (Daniels & Kitano, 1970:74). The victim was a young Mexican American, José Diaz, apparently slain as the result of in-traethnic gang rivalry. Throughout that summer, an artificial crime wave was fabricated by the press and local police and attributed to Mexican Americans. When the press made a sensation of Diaz's murder (ordinarily not considered newsworthy), the police followed suit with a mass roundup of suspects. Some twenty-four youths were arrested for the murder, and seventeen of them were actually indicted. There was no tangible evidence against any of them, but nevertheless the local authorities embarked on the largest mass trial for murder ever held in the United States. The defendants were beaten by police and were forced to appear in court with unkempt appearances (for a time they were not even allowed to have their hair cut). Eventually, after a long trial, nine were convicted of second-degree murder, and the other eight found guilty of lesser crimes. More than two years after the crime, which remains unsolved, the California District Court of Appeals unanimously overturned all of the convictions.

What made this homicide significant was the illegal behavior of local law-enforcement officers, the reaction of the Mexican community to this incident, and the overt message of prejudice directed at the Mexican community.

The hostility of the local police to the Mexican American population is hard to overstate and was of long duration. Innumerable instances of prejudice could be cited, but perhaps most illuminating are the following excerpts from a report given to the Los Angeles County Grand Jury by the sheriff's expert on Mexican American behavior, Captain E. Duran Ayres. After presenting rather fanciful statistics on ethnicity and crime—the official taxonomy was black, yellow, and red for Black, Oriental, and Mexican respectively—Captain Ayres embarked on a historio-sociological account of the Mexican in California.

Mexicans, he reported accurately enough, are restricted in the main only to certain kinds of labor, that being the lowest paid. It must be admitted that they are discriminated against and have been heretofore practically barred from learning trades. This has been very much in evidence in our defense plants, in spite of President Roosevelt's instructions to the contrary. Discrimination and segregation in certain restaurants, public swimming plunges, public parks, theaters, and even in schools cause resentment among the Mexican people. There are certain parks in the state in which a Mexican may not appear, or else only on a certain day of the week. There are certain plunges where they are not allowed to swim, or else only on one day of the week (and that invariably just prior to cleaning and draining), and it is made evident by signs reading "Tuesdays reserved for Negroes and Mexicans." All of this (and much more) applies to both the foreign and American-born Mexicans. (Daniels & Kitano, 1970:75)

Ayres followed this narrative with a blatantly racist explanation for Mexican American crime and delinquency, an explanation apparently accepted by the grand jury, most of the press, and probably most of the population.

> The Caucasian [and] especially the Anglo-Saxon, when engaged in fighting resort[s] to fisticuffs ; but this Mexican element considers [good sportsmanship] to be a sign of weakness, and all he knows and feels is a desire to use a knife or some other lethal weapon. In other words, his desire is to kill, or at least let blood. That is why it is difficult for the Anglo-Saxon to understand the psychology of the Indian or even the Latin, and it is just as difficult for the Indian or Latin to understand the psychology of the Anglo-Saxon or those from northern Europe. When there is added to this inborn characteristic that has come down through the ages, the use of liquor, then we certainly have crimes of violence. (Daniels & Kitano, 1970:75)

The Zoot-Suit Riots

These riots,[1] in the late spring of 1943, have been largely ignored by historians, but when they are discussed, it is usually made to appear that the young Mexican Americans were the aggressors (Daniels & Kitano, 1970:76). For instance, A. A. Hoehling, in *Home Front, U.S.A.* (1966), wrote:

> the zoot-suiters of Los Angeles were predominantly Mexican youths with some Negro disciples, between the ages of sixteen and twenty. They wore absurdly long coats with padded shoulders, porkpie hats completed by a feather in the back, watch chains so long they almost touched the ground, and peg-top trousers tapering to narrow cuffs. At best, as one pundit observed, they were not characterized primarily by intellect. They formed themselves into bands with flamboyant names: the Mateo Bombers, Main Street Zooters, the Califa, Sleepy Lagooners, the Black Legion, and many more. Their targets for physical harm were members of the armed forces, with a special predilection for sailors. The latter fought back with devastating effect. The situation quickly deteriorated to the point that the Navy declared Los Angeles out of bounds. The city council outlawed the wearing

---

[1]A play entitled "Zoot Suit," based on this incident became a hit in Los Angeles in 1978, but did not fare too well in New York in 1979.

Mexican American youth in their zoot suits, 1942.

of zoot suits for the duration and the city simmered down. (Daniels & Kitano, 1970:76)

This account, more fantasy than fact, faithfully summarizes what Hoehling read in the newspapers. The facts are that after certain clashes between sailors on pass or leave (not generally the most decorous group in the population) and civilian teenagers, the sailors, with the tacit approval of both the naval authorities and the police, made organized assaults not just on zoot suiters, who were a tiny fraction of Mexican American youth, but on any Mexican they could catch. Carey McWilliams, in *North from Mexico* (1968), described one organized foray in which about 200 sailors hired a fleet of twenty taxicabs and cruised around town beating up Mexicans in ones and twos. After receiving accolades from the press—"Sailor Task Force Hits L. A. Zooters"—the "heroic" servicemen came in even greater force the next night. The police, although forewarned, did little if anything to inhibit the violence against Mexicans, although they did arrest twenty-seven Mexican youths. For several nights the streets of Los Angeles were turned over to informal posses of servicemen, who proceeded to beat, strip, and otherwise humiliate every Mexican American (and some blacks) they could find. Bars were wrecked and movie theaters invaded, all with the same kind of impunity once granted to vigilantes in San Francisco. Throughout it all, the press made it appear that the Mexican American youths were the aggressors rather than the victims, with headlines like:

44 Zooters Jailed in Attacks on Sailors

Zoot Suit Chiefs Girding for War on Navy

Zoot Suiters Learn Lesson in Fight with Servicemen

An exception to this biased coverage was a small community paper, *The Eastside Journal,* which published eyewitness accounts by reporter Al Waxman. He described coming upon

> a band of servicemen making a systematic tour of East Street [in the heart of the main Mexican quarter]. They had just come out of a cocktail bar where four men were nursing bruises. Three autos loaded with Los Angeles policemen were on the scene but the soldiers were not molested. Farther down the street the men stopped a streetcar, forcing the motorman to open the door and proceeded to inspect the clothing of the male passengers . . . (Daniels & Kitano, 1970:77)

When Waxman pleaded with local police to put a stop to these activities, they answered that it was a matter for the military police. But the local police themselves contributed positively to the disorder. Waxman continued:

> Four boys came out of a pool hall. They were wearing the zoot suits that have become the symbol of a fighting flag. Police ordered them into arrest cars. One refused. He asked, "Why am I being arrested?" The police officer answered with three swift blows of the night-stick across the boy's head and he went down. As he sprawled, he was kicked in the face . . . At the next corner, a Mexican mother cried out, "Don't take my boy, he did nothing. He's only fifteen years old. Don't take him." She was struck across the jaw and almost dropped [her] baby. (Daniels & Kitano, 1970:77)

If they had not already known, Sleepy Lagoon and the zoot-suit riots made it clear to California's Mexican population just how second class their citizenship was. At the same time that the community's older sons were dying on foreign battlefields, some of the younger ones were casualties in their own neighborhoods. Before these wartime incidents, a paternalistic myth had somewhat obscured the real relationships between the Mexicans and their Anglo neighbors; from that time until the present day, that relationship has been more and more resented. Both the Sleepy Lagoon murder case and the zoot-suit riots were important realities to be faced by the Mexicans. Perhaps the most dramatic was the realization that racism could turn into violence toward any nonwhite group. Furthermore, "officialdom," in the form of consuls and Mexican establishment leaders, was not as influential as had been previously supposed. Finally, the riots were aided by the racist attitudes of many officials, such as the police and those in city hall, who were supposed to protect, rather than to persecute the victims.

World War II exposed many Mexicans to a broader world. A large number went into military service and were transported to different parts of the globe. New ideas, new perceptions, and new styles were being tried, and as with most people who benefited from these new exposures, things were never the same again.

Illegal or Undocumented Aliens (Wetbacks)

A group that has had a pronounced impact on the Mexican American community is the illegal alien, or "wetback"—an epithet invented by the Anglo community, but thankfully now out of favor. A more recent term is the undocumented, and the recession from the late 1970s to the 1990s has brought renewed attention to this group. No one can provide exact figures on the current number of undocumented Mexicans in the United States, but estimated figures range anywhere from one million to ten million or higher.

It is reasonable to assume that the undocumented worker has very little power and can be the victim of abuse and exploitation. A study by Salcido (1977) described the experiences of such a group and its ability to survive through the development of its own network of health and welfare services. Although most are employed in jobs that the native-born shun, they are constantly accused of taking jobs away from Americans.

Californians in 1995 voted on Proposition 187 whereby the undocumented would no longer be eligible for social welfare and educational services. The measure would also restrict services to other groups, including citizens, so that the purpose was to discourage immigration, both legal and illegal, by denying them governmental support.

It is interesting to note that Mexican laborers were also scapegoats in an earlier depression; Betten and Mohl (1975) pointed out that in the 1930s Mexican-born immigrants, numbering over 9,000 in Gary, Indiana and East Chicago, were partially blamed for the depression and were repatriated, rather than being put on welfare.

The ease of crossing a border that has no differential markings was emphasized by McWilliams (1968). Rather than taking a ship and crossing an ocean, the Mexican immigrant moves north into an environment that is geographically, culturally, and historically familiar. Mexicans emigrating to the Southwest have had a feeling of being close to their ancestral roots, and it would not be farfetched to say that no Mexican is really an immigrant or alien in this territory.

The situation has led to complicated legal entanglements governing immigration, citizenship rights, and deportation between the two countries. It also has generated great animosity between the Mexicans and the law-enforcement agencies. Since there is no immediate way of differentiating between citizens and aliens, anyone who looks like a Mexican is halted, searched, identified, and sometimes arrested by immigration and naturalization officers at the border. United States citizens of Mexican origin have often been deported because they could not immediately produce the proper documents.

The issue of the undocumented has also created divisions in the Mexican American community. Some Chicano leaders favor immigration restrictions, since the undocumented worker serves as labor competition to local Mexican Americans; other leaders perceive the issue in terms of civil rights, arguing that the search and seizure role of the Immigration and Naturalization Service (*La migra*) and its resulting violence is a graver danger to the local community.

It should be noted that a Department of Labor study in 1976 estimated that 73 percent of the undocumented workers paid federal income taxes; that 77 percent paid into Social Security although very few would receive its benefits; that less than 4 percent had children in U.S. schools; and that only 0.5 percent received welfare benefits (Cortés, 1980:704).

Halt of Unrestricted Immigration

Until 1965 there was unrestricted immigration between the United States and Mexico. There was no official quota limiting the entrance of Mexicans, but in 1965 Congress imposed a ceiling of 120,000 immigrants from all western hemisphere countries, which took effect in 1968. Although there has been no formal evaluation of the effects of this legislation, it is expected that the imposition of quotas will simply increase the traffic on the illegal immigration routes.

The history of Mexican immigration can be summarized by the following statements (Moore & Pachon, 1976:38–40):

1. Mexican immigration has never been regulated by formal quotas; therefore, records of early immigration are useless.
2. Immigration has been continuous, but the greatest numbers have migrated in recent times.
3. The various types of immigration have resulted in complicated legal definitions. There are permanently legal and permanently illegal immigrants. There are those who contract on a seasonal basis; others commute daily across the border. Then there is the two-way flow of businessmen, tourists, and students to add to the complexity and confusion.
4. It is still easy for Mexicans to enter the United States by rail, car, and bus.
5. No other minority has ever been deported in such large numbers as the Mexicans. Massive roundups of illegal aliens—such as "Operation Wetback"—have been regular procedures. Moore reports that in five years, Operation Wetback had rounded up the astonishing total of 3.8 million

illegal Mexican immigrants. Most of them were simply expelled without formal proceedings.

6. As long as the discrepancy of wealth and opportunity remains between the two countries, there will continue to be problems of immigration.

After years of debate, the Immigration Reform Act of 1986 was passed. Its primary aim was to deal with the undocumented. One feature was to provide amnesty for those who could provide proof of continuous United States residence for a specified length of time. It also attempted to make America less economically attractive by penalizing employers who hired illegal aliens.

THE CURRENT IMMIGRANT

Most recent Mexican immigrants come from the central area of Mexico, where there is great poverty. Most of them are young, unskilled male laborers with limited education. They are generally of mixed Indian and Spanish ancestry, so that in addition to the ethnic, cultural, and linguistic discrimination faced by most immigrants, they are also victims of racial discrimination (Cortés, 1980:704). They face a difficult time in the United States. Earlier, the United States might have absorbed them into its economy, but current opportunities, especially in the less industrialized Southwest, are limited. The additional barrier of the racist stereotype—that Mexicans are lazy, slow, uneducable, and ignorant—will continue to block their mobility for a long time to come.

Moore and Pachon (1976) wrote that, except for the relatively small Indian group, no population in the Southwest is as economically impoverished as the Mexican. The Chicano head of family must make his lower income support a large household, and his chances of earning an adequate income are relatively low and are improving only slowly.

The Chicano is significantly below the white Anglo male on most indices of inequality, including education, income, occupation, and housing. Most Mexican males are no longer underrepresented in skilled blue-collar operations, but they are still overrepresented in the operative category and among farm workers. But the majority of Mexican-American workers are no longer farm laborers (Feagin & Feagin, 1996). Although there have been improvements over time, the average Mexican American remains marginal in the job market. Mexicans hold the low-paying, less desirable jobs in most occupations. Those in the managerial category are usually self-employed in marginal occupations. They are excluded, except in token numbers, from civil service jobs such as those in fire and police departments, and are not found in large numbers in higher paying, unionized jobs (Moore and Pachon, 1976). Other discriminatory trends indicate that even in similar kinds of work, Mexicans are paid less than Whites. Unrealistic standards (for example, the high school diploma requirement for unskilled jobs) keep the unemployment figures high.

EDUCATION

Education has not provided Mexican Americans with a ladder to success. Segregation, isolation, inappropriate curricula, and poor teaching are partially responsible for this state of affairs. The incidence of functional illiteracy (0 to 4 years of elementary school) is seven times that of the Anglo population and nearly twice that of nonwhites (Moore & Pachon, 1976:66–67).

High dropout rates and low achievement are the principal problems. Educators have blamed bilingualism, implying that the Spanish language is a major handicap and therefore should be abolished. Others blame the lack of motivation, apathy, and noncompetitive outlook.

The ethnic community blames the irrelevance of the school curriculum and Anglo teachers' prejudiced, stereotyped responses to Mexican children. For example, community members feel that Mexican students are often arbitrarily advised to take nonacademic courses; sometimes they are placed in classes for the mentally retarded (the language handicap may be an important factor in this placement). Whatever the reason, the American educational system is not meeting the Mexicans' needs.

A movie, entitled "Stand Up and Deliver," was based on the experiences of Jaime Escalante, a teacher in a predominantly Mexican "ghetto" high school in Los Angeles. The basic message was that hard work, discipline, and study would eventually lead to academic honors and success.

THE CHURCH

The Roman Catholic Church has been presumed to have a strong influence on Mexican Americans ever since the days of the Spanish conquistadors, who arrived with a sword in one hand and a cross in the other. But it is difficult to assess the influence of the Church on modern Mexican-American life. Generalizations differ by area. There certainly is an overall lessening of religious influence on most facets of American life, and it is occurring within this ethnic group as well. There also is some indication that at an earlier time the Catholic Church lost its place as a relevant instrument of social change. Rather than serving as a vehicle for understanding the unique problems faced by a disadvantaged ethnic community and providing leadership in effecting social change, the Church, dominated by white leadership, instead adopted a much more conservative, static position. But there have been changes: pastoral concerns have been modified in the past to answer the needs of "Americanization," and current appeals for social justice may accelerate the process of making the Church more responsive (Moore & Pachon, 1976:90–91).

Grebler, Moore, and Guzman (1970:449) stated that two factors conditioned the relationship between the Church and Mexican Americans. One was the clergy's view that Mexicans were uninstructed in their faith and deficient in their adherence to the norms of church practice. Therefore, much of the clergy's time and energy was spent in ministering to the religious needs of the group, rather than providing a place where the immigrants could find support and comfort in a new and strange land. The other factor was the general poverty of the Catholic Church in the Southwest. The constant shortage of funds and priests has made it difficult to plan and expand programs beyond narrow ministerial functions.

MacNamara (1973) indicated that the Catholic Church has made assimilation and patriotism its priorities. The Church's goals were to aid Mexican Americans to become loyal, trustworthy, law-abiding citizens; to protect them from the social evils of the day, such as Protestantism, Bolshevism, Communism, delinquency, and relativism in doctrine and morality; to equip them with the means to move upward in the socioeconomic system; and to accomplish their goals without resorting to violence and social disturbance.

The Church has had some influence. Values, rules of conduct, and other standards have been an integral part of its programs. Parochial schools have been important to the education of many Mexican Americans. But the Church, with a few exceptions, has not provided the leadership in addressing the primary problems facing the Mexican American—discrimination, poor education, lack of economic opportunities, and poverty. It would be important for the Church to provide leadership in addressing some of the problems facing Mexican Americans—discrimination, poor education, lack of economic opportunities, and poverty. Newer leadership appears to be taking steps in this direction.

OTHER INSTITUTIONAL CONTACTS

Law enforcement

There has been a strain between the Chicano community and representatives of the American legal system from the very beginning. For example, the well-publicized Texas Rangers were founded in 1835 to deal with the Mexican "problem." The Western tradition of vigilante law enforcement aided Arizona mine owners, Texas ranchers, and California fruit growers in dealing with Mexican Americans under the sanction of dominant-group definitions of law and order. Chicanos feel that they have been the victims of much unnecessary brutality and overzealous law enforcement.

Social Welfare and Other Public Agencies

Poverty has forced many Mexican Americans to depend on the public welfare system. The problem of public welfare is a recurring one that goes far beyond its implications to one ethnic minority. Upward economic and social mobility is extremely difficult for any ethnic group that finds significant proportions of its members on public welfare, especially when occupational opportunities are limited.

Relations between Mexicans and the American social welfare establishment were especially difficult during the Great Depression. The need for Mexican labor quickly vanished as jobs became scarce, and there was a great push to deport both citizens and aliens by a variety of strategies. Voluntary repatriation was encouraged, and subsistence money was cut off. A bureau was set up for Mexicans applying for relief; it served as a deporting agency and waived questions of constitutionality, justice, and morality in order to save the taxpayers' dollars. It was cheaper simply to transport large groups of Mexicans back to Mexico.

At present, Mexican Americans are very reluctant to use the larger community services available to them. The number of Mexican clientele at health, psychiatric, and counseling clinics is so low that they are often referred to as the "hard to reach." They tend to visit hospitals, child-guidance clinics, family-service agencies, and psychiatric facilities only as a last resort.

A study by Miranda and Kitano (1976) indicates several reasons for the lack of use of mental health facilities by Mexican Americans as well as Asian Americans. They include the fragmentation and bureaucratic nature of services; the inaccessibility, both physical and psychological; the discontinuity of American styles with their own historical experiences; and unaccountability, whereby facilities are managed and manned by "outsiders," with little input from the ethnic community. It is also reasonable to suggest that American models of services and therapy may be only appropriate for those with a high degree of acculturation.

Quiroz (1986) comments on the similarity between the plight of many of the newly arrived Mexicans and the Southeast Asian refugees. Both groups had similar experiences of separation from family, political harassment, and difficulties in employment. Both groups, although from widely disparate geographical areas, had much more in common with each other than with their respective "ethnic" counterparts who had been in the country much longer and were more fully acculturated.

The low usage of mental health services occurs in spite of conditions which may foster ill health—poverty, poor housing, low educational attainment, unemployment, identity issues, and competing in a new culture (Chavez, 1986). The necessity for developing culturally relevant services seems obvious.

THE FAMILY AND COMMUNITY

The significant aspects of the Mexican family cannot be covered by any easy generalization, but some broad statements on social class and the urban-rural factor can be made. For example, the lower-class rural family generally has an extended family structure. Relatives on both sides provide emotional and economic support, as well as a reference group for accomplishment. The family patterns in the city are varied. Increasing numbers are moving out of the

Mexican American festival depicting dedication to the family and community.

barrios (Spanish-speaking neighborhoods)—some to the periphery and others to the suburbs. Generally, there are differences in lifestyle between those families remaining in the *barrio* and those surrounded by white neighbors. The rates of assimilation, integration, and change are closely related to the housing patterns.

The traditional family is arranged hierarchically: the father occupies the top, followed by the sons; together they shelter and protect the wife and daughters. The women are expected to cook, raise the children, and serve the needs of the men. Male and female roles tend to be clearly proscribed; masculinity (*machismo*) is of great importance, even outside marriage. The family remains the most important unit; close relationships outside the family are mostly with age peers. Godparents (*compadrazgo*) provide another linkage.

Middle-class family patterns are generally similar, but their more adequate income gives them more freedom of choice. For example, middle-class Mexicans may go to a physician rather than a *curandera*, to an attorney rather than a priest; and their children may go to college. Nevertheless, most Mexican families remain quite isolated from the Anglo world, since they prefer to associate with their own relatives and the ethnic community.

In urban areas, poverty has shifted the burden of family financial responsibility to the public services and public welfare agencies. It offers an option to many who previously had no recourse but to depend on relatives; now they may choose to be more independent of the kinship system. Such a breaking away will have both positive and negative consequences, although the underlying factors of poverty and dependence remain untouched.

Urbanization and acculturation are changing family roles, especially that of the Mexican male. He now helps care for the children and shares family decisions with his wife. The input of the mass media showing models at variance with the traditional roles is important, especially in cities like Los Angeles. The extended family system is also being modified. But much is hidden from majority eyes because of the highly segregated living conditions and the constant flow of new immigrants (Becerra, 1988).

In the early days there was the *patron* system. The *patron* was a large landowner who lived on or near his property surrounded by his peasants. There was a personal dependence on the *patron* by the workers and a reciprocal obligation by the owner. The unit was highly self-sufficient and paternalistic; the *patron* served as legislator, judge, and jury, as well as protector, provider, and employer (Taylor & West, 1975).

The vertical structure is similar to some of the family and economic structures in Asia, and significantly, these structures seem to discourage horizontal organizations. At present, the Mexican American does not have a nationwide organization similar to the NAACP for blacks or the JACL for Japanese Americans. Fishman (1985) comments that although the number of Mexican Americans is large, there is little fear of ethnic politics and ethnic loyalty. Instead the depolitization of the group is more common than that of its politization. Political separatism, terrorism, and other calls for more militant activities are rare and political organization along Anglo lines is weak. The number of Mexican American governors, senators, and other representatives is much smaller than would be expected given the population base, and underrepresentation appears to be the current status.

But more recent evidence indicates that 81 percent of naturalized Latinos have signed up to vote (Davis, 1980). The article does not specify the proportion of Mexican Americans in the sample, but shows some of the differences by ethnic group: 42 percent of the Mexicans identified themselves as Democrats, while 16 percent were Republicans. Conversely, naturalized Cubans preferred the Republican party over the Democrats, 63 percent to 9 percent. An estimated 5 million non-naturalized Latinos reside legally in the country so that in order to maximize Latino representation, a drive for naturalization might be a wise strategy. But it is clear that Latinos will not vote as a bloc.

Weyr (1988) indicates that, although many Hispanics depend upon government support (that is, food stamps, Medicaid), they favor a conservative position. For example, most of them oppose abortion, are lukewarm about busing, tend to favor prayer in school, and are apt to support a strong national defense.

Social Class

Most Mexican-American families are very poor, though other groups "above" them are constantly changing and evolving away from the older traditions (Moore & Pachon, 1985). Before the American annexation, the upper class was reserved for the Spanish, and when the United States acquired the territories, most retained this status, the "half-breeds" (*mestizos*) and the native Indians filling the lower positions. The upwardly mobile wanted to be identified as Spanish, "the purer the better," and traces of this point of view remain.

The mobility pattern for Mexican Americans has several forms. As income and other related circumstances rise, individuals may begin to lead more comfortable lives within the ethnic community. But their contacts and interactions are confined to their ethnic group. Although there may be strong resemblances to the Anglo middle-class, Mexicans and Anglos are generally ignorant of each other, especially since the Anglo stereotype usually does not include a middle-class Mexican.

Another type of mobility leads away from the Mexican community. Education, income, and other marks of status result in increased majority-group contacts and perhaps a conscious decision to leave the barrio. The success of this pattern depends on the accessibility of the Anglo world; if it is perceived as open, there may be a permanent move into the larger community. Individuals choosing this path take serious risks. Even if they have tried to think and behave like Anglos, they may find their new world inhospitable and may alienate their old friends in the ethnic community.

The third type is bilingual and bicultural, most often college students, who partially integrate without assimilating. They learn the Anglo system very well but retain many ethnic contacts; their life does not center exclusively on the ethnic enclaves or on the academic world. As their numbers grow, they may develop a subcommunity of ethnic intellectuals.

College students, especially those recruited from the *barrios*, are often subject to serious conflicts. Much of the initial impetus for going to school came from community members who wanted to be proud of the fact that some of their own could enter a university. Ethnic students' interests change, however, and their former friendships in the *barrio* become strained. Some college students report being called "sell-outs" by those who have remained in the community.

GOALS

In spite of discrimination, poor treatment, and poverty, the long-range goal of most Mexicans is eventual assimilation into the broader society. Modifications of this goal include a retention of ethnic identity and a degree of cultural pluralism, but there seems to be no strong movement toward separatism, a separate state, or a mass return to the homeland.

But, as with most groups there are opposing points of view. Abalos (1986) says to assimilate is to make one's self image over in the image of others. Acknowledging that assimilation means gaining desirable things such as travel, money, security, power and respect, it also means becoming like the dominant white. To assimilate means acquiring a degree of power, but also choosing a way of life that strips spontaneity, and lacks emotional depth, creativity and imagination. There is also the chance that one can never be like the dominant group—the pain of being called a dirty Mexican, greaser or spic also limits the desire to integrate.

Fishman (1985) uses the term "sidestream ethnicity" to describe the Mexican adaptation to the United States. Ethnicity can now be open, and even flaunted; and one's ethnic heritage can now be presented in public places. It is thought of as being for the general societal good: ethnic communities, neighborhoods, restaurants, theaters, churches, radio and television programs are viewed as adding spice to the bland, Anglo world. Ethnicity is thought of as being a good influence, rather than a hindrance and that it helps groups such as the Mexicans to find their "roots." Nevertheless, sidestream ethnicity does not prevent a group from entering into the mainstream, nor is it inimical to a pluralistic version of society.

Rodriguez (1989), in a newspaper article, indicates that many newcomers come to find work, not to find an American identity. They come because of necessity—there is no work at home, but there are jobs in America. But they perceive America as a confusing place, having high conflict and dangerous freedom. They fear losing Mexican "values," and do not wish to have "Americanized" children, but are willing to take the risks in order to find employment.

Many practice what Rogers (1985) calls a "circular migration," wherein they live partially in the United States, but frequently return to Mexico. Rodriguez indicates that in his childhood in California's Central Valley, Mexicans were noted for pulling their children out of school in November after the harvest and returning to their "homes" in Mexico. But they came back again in early spring, and many eventually stayed. Although such patterns are not entirely uncommon, the frequency of the circularity may be more unique.

Norms, Values

Mexican middle-class norms—the dominant ideal for most Mexicans—are congruent with Anglo prescriptions. There is an emphasis on respect and deference to elders, on getting along with people, and on getting ahead in the world. As they prepare for their first school experience, most Mexican American children are willing to learn and to respect, obey, and please the teacher.

Many consider the Mexicans' values to be the cause of their problems. The literature of the social sciences abounds with comparisons of Mexican and American values and cultural explanations for the low collective achievements of the Mexican. Perhaps the most widely disseminated study was that of Kluckhohn and Strodtbeck (1961), which reinforced the impression that Mexican Americans were distinct from Anglos. Subsequent interpretations and generalizations of this study ignored two major points that they had made: (1) that the Mexican American sample was from a remote village in New Mexico, and (2) that basic changes were predicted, even in this isolated village.

Therefore, the "scientific" generalization that the Mexicans were "fate-oriented" and focused on the present rather than on the future became rather widely accepted in social science circles.

Current information indicates that the range of responses of urban Mexican residents is "generally within the range of American cultural values in such critical arenas of life as family, neighbors, and social class" (Grebler et al., 1970:423). Most Mexicans are no different from most Americans. The stereotyped Mexican peasant could not survive in an urban environment without some change. Most Mexican Americans, like other Americans, want to get ahead in their work; they want job satisfaction, security, and a higher income. They direct their young toward the professions and, on the whole, "Mexican Americans are not notably more passive, nor do they value integration with relatives more than most populations on which data are available" (Grebler et al., 1970:439).

Those Anglos who do interact with Mexicans often select information that supports their prejudices. For example, interethnic contact between middle-class Anglos and Mexicans most often takes place under institutionalized auspices; professionals such as social workers, nurses, teachers, probation and other law enforcement officers generally see only the Mexicans who are in trouble. Their contacts are often limited to those Mexicans exhibiting social problems, but their observations become the inferred norm for all Mexicans.

The predictable outcome of these perceptions, therefore, has been the tendency to blame the Mexican culture for the lack of progress. As we have and will continue to emphasize, ethnic groups do not live in a vacuum; the problem lies in the *interaction* between the majority and the minority, not in the culture of the minority.

It is also our impression that the Mexican American belongs to the ethnic group with the widest spread of political views and ideologies. It is not unusual to see spokespersons advocating both extremely liberal and extremely conservative points of view, whereas it is often difficult to find many right-wing spokespersons in the other ethnic groups.

Visibility

Mexican Americans exhibit a wide range of skin colors—from light Caucasian to dark Indian, and all shades in between. Color was an important stratification variable within the group even before contact with the United States.

Spanish surnames provide another index for identification, although they are not infallible guides; Latin Americans, Puerto Ricans, Cubans, and Philippinos share many of the same surnames. Dress, food, and music reflect other highly visible cultural styles. But because most Mexicans remain isolated, such visibility is confined to typical tourist havens, such as Olvera Street in Los Angeles.

One conspicuous Mexican American style in the urban areas is the gang. The gang phenomenon, especially as an adolescent socialization force (which may continue through adulthood), is especially intriguing. One common stereotype, even before the zoot-suit riots, was that Mexican American youngsters generally belonged to gangs and that there was continuous fighting among them. Cortés (1980:715), in writing about Mexican gangs, indicated that on the positive side they provided comradeship, community services, a feeling of belonging, and an identity. But on the negative side there was the tendency to defend their turf, even by violence, and an exaggerated sense of honor and seemingly senseless behavior.

The Chicano gang subculture appears to be age-graded, so that the gang ensures a place for everyone, even the very young: It allows for regeneration with the inclusion of each new generation and provides the social arena for youngsters to learn about social customs, norms, roles and values among themselves.

THE CHICANO PATTERN

It is difficult to envisage any one model to encompass the diversity within the group. The *Californios* (Pitt, 1966) are different from the undocumenteds, who are different from the legal immigrants, who are in turn different from the *braceros*. Their motivations, the local conditions, and resources are all different.

One model for understanding the group is the colonial one. The land of the original inhabitants was invaded and occupied by military force, and the native Mexicans became involuntary subjects. The conquerors imposed an alien culture and an alien form of government on the vanquished. They were denied access to the structures of the dominant group through discrimination and racism, and were relegated to a subordinated status. The conquerors attempted to dismantle the ethnic institutions and the ethnic culture, and were able to gain control over the political, economic, and educational lives of the conquered. The distinguishing characteristics of this model are invasion, subjugation, cultural genocide, imposition of an alien culture, and political and economic disenfranchisement.

Keefe and Padilla (1987) use the concept of generations to indicate that the first generation immigrant fits the colonial interpretation of ethnic relations. They are primarily lower class, ethnically set apart and socially isolated. As one consequence, acculturation is slow and they are powerless in dealing with the larger community. Conversely, the second generation (and each of the following ones) have the backing of an integrated, kinship-based community with knowledge of dominant community ways.

When issues are framed along the lines of immigration, the ethnic lens may be very strong; other areas of ethnic solidarity are in the area of bilingual and bicultural issues. However, there is a wide divergence within the population. There are descendants of the early Californios to barely arrived immigrants, there are legal and undocumented immigrants, and in common with all of our groups, there are differences in age, generation, social class, ethnic identity, personality, and whatever other differences that are a part of the human condition. But because of racism, the ethnic lens may remain as the most salient.

REFERENCES

ABALOS, D. (1986). *Latinos in the United States*. Notre Dame, Ind.: University of Notre Dame Press.

AGUIRRE, L. (1973). The Meaning of the Chicano Movement. In *We are Chicanos*, (Ed.). P. Ortega. N.Y.: Pocket Books.

BECERRA, R. (1988). The Mexican American family. In C. H. Mindel, R. W. Habenstein, & R. Wright, Jr. (Eds.), *Ethnic families in America* (pp. 141–159). New York: Elsevier.

BETTEN, N., & MOHL, R. (1975). From discrimination to repatriation: Mexican life in Gary, Indiana during the Great Depression. In N. Hundley, Jr. (Ed.), *The Chicano* (pp. 124–142). Santa Barbara, Calif.: Clio Press.

CHAVEZ, N. (1986). Mental health services delivery to minority populations: Hispanics—a perspective. In M. Miranda & H. Kitano (Eds.), *Mental Health Research and Practice in Minority Communities* (pp. 145–156). Rockville, Md.: National Institute of Mental Health.

CORTES, C. (1980). Mexicans. In S. Thernstorm, A. Orlov, & O. Handlin (Eds.), *Harvard Encyclopedia of American Ethnic Groups* (pp. 697–719). Cambridge, Mass.: Harvard University Press.

DANIELS, R., & KITANO, H. H. L. (1970). *American racism*. Englewood Cliffs, N.J.: Prentice-Hall.

DAVIS, K. (1980). 80% of naturalized Latinos sign up to vote, study says. *Los Angeles Times*, September 8, part I, p. 27.

DEL OLMO, F. (1989). Cuban in Congress spells end of Hispanics. *Los Angeles Times*, September 5, part II, p. 7.

DIAZ, P. (1963). The Conquest of New Spain. Trans. J. M. Cohen. Baltimore: Penguin.

FEAGIN, J. R. AND FEAGIN, C. B. (1996). *Racial and ethnic relations*. Upper Saddle River, New Jersey: Prentice Hall.

FISHMAN, J. (1985). The ethnic revival in the United States: Implications for the Mexican-American community. In W. Connor (Ed.), *Mexican Americans*. Washington, D.C.: The Urban Institute Press.

GREBLER, L., MOORE, J., & GUZMAN, R. (1970). *The Mexican American people*. New York: Free Press.

HRABA, J. (1979). *American Ethnicity*. Itasca, Illinois: F. E. Peacock.

KEEFE, S., & PADILLA, A. M. (1987). *Chicano ethnicity*. Albuquerque: University of New Mexico Press.

KLUCKHOHN, F., & STRODTBECK, F. L. (1961). *Variations in value orientations*. Evanston, Ill.: Row, Peterson and Co.

MACNAMARA, P. (1973). Catholicism, assimilation, and the Chicano movement: Los Angeles as a case study. In R. De La Garza et al. (Eds.), *Chicanos and Native Americans* (pp. 124–130). Englewood Cliffs, N.J.: Prentice-Hall.

MARDEN, C., & MEYER, G. (1978). *Minorities in American society* (5th ed.). New York: Hill & Wang.

MCWILLIAMS, C. (1968). *North from Mexico*. New York: Greenwood Press.

MEIER, M., & RIVERA, E. (1972). *The Chicano: A history of Mexican Americans*. New York: Hill & Wang.

MIRANDA, M. R., & KITANO, H. H. L. (1976). Mental health services in third world communities. *International Journal of Mental Health*, 5 (2), 39–49.

MOORE, J., & PACHON, H. (1985). *Hispanics in the United States*. Englewood Cliffs, N.J.: Prentice-Hall.

MOORE, J., & PACHON, H. (1976). Mexican Americans. (2nd ed.). Englewood Cliffs, N.J.: Prentice-Hall.

PITT, L. (1966). *The decline of the Californios: A social history*. Berkeley: University of California Press.

QUIROZ, R. (1986). Hispanic human resource issues: A reassessment of mental health manpower needs. In M. Miranda & H. Kitano (Eds.), *Mental health research and practice in minority communities* (pp. 133–143). Rockville, Md.: National Institute of Mental Health.

ROGERS, R. (1985). Migration theory and practice. In W. Connor (Ed.), *Mexican Americans*. Washington D.C.: The Urban Institute Press.

SALCIDO, R. (1977). Utilization of Community Services and Immigrant Experiences of Documented and Undocumented Mexican Families. (Unpublished doctoral dissertation), University of California, Los Angeles.

TAYLOR, W., & WEST, E. (1975). Patron leadership at the crossroads: Southern Colorado in the late nineteenth century. In N. Hundley, Jr. (Ed), *The Chicano* (pp. 73–95). Santa Barbara, Calif.: Clio Press.

WEYR, T. (1988). *Hispanic U.S.A.: Breaking the melting pot*. New York: Harper & Row.

Chapter 10

Puerto Ricans and Cubans

In addition to the Mexican Americans, covered in Chapter 9, and the Puerto Ricans and Cubans, covered in this chapter, there are many other groups under the rubric of Hispanics and Latinos. They include Salvadoreans, Dominicans, Colombians, and Ecuadorians, as well as those whose former residences were in Central and South America.

The purpose of this chapter is to concentrate on the Puerto Ricans and Cubans, since after the Mexican Americans, they represent the two largest Spanish-speaking minorities. In terms of growth, the Latino populations have grown from approximately 14.5 million in 1980 to over 22 million in 1990. They now comprise over 10 percent of the total population in the United States. There were 13,495,938 Mexicans; 2,727,754 Puerto Ricans; 1,086,435 Cubans and 5,086,435 other Hispanics in the United States.

In many ways all the Hispanics have had similar experiences in the United States. Most have faced discrimination, have generally lived in the poorest areas of large cities, and have had difficulties with language, the U.S. educational system, and employment. Their countries lie in close proximity to the United States, and with the exception of the Cubans, they have a history of circular migration, where large numbers are known to go back and forth between the home country and the United States. And a common error is to reserve the term "American" for people in the United States, when all inhabitants of the Americas, both North or South, can lay claim to the term.

THE PUERTO RICANS

The majority of Puerto Ricans reside in New York City, which has been host to several generations of immigrants—the Irish, the Italians, and the Jews, to name but a few. The Puerto Ricans are entering the city when symptoms of social disorganization are especially prominent. Large cities have always been plagued by outbreaks of violence and disorder, and residents have constantly feared for their personal safety, but such anxieties appear to have reached a zenith in present-day New York.

Further, the changes in our economic system have been such that unskilled immigrants may no longer be able to follow the road to success laid down by earlier immigrant groups, even though they may arrive with a strongly internalized work ethic. As Padilla (1977) pointed out, Puerto Rican concepts of work are historically linked to agrarian, colonial experiences and reflect obligation, family background, and personal worth. Despite this value placed on work, Puerto Ricans in New York, especially those with nontransferrable or inadequate skills, face unemployment or employment in the least desirable jobs and welfare. Prejudice and discrimination exacerbate the situation, but the fundamental problem may lie in the structural conditions of the economy, which has attracted a large number of displaced people to the urban ghettos.

A Puerto Rican community.

Background

Puerto Rico was ruled by Spain for over 400 years. The Spanish American War and the Treaty of Paris in 1898 ceded the islands to the United States, and formal interaction between the two countries is acknowledged from that year. The significant migration of Puerto Ricans to the United States, however, did not take place for several decades. World War I and the need for labor provided the impetus for a small migration; and by 1930, approximately 53,000 Puerto Ricans were residing on the mainland. But the depression years and World War II brought a virtual halt to immigration.

The great migration came after World War II. There were several reasons for this: First, Puerto Ricans were American citizens and were therefore under no quota restrictions; second, there was unemployment at home and employment on the mainland; third, there was cheap transportation; finally, many had friends and relatives living in New York and elsewhere on the East Coast. In 1960 the U.S. Census reported almost 900,000 Puerto Ricans living in the United States, and by 1970 there were 1,429,604 first- and second-generation Puerto Ricans in the continental United States, with almost one million in New York City (Marden & Meyer, 1978:266). The 1980 census reported 2,013,945 Puerto Ricans, making them one of the largest minorities in the United States.

The Puerto Rican immigration pattern is unusual because of its large departure rate. Although figures for net migration are difficult to ascertain, in 1969 the Puerto Rican Planning Board reported 2,105,217 departures and 2,112,264 arrivals. Fitzpatrick (1980) reports that as many as five million Puerto Ricans were coming and going to the United States in 1973. There is, of course, no way of identifying how many Puerto Ricans were coming to the mainland for the first time, how many were tourists, or how many planned to stay permanently. However, migration back to the island has been heavy, and some even refer to the Puerto Ricans as commuters.

From an analysis published in 1972 by the Puerto Rican Resources Center for the Federal Office of Civil Rights, Padilla noted that the Puerto Rican immigration may be a lengthy one because of the structural weakness of the Puerto Rican economy. The lack of integrated planning has led to the export of Puerto Ricans as the only way of achieving economic growth (1977:156). Island unemployment has been high; in 1979 it was 16.5 percent; in 1981, 18 percent; and in 1982, 24 percent (Digby, 1982).

Relationship with the United States

A major unresolved Puerto Rican issue is its relationship with the United States. Puerto Rico was turned over to the United States by the Treaty of Paris (1894) at the end of the Spanish American War; in 1900 the island was given a measure of self-government; and in 1917 the Jones Act unilaterally declared that Puerto Ricans could become citizens of the United States. In 1952 Puerto Rico was designated as a commonwealth, which meant that it was subject to most American laws, including military conscription. However, Puerto Ricans could not vote in United States elections and did not have formal representation in Congress, except for an elected residential commissioner who did not have a vote (Fitzpatrick, 1980). The relationship can be likened to a colonial one, with major decision-making power in the hands of Congress.

Puerto Rico is an important part of the western Atlantic defense system. Under Spain, the island served as a garrison outpost protecting the sea lanes to the rich colonies of Mexico and Central America. Commonwealth status insures that the island remains dependent on the United States, with no senators or congressional representatives to mount protests or raise inconvenient questions. Carrion and others (Carrion, Babin, Costas, Santana, & Vales, 1983) emphasize that the fundamental relationship between Puerto Rico and the United States is that of dependence, with Congress serving as the paternal body authorizing handouts to bail out an ailing island economy. For example, 60 percent of Puerto Rico's population was on food stamps in 1980.

The recession of the 1980s, combined with the Reagan cuts in social programs, had severe effects on Puerto Rico. The switch from food stamps to block grants, cuts in the Comprehensive Employment Training Act (CETA), a drop in tourism, and a slackening demand for Puerto Rican products have resulted in added pressure for migration.

There are a number of possible alternatives to the present relationship between the United States and Puerto Rico. One is total independence; another is statehood; while another route is to retain the status quo. It has been difficult to arrive at a consensus on any of these options; the pattern of colonial politics has persisted, so that the question of the most desirable relationship has been clouded by the differences in goals and divisions between the Puerto Rican elites and the electorate. And most important is the power of the United States, so that congressional indifference, American ignorance, and the lack of consensus among Puerto Ricans serve to maintain the unsatisfactory status of a basic colonial relationship.

New York City

The rise of the Puerto Rican population in New York City has been dramatic. The 1920 census reported 7,365 persons; the 1940 figures were 61,463; in 1960 there were 612,574; and by 1980 it was at 1,000,000. In 1974–1975 Puerto Rican children in the New York City schools numbered 253,000, or 23 percent of the enrollment. The heaviest concentration of Puerto Ricans is now in the South Bronx, but the East Harlem community is considered to be the original *barrio*.

The Puerto Ricans have been a very mobile people. They have spread out rapidly in their search for better housing, not being content to stay long in one place. One consequence of their housing patterns (also due to overcrowded conditions in New York) has been the lack of a tightly knit, strong, physically contiguous ethnic community. They have not developed Little Italies or Chinatowns. Such self-contained ethnic enclaves (despite many of their handicaps) were often very functional: The culture could be maintained while the groups became familiar with the new country; friends and relatives could move in; ethnic blocs could wield a degree of political power; and a consensus of norms and a high degree of social cohesion could serve to control deviant behavior.

Color and Visibility

There are many contradictory findings concerning color prejudice in Puerto Rico, as there are in most Latin American countries. Some claim that Puerto Ricans are completely integrated and colorblind; others claim that they are highly but subtly stratified. Color does not seem to be as important an indicator of social status as social class is, but there is a correlation between darker skin color and low status. However, color is less a sign of pariah status among Puerto Ricans than among Americans.

There is a high degree of color integration in Puerto Rico. They did not develop the two-category, black-white structure found in the United States; rather, the differentiations of color were spread over a wider spectrum. For example, words such as *pardo, moreno, mulatto*, and *trigueño* classify a range of colors other than black and white. Terms such as *indio* and *grifo* denote other identifying characteristics. The United States' practices of segregation and antimiscegenation laws were not a part of the Puerto Rican experience.

Social class is an essential part of the Puerto Rican stratification system. Although whiteness may be considered desirable, an individual's status is more clearly demarcated by class position. Fitzpatrick quoted a saying that provides some insight concerning color and class: In the United States, a man's color determines what class he belongs to; in Puerto Rico, a man's class determines what his color is (1971:103). Therefore, living in a *barrio* is an indication of one's status—whether black, *trigueño*, or white—as is occupation, income, and education. Color is viewed within the context of other role signs and is not the sole criterion.

Fitzpatrick mentioned a number of cultural and historical factors in Puerto Rico that have contributed to their more tolerant racial attitudes (1971:103).

1. The long Spanish experience with people of dark skin color (Moors), including intermarriage.
2. Different experiences under slavery. In the wars of the Christians against the Moors and Saracens, captured whites also became slaves. Therefore, there were attempts to protect slaves who were white, and such attitudes were carried over to the blacks.

3. Upper-class men in the Spanish colonies baptized and recognized their illegitimate children by colored women.

4. The practice of *compadrazgo*, in which outstanding white members of a community would frequently be the godparents of colored children at baptism. The *padrino* or *compadre* could become a significant person in a child's life, and although the real father might be obscure, the godparents would be well known.

As a consequence, color was not a strong barrier, and upward mobility under this more open system was a theoretical possibility. But Puerto Rico has advanced very rapidly in education, industry, government services, and the like and a middle class has formed. Upward social and economic mobility complicates the role of color and class, and color prejudice is growing. For example, Fitzpatrick (1971:105) observed that societies and clubs are now not as open to people of color. Puerto Ricans quickly learned that color is an important role sign in the United States. They saw that the two-category system abolished the intermediate categories and that social acceptance and economic advantages are easier to obtain if one is white.

Perhaps the most difficult position is that of the *trigueños* of intermediate color. In one study (Padilla, 1958), they showed the least evidence of assimilation into the New York community. They were not accepted as white; many did not want to be classified as blacks, and they were therefore caught in a marginal position. Many responded by retaining a strong Puerto Rican identity. Another early study (Berle, 1959) of twenty young Puerto Rican drug addicts showed that nineteen of them were the darkest members of their families.

Assimilation

It is difficult to find consistent evidence on the extent of Puerto Rican intermingling in New York City. They have brought their more relaxed racial attitudes with them, and Puerto Rican gatherings present a wide range of color mixtures. But as they advance to middle-class status, they may become more sensitive to U.S. definitions of race.

The relations between Puerto Ricans and blacks have been strained. Both are involved in similar struggles for power and control and are sometimes pitted against each other. Among the more militant young there is some degree of cooperation.

Data concerning the rates of intermarriage are difficult to find, although Fitzpatrick (1971) notes that there has been a significant increase in the rate of out-group marriage between 1949 and 1969. He concludes that if out-marriage is accepted as a sign of assimilation, the group is rapidly moving towards assimilation. However, there is a lack of available data, especially outside New York City.

The Role of Church and Family

The Puerto Ricans come from a predominantly Roman Catholic country. Church membership there was somewhat different from the United States model of organized membership and a consistent church affiliation. Rather, they had a much more personalized spiritual relationship, and this often took place outside the organized church structure. Adherence to Roman Catholic practices was not so strict that native cult practices, spiritism, and other religious variations could not flourish. Although most of the immigrants were Catholic, they came to the United States without their own clergy. Therefore, they did not develop ethnic parishes, a resource that served as an important support system for other immigrant groups. Church influence is diffused on the mainland. There are, of course, many parochial schools, but partly because of the distribution of the group, it is difficult to assess the specific influence of religion (Fitzpatrick, 1971).

The family structure in Puerto Rico was described by Fitzpatrick (1971:83) as falling into the following fourfold typology:

1. An extended family system. These families have strong bonds, and grandparents, parents, and children may often live together in the same household. It may include consensual unions as well as regular marriages.
2. The nuclear family. The rise of the middle class has increased the number of families following the United States pattern of an independent unit of father, mother, and children.
3. Father, mother, their children, and children of another union or unions of husband and wife. This is not an uncommon pattern in Puerto Rico, with children of different names residing in the same household.
4. The mother-based family, with children of one or more men, but with no permanent male in the home.

All four typologies are present in the United States. The greatest white animosity is directed toward the type 4 family unit, often found in welfare families. Pragmatic politicians are especially adept at laying the blame for much of society's ills on those welfare chiselers, who, if one were to believe the claims, are the main contributors to the financial and moral crises of our time. Because certain ethnic groups are stereotyped in this fashion, prejudice and discrimination against them are strengthened.

Values

Personalism.   A number of values have been hypothesized to explain Puerto Rican behavior in a broad context. The most important is personalism, which Fitzpatrick described as a form of individualism which focuses on the inner importance of a person—those inner qualities that constitute the uniqueness of the person and his goodness or worth in himself (Fitzpatrick, 1971:90). This value derives its strength from the relatively rigid class structure in which individuals are respected if they know their position and behave with dignity and sensitivity. They take family obligations seriously.

Puerto Ricans have developed a strong sense of the hierarchical class structure. Lower and upper classes were taken for granted; therefore, a person's personal worth was distinct from his or her position in the social class structure. The idea of upward mobility was not a common aspiration in Puerto Rico; rather, the acceptance of playing a designated role with dignity was valued highly.

The Puerto Rican values of personalism are in conflict with U.S. values. In the Latin system, the individual is to be trusted above all; life is a network of personal relationships, and a person's word, honor, and style are to be reckoned with and respected. In contrast, the American style of individualism emphasizes the ability to compete aggressively for social and economic gain. Americans have a high regard for systems, organizations, legal regulations, and efficiency; they become uneasy when the system fails. It is said, however, that Latin Americans become uneasy when the system works too well—they feel that impersonal elements have taken precedence over personal relationships.

Machismo. Machismo connotes masculinity and personal daring by which one faces challenge, danger, and threat with calmness and self-possession; this sometimes takes the form of bravado (Fitzpatrick, 1971:91). Associated attributes and qualities include personal magnetism, sexual prowess, and power over women, including the jealous protection of wife or sweetheart.

Fatalism. The fatalistic attitude is best summed up by the phrase *Que será, será*—Whatever will be, will be. There is a strong sense that certain events are inevitable and are dictated by God. This modifies the impact of failure or success and the attendant sense of guilt or satisfaction because God willed it.

Social Problems

Education and the School System. An early study, titled *The Puerto Rican Study, 1953–57* (Board of Education, 1958), pointed out some of the difficulties faced by Puerto Rican students in New York City. Special problems included the language handicap and the tenuous relationship between the school system and Puerto Rican parents. Subsequent studies have shown that these problems have grown progressively worse. Very few survive the competition to enter colleges and universities, although the open admissions policy in New York may have increased Puerto Rican attendance in the city college and university system. The route to success by way of education, used by many other immigrant groups, remains an expectation rather than a reality for most Puerto Ricans.

One fundamental issue, difficult to resolve, centers on cultural pluralism in education. Bilingualism and English as a second language are unresolved issues, and the debate over the validity of various models continues.

Welfare.   A special problem for the Puerto Ricans has been their relatively high numbers on public welfare. For example, one study estimated that as many as 35 percent of Puerto Rican families were receiving Aid to Families with Dependent Children (AFDC) benefits. Without going into the accuracy of these figures, it is of critical importance to understand that dependence on public welfare affects Puerto Rican adaptation to the United States. Although the goals of AFDC and other welfare programs are appealing, and although the planners no doubt had the best intentions, the actual programs have become an embarrassment to the U.S. public. It would be difficult to conceive of a worse institutionalized alternative to U.S. life, considering the current attitudes toward welfare recipients. The degradation of the recipients is a result of both inadequate resources and an unpopular program.

Mental Illness.   Rogler and Hollingshead (1965) offered systematic data on mental illness in Puerto Rico and identified several contradictory strains that contributed to the problem. Girls were carefully protected from sexual experience, while boys were allowed great freedom; the housewife was expected to be submissive, while the husband had to embody all aspects of *machismo*; there was a great discrepancy between expected and achieved standards of living, and poverty exerted severe pressure on everyone's life.

Rates of mental illness are higher for the Puerto Ricans than for the general population. For example, Malzberg (1956) noted that the rate of first admissions for schizophrenia for Puerto Rican males in New York State was 122 per 100,000, as compared to the general population rate of 36.6 per 100,000. He could find no convincing reason for this differential, which is apparently related to such diverse variables as the experience of migration, language difficulties, occupational problems, and segregation into areas that have a high incidence of mental illness. A major problem, of course, is that the poor have little access to health services because of high cost and superstition.

The Midtown Manhattan Study (Langner & Stanley, 1963) also noted a high incidence of mental illness among Puerto Ricans, mostly because of the shortage of Spanish-speaking professionals, the lack of communication and understanding, and other cultural disparities.

In spite of certain biases in the statistics on mental illness, the available evidence indicates that the stress and tension of migration and urban living have exacted a high toll in mental illness from Puerto Ricans. The question now is whether this is a preliminary adaptive stage for any newly arrived immigrant group, and whether it is followed by another stage.

There is also evidence of high drug use in certain census tracts in New York City. These areas are also characterized by poverty and by a large proportion of blacks and Puerto Ricans. The relationships among poverty, drug use, and ethnicity should be targets for future research.

Parrillo (1985) lists some of the overall problems of the group, which includes high levels of tuberculosis, venereal disease, drug addiction, illegitimate births, and chronic unemployment. However, these problems are shared by most poor minorities who live in deteriorating urban neighborhoods with low income. The prediction is that as long as United States-aided technological development in Puerto Rico continues, there is the creation of a surplus of unskilled labor that migrates to the mainland. Puerto Ricans will therefore continue to come and join the ranks of the lower working class or even the nonworking poor. However, Sanchez-Ayendez (1988) indicates that little is known about Puerto Ricans. Gender, generation, age, income, age at arrival, length of residence, and other important variables have yet to be systematically studied, especially in areas outside of New York City, so that generalizations about the group are tenuous. Nevertheless, it is predicted that those Puerto Ricans with higher levels of education, occupational status, knowledge of English, and with lighter skin color will have an easier time in adapting and will move out of the ethnic ghettos into more middle class neighborhoods.

The Puerto Rican Model

Puerto Ricans form a large part of New York's unskilled labor force. Their incomes are low; their unemployment is high; their occupational prestige is low; their rates of poverty are high; and their housing conditions are among the poorest. They face discrimination by the unions, in licensing procedures, in the courts, and in housing (Marden & Mayer, 1978:271). They form an underclass.

Rosenberg and Lake (1976) believe that neither the melting pot nor the black model can be used for the Puerto Rican. They cited the competition between the Puerto Rican and the larger, more established black population as one factor, and the constant return to Puerto Rico as another that has to be considered in any model.

The persistence of the Spanish language is another factor. Most social planners assumed that the Puerto Ricans (as well as other Hispanics from the Dominican Republic, Peru, Colombia, and Ecuador) would become mainstream Americans over a period of time, but an estimated 70 to 80 percent still rely on Spanish as their primary language (Cowan & Cowan, 1977). They find it both comfortable and functional; they can read their hometown newspapers flown in from Latin America and live their lives in a Hispanic atmosphere.

The frame for viewing Puerto Ricans is that of ethnicity, race, nationality, and class. Marger (1991) indicates that the nature of their entry into society, their racial characteristics, and their class handicap deters assimilation and leads to some aspects of the internal colonial model. Because of their visibility, their culture, and their Spanish surnames, they may find it easier to identify and to integrate with Hispanics from other countries.

THE CUBANS

Historically, Cuba has had a number of foreign influences including Spain, West Africa, the United States, and the Soviet Union. Each has played a role in shaping Cuban culture, although the Spanish influence—who ruled from 1511 to 1898—probably had the greatest impact on the Cuban value system and institutions. One important facet was the sugar industry; labor demands for sugar meant that approximately one million slaves were imported from West Africa.

In 1846, a census of Cuba's population indicated a slave population of 660,000; 220,000 free Blacks and mulattoes, and 565,000 Whites. An Emancipation Law was passed in 1880, but the continual demand for cheap labor led to the importation of Chinese; so that after the Blacks, the Chinese constituted the most important ethnic minority in the twentieth century (Szapocznik & Hernandez, 1988).

The United States acquired Cuba, along with Puerto Rico, as a result of the Spanish American War in 1898. After the American victory, Cuba was ruled by an American army of occupation for a short period of time, then be-

Congresswoman Ileana Ros-Lehtinen comforts José Basulto, president of "Brothers to the Rescue" after two of their planes were shot down off the coast of Cuba, February 24, 1996.

came an independent nation in 1902, but with close, dependent ties to the United States.

There was an early, small, steady migration from the islands—an estimated 18,000 Cubans lived in the United States in 1930, and about 79,000 in 1960. But with the Fidel Castro takeover of Cuba in 1959, large numbers of refugees fled to the United States so that by 1973, 273,000 new immigrants were in this country. In addition, in 1980, more than 10,000 Cubans took refuge in the Peruvian embassy in Havana, with the hope of emigration to the United States. This group, as well as many others—totalling about 118,000— were eventually granted permission to leave; they left from the Cuban port of Mariel, so that they are often referred to as the Marielitos.

Moore and Pachon (1985), in discussing Cuban immigration, refer to three waves of immigrants (excluding those who were in the United States prior to the Castro era). Each of the waves represented a different sample: The first wave was 94 percent white, with an average age of 34 and with a high educational background (fourteen years of school). They came primarily from the more privileged classes—many were wealthy businessmen, government officials, professionals, and managers with influence and power.

The second wave, although primarily white (80 percent), was younger and poorer. The third wave, or the Marielitos, were 60 percent white, and also much younger and even poorer. The media publicized this third wave in sensationalized accounts—that these new immigrants were drawn from the deviant sectors of the society and included criminals, homosexuals, and the mentally ill. Although there was some validity to these charges, the majority were not drawn from the ranks of the deviant, but one consequence was that the third wave faced a resentful American public, already burdened by the economic recession in the 1980s and feeling overrun by immigrants, especially the refugees.

It is interesting to note that the majority of our political refugees are fleeing from communism, so that the initial wave is often composed of the more politically conservative elements of a society, such as government officials and people of wealth. The Cuban migration fit this model, and also in common with many political refugees, there were thoughts of retaking the homeland. An actual attempt was made by the refugees on April 17, 1961, when a group invaded Cuba, but suffered a defeat in what is referred to as the Bay of Pigs incident.

Moore and Pachon mention some other characteristics of the Cuban migration. The great majority settled in Miami, so that parts of Miami bear a close resemblance to Havana. Aside from being very close to Cuba, the city offered the refugees a familiar climate and a large ethnic community where monolingual immigrants could survive. There were enough wealthy Cuban entrepeneurs to provide resources to sustain many of the poorer arrivals during their early period of adjustment.

Another facet of the Cuban migration has been the diversity in terms of social class. There has been a full range, from the wealthy to the poor, which is unusual for most immigrant groups, although perhaps more common among the refugees. But a common unifying theme has been that of an anti-Castro and anti-communism stance, and an identification as freedom fighters. It will be interesting to see how long such an ideology is retained in subsequent, American-born generations.

The Family

Szapocznik and Hernandez (1988) note that the modern Cuban family in the United States has already begun the transition from the extended to the nuclear family structure, although there remains an allowance for the inclusion of relatives and godparents (*padrinos*). Although there is an expectation of hierarchical family relations with the father at the top, the American model of equality continues to exert influence over time.

One of the more important changes has been the role of women. Whereas females in pre-Castro Cuba were not an important part of the labor market, in many instances, the first to be employed in the United States were women. As a wife's economic contribution to the family became important, her decision-making power has also increased, with a corresponding diminution of the power of the husband. There has also been the familiar story of acculturation, stress, disorganization, and alienation between parents and children. Parents cannot understand their highly Americanized children, in turn, the children cannot understand their less acculturated and old-fashioned parents. These conflicts appear inevitable—all immigrant families face them, and somehow or other, they all seem to survive, although with varying degrees of pain, frustration, and success.

Parrillo (1985) comments on some of the value differences between the Cubans and the Americans. Americans stress hard work as a means of achieving material gains; Cubans value material success for personal freedom, not physical comfort. Anglos live for work as an end in itself, whereas Cubans believe that one should work to enjoy life. Cubans prefer an open-hearted generosity over the Puritan values of thrift and frugality. There is also an emphasis on the group in contrast to the American value of individuality.

The clash between old-world and new-world values is again typical of immigrants and their children, and in the experience of most immigrant groups, succeeding generations generally adopt the newer values.

The current adaptation of the Cubans resembles a bicultural model (Szapocznik & Hernandez, 1988). They must learn to interact successfully with both the American and ethnic cultures since they live in a bicultural environment. Those who underacculturate (that is, fail to learn and act in an American context), or overacculturate (that is, reject the skills of dealing within the Cuban cultural milieu) will not have the necessary flexibility to operate in their current environment. The current situation calls for a balance between the two cultures; it will be interesting to see if such a balance will remain in future American-born generations. A more acculturated stance may be more relevant for those who migrate away from the tight ethnic community.

The basic frame for the Cubans is that of ethnicity, nationalism (a strong lens is anti-Castro), and class. Individualism is not a strong focus, although those who are the most upwardly mobile may tend to become more individualistic.

SUMMARY OF HISPANICS

In terms of placement in the ethnic hierarchy, the Hispanics are slightly above the blacks and below the Asians. The groups are concentrated in different regions; the Mexicans in the Southwest, the Puerto Ricans in New York City, and the Cubans in Florida, especially Miami. They are generally below average in wealth—the Cubans are the highest, followed by the Mexicans and Puerto Ricans. They have been the object of discrimination, albeit less so than the Blacks, but much more than Euro-Americans. Factors such as proximity, constant in- and out-migration, and relatively dense ethnic populations have slowed cultural assimilation. They have been relatively slow in political participation, but both the Mexicans and the Cubans are in a position to exert political power with their numbers, ethnic identity, and relevant causes.

REFERENCES

BERLE, B. (1959). *Eighty Puerto Rican families in New York City*. New York: Columbia University Press.

BOARD OF EDUCATION. (1958). *The Puerto Rican study*, 1953–57. New York: Author.

CARRION, A. M., BABIN, M. T., COSTAS, A. C., SANTANA, A., & VALES, L. G. (1983). *Puerto Rico: A political and cultural history*. New York: Norton.

COWAN P., & COWAN, R. (1977). For Hispanics it's still the promised land. In L. Dinnerstein & F. Jaher (Eds.), *Uncertain Americans* (pp. 307–316). New York: Oxford University Press.

DIGBY, S. (1982). Puerto Rico is mired in unemployment rivaling that of 30's depression in U. S. *Los Angeles Times*, November 27, part I-A.

FITZPATRICK, J. (1971). *Puerto Rican Americans*. Englewood Cliffs, N.J.: Prentice-Hall.

FITZPATRICK, J. (1980). Puerto Ricans. In S. Thernstrom, A. Orlov, & O. Handlin (Eds.), *Harvard Encyclopedia of American Ethnic Groups* (pp. 858–867). Cambridge, Mass.: Harvard University Press.

LANGNER, T. S., & STANLEY, M. T. (1963). *The Midtown Manhattan Study*. New York: Free Press.

MALZBURG, B. (1956). Mental illness among Puerto Ricans in New York City, 1949–51. *Journal of Nervous and Mental Disease, 123,* 457–465.

MARDEN, C., & MEYER, G. (1978). *Minorities in American society* (5th ed.). New York: D. Van Nostrand.

MARGER, M. (1991). *Race and ethnic relations*. Belmont, Calif.: Wadsworth.

MOORE, J., & H. PACHON (1985). *Hispanics in the United States*. Englewood Cliffs, N.J.: Prentice-Hall.

PADILLA, E. (1977). Concepts of work and situational demands on New York City Puerto Ricans. In H. R. Kaplan (Ed.), *American minorities and economic opportunity* (pp. 148–169). Itasca, Ill.: F. E. Peacock.

PADILLA, E. (1958). *Up from Puerto Rico*. New York: Columbia University Press.

PARRILLO, V. (1985). *Strangers to these shores*. N.Y.: John Wiley.

ROGLER, L. H., & HOLLINGSHEAD, A. B. (1965). *Trapped: Families and schizophrenia*. New York: John Wiley.

ROSENBERG, T., & LAKE, R. (1976). Towards a revised model of residential segregation and succession: Puerto Ricans in New York. *American Journal of Sociology, 81,* 1142–1150.

SANCHEZ-AYENDIZ M. (1988). Puerto Rican Elderly Women: The Cultural Dimension of Social Support Networks. *Women & Health* V. 14, Fall p. 239.

SZAPOCZNIK, J., & HERNANDEZ, R. (1988). The Cuban American family. In C. H. Mendel, R. W. Habenstern, & R. Wright, Jr. (Eds.), *Ethnic Families in America* (pp. 160–172). New York: Elsevier.

U.S. BUREAU OF THE CENSUS. The Hispanic Population in the United States: March 1993, Current Population Reports, pp. 20–475 (Washington, 1994) p. 11.

Chapter 11

Native Americans

The group that has had the most disruption in their lives has been the Native Americans. Although there were warfare and conflicts under tribal identities, the American Indians were remarkable in their ablity to come to grips with nature and to develop a culture based on human relationship to nature. Therefore, with the advent of the white people, bringing with them the European culture, the natives were forced to deal with the more powerful newcomers. In the process the natives were conquered, their lands taken away, tribes were decimated, and the survivors were forced to live on reservations and on government handouts. The notion that a "good Indian was a dead one," summarizes the thoughts of the early European settlers.

The American Indian has been the product of a series of perceptions fostered by the dominant group. They were savages, they were noble savages, they were drunkards, and they were the guardians of nature. There was the picture of war dances, of scalps and tomahawks, and of sitting in a circle smoking peace pipes. Even today, the picture of Indians includes feathers, teepees, and bows and arrows, rather than their current adapation to modern-day life. The historical picture remains the reality.

At one time American Indians were one of our most visible minorities. They were featured in the movies and on television—the cowboys and Indians era. In addition, there was the cigar store Indian, and even the face of an Indian engraved on the five-cent piece. Although remnants of these images remain, Indians have become an "invisible minority." One reason is that, although many are leaving the reservations to live in the cities, they have not developed a "Little Tokyo," a Chinatown, or a Koreatown, so that there are no visible ethnic centers with their stores, restaurants, and organizations. Instead, Indians tend to scatter in the low-rent areas of most cities or remain in isolated reservations (Larsen, 1989).

The most recent development has been their entrance into large-scale gambling, including bingo parlors, casinos, and slot machines. In 1994, Native American groups in more than twenty states operated some 220 gambling operations. Revenues have paid for educational and health-care facilities, water and sewage treatment plants, job training, roads, and housing, and have reduced unemployment. Yet white investors and management firms have claimed the bulk of the revenue. Many tribes have been vicitms of economic exploitation, theft, and embezzlement by white management firms (Leudors, 1994).

Because they were the original inhabitants, American Indians have no connection with a foreign government, so there are no embassies, diplomats, or businessmen who show a special concern for their people. As a consequence, American Indians cannot benefit from political alliances and trade policies that often enhance the treatment of immigrants and nationals.

The basic question faced by the group is a familiar one: Should acculturation, assimilation, and entrance into the mainstream be the primary goal, or should there be pluralism and separation? As we shall see, the U.S. government has wrestled with this issue ever since the "conquest" of the Native American, with minimal success. The tendency, then, seems to place the blame on the victim: that it is the fault of the Native Americans and their culture that hampers any successful resolution.

BACKGROUND AND HISTORY

The European view of the Indians is perhaps best exemplified by the name "Indian," which was given to the natives of North and South America by explorers such as Columbus who were actually seeking a direct route to the East Indies and Southeast Asia. The epithet "Indian," which has stuck up to the present day, covers a widely disparate group of peoples with different languages, cultures, political divisions, and levels of civilization and organization. Rather than indicating differences, the term conceals them and automatically demotes all Indians to the lower level of the ethnic stratification system. The most important ignored fact about the American Indians is their diversity. There was, and still is, no one kind of Indian, nor one tribe, nor one nation. Rather, the American Indians represent as much variety as the peoples living on the Eurasian land mass. Their linguistic resources include at least a dozen distinct stocks, and within each stock are languages as disparate as English and Russian.

Native American technology and culture also reflect this diversity. The Mayas, Aztecs, and Incas developed complex social organizations and a so-

Painting by Robert Lindneux showing the "Trail of Tears".

phisticated technology, while tribes such as the Paiute had a much simpler social system.

Contrary to popular belief, the majority of American Indians in the 1800s were not wandering nomadic hunters but were farmers and fishermen living in stable villages and communities. But the richness of their culture has been lost, primarily because they did not leave behind written records, documents, or artifacts that could be used to reconstruct their history.

One explanation for the origin of the Native Americans is that they emigrated over the Alaskan land bridge from Asia over 20,000 years ago. By the time Columbus—their "official" discoverer—arrived in 1492, they numbered several million, but because they were militarily weaker than the Europeans, they soon lost their land and have had to struggle ever since to retain their cultures and their ways of life.

At the time of the European invasion, the numerous Native American societies could be divided into seven major geographical areas, each linked to cultural adaptations based on local conditions. These seven areas were: (1) the Eastern tribes, who hunted, farmed, and fished and whose first encounters were with the English; (2) the Great Plains hunters and agriculturists, whose first encounters were with the Spanish; (3) the fishing societies of the Pacific Northwest; (4) the seed gatherers of the California area; (5) the shepherds and pueblo farmers in the Arizona and New Mexico area; (6) the desert societies of southern Arizona and New Mexico; and (7) the Alaskan groups, including the Eskimo (Feagin & Feagin, 1995:198).

Views of the Native American varied—some even being friendly—during the early stages of European contact. But as accommodation changed into conflict and a fight for Indian land, the stereotypes and prejudices came to share one common denominator—that the Native Americans did not deserve to own their own land (Hraba, 1979:210). Several principles were implicit in the American treatment of Native Americans, based primarily on England's experiences with territory and control in Europe. These included diplomacy, armed conflict, and treaties, with the notion that warfare could be avoided between the colonists and the Indians if there were clear boundaries and signed treaties. Disputes could be adjusted by new treaties (Spicer, 1980).

For a period of time, from the sixteenth to the late eighteenth century, Native American tribes were viewed as "nations," and they often held the balance of power as the Americans, British, Dutch, French, and Spanish struggled for control of North America. The European powers generally accommodated Native American rights and were concerned with protecting Native American lands. Some tribes were even sought as allies. But most of the tribes allied themselves with losing European factions, so when the Americans eventually established dominance, the Native Americans found themselves in a vulnerable position.

Nevertheless, during the early years the British colonies promised good-faith treatment of the Indians. The 1787 Northwest Ordinance emphasized respect for property rights, due process, and justice (Deloria, 1972a). Written policy could be interpreted as sincere, although the empirical facts showed recurrent land thefts, with or without the sanction of federal officials (Feagin, 1978:195).

The principal conflict was over land, and it took several forms. One pattern that did not necessarily involve violence was the encroachment of white settlers on Native American land, bringing diseases that often decimated Native American populations. The settlers also drove away the game that hunting tribes needed, so that very soon the Native Americans had to move to new lands, leaving the territory to the encroachers. When the American Indians might stage retaliatory raids against the white settlers, the colonists would call for the protection of federal troops; they would fight, and the conflict would end in a signed treaty. The result was the same: The Native Americans were moved out and lost their land. The pattern might then be repeated with the encroachment of white settlers on the new Indian land.

The election of Andrew Jackson to the presidency instituted a much more overt policy of taking away Native American lands. Congress passed the Indian Removal Act in 1830, and within a decade many of the Eastern tribes migrated to lands west of the Mississippi River, voluntarily or at gunpoint. The most infamous was the "Trail of Tears" of the Cherokees, a forced march that resulted in 4,000 deaths and terrible suffering (Cunningham, 1930). Vogel (1972) compared the forced move of American Indians to Oklahoma to a move to concentration camps, citing the fact that Native Americans from as far away as New York and California were "concentrated" into a territory that already had five large tribes.

Indian resettlement in Oklahoma and the Great Plains states was only a temporary respite, since the westward expansion of the American settlers continued. Plains tribes such as the Sioux and the Comanches fought with the white people. These struggles have been popularized in Hollywood westerns.

The most effective Army strategy was to destroy the tribes' food supply and possessions, leaving them helpless and unable to fight back. The actual war on the Plains resulted in men, women, and children dying from cold, disease, and starvation in less than epic circumstances. Although the Plains Indians had long participated in limited-scale intertribal warfare, they had never experienced the genocidal actions of federal troops and settlers (Feagin, 1989).

Another factor leading to the destruction of tribal life was the lifestyle of the white settlers, which included the slaughter of the buffalo, the clearing of the forests, and the commercial use of rivers and streams. By drastically altering the economic and cultural bases of tribal survival, the Whites were able to destroy Native American groups such as the Comanches (Fehrenback, 1974).

The Plains Indians did not passively accept the encroachment into their territory. Their war parties attacked white settlers and used guerrilla tactics extensively, with much cruelty and savagery on both sides. As Andrist (1964) indicates, the White versus Native American struggle on the Plains was a gruesome and bloody one.

A particularly bloody incident occurred in 1864, when Colonel John Chivington, a minister, and a band of Colorado volunteers massacred nearly 200 peace-seeking Indians in Sand Creek. Meyer (1971) described it as one of the most brutal incidents in Western history: "Both male and female genitals were later exhibited by the victors as they marched into Denver" (p.32).

Perhaps the symbolic end to overt Indian resistance was the massacre at Wounded Knee, South Dakota, in 1890. The "battle" was the culmination of the army's attempt to disarm and herd the Native Americans under Chief Big Foot into a cavalry camp. By the end of the massacre, an estimated 300 (out of 350) Indian men, women, and children had been gunned down (Brown, 1973). The army had been aroused to panic by a Pan-Indian movement centered on the Ghost Dance. In 1890 Kicking Bear related that a voice had commanded him to go forth and meet the ghosts of Indians who were to return and inhabit the earth. He had had visions of a messiah, a crucifixion, and the return of great herds of buffalo and wild horses. The Indians who danced the Ghost Dance would be suspended in the air to await the coming of a new earth, inhabited only by Indians. The Ghost Dance spread rapidly, and white agents were empowered to stop it (Brown, 1970:434–435). The Ghost Dance caused rumors of potential Indian unity and was one factor leading to the massacre at Wounded Knee.

From this time on, the Indians were supervised by various bureaucracies created to "help" them. Wax concluded:

> Wounded Knee was not the only massacre by whites of defenseless Indians, nor was Custer's Last Stand the only defeat by Indians of an Army unit; however, both involved flamboyant and heroic people, and so have been remembered by Americans and added to their folklore. Both events were also to be the last of their kind, not only for the Sioux, but for the Plains Indians; thereafter, the history of the peoples becomes a matter of reservation life under the aegis of the Indian service. (1971:21–22)

Treaties

Because of their status as an independent nation, the main legal process in dealing with the Indians was the treaty. "The treaties, part of United States law, were often masterpieces of fraud; consent was often gained by deception or threat" (Feagin, 1989:181). Between 1790 and the Civil War, up to 400 treaties had been signed, the great majority related to land issues. Burkey observed that scarcely one remained unbroken (1978:176).

But it is also important to realize that some of the few Indian "victories" have been through litigation. Wilkenson (1987) cites the Supreme Court decision on Williams v. Lee in 1959 as spurring the resurgence of tribal activity in the courts. The case involved state court or Indian tribal jurisdiction over a contract claim on the reservation. The Court recognized a broad tribal jurisdiction and diminished the role of the state.

The Reservations

By the 1860s Native Americans were no longer viewed as quasi-nations, to be dealt with through treaties, but as wards of the government. Administrative regulations were set up by federal bureaus, which exercised tremendous control over the lives of the Native Americans in a manner analogous to that of a parent or guardian over a child (Burkey, 1978:234).

For the next several decades, the reservation became the accepted administrative and political solution to the question of what to do with the Native Americans. Although the ostensible purpose of the system was to assimilate the Native Americans, Hraba (1979:224) noted that the reservation became an evolutionary dead end. The American Indians were without capital or technology and had little access to industrial work or to educational institutions, so that reservation life left most of the residents totally unprepared to understand and to cope with the vast industrial changes taking place in the American economy and in the "outside world."

The government attempted to Christianize the Native Americans, to teach them the English language, and to practice American agricultural methods and mechanical arts. In the early 1880s off-reservation schools were established to hasten the acculturation of the American Indian children, with generally unfavorable results (Burkey, 1978:235). By the end of the 1880s those interested in Native American welfare became convinced that the reservation system, with its attendant paternalism and corruption, would not accomplish its mission of assimilating the Native American into the U.S. mainstream. One result of this new thinking was the Dawes Act, or the General Allotment Act of 1887, which visualized the Native American as an independent landowner (Burkey, 1978:235).

Under the act, which served as official government policy for the next forty years, reservation Indians were supposed to act like white settlers by becoming farmers and tillers of the soil. European conceptions of the meaning of property and the management and use of farm lands, both unfamiliar practices to the Indians, meant that soon thereafter much of the better farm lands ended up in the control of the Whites. Instead of aiding in the assimilation of the Native Americans into the mainstream, the act instead deprived them of whatever base they had had on the reservations.

By the 1930s the government was ready to shift to another Indian strategy. John Collier, who later became Commissioner of Indian Affairs, and other influential Whites helped draft the Indian Reorganization Act of 1934, designed to improve the reservation system and to encourage cultural and structural pluralism. Its provisions included a return to tribal management of reservation land, replacement of the Indian boarding schools, and respect for tribal practices, including native religions (Hraba, 1979:230).

Burkey (1978:275) found that many Indians were against the Reorganization Act for a variety of reasons. Some were assimilationists and did not support the return to pluralism. Others with private land holdings resulting from the Dawes Act opposed a provision that called for a return of family-owned land to the reservation. Some were antitribal, and many opposed the act on the basis that anything the United States government supported was bound to be detrimental to the Native Americans. The vote of the Navahos illustrates the divisive nature of the issue: 8,197 opposed the act, while 7,679 voted for it. According to Burkey (1978:275), instead of strengthening tribal governments, the unintended consequence of the Reorganization Act was to increase federal control and Indian dependency.

The Present

The spirit of protest can be seen in American Indian activity over the past several decades. Feagin & Feagin (1995) reported that between 1961 and 1970 there were 194 instances of protest. The largest number were legal suits and formal complaints.

Protest activities included tribes in the state of Washington fishing with nets outside the boundaries of their reservations and a sit-in by some Passamaquoddy Indians in Maine against a logging company. The most publicized event was the occupation of Alcatraz Island from late in 1969 to 1971, which helped to dramatize the plight of the American Indian.

The Alaskan Native Claims Settlement Act of 1971 (Havighurst, 1977) restored forty million acres of land to the natives. The program included $962.5 million as compensation for land taken over by the state and federal governments and the development of regional corporations to invest in productive enterprises such as hotels, supermarkets, mineral exploration, reindeer herds, and fish canneries.

In 1968 the American Indian Movement (AIM) was organized to focus on problems of discrimination in employment and housing, and police brutality. AIM organized an occupation of Wounded Knee, South Dakota in 1973, and in the 1990s protested the use of Indian nicknames (i.e., Redskins, Braves, Indians) for athletic teams. There was also the "tomahawk chop," popularized by the Atlanta baseball team, which was viewed as a degrading caricature and a mocking stereotype. As the AIM director told a reporter, "Imagine if they named a team the Atlanta Bishops, and fans came to the game waving crucifixes, (and) there was a guy dressed like the Pope running up and down the aisles throwing holy water on the crowd."

TRIBAL HISTORIES

An analysis of the interaction between the Europeans and specific Indian tribes will be presented here to demonstrate the different types of experiences and adaptations. The California Indian, a case of genocide; the Iroquois, a tribe fleeing to Canada; and the Dakota Horse Nomads, a group going through almost every phase, ending up on reservations and now beginning to move into American cities.

The California Indian: The Yahi

The California Indians met two major invaders—the immigrants who came north from Mexico and west from the states. According to Daniels and Kitano:

> Each group brought with it a common contempt for the native Indian, but a contempt shaped by the quite different values of Ibero- and Anglo-America. Each group subjugated and suppressed the Indian in the quite different ways suggested by its own culture and its own experience in white-Indian relations. Each ran roughshod over the natives and neither considered, in any way, their wishes. Each group regarded the Indian as subhuman; neither accorded him any real say about his own destiny, except perhaps, giving him a choice of how he wanted to die—in hopeless battle or in an even more hopeless existence. California racism, then, dates back to the eighteenth century, back to the earliest settlement by Europeans and their descendents. (1970:29)

One California Indian is known, and his story, as written by Theodora Kroeber (1964), will have to stand as proxy for an otherwise unknown people.

Whether Ishi, as he was called, was representative, is, of course, a question that cannot be answered. There is no doubt about the quality of his story; it is one of almost unsurpassed horror. By a historical accident, he was perhaps the last "wild" Indian—the sole survivor, by a few years, of the Yahi tribe.

The Yahi were a tiny "tribelet" of perhaps 2,000 souls occupying a few dozen square miles of territory north of Sacramento. In the space of one bloody year, 1864, when Ishi was a small boy, all but a few dozen of his people were hunted down and destroyed by organized and legally sanctioned parties of armed Whites. The survivors of this bloody year, perhaps fifty in all, were further harassed and hunted and killed for the next few years. Then the surviving handful, a remnant of a remnant, went into what Kroeber called "the long concealment," which lasted about four decades. When, on August 29, 1911, an exhausted, middle-aged male Yahi Indian was captured near Oroville, California, the "tribelet" was down to a lone survivor, Ishi. He lived four and a half more years in the friendly "custody" of anthropologists at the University of California. When he died of natural causes on March 25, 1916, a minor variety of *homo sapiens* ceased to exist; the Yahi had become, in the words of our pioneer ancestors, "good Indians."

The fate of the Yahi, symbolically at least, stands for the majority of California's Indians and is an extreme example of the way Whites have treated nonwhites. But thousands of other Indians did survive. Some merged into the general population; the majority of ethnically identifiable American Indians continued to exist on the fringes of U.S. life, technically within our society, but actually almost wholly apart from it. These surviving, less dramatic casualties of what one writer called the "transit of civilization" from the Old World to the New also represent an extreme form of White-nonwhite relations in the United States: physical and legal separation—what we would call apartheid in another land (Daniels and Kitano, 1970).

The Iroquois

Where the Spanish had sought precious metals and had been zealous missionaries, the English, French, and Dutch had been primarily interested in furs. The exchange of animal pelts for guns, ammunition, and other manufactured goods established a trade relationship between the Europeans and the Native Americans of the Northeast.

The name *Iroquois* was given to the League of Five Nations, consisting of the Seneca, Onondaga, Cayuga, Oneida, and Mohawk. Later, a sixth tribe, the Tuscaroras from North Carolina, was added. According to Wax:

> Its peoples had been living in settled villages near streambeds where the women could plant their gardens of maize, beans and squash. In addition to serving as warriors, the men contributed fish and game to the diet. The machinery of their League was primarily an arrangement for maintaining peace and harmony among the member tribes, and except for issues of con-

flict among tribes, affairs were largely in the hands of the separate tribes and villages. (1971:13–14)

By the middle of the seventeenth century, the Iroquois had exhausted the furs (especially beaver) in their own territory. They began to look for new lands and became an expansionist nation. They eventually came into conflict with tribes of the northern confederacy, such as the Huron, who were active in the French trade. By forming a much more aggressive military and commercial alliance, the League was able to achieve large-scale military victories and expand its hegemony. It appeared for a time that the Iroquois would extend their power over the entire eastern seaboard, but the Creek confederacies in the South were too powerful, and the Canadian tribes remained more closely allied to the French.

The league fought with the British in the French and Indian Wars, and by the 1700s:

> The Iroquois were becoming both powerful and acculturated: eleven Indian nations were living with the Seneca, numerous whites were intermarrying and a distinctive blend of cultures was emerging. (Wax, 1971:14–15)

Many white colonists were not pleased by the success of the Iroquois. Nevertheless, the British Crown perceived the Indians as powerful allies against the French; the Royal Order of 1763 sealed off the western lands from white settlers and recognized Indian ownership. Wax stated:

> The Order was not received well among the colonists, and was one of the grievances that was to lead to the Revolutionary War. During the conflict, the League, following its successful system of neutrality in the wars of the whites, tried at first to hold itself aloof. (1971:15)

The peace treaty that followed the end of the Revolutionary War made no provision for the Indian allies of the British. Settlers and land speculators seized the opportunity to invade Indian lands. Maltreatment and conflict led to the decimation of the Iroquois. The national government preferred the friendship of the Indian allies, but they could not control the actions of the settlers and speculators, who often threatened to organize new border states and to secede. Eventually the Iroquois were forced to flee to their English friends in Canada.

The Dakota Horse Nomads

Wax gives the name *horse nomads* to those Native American tribes who developed elegant skills on horseback and who adopted a nomadic existence following the buffalo. These tribes devised skin tepees and other features of light travel that enabled them to carry on their nomadic activities. In the process, they became competitive and aggressive warriors who could travel long distances swiftly and quietly, constantly in search of horses, buffalo, scalps, loot, and fame.

Among the tribes who took up this style of existence after the early Spanish colonists had brought horses to the Rio Grande Valley in 1598 were the Blackfoot, Arapaho, Cheyenne, Comanche, and the Crow. The Tetons, one of the tribes making up the Sioux, were among the earliest to take to the Plains. Said Wax:

> The Teton became the scourge of the northern Plains, acquiring a reputation for irascibility, impetuosity and stealthy ferocity. The settled agriculturalist tribes, which had built a rich ceremonial existence and complex societal organization, could not cope with the Dakota raids, even though they themselves acquired the horse and some of the traits of the horse nomads. The Teton harassed the traders who attempted to utilize the Missouri River; later they continued the sport with the wagon trains crossing the Plains. Peaceable contact with the whites was mainly via French traders who established their posts along the riverine routes and took Indian women to wife. (1971:18–19)

The development of the rapid-fire revolver and the introduction of cattle ranches spelled the end of the horse nomad. With the advent of barbed wire, the Homestead Act, cattle ranches, and the railroad, the Plains Indians came to be seen as a menace to law and order. Although pitched battles were generally won by the Whites, the most effective means of gaining control over the Native Americans was by paper and pencil—the treaty. These documents, of which there were many, provided certain conditions that both sides promised to live up to in order to guarantee a more peaceful coexistence.

Relationships under various treaties were periodically strained. In 1874 the discovery of gold in the Black Hills brought a flood of new white settlers. Many of them complained about harassment from the Sioux and demanded that they return to their reservation; this conflict ended with the defeat and annihilation of General Custer at Little Big Horn in 1876. But the Indian victory was only temporary, and in the long run, they were the losers. Reservation life, dependency on congressional appropriations, white opportunism, and swindling left most Indians half-starved and diseased.

The history of the Native American is one of maltreatment—forced acculturation, extermination, genocide, and isolation on the reservations. Of all the ethnic groups, the Native American has the strongest reason to question "law and order," "justice," and the credibility of the Whites. Deloria (1973) traced the logic of white people in their quest for Indian lands and territory. Although much of the land was conquered by simple armed force, a more powerful weapon was the concept of the Doctrine of Discovery. This doctrine had been used by Christian nations and the church to establish hegemony over large portions of the earth by simply declaring them "discovered." By a few simple statements ("I plant this flag in the name of my King"), aboriginal lands came under Christian mandate. Spicer (1980) summarized the five methods used by the dominant white culture in dealing with the Indian:

1. By separation, with the goal of removing the Indians from their lands and erecting boundaries between the groups.
2. By coercive assimilation, with the goal of replacing the Indian culture and way of life with American lifestyles. Indians were to become farmers and artisans. Missionaries attempted to convert the Indians, and the process was deemed to be successful when the Indians became more like the Whites.
3. By tribal restoration, whereby Indians were encouraged to maintain their tribal existence.
4. By terminating the dependency relationship with the federal government, so that Indians could be freed of the protection and assistance of the Bureau of Indian Affairs.
5. By reintroduction of tribal restoration, but this time with an emphasis on corporate adaptation (Indian business corporations) to the mainstream society.

There are current attempts to encourage Indians to settle in urban areas. The urban migration is still in process. The basic reason for the various changes in federal policy toward the Indians has been the lack of success of these policies, both from the dominant-group perspective and the minority-group response. For example, Spicer (1980:63) noted that the period of forced cultural assimilation did not necessarily mean that the Native Americans identified with the ways of the dominant culture. Rather, there was considerable alienation and aversion to white beliefs, behavior, and organization. Indian identity was retained through a variety of ways: Native dances, religion, and music became symbols; Indian headbands, moccasins, and dress were worn; and tribal lore and Indian heroes and heroines were resurrected. These actions served to counterbalance acculturative pressures and to hinder Indian absorption into the dominant society.

WHO IS AN INDIAN?

In one area—that of individual racial intermingling—the Indian has been highly successful, so that there is a problem of identifying just who is an Indian. In the past, white soldiers, vagabonds, trappers, hunters, and traders—primarily adult, single men—invaded Indian lands and mated with Indian women. Of course, there were strong taboos against half-breed offspring, but the number of Americans with some percentage of Indian blood must run in the millions.

At the time of European settlement, the number of Native Americans in the United States had been estimated as low as one million and as high as ten million. By 1800 the native population was about 600,000, and by 1850 it had shrunk to about 250,000; malnutrition and disease (with extermination and genocide thrown in) were the primary causes. The 1960 Census showed a total of 523,591 Native Americans; the 1970 figures were 792,730, the 1980 figures were 1,364,033. From 1970 to 1980, the American Indian population increased by 72 percent from 827,268 to 1,420,400 (O'Hare, 1992) and the 1990 Census counted more than 1.9 million Native Americans, so that it is one of the fastest growing younger populations. It should be noted that the number of American Indians varies, even though they are all figures reported by the U.S. Census. The dramatic growth in the population can be attributed to the use of self-identification in the U.S. Census, births, and greater efforts to more accurately count the Native American population. In addition, there were another 6.7 million who claimed partial Native American ancestry.

John (1988) indicates that the American Indians are the most rural of any ethnic group in the country. One half live in non-metropolitan areas, 21 percent in central cities, and the rest live in metropolitan areas outside of the central cities. Twenty-four percent live in one of the 278 recognized reservations. Most of the American Indians live west of the Mississippi River, with California, Oklahoma, Arizona, and New Mexico (each with over 100,000) accounting for 44 percent of the American Indian total.

The Native American is a young population; the median age for females is 23.5 years as compared to the general population where the median age is 31.2 years. Therefore, many are of childbearing age (John, 1988).

NATIVE AMERICAN PROBLEMS AND SURVIVAL

The Family and the Band

The ethnocentric ideal of white America is the nuclear family—husband, wife, and two children. One of the targets for many reformers was the Indian *band,* composed of kinspeople "who recognized obligations to each other, including the sharing of certain kinds of property, and the joint organization of rituals and festivals" (Wax, 1971:75). Bands were most common to reservation life; decisions and actions emerged from group discussion and concensus, rather than from a leader.

Bands were quite egalitarian and served as mutual assistance societies. There was much sharing, and there might be a massive redistribution of property when someone died. Therefore, there was little opportunity for one man or one family to accumulate and maintain vast amounts of property for any length of time. Band organization limited the opportunities for individual Indians to become wealthy, but it also prevented others from being ignored or left to starve.

Another characteristic of the band was its particularistic pattern. Members of one band network were not obligated to share with those outside their own network. This "ignoring" of outsiders has caused much white misunderstanding.

There is no single Indian nation per se. There are, instead, many local units, such as bands of kin. But white administrators are used to dealing with such units as countries and nations or with smaller units, such as the family. They frown upon band interdependence, especially when there appears to be much freeloading. There is no incentive to gather, hoard, and save, because those Indians who have accumulated some food or cash are visited by their band members until the surplus is exhausted. This band culture conflicts with the American values of individual achievement, accumulation of wealth, saving for the future, and individual industry.

Although recognizing some of the problems caused by the band, Wax feels that it is the strength of the band organization—its vitality, tenacity, and flexibility—that has enabled Native American communities to survive at all. The patterns of sharing, voluntary cooperation, equality, and solidarity have sustained the Native American under the most severe conditions of hardship, whereas other forms of organization (such as the individual family) probably would have led to the total destruction of the group.

Money

Acculturated and urbanized Native Americans use money in the same manner as the majority culture does. However, money takes on a different value for those on reservations, where there is little opportunity for agricultural or industrial employment and low cash incomes. The Indian is able to survive on little money because of the band organization, with its mutual assistance, sharing, and pooling. This unit goes far beyond the nuclear family and the extended family, and includes a complex of families living close together. There are also many free services: Surplus foods and health care are provided; wood and water are available; and while they are not grand, there are cabins. Since everyone lives under similar circumstances, the competitive strains of the U.S. social system (having a bigger house, keeping up with the Joneses) are absent.

Under these circumstances, the Native Americans may use money for specialties and luxuries. Cash is paid out for sweets, clothes, and trips to relatives, which appalls the "sensible" welfare workers, who have nuclear families and live on fixed, scheduled incomes. They accuse the Indian of being irresponsible, haphazard, and ignorant of the value of money; they try to deprive the Indians of their cash and instead provide the goods and services they think are necessary.

A similar situation exists in some colleges and universities that are granted large amounts of money to teach and train Native Americans. According to Wax:

In a sense, the universities have inherited the social role played in the nineteenth century by missionary groups who came to control the reservations because the federal operations could not be kept free of the taint of political corruption. But, just as the missionaries, the universities are insulated from the influence of local Indian communities, and organize their programs according to ideologies, professional codes, and bureaucratic procedures that exclude any control by the relatively uneducated Indian. As the universities build staffs and operate programs, they become increasingly dependent upon these monies, and constitute a vested interest of some potency in maintaining reservations in a subordinated state. (1971:82)

Education

Immigrant groups have always believed education to be the major route to success; they think education will allow them to be assimilated into the American way of life. Many of them give up their ethnic ways, only to find their entrance into the American system blocked. This leaves them in the category of part-white ethnics, with the subsequent problems of identity, alienation, and marginality. Native American children who do extremely well in school may be regarded as marginal or deviant if the majority of their peers adopts other norms.

The interaction between American Indians and the white society's schools is often painful. There is a gulf between the parents and the school system, especially on the reservations. The cultural separateness of the children and their teachers is another barrier. The outsider (the teacher) vainly tries to impose unfamiliar and even dysfunctional styles on the lives of the insiders (the Native American children). There may be much confusion, inattention, and little actual learning, even though by the middle grades there may be a semblance of order and quietness. Predictably, scholastic achievement test scores reveal a steady decline with advancement in grade.

Wax writes that the failure of educators to recognize and integrate the Indian peer society in educational tasks is at the root of the difficulty. Other explanations include the alienation of the children from both schools and parents, the inadequate curriculum of the schools (English as a second language), the simple lack of linguistic facility, and the questions of motivation, identification, and confidence. One could also question the meaning of an American education for the Indian.

Wax cited some typical conflicts that occur in the schools when teachers are unaware of the peer society. Native American pupils hesitate to perform individually before the class, not only because they do not want to be exposed as inadequate, but also because they do not want to demonstrate their individual superiority and thereby the inferiority of their peers. If competition is based on a peer-group basis (such as on athletic teams), however, they can become excellent participants.

The Cherokees have an ethic of harmony. Gulick (1960) emphasized that the self-assertive, aggressive individual destroys this harmony, and yet many teachers promote "self," aggressiveness, and assertiveness as student ideals. For the tribal Cherokee, this individuated emphasis is morally very troublesome. Individual victory, achievement, and exposure—desirable norms in the larger society—are met with uncomfortable and passive resistance by the minority. Wax claimed that a blindfolded person could discern the sharp differences between the Oklahomans of white and Cherokee backgrounds. The timbre and loudness of the voices and the frantic attempts to get the attention of the teacher clearly differentiate the Whites from the Native Americans.

The error of many teachers is their desire to disrupt the peer society for individual reward and effort. It is the peer society that provides the Indian with a sense of identity and self; destruction of this tie deprives the individual of one of his or her most important sources of security and worth.

Educational reforms have proved to be as difficult to carry out as reforms in other areas of Indian-white relationships. More and more Native Americans are moving into urban areas, and federal monies set aside for their special education are probably absorbed into the general fund. The BIA schools continue to have their problems and tend to reflect the interests of the local pressure groups. There are few Native Americans in colleges and universities; education has not been the "ladder to success" for most Native Americans.

Means (1995) and Deloria (1995) question the "European"-based emphasis of the educational system. Science conflicts with many of the Indian ways; capitalistic and Marxist models emphasize production and materialism, which contrasts with the Indian views of production and sharing. Deloria indicates that many Native Americans have become successful; tribal chairmen have become well-heeled Republicans, and are now concerned about the moral fiber of the young and prayer in the schools. The push for education has taken hold in the new generations; they have become technically proficient, but in the process, they have thrown away their Indian heritage.

Alcoholism

The vulnerability of the Native American to alcohol has become a legend. The Indian style of drinking does not consist of demure cocktails before dinner or "holding one's liquor like a gentleman." Rather, it is what Wax called "binge drinking." This drinking takes place in peer groups, usually of young males, and is often associated with driving at high speeds and encounters with the police, with the promise of danger and possible disaster. Some have argued that the relative newness of liquor in Indian life has led to some of the current problems, and that the Native American has not yet had time to work out a culturally acceptable way of drinking (at least according to majority norms). The problem is compounded by the fact that many Indians value states of trance and euphoria, and that the all-important warrior rituals are recreated under the influence of alcohol. The conflict between being an Indian warrior or a "failure" in Western terms can be partially forgotten when one is inebriated.

May (1989) acknowledges that Native Americans have problems with alcohol, but also notes that Indian adults, particularly females, drink less than non-Indians and that the percentage of abstainers who have quit drinking by the age of 30 and above far exceed the United States average.

Dozier (1966) provides a sociocultural explanation for the Indians and alcohol. Wars, contemptuous settlers, cultural invasion, military subordination, loss of property, and invasion of their hunting and fishing grounds are historical factors that have led to sociocultural deprivation and consequent drinking among present-day Native Americans.

Whatever the reason, liquor has often gotten Native Americans into trouble with law-enforcement agencies. The rate of Indian arrests for crimes related to alcohol is many times the national average, and drunkenness seems to rise as the American Indian migrates to urban areas.

Statistics also show a high proportion of Native Americans in penal institutions. For example, in South Dakota, where the Native Americans represent about 5 percent of the total state population, they constitute over 33 percent of the prison population. As with most official statistics, the reasons behind the incarcerations may be questioned; nevertheless, it is one indication of a continuing social problem.

The Indian Model

The Native Americans' adaptation to their conquerors covers the entire range of intergroup interaction. On the one hand, individuals and tribes have acculturated and integrated to such an extent that a measure of their "Indianness" may be "a drop of Indian blood" from a distant ancestor; other tribes have been completely annihilated; and there are those Indians who have retained a strong tribal affiliation and are deeply committed to a pluralistic perspective.

The Native Americans are probably the closest example of the paternal or colonial model among all of our ethnic groups. As Jorgensen asserted: ". . . the metropolis-satellite capitalist economy has harnessed the military and the BIA to conquer and control North American Indians, and it is this political economy that has maintained Indian deprivation" (1977:190).

There are, no doubt, facets of the Indian economy and culture that have contributed to the problem, but the greatest burden lies with the dominant group. It expropriated and exploited the resources of the Native Americans; it put them on reservations and ran their lives; and it established political, economic, and welfare systems that rendered most Native Americans powerless and alienated. It attempted to destroy the Native American culture and life. It is a credit to the tenacity of some Native Americans that any part of that cultural integrity still survives.

Thomas (1975), in writing about the internal-colony system, emphasizes that many of the intentions of the federal programs are benevolent, but that their effects are negative (institutional racism). No matter how well intentioned, the administration and leadership still come from outside the group. The structure impedes Indian advancement. For example, in Pine Ridge, South Dakota, the Sioux cannot get loans from private banks because the land is held in trust. Their few, small industries are accountable to the BIA, not to the tribe. Their main resource, the land, is leased out to white ranchers, so that the majority of the Sioux end up as migrant workers, recipients of social welfare, unskilled workers in low-paying government jobs, or in tribally subsidized industries. The structure helps keep the Sioux people away from the mainstream economy, exploits the land resources for the benefit of others, and keeps the majority of the tribe as a reservoir of unskilled migrant workers for the surrounding area. If they complain too loudly, they fear that Congress may dismantle the costly BIA, the bureau that has trapped the tribes in a dependency relationship.

Dependency

The United States' treatment of the Indian has encouraged dependency and irresponsibility, especially in relation to inheritance laws. Instead of considering rights, duties, privileges, and responsibilities in the complex net of Indian social relationships, the United States views the membership of each person as a case of heirship to a piece of property (Wax, 1971). This encourages the individual to think solely in terms of rights, privileges, and rewards, and not in terms of duties, responsibilities, and obligations. For example, anyone who can prove having Indian blood may be eligible for various federal benefits (in health, education, employment), regardless of whether he or she participates in an Indian community or contributes to its existence. A similar logic is applied to voting on tribal matters, the sale of property, and other proceedings, with the result that the functioning Indian tribal society is constantly disrupted by those whose only bond with the group is that of blood. Dependency continues to be encouraged by a decision-making apparatus that has historically been under the control of outsiders. Indian "experts" continue to make decisions on what is good for the Native Americans, ignoring the needs and desires of the population.

Another important structural factor that maintains the dominant/subordinate relationship has been the BIA community and the tribes that it serves. A BIA complex in Barrow, Alaska was studied by Hennigh (1975), who found that highly competent federal officials maintained negative stereotypes of the Eskimo. The source of the stereotype was the aloofness and autonomy of the BIA community as it viewed the more "primitive" Eskimo community and the vast discrepancy in creature comforts and lifestyles.

General Nguyen Cao Ky, a former prime minister of Vietnam, also discussed the impact of U.S. culture on less developed, poor nations. He talked about the hidden price of United States' aid and warned that it was the American technician who took the first step in destroying the culture. The example of the highly paid American technician living in luxury apartments and freely spending money creates a conflict between the foreign and the native way of life, and reminds the citizenry of just how far they must go to reach a comparable standard of living (Wood, 1979).

The Immigration

It seems incredible to think of the original inhabitants of the country as immigrants; yet in one of the ironies of the interaction between groups, this appears to be the case for the Native American.

In 1952 the BIA established a national program of relocation assistance, which encouraged the employment of Native Americans outside the reservation. In 1956 vocational planning programs were added for Indian youths, and in 1962 a program of employment assistance was started at seven urban centers (Miller et al., 1975). One result of these programs has been the rise in the number of Native Americans in urban areas. In 1910 only 10 percent of the Native Americans lived in urban areas; by 1970 the number of urban-dwelling Native Americans was estimated at over 50 percent.

Senator Ben Nighthorse Campbell at a news conference for newly elected Senators, 1992.

A study by Miller, herself a Native American, and a group of Native American researchers analyzed the adaptation of 120 Indian families to urban life (1975). These are the urban Indians, or the "new immigrants"—made up of many tribes, attempting to succeed in the city by speaking English, going to school, working for wages, and behaving as most working-class Americans are supposed to. But very few have become "Americanized," and Miller's group developed three hypotheses for this resistance to acculturation.

1. The land still belongs to the Native Americans. They did not come here from another place; they are the original inhabitants. Who has to adapt to whom?

2. Native Americans do not see the white way as superior to or more desirable than their own cultural ways.

3. The majority society does not wish Native Americans to be equal partners and has created legal and structural barriers to deny them full and equal access.

Steele (1975) questions the assumptions behind the acculturation-assimilation model for the new Indian immigrant, based on a small number of Indian migrants and the assumed contrast between urban and reservation life. More relevant questions include discrimination, realistic possibilities for decent employment in the cities, and constructive assistance available to low-income migrants in large cities. The other major question is not concerned with the "superiority" of the white culture to Indian culture but with the political and economic power of the white society, which can almost totally change Indian life.

Denton (1975), in a Canadian study, showed that in the move from rural to urban areas, Native Americans found themselves stigmatized. They adapted to this negative situation by concealing their Indian identity or by admitting that they were Native Americans but acting in such a way as not to be discredited by this identity.

Price (1975) argued that in order for Indian migration to be successful, tribal identities must be fostered. The urbanization process that has decimated the tribes and is leading to a Pan-Indian identity in a white racial society is seen as trivializing and confusing. Miller's study (1975) found that those Native Americans following a bicultural model and achieving a degree of comfort with both the Indian and white world exhibited a greater ability to survive and to adapt to the city than those families who were comfortable with only the Indian world.

Another important factor remains the accessibility of the homeland, or reservation. Very few of the other immigrant groups had available such an easy option, and there is some evidence that many Indians are taking advantage of returning "home." A study of a group of Spokane Indians (Chadwick & White, 1973) focused on reasons why some decided to stay in the cities and others chose to return to the reservation. Contrary to expectations of the importance of economic factors, the most significant variable was the Native Americans' feeling of acceptance by the white community.

There have been attempts to help keep the Native Americans on the reservations. Stoffle (1975), in describing an electronics factory on a Zuni reservation, emphasized the necessity of understanding both the functional requisites of the industry and the culture of the tribe. Conflicts were satisfactorily resolved when cultural and subcultural differences were accommodated by all parties.

Lack of Cohesion

A major handicap for the Native American has been the lack of a cohesive, united front. Because they were the original inhabitants, they already had developed tribal loyalties that included centuries-old enmities, feuds, and differences. Thus, the Native Americans fought the Whites as separate tribes, often while continuing to fight one another (Josephy, 1977). The threat of white conquest did not serve as a unifying element for the tribes; in fact, it may have even exacerbated the differences. On the other hand, the loosely organized white settlers from vastly different backgrounds who were almost total strangers to each other found the Indian threat a unifying and organizing influence. They submerged their differences and achieved cohesion under the threat of the "Indian menace."

Poverty

The major problem on the reservation is not the Indian culture or its distinctiveness, but rather, economic exploitation and poverty. The same is true wherever the Native Americans live in America, for they, like the Blacks, are considered unequal to white male norms on all measures of inequality.

To a considerable extent, poverty is responsible for the lack of education, especially at the college level, the unemployment, and the lack of skills. Poverty is also related to powerlessness. As Deloria (1970) indicated, Indian children were "kidnapped" and taken away to government boarding schools, often thousands of miles away. They were whipped if they used their native language. Indian ceremonies were banned, even on their own reservations. "People thought that by banning everything Indian, they could bring the individual Indians from the Stone Age to the Electric Age in one generation" (Deloria, 1970:109). The tragedy of the Native Americans' plight is, in a sense, the irony of America. In their rage for progress, white people have not only threatened the Native Americans with extinction; they also have plundered the land, decimated its natural resources, produced overcrowding and pollution, and destroyed much of the natural richness of the country. One national magazine put it this way:

From its Indian citizens, the United States may yet learn some lessons about restoring the balance between man and his surroundings. The Indian has always been a partner of nature, not a destroyer of it. In the legends he wrote about mountains, trees, lakes and canyons, in his understanding of the spiritual force of nature, he has maintained a vision of coherence and beauty: the land and the men upon it must exist in harmony. (*Life,* 1971:38)

REFERENCES

ANDRIST, R. (1964). *The long death*. London: Collier-Macmillan.

BROWN, D. (1973). *Bury my heart at Wounded Knee*. New York: Holt, Rinehart & Winston.

BURKEY, R. (1978). *Ethnic and racial groups*. Menlo Park, Calif.: Cummings Publishing.

CHADWICK, B. A., & WHITE, L. C. (1973). Correlates of length of urban residence among the Spokane Indians. *Human Organization*, *32* (1), 9–16.

CUNNINGHAM, H. T. (1930). A history of the Cherokee Indians. *Chronicles of Oklahoma*, *8* (3), 291–314; *8* (4), 407–440.

DANIELS, R., & KITANO, H. H. L. (1970). *American racism*. Englewood Cliffs, N.J.: Prentice-Hall.

DELORIA, V. (1970). *We talk, you listen*. New York: Macmillan.

DELORIA, V. (1972a). *Of utmost good faith*. New York: Bantam.

DELORIA, V. (1973). Burying our hopes at Wounded Knee. *Los Angeles Times*, April 1, p.1.

DELORIA, V. (1995). *Red earth, white lies*. New York: Scribner.

DENTON, T. (1975). Canadian Indian migrants and impression management of ethnic stigma. *Canadian Review of Sociology and Anthropology*, *12*, 65–71.

DOZIER, E. P. (1966). Problem drinking among American Indians: The role of sociocultural deprivation. *Quarterly Journal of Studies on Alcohol*, *27* (1), 72–87.

FEAGIN, J. (1978). *Racial and ethnic relations*. Englewood Cliffs, N.J.: Prentice-Hall.

FEAGIN, J. (1989). *Racial and ethnic relations*, 3rd ed. Englewood Cliffs, N.J.: Prentice-Hall.

FEAGIN, J. & FEAGIN, C. (1995). *Racial and ethnic relations*. Upper Saddle River, N.J.: Prentice-Hall.

FEHRENBACK, T. R. (1974). *Comanches: The destruction of a people*. New York: Knopf.

GULICK, J. (1960). *Cherokees at the crossroads*. Chapel Hill: University of North Carolina, Institute of Research on Social Science.

HAVIGHURST, R. (1977). Indian education since 1960. Paper presented at the meeting of the American Sociological Association, Chicago, September 5.

HENNIGH, L. (1975). Negative sterotyping: Structural Contributors in a BIA Community, *Human Organization, 34* (3):263–268.

HRABA, J. (1979). *American ethnicity*. Itasca, Ill.: F.E. Peacock.

JOHN, R. (1988). The Native American family. In C. Mindel, R. Haberstein, & R. Wright, Jr. (Eds.), *Ethnic families in America* (3rd ed.) (pp. 325–363). New York: Elsevier.

JORGENSEN, J. (1977). Poverty and work among American Indians. In H. R. Kaplan (Ed.), *American minorities and economic opportunity* (pp. 170–197), Itasca, Ill.: F.E. Peacock.

JOSEPHY, A. (1977). What the Indian wants. In L. Dinnerstein & F. Jaber (Eds.), *Uncertain Americans* (pp. 277–288). New York: Oxford University Press.

KROEBER, T. (1964). *Ishi*. Berkeley, Calif.: L. Parnassus Press.

LARSEN, D. (1989). The invisible minority. *Los Angeles Times*, October 8, part IV, p. 1.

LEUDORS, B. (1994). Casino cowboys take Indians for a ride. *Progressive*, August, 30-33.

LIFE, July 2, 1971, *71* (1):38–59.

MAY, P. (1989). Alcohol abuse and alcoholism among American Indians: An overview. In T. D. Watts & R. Wright, Jr. (Eds.), *Alcoholism in minority populations* (pp. 95–119). Springfield, Ill.: Charles C. Thomas.

MEANS, R. (1995). *Where white men fear to tread*. New York: St. Martin's.

MEYER, W. (1971). *Native Americans*. New York: International Publishers.

MILLER, D. ET AL. (1975). *Native American families in the city*. San Francisco: Scientific Analysis.

O'HARE, W. (1992). America's Minorities: The Demographics of Diversity. *Population Bulletin, 47, 4.*

PRICE, J. (1975). U.S. and Canadian Indian urban ethnic institutions. *Urban Anthropology, 4* (1), 35–52.

SPICER, E. (1980). American Indians. In S. Thernstrom, A. Orlov, & O. Handlin (Eds.), *Harvard Encyclopedia of American Ethnic Groups* (pp. 58–122). Cambridge, Mass.: Harvard University Press.

STEELE, C. H. (1975). The acculturation-assimilation model in urban Indian studies: A critique. In N. Yetman & C. H. Steele (Eds.), *Majority and minority* (2nd ed.) (pp. 305–314). Boston: Allyn & Bacon.

STOFFLE, R. (1975). Reservation-based industry: A case from Zuni, New Mexico. *Human Organization, 34* (3), 217–225.

THOMAS, R. K. (1975). Powerless politics. In N. Yetman & C. H. Steele (Eds.), *Majority and minority* (2nd ed.) (pp. 394–401). Boston: Allyn & Bacon.

VOGEL, V. (1972). *This country was ours*. New York: Harper & Row.

WAX, M. (1971). *Indian Americans*. Englewood Cliffs, N.J.: Prentice-Hall.

WILKENSON, C. F. (1987). *American Indians, time, and the law*. New Haven and London: Yale University Press.

WOOD T. (1979). Ky reflects on hidden price tag of U.S. aid. *Los Angeles Times*, January 20, section 1, p.18.

Section III

Groups in the Second Tier of the Stratification System

Part of the third section of the book deals with two groups of Europeans, the Irish and the Italians—both have faced prejudice, discrimination, and segregation, but have achieved a degree of mobility to the middle of the ethnic stratification system. They may have even surpassed the societal norm in terms of income and education; yet, many have retained an ethnic identity so that an ethnic lens is retained, although not as strongly as the groups in the previous section. More importantly, the society may see them as ethnics, although generational changes continue to erode the strength of the identity.

The Asian Americans represent another group who have achieved a degree of mobility from the bottom of the ethnic stratification system. Not all of the many groups that make up the Asian Americans have advanced, but the Chinese and Japanese are two who have been upwardly mobile. Asian Americans have suffered through intense prejudice, discrimination, and segregation, primarily because of their racial visibility, so that their history and treatment are viewed from both a racial and ethnic lens.

Table III–1 shows persons of Western and Northern European ancestry in the United States for 1980 and 1990. The Germans are the most numerous (over 57 million) followed by the Irish (over 38 million). This chapter will present the Irish as a group from Western Europe.

Table III–2 shows persons of Eastern and Southern European ancestry for 1980 and 1990. The Italians, who will be covered in this section, are the most numerous with over 14 million, followed by the Polish with over 9 million.

Data on Jewish Americans is more difficult to obtain since the U.S. Census does not ask for religion. The best guess by Farley (1995), based on data from Goren (1980) is that the Jewish population is above 6 million or 3 per-

Table III–1   Persons of Western and Northern European Ancestry, 1980 and 1990

Ancestry[1]	1980 Population	1990 Population
English	49,598,000	32,556,000
	26.3%[2]	13.1%
German	49,224,000	57,986,000
	26.1%	23.3%
Irish	40,166,000	38,740,000
	21.3%	15.6%
French	12,892,000	10,321,000
	6.8%	4.1%
Scottish	10,049,000	5,394,000
	5.3%	2.2%
Dutch	6,304,000	6,227,000
	3.4%	2.5%
Swedish	4,345,000	4,681,000
	2.3%	1.9%
Norwegian	3,454,000	3,869,000
	1.8%	1.6%
Welsh	1,665,000	2,034,000
	0.9%	0.8%
Danish	1,518,000	1,635,000
	0.8%	0.7%
Swiss	982,000	1,045,000
	0.5%	0.4%
Austrian	948,000	871,000
	0.5%	0.4%
Finnish	616,000	659,000
	0.3%	0.3%
French Canadian[3]	780,000	2,167,000
	0.4%	0.9%
Canadian[3]	456,000	561,000
	0.2%	0.2%

[1]Includes both single and multiple ancestry. Persons who reported more than one ancestry group may be counted in more than one category.

[2]In 1980, percentage of those who reported ancestry in that census. In 1990, percentage of total population.

[3]Included because most Canadians and French Canadians are of western or northern European ancestry.

Source: 1980: U.S. Bureau of the Census, 1983c, pp. 12–14, 1990: U.S. Bureau of the Census. *1990 Census of Population, Social and Economic Characteristic*s, United States, p. 12.

Table III–2   Persons of Eastern and Southern European Ancestry, 1980 and 1990

Ancestry[1]	1980 Population	1990 Population
Italian	12,184,000	14,715,000
	6.5%[2]	5.9%
Polish	8,238,000	9,266,000
	4.4%	3.8%
Russian	2,781,000	2,953,000
	1.5%	1.2%
Czech	1,892,000	1,615,000
	1.0%	0.6%
Hungarian	1,777,000	1,582,000
	0.9%	0.6%
Portuguese	1,024,000	1,153,000
	0.5%	0.5%
Greek	960,000	1,110,000
	0.5%	0.4%
Ukranian	730,000	741,000
	0.4%	0.3%
Slovak	777,000	1,883,000
	0.4%	0.8%
Lithuanian	743,000	812,000
	0.4%	0.3%

[1]Includes both single and multiple ancestry. Persons who reported more than one ancestry group may be counted in more than one category.
[2]In 1980, percentage of those who reported ancestry in that census. In 1990, percentage of total population.
Source: 1980: U.S. Bureau of the Census. 1983c, pp. 12–14, 1990: U.S. Bureau of the Census. *1990 Census of Population, Social and Economic Characteristics, United States*, p. 12.

cent of the U.S. population. This constitutes about half of the world's Jewish population. It is a highly urbanized and successful population and is growing very slowly because of its low birthrate.

Table III–3 shows the Asian, Southeast Asian, and Pacific Islanders in the United States in 1990. The total number of Asian/Pacific Islanders, over 7 million, is small, barely approaching 3 percent of the total population in the United States. The Chinese are the most numerous (1,645,472), followed by the Filipinos (1,406,770) and the Japanese (847,562).

There remains a strong racial and ethnic identity among the Asian American groups; the Catholic identity remains a strong source of identity among the Irish and Italians. But, as in common with individuals who feel

Table III–3   Largest Asian or Pacific Islander Groups in the United States, 1990

Group	Total	Share of U.S. Population (%)
Total Asian or Pacific Islander	7,273,662	2.9
Total Asian	6,908,638	2.8
Total Pacific Islander	365,024	0.1
Chinese	1,645,472	0.7
Filipino	1,406,770	0.6
Japanese	847,562	0.3
Indian	815,447	0.3
Korean	798,849	0.3
Vietnamese	614,547	0.2
Hawaiian	211,014	0.1
Laotian	149,014	0.1
Cambodian	147,411	0.1
Thai	91,275	0.0
Hmong	90,082	0.0
Samoan	62,964	0.0
Guamanian	49,345	0.0
Tongan	17,606	0.0

Source: U.S. Census Bureau.

that racial, religious, and ethnic identity are no longer relevant, a stronger individual identity has also developed in the groups.

Chapter 12 will present the Irish and Italians; Chapter 13, the Chinese; Chapter 14, the Japanese; Chapter 15, the Koreans and Filipinos; and Chapter 16, the Southeast Asians and Pacific Islanders. I have focused on the Asian American groups with more detail since they are not covered as thoroughly in other books on race and ethnicity, and because I am an Asian American.

REFERENCES

FARLEY, J. (1995). *Majority Minority Relations*. Englewood Cliffs, N.J.: Prentice-Hall.

GOREN, A. (1980). *Jews*. In S. Thornstrom, A. Orlov, and O. Handlin. (eds.) Harvard Encyclopedia of American Ethnic Groups, Cambridge Mass.: Harvard University Press, pp. 571–98.

Chapter 12

Irish and Italians

THE IRISH

The Irish are often cited as an example of the rapid assimilation of European immigrants to the American society. Although they have achieved success in the political, educational, and economic areas, many still carry an Irish, or Irish American identity. There is also a religious identity among Irish Catholics.

Immigration History

The first significant immigration of the Irish occurred in the 1700s, so by the time of the first U.S. Census in 1790, they were about 10 percent of the white population of 3.2 million. Many came as indentured servants and subsistence farmers. They entered into an English dominated country, where English Americans viewed the Irish as subordinates, even as an inferior race (Feagin & Feagin, 1996).

Akenson (1993:250) indicates that the estimated number of Irish who arrived before 1820 was composed of 60 percent Scotch Irish, 7 percent Anglo Irish, and the remainder as Catholic Irish. Many of the group were Protestants who represented the middle and upper classes, while the Catholic Irish who arrived during this period were agricultural laborers, servants, and exiled criminals.

In common with most European immigrants, the "push" was famine and failure of potato crops[1] between 1845–1849, and the brutal English colonization of Ireland, which began in 1649 and lasted until 1920 with the partition of Ireland, while the "pull" was for a better life in America. Irish immigration was also a part of a larger movement that included migrants to England, Canada, Australia, South Africa, and New Zealand (Akenson, 1993).

The Irish Protestants were not subject to religious persecution, but ran into conflict with the English, nativists of other established groups, and with Native Americans (Leyburn, 1962). In addition, Catholic migrants of the colonial era were met with religious prejudice and discrimination, which occasionally spilled over into violent attacks on their communities and churches (Wittke, 1956).

The Irish Catholics settled primarily in the large urban areas in the northeastern states, while the Irish Protestants were more likely to settle in the rural areas of the middle and southern states. New York, Boston, and Philadelphia were major centers, although the Irish did not form large ethnic communities but instead spread out in small clusters in working class neighborhoods, close to their place of employment. They often lived in crowded, undesirable conditions; Greeley (1981) estimated that in 1863, 18,000 migrants lived in disease-ridden cellars in New York City. Life was harsh and short; employment was in the low-skill, low-wage jobs. They were overrepresented in the almshouses; crime rates were high and they faced continual discrimination.

Discrimination

The prejudice and discrimination had its roots in the English conquest and subsequent oppression of Ireland. Much of the antagonism arose from anti-Catholicism, and the Irish were seen as different and inferior race. Racial inferiority justified Irish oppression.

In North America, the hatred of Catholics was reinforced by the specter of colonies of French Catholics to the north, and Spanish Catholics to the south. There was widespread fear of a Catholic conspiracy to take over British North America, which led to anti-Catholic laws in many colonies. By the time Irish Catholics began to arrive in the 1830s, hatred of Catholics had become a part of the American culture. Signs stated, "No Irish Need to Apply," and individuals with a Gaelic surname and a strong brogue had difficulty in finding employment (Lovejoy, 1987).

---

[1]Feagin and Feagin (1996) indicate that during the famine years in Ireland in the 1840s, Ireland actually produced more than twice the food necessary to feed the hungry. However, oppressive English landlords saw to it that most of the foods were exported to England, or consumed by those in Ireland with money. "God sent the blight, but the English landlord sent the famine." (p. 103)

The stereotypes used against the Irish were similar to those used against African Americans. They included apelike features, low intelligence, wickedness, a fighting stance, a jug of whiskey, ignorance, and a threat to orderly politics (Greeley, 1972; Feagin and Feagin, 1996).

In 1932, traits associated with the Irish still included pugnacious, quick tempered and quarrelsome, although some positive images included intelligence and loyalty to the family. In the 1980s a nationwide opinion poll indicated that Irish Americans received the second highest percentage of positive answers (the English were the first) in response to the question of which groups had been good or bad for the country (Feagin & Feagin, 1996:105).

Irish women also played a significant role. One distinctive aspect of Irish immigration was the presence of a large number of young single women. Because they had little hope of inheritance and marriage in their poverty stricken homeland, they saw America as the land of opportunity.[2] Once in the United States, they did not subscribe to the norm that a woman's place was in the home; rather, many became self-sufficient persons with distinctive work histories and made important social and economic contribution to the upward mobility of Irish Americans into middle-income America (Feagin & Feagin, 1996:103).

By the 1960s and 1970s, Irish Catholics were second only to Jews in annual income and educational levels. In high-prestige occupations, such as media personalities and college professors, they ranked behind the Jews and British Protestants. Akenson (1993) indicates that although there is lingering discrimination in high-prestige public roles, they are among the most privileged white ethnic groups in the United States.

There is less data on Irish Protestants, primarily because they located in the rural areas of the middle and southern states. In the 1960s and 1970s they represented the lowest white ethnic group in terms of income, education, and occupational prestige, and as opposed to the overwhelmingly urban Catholics, they were still almost 30 percent rural (Greeley, 1988; Akenson, 1993).

Irish Identity

In spite of their relatively long history in the United States, their dispersal, the high levels of education and their ability to blend into the mainstream, there remains a closeness to Ireland and an Irish identification. There is a persistence of the identity, often closely linked with Catholicism, but even among the Protestants, the vast majority still identify themselves as Irish.

---

[2]Many of the conditions of women were also similar in many other countries. For example, in a similar time period, Japanese women faced similar circumstances, yet there was no significant emigration of single women.

*Francis Scott Fitzgerald
(1896–1940), famous Irish
American writer.*

Politics

Irish participation in politics was as early as the signers of the Declaration of Independence, where 8 of the 56 signers were Irish. They participated in the election of Thomas Jefferson and their vote was important in electing the first Irish-American (Protestant) president—Andrew Jackson—in 1829 (Feagin & Feagin, 1996:110).

But no other Irish competed in presidential elections until 1928 when Alfred E. Smith ran unsuccessfully on the Democratic party ticket. Smith was defeated in "a veritable firestorm of unabashed bigotry" (Reedy, 1991:138). The election of John F. Kennedy, a descendant of the potato famine in 1960 was a landmark for the Irish and Catholics.

The Irish were much more active on the local level. In the pre-Welfare State Society (the Franklin D. Roosevelt New Deal era, beginning in 1932), Irish political machines provided jobs, construction contracts, schools and social services to urban residents as well as social status, political power, and wealth to the politicians. They were often corrupt patronage systems but nevertheless provided major social programs and assistance to the needy poor of various ethnicities. William "Boss" Tweed's organization, which captured Tammany Hall in the 1860s, was one of the best known early political machines.

Reedy (1991) writes that the Irish made significant contributions to politics, which included the concept that government has an obligation to assist individual citizens when they are in need; a personal, pragmatic, and nonideological style of politics; and of governance as a give-and-take process leading parties to compromise in order to get things done.

In summary, Irish Americans have been the victims of prejudice and discrimination, including racism and anti-Catholicism. They have managed to rise up in the economic and ethnic stratification system, and yet many have retained an Irish identity. They have been stereotyped as conservative and racist, have been the supporters of the Democratic Party, and have played important roles in the American political system.

An important issue remains the conflict in Northern Ireland. A cease fire and peace talks have lead to a unity among Irish Americans and a renewed interest between the Irish in the United States and in Ireland (Candaele, 1995).

THE ITALIANS

From their migration in the late 1800s and early 1900s, the Italians have become one of America's more successful minorities. Starting from largely poor, illiterate farm workers unable to speak English, they have blended into the mainstream so that their ethnic distinctiveness has been threatened. However, some scholars indicate that there is a reawakening of a sense of ethnic community (Alba, 1985; Vecoli, 1985), although generational changes have meant a loss of the Italian language, and increased marriage to non-Italians.

Early History

Although the early Italian explorers such as Columbus, Giovanni Cabototo (John Cabot), and Amerigo Vespucci are well known, very few Italians emigrated to the United States. For the period between 1820 and 1870, only 25,518 Italians entered the United States (Battistella, 1989). Mangione and Morreale (1992) indicate that these early migrants were different from the bulk of immigrants who came between 1880 and 1924 in that they were artists, musicians, teachers, and political refugees with skills and resources. They came primarily from northern Italy with the intention of staying and only a few had an agricultural background.

In contrast, the bulk of the Italians who came after 1880 were from the rural areas of the south. They were primarily farmers, males, and dislocated peasants who lacked the skills and resources of the earlier migrants. Many were illiterate and half of those who arrived during this period returned to Italy (diFranco, 1988). In common with many of the Asian immigrants (to be presented later), there were sojourners who returned after earning enough money to invest in enterprises in Italy.

The unification of Italy gave dominance to the north over the south so that southerners were faced with heavy taxes and political oppression. In addition, the south was faced with poor soil conditions, low rainfall, chronic shortages of food, conscription, and corruption in government. As a consequence, the push towards America was great, while the rapidly expanding U.S. industrial economy stimulated a need for large pools of labor. In addition, there were labor recruiters, returning immigrants, and family members already in America, so that millions of mostly poor Italians embarked on the voyage to the United States (Gambino, 1974; Lopreato, 1970; Mangione & Morreale, 1992; Nelli, 1983).

The migrants clustered in industrial centers in the northeast and New York where the need for cheap, unskilled labor was great. There was a chain migration of family and village groups; identity was based more on kinship, village, and region rather than a national identity since Italy as a nation was just beginning. By 1910 the greater New York metropolitan area housed up to seventy Italian neighborhoods (Mangione & Morreale, 1992).

Prejudice and Discrimination

The historian Higham (1971) writes that the Italians were one of the most hated groups, in part because of their large numbers and their physical distance from the WASP norm. In addition, economic downturns, fear of foreigners, and the Catholic background fed prejudice and stereotypes. Many in the dominant society felt that the Italians, as well as the Jews, were considered as members of biologically inferior races.

An editorial in the *New York Times* appearing in 1882 was indicative of the prejudice against Italians:

> There has never been, since New York was founded, so low and ignorant a class among the immigrants who poured in here as the Southern Italians who have been crowding our docks during the past year . . . They are the provinces South of Naples whose principal export to foreign countries is rags . . .

The northern Italians often attempted to distance themselves from the southern Italians, who were looked upon as swarthy peasants who were dirty, ignorant, poor, and stereotyped as highly emotional, cynical, lazy, cruel, and prone to violence and criminality. They were also blamed for the city slums, public health problems, class conflict, and corruption and graft in city politics (Rolle, 1980:56–57).

Probably the most prominent stereotype was the image of criminality, violence and crime which had its beginning with their large scale immigration in the 1880s and continues to the present day. Although the incidence of criminal convictions among Italian immigrants is similar to that of other immigrant groups and lower than that of the native born population, the picture of the Mafia, Godfathers and organized crime remains as popular subjects. But Rolle (1980) indicates that the vast majority of Italians have been and continue to be hard-working, law-abiding members of the society.

Social Mobility

In the period prior to the end of World War II, most Italians were relegated to low-paying unskilled jobs. Alba (1985) writes that the combination of their occupational and cultural background, widespread discrimination, and the intention of returning to Italy resulted in their low socioeconomic position in U.S. society.

In contrast with the Irish, few Italian women found outside employment. Cultural prescriptions limited contact with men outside of the home so that Italian women contributed to the family income through a highly exploitive system of homework and by taking in boarders. As late as 1950, 77 percent of Italian American women still worked in the needle trades where they could work in a predominantly female workplace (Mangione and Morreale, 1992: 304–308).

Since a large proportion of the early immigrant population intended to return to Italy after a period of work and saving, many Italians placed little emphasis on learning English and becoming citizens. Kessner (1977) suggests that this relatively slow adaptation to the mainstream society placed the Italians at a distinct disadvantage to other immigrant groups who did not possess the sojourner orientation.

Ethnic banks, mutual aid societies, and Italian labor contractors helped to mitigate discrimination and urban poverty. They provided a sense of community, although there were instances of exploitation by fellow countrymen (Mangione & Morreale, 1992; Vecoli, 1985).

Vecoli indicates that World War II was a major turning point for Italians. Full employment and high wages, both during the war and the postwar economy, helped fuel upward mobility. In addition, the G.I. Bill assisted many Italians to acquire college educations and professional training. A study of occupational patterns conducted in the early 1960s revealed that 48 percent of the respondents held white-collar jobs in contrast to 26 percent of their fathers. In addition, 52 percent of the respondents held blue-collar jobs, compared to 71 percent of their fathers (Nelli, 1985:83).

By the mid-1970s, Greeley (1974) indicates that Italians were on a par with the national average in terms of persons employed as managers, owners, professionals, and technical workers. Other studies conducted in the 1970s indicated that Catholic Italian families ranked third in terms of average income behind Jews and Irish Catholics (Nelli, 1985:83). By the 1980s, they had attained a position in the economy that was well above the average of the white population.

Recent data indicates that Italians have continued to move away from the lower paying blue-collar positions to more well-paying prestigous occupations. Italian Americans are entering into law and medicine as well as business ownership, although very few have reached the highest positions in large, or even medium-sized, corporations (Bonutti, 1989:63–66; Nelli, 1985:85).

Major concentrations of Italians outside of the Northeast and Midwest are found in the San Francisco Bay area, Florida, Arizona, and Southern California. As the third and fourth generations have begun to dominate the ethnic community, there is an increase in the distance from the ethnic group, and their location in urban areas has brought about conflict with other urban groups. Based on data collected in the 1980 Census, Velinkonja (1989) notes that the Italian ancestry population is now similar to other U.S. white populations in most measures, including educational achievement, literacy, and cultural background.

Alba (1985) suggests that the assimilation process has been completed so that there will be a disappearance of Italian identity in the near future. Others note a resurgence of ethnic pride and a reaffirmation of ethnic community, even among the upwardly mobile. Historian Furio Columbo (1985) comments that there is an ethnic resilience of the Italian American identity, while Vecoli (1985), although decrying the failure of Italian Americans to create an infrastructure of institutions and organizations to sustain an ethnic identity, reinforces the search for such an identity by stating: "Of one thing I am sure: the search for an Italian American will continue" (p. 112).

Politics

The bulk of the Italian immigration came too late to shape the political machines that the Irish had captured and harnessed before them. But Reedy (1991) notes that the Italians constituted an important base of support for the Irish political machines, which provided jobs and services in exchange for votes.

The first generation from southern Italy brought with them a distrust of politics, and since many had planned to return to Italy, they did not become citizens. However, there was an identification with Mussolini, a promoter of national power and pride, as he rose to power in the 1920s and 1930s. But when he joined forces with Hitler, Italians, "with almost complete unanimity . . . proclaimed their undivided loyalty to the United States" (Vecoli, 1985:97; Mangione & Morreale, 1992).

World War II was the turning point for Italians in politics. In part to avoid the repression brought on by being identified as an enemy alien group—such as the concentration camps for the Japanese Americans—there was a rapid move towards acculturation and Americanization. They disbanded ethnic festivals and ethnic societies and enlisted in the Armed Forces, so that the second generation set the stage for more active participation in the American society (Vecoli, 1985:97).

Prior to World War II, Vito Marcontonio, a socialist, served in the Congress (1934–1948) and Peter Cacchione was the first Community Party mem-

Film director Martin Scorsese accepts the American Society of Cinematographers' 1995 Board of Governors Annual Award from actor Robert DeNiro, at the Beverly Hilton.

ber elected to public office (Mangione & Morreale, 1992:397–401). McCarthyism and the Cold War influenced Italians away from the left and more towards the center. In recent times, Italian American politicians have tended to run as conservatives from both parties. Antonio Scalia was the first Italian American to be appointed to the U.S. Supreme Court.

No Italian has been nominated or elected to the Presidency, although Geraldine Ferraro was nominated for the office of Vice President and Mario Cuomo, former Governor of New York was considered a Presidential nominee. Barone (1985) has noted as the Italian Americans have entered into the mainstream, they have tended to become more conservative with less emphasis on an ethnic identity.

In summary, the Italians have changed, generation by generation. The first generation was peripheral and marginal to the U.S. mainstream; subsequent generations have become much more active in terms of acculturation, upward mobility, and becoming a part of the American society. The question of disappearing as an ethnic group remains as the central question; it is our perception that the ethnic lens has grown dimmer, and that an individual lens, based on individual qualities and individual stands, has taken over. Rather than an Italian American identity, variables such as occupation and social class will provide the main sources of an identity.

REFERENCES

AKENSON, D. H. (1993). *The Irish diaspora: A primer.* Toronto: P. D. Meany Company.

ALBA, R. (1985). *Italian Americans into the twilight of ethnicity.* Englewood Cliffs, N.J.: Prentice-Hall.

BARONE, M. (1985). Italian Americans and politics. In L. F. Tomasi (Ed.), *Italian Americans: New perspectives in Italian immigration and ethnicity* (pp. 378–384). New York: Center for Migration Studies.

BATTISTELLA, G. (Ed.) (1989). *Italian Americans in the '80s: A sociodemographic profile* (p. 1–21, 100). New York: Center for Migration Studies.

BONUTTI, K. (1989). Economic characteristics of Italian Americans. In G. Battistella (Ed.), *Italian Americans in the '80s: A sociodemographic profile* (pp. 62–79). New York: Center for Migration Studies.

CANDAELE, K. (1995). The power of history: The famine and peace. *Los Angeles Times,* part M, p. 2, 6.

COLUMBO, F. (1985). The Italian American identity. In L. F. Tomasi (Ed.), *Italian Americans: New Perspectives in Italian Immigration and Ethnicity* (pp. 113–116). New York: Center for Migration Studies.

DIFRANCO, P. (1988). *The Italian American experience.* New York: Tom Doherty Associates.

FEAGIN, J. & FEAGIN, C. (1996). *Racial and ethnic relations.* Upper Saddle River, N.J.: Prentice-Hall.

GAMBINO, R. (1974). *Blood of my blood: The dilemma of the Italian Americans.* Garden City, N.Y.: Doubleday & Co.

GREELEY, A. M. (1972). *That most distrustful nation.* Chicago: Quadrangle Books.

GREELEY, A. M. (1974). *Ethnicity in the United States: A preliminary reconnaissance.* New York: John Wiley and Sons.

GREELEY, A. M. (1981). *The Irish Americans: The rise to money and power.* New York: Harper & Row.

GREELEY, A. M. (1988). The success and assimilation of Irish Protestants and Irish Catholics in the United States. *Social Science Review, 72* (4), 229–235.

HIGHAM, J. (1971). *Strangers in the land, patterns of American nativism, 1860–1925.* New York: Athenum.

KESSNER, T. (1977). *The golden door: Italian and Jewish immigrant mobility in New York City, 1880–1915.* New York: Oxford University Press.

LEYBURN, J. G. (1962). *The Scotch-Irish.* Chapel Hill: University of North Carolina Press.

LOPREATO, J. (1970). *Italian Americans.* New York: Random House.

LOVEJOY, D. S. (1987). *The glorious revolution in America.* Middletown, Conn: Wesleyan University Press.

MANGIONE, J. & MORREALE, B. (1992). *La Storia: Five centuries of the Italian American experience.* New York: Harper Collins.

NELLI, H. (1983). *From immigrants to ethnics: The Italian Americans.* New York: Oxford University Press.

REEDY, G. E. (1991). *From the ward to the White House: The Irish in American politics*. New York: Charles Scribners Sons.

ROLLE, A. (1980). *The Italian Americans: Troubled roots*. New York: Free Press.

VECOLI, R. J. (1985). The search for an Italian American identity: Continuity and change. In L. F. Tomasi (Ed.), *Italian Americans: New Perspectives in Italian Immigration and Ethnicity* (pp. 88–112). New York: Center for Migration Studies.

VELIKONJA, J. (1989). Demographic and cultural aspects of Italian Americans. In G. Battistella (Ed.), *Italian Americans in the '80s: A Sociodemographic Profile* (pp. 22–35). New York: Center for Migration Studies.

WITTKE, C. (1956). *The Irish in America*. Baton Rouge: Louisiana State University Press.

Chapter 13

Chinese Americans

A number of errors are made when discussing Asian Americans. Among the most common are the following:

- That because they look alike, they are similar, so that knowing one Asian American group leads to generalizations concerning all Asians. Or that because they are still relatively small in number, combining them into one Asian American category is appropriate.

  The fact is that Asian American groups represent a diversity in terms of history, culture, demography, area of settlement, and time and circumstances of their entry into the United States. Lumping this diversity into one category ignores the diversity within the population. Unfortunately, many articles ignore the diversity.

- That there is a tendency to assume an intimate relationship between the immigrant and the ancestral homeland.

  It is important to view generation, acculturation, and other variables as indicative of the ties between Asian Americans and the home country. One of the tragedies of the assumption was during World War II when all Japanese, whether citizens or aliens, were placed in concentration camps because of their presumed ties with the Japanese nation.

It is difficult to ignore the fact that the term, Asian American, is still in frequent use. For example, Seo (1995), writing in the *Los Angeles Times,* indicates that "Asian Americans" at Arcadia High School (a suburb of Los Angeles) are no longer a minority. They have become a significant force in campus politics, in academic and in social organizations so that Korean American Caroline Sim, this year's student body president, when seeing pictures of past student leaders on the wall, said:

> When I first saw the wall, it was intimidating because all I saw were pictures of Caucasians. Then all of a sudden I saw the Asians and it's like, whoa! The change has finally happened and everyone can see it (p. A1).

The change has been especially noticeable in California schools, and the stereotype of high-achieving Asian students has also seen changes. Sally Chou, an assistant principal at Alhambra High School near Los Angeles indicates that there is no such thing as a typical Asian American student. Rather,

> These days, we have all kind of Asian kids—truant kids, dropouts, pregnant girls, gang members, high achievers, and low achievers (p. A30).

An article with an Associated Press byline (1995), using the term Asian Americans and Pacific islanders (API), indicated that the group grew to an estimated 8.8 million in 1994. Nearly 90 percent of men and 80 percent of women were high school graduates, while 41 percent held at least a bachelor's degree, compared with 22 percent of Americans overall. But there were income disparities; college educated API men earned a median income of $41,220 compared to $47,180 for Whites. The income disparities were greater among those without a college education; API women earned $17,330 and men earned $23,490 compared with $19,850 for white women and $28,370 for white men.

It is interesting to note that the first Asian American group to come to America, the Chinese, were at one time the principal target of racism and were deemed to be totally unable to fit into the society. Yet they have achieved a degree of mobility that places them in the middle category of the three-tiered ethnic stratification system.

Like the Irish and Italians presented in Chapter 12, they faced prejudice, discrimination, and segregation and were viewed as less than human by the dominant society. In addition, they belonged to a different race and were easily identifiable so that racism of an especially virulent kind was directed at them. Terms such as heathens and unassimilable and animal-like metaphors were common; special discriminatory legislation was passed to guarantee second-class citizenship.

The two groups most commonly mentioned as "successful" are the Chinese and the Japanese. The purpose of this chapter is to provide a historical context and to present some of the models that help to explain Chinese interaction with the dominant community.

EARLY YEARS

Although there may have been earlier Chinese contact across the Pacific, the significant immigration came just before the California Gold Rush in 1849. By 1860, there were more than 30,000 Chinese in the United States, with the majority residing in California. Most were single males, drawn from the peasant classes, and one expectation was to make enough money and to return to the homeland in triumph. This sojourner orientation has often been used to explain some of the problems of the group; that is, that they were not real immigrants, but as Kitano and Daniels (1988:20)[1] indicate, this was also a common orientation among many European groups such as the Italians and the Greeks.

There were problems involving the Chinese, but the dominant group framed the issue in racist terms. For example, there were negative attitudes towards the newly arrived race and their culture, which lead to restricted areas of residence and discriminatory legislation. Further, the early experiences of the Chinese were eventually to be played out with later Asian arrivals.

The Chinese were the first Asian immigrants to enter the United States in significant numbers. Most of the early immigrants came from two southern provinces, Fukien and Kwangtung (Purcell, 1965). The push was primarily poor economic conditions; the pull, bettering one's economic position. As Ichioka (1988) says, immigrant history is essentially labor history. At first the Chinese immigrants were well received in California. They were regarded as objects of curiosity, and because they were willing to provide supplementary rather than competing economic services, there was little or no objection to them. In fact, in August 1850, when Chinese participated on two occasions in San Francisco civic ceremonies, their colorful costumes, according to a local chronicler, made a fine and pleasing appearance. This warm reception can be better understood if the fantastic inflation that the gold rush produced in California is taken into account. In San Francisco in 1850 a common laborer received a dollar an hour; on the East Coast he would have received a dollar a day. A loaf of bread, priced at about a nickel elsewhere, cost fifty cents. Laundry rates were astronomical; prices as high as $20 per dozen items have been reported. Some Californians actually sent their dirty clothes to Honolulu and Canton. This inflation was a result of the gold strikes and the extreme shortage of women; those women who were in the labor force worked at more glamorous occupations than domestic service. The Chinese (and later, the Japanese) quickly filled the jobs that were generally regarded as women's work.

But most Chinese, like other forty-niners, eventually made their way into the diggings, and it was in the lawless mining regions that anti-Chinese feeling broke out. By 1852 hostility toward the Chinese was already well de-

[1]Much of the material is drawn from Roger Daniels and Harry Kitano, in *American Racism*, Englewood Cliffs, N.J.: Prentice-Hall, 1970.

veloped and showed that curious mixture of class and race antagonism that was to be one of its hallmarks. One writer reports the following resolution passed by a miners' meeting:

> Be it resolved: That it is the duty of the miners to take the matter into their own hands—to erect such barriers as shall be sufficient to check this Asiatic inundation. That the Capitalists, shipowners and merchants and others who are encouraging or engaged in the importation of these burlesques on humanity would crowd their ships with the long-tailed, horned, and cloven-hoofed inhabitants of the infernal regions (if they could make a profit on it).
>
> Resolved: That no Asiatic or South Sea Islander be permitted to mine in this district either for himself or for others, and that these resolutions shall be a part and parcel of our mining laws (Daniels & Kitano, 1970:36).

Despite such resolutions, the Chinese population of California continued to grow: In 1852 there were perhaps 25,000 in the state; a decade later there were more than 50,000. Almost all were adult males. Among the Chinese migrants, males outnumbered females by at least 15 to 1; among contemporary European immigrants, the figure was about 2.5 to 1. Throughout the period of 1850–1880, Chinese accounted for 10 percent or more of California's population.

Despite virulent opposition, the economic opportunities for Chinese in California were so great that they continued to come for three decades. Hostility was more than verbal. First in the mining districts and then in the cities, Chinese were robbed, beaten, and murdered. These crimes were seldom punished because of the notorious laxity of law enforcement in California at the time. Whatever chance a Chinese might have had to obtain justice vanished because of a ruling that no Chinese could testify against a white person.

An 1849 law had provided that no Black, or mulatto person, or Indian, shall be allowed to give evidence in favor of, or against a white man. Five years later, the chief justice of the California Supreme Court, himself a member of the anti-immigrant Know Nothing, or American Party, ruled that Chinese were included within the prohibition:

> The anomalous spectacle of a distinct people, living in our community, recognizing no laws of this State except through necessity, bringing with them their prejudices and national feuds, in which they indulge in open violation of the law; whose mendacity is proverbial; a race of people whom nature has marked as inferior, and who are incapable of progress or intellectual development beyond a certain point, as their history has shown; differing in language, opinion, color, and physical conformation; between whom and ourselves nature has placed an impassable difference, is now presented and for them is claimed, not only the right to swear away the life of a citizen, but the further privilege of participating with us in administering the affairs of our Government (Daniels & Kitano, 1970:37).

The chief justice was perhaps the first Californian to speculate publicly on the possibility of an Oriental inundation, a fantasy that would later grip the Western imagination under the rubric of the Yellow Peril. By the 1860s anti-Chinese sentiment had developed to the point where it was political suicide for anyone to take their side. The presence of the Chinese promoted all white persons to a superior status. It also blurred differences within the white majority and solidified it to the extent that Jews and Catholics, who were usually scapegoats elsewhere, were more readily accepted in places like San Francisco and Los Angeles. Chinese competition also forced white workers to band together.

The Chinese issue smoldered in California during the late 1850s and early 1860s; at the end of the 1860s it burst into flame. The census of 1870, which probably underestimated their number, showed that a fourth of the state's 50,000 Chinese lived in San Francisco, which had become the undisputed center of anti-Chinese agitation. The situation in San Francisco was exacerbated by the constant influx of new immigrants (some 15,000 had arrived between 1870 and 1871), the continued expulsion of Chinese from the mining districts, and perhaps most crucial, the arrival of 10,000 Chinese laborers after the completion of the Central Pacific Railroad. The increase in Chinese population, together with a severe economic depression, produced an explosive situation throughout the state. In the sleepy village of Los Angeles, for example, some twenty Chinese were killed by gunfire and hanging on October 24, 1871—an outrage that must have involved, in one way or another, most of the adult male inhabitants. But it was in San Francisco in 1870 that the anti-Chinese movement came to a head.

Throughout California the Chinese lived in distinct communities, such as those who were clustered in the twelve-block confines of San Francisco's Chinatown. After the completion of the Central Pacific Railroad, the Chinese, who already dominated the laundry business and had filled most of the positions for domestic servants and menials, began to work in various manufacturing enterprises. In the shoe industry, for example, Chinese shoemakers soon outnumbered Whites by four to one; in the process, wages fell from $25 to $9 per week. In the cigar industry their dominance was even more marked: 91 percent (1,657 workers) of all those employed were Chinese. In the textile industry the figure was 64 percent. In addition, Chinese operated many small retail and service shops.

During the summer of 1870, anti-Chinese mass meetings flourished in San Francisco and other northern California cities, featuring slogans like:

We Want No Slaves or Aristocrats.

The Coolie Labor System Leaves Us No Alternative—Starvation or Disgrace.

Mark the Man Who Would Crush Us to the Level of the Mongolian Slave—We All Vote.

Women's Rights and No More Chinese Chambermaids.

These meetings were addressed by labor leaders and agitators; they passed resolutions demanding an end to Chinese immigration and calling for a battery of discriminatory acts against Asian immigrants.

State and local governments responded quickly to the voice of the people. The state legislature passed a patently unconstitutional act requiring a $500 bond for each Asian immigrant (regulation of immigration is exclusively a federal concern), while the city of San Francisco passed a number of frankly harassing ordinances to drive [the Chinese] to other states. These included special taxes on Chinese laundries; a cubic air ordinance, enforced only in Chinatown, which jailed the tenants rather than the landlords of overcrowded slum dwellings (critics quickly pointed out that the city jail provided much less than the statutory 500 cubic feet per prisoner); and a queue ordinance, which placed a tax on pigtails. All of these invidious acts eventually were declared unconstitutional, thus adding to popular frustration.

By the mid-1870s, the California anti-Chinese agitation attracted a congressional investigating committee, which visited San Francisco in 1876. The testimony against the Chinese was blatantly racist: They lowered wages; they were unassimilable; they were heathens; they were disgusting and tended to debauch those around them. Their defenders emphasized their ability to work and their productivity.

In 1877—a year punctuated by labor violence, riots, and the use of state militia and federal troops throughout the country, during which many conservatives thought that the Paris Commune was being reenacted in America— the anti-Chinese movement found its most volatile leader in Denis Kearney, a San Francisco teamster and a recent immigrant from Ireland. Kearney, a born orator, kept reiterating an almost classic refrain—the Chinese must go—and embellished his tirades with incendiary slogans like "Every Workingman Should Get a Musket." For the despised Chinese capitalists, he suggested "a little judicious hanging," and for San Francisco, where he and his "sandlotters" flourished, he sometimes suggested burning. Like most American demagogues, Kearney's bark was worse than his bite, but he was the spokesman for large groups—probably the majority—of the population who had legitimate grievances in the harsh depression decade of the 1870s.

California's nativist forces, in conjunction with racism in other parts of the country, were able to put into practice overt discriminatory laws. The American labor movement gave its support, but it is clear that political expediency, rather than principle, was responsible for many of the congressional votes. Within the state, the old demand that the Chinese must go quickly lost most of its force. Within a few decades Californians, faced with a new threat of "yellow inundation" from the Japanese, were already remembering the Chinese with a trace of nostalgia that would have shocked both the Kearneyites and their hapless targets.

One other fact about the Chinese experience in the United States should be remembered. In the late 1930s and during World War II, the Chinese became our friends and allies, although the general tone of the friendship was condescending. Their peace-loving nature was emphasized; they had fought valiantly against the "sly, tricky Jap"; they were different from their more aggressive neighbor; and they were honest, hard-working, gentle, and compliant. In many ways, this praise alleviated the everyday humiliation, harassment, and deprivation faced by many Chinese, even with the relatively favorable attitude toward all orientals (except the Japanese) at this time (Daniels & Kitano, 1970).

The Chinese "exclusion era," which had its beginning in 1882, terminated in 1943, during World War II, with the repeal of the Chinese Exclusion Acts. The fact that China was an ally at that time in the war against Japan was probably the most important reason behind the repeal; a token quota of 105 immigrants per year was assigned to China, and permanent resident aliens became eligible for naturalization (Lai, 1980).

The significant postwar immigration began after passage of the 1965 Immigration Act, and by 1990, the census reported that the 1,645,472 Chinese comprised the largest Asian group in the United States. The postwar immigration repopulated the old Chinatowns with a new population seeking housing, goods, and services. Living styles from the diverse areas of embarkation were mixed with the heterogeneous local mixture. Most of the immigrants settled in cities with large Chinatowns, such as San Francisco, Los Angeles, and New York, which were ill equipped to absorb the influx, so that overcrowding remains one of the major unsolved problems.

FAMILY AND KINSHIP PATTERNS

There are no "typical Chinese families," just as it would be difficult to single out one American family and label it as typical. The variations within a culture are as wide as between cultures.

The changes in the structure and style of Chinese family life that the immigrants brought with them developed from acculturation, exposure to newer models, and challenges in the new country. It is the interaction of the power, culture, and visibility of the ethnic community with the American culture that explains the development of the Chinese family style in the United States.

One type of family was described by Hsu (1971). It has a cohesive, extended family structure and stresses duty, obligation, importance of family name, and ancestor worship. Roles are clearly defined, with the father and eldest son having the most dominant. The duty of the woman is to please her husband, his family, and to provide sons. As with most such traditional family units across the world, there are definitions of good and bad children, attempts to arrange suitable marriages, and sacrifice of self for the larger family unit.

Hsu (1971) pointed out some of the advantages of the extended kinship system. The Chinese way gives individuals a greater sense of security and a means of dealing with the world. Unattractive women do not have to become lonely old maids; men with less ability or motivation do not have to strive constantly for an individual identity; old people do not live in fear of being thrown out of the home as their productive years decline, to face their last years in a home for the aged. (There are risks and consequences in any type of family or kinship system, and preferring one over the other is essentially a matter of values.)

Weiss (1977) and Wong (1976) have described the following types of Chinese families in America. They are:

1. The traditional family. The family described by Hsu fits this description—male-dominant, hierarchical in structure, traditional roles of parent and child, values from the old country.

2. The bicultural family. This type of family is usually of the second or third generation, although there may be some first-generation biculturals, depending upon age of arrival in the United States. They are products of the exposure to both cultures; although there may be instances of culture conflict and marginality, the majority have successfully integrated Chinese and American models.

3. The modern family. This family type is described as modern and cosmopolitan, more American than Chinese. They desire full acculturation and they think, speak, and are "American" in every way except for their physical features.

Sung (1967) pointed out several other patterns of marriage and family life. These include the "mutilated family"—a family united in bond, such as marriage, but separated physically. "In other words, the Chinese men in the United States were [often] family men without the presence of family members, which explains why there were four times as many married men as married women in the census of 1930" (Sung, 1967:155). Chinese tradition was certainly one bar to these families getting together; another was the discriminatory features of the Immigration Act of 1924, which made it practically impossible for a married Chinese man to send for his wife and family. The mutilated family was the predominant form of family life among the Chinese in the United States until more liberal legislation was passed after the end of World War II (Sung, 1967:156). After many years of separation (for some as long as thirty years), there was the chance to rejoin their spouses again. These reunions tested the old phrase, "Absence makes the heart grow fonder." The husband and wife were each brought up in a different culture under completely different circumstances. Sung (1967) described a number of marital failures arising from clashing expectations; Rose Hum Lee (1960) cited a divorce rate of 8.5 percent among the Chinese in San Francisco.

There was also another way of marrying. Although many of the Chinese immigrants remained bachelors during most of their lives in the United

States, the liberalization of immigration laws after World War II enabled many to go to Hong Kong in search of wives. The courtship was instantaneous, and complete strangers often found themselves married to each other. In many cases, older men, accustomed to a life of hardship in the United States, married younger, more "modernized" Chinese women. After marriage, they returned to the crowded, dilapidated quarters of the urban Chinatowns on the West Coast, and it is probable that many became seriously disillusioned.

But, as Sung found, "In spite of the stresses and strains borne by both husband and wife in the transition, the Chinese family usually remains intact. Discord and unhappiness are generally turned inward toward the self and are reflected in a higher suicide rate rather than divorce statistics" (1967:161–162). Suicide has been one form of protest for Chinese women caught in unbearable matrimonial situations.

Tong (1971) indicates that most of the studies on Chinese families have focused on the upper classes. His view of the Chinese American heritage is different from those of most traditional writers. Rather than discussing the scholar-official class, which did not immigrate to the United States in any significant numbers, he focused on the powerless peasant and considered him to be a major figure in Chinese immigration. The peasant was dominated by the psychology of survival; he minded his own business and took care of his own problems, expecting to be left alone. The peasant had little power to define culture, to control relationships, or to develop a vigorous individual identity. Rather, his best chance for survival was to be ignored by those who were more powerful. Those were the conditions for most peasants in China, and the similarity of their treatment under California racism shaped a similar adaptation.

Today, family patterns reflect age and class differences. The extended kinship patterns of old China are uncommon. Sung observed that the husband generally occupies a stronger position than the wife in the Chinese-American family. Unless the woman is an aristocrat, highly educated, or quite modern, she will tend to stay in the background.

Huang (1976) discussed both the Chinese ghetto family and the professional family. One type of ghetto family is composed of the hard-working but poorly paid Chinese male and his imported, much younger wife from Hong Kong. The preference in this case seems to be for Chinese-born women, since the American-born woman is felt to be too "modern." Huang found that the professional Chinese male rejects the Chinese American woman in favor of Caucasian partners. One of her respondents joked about awarding a fifty-dollar prize to the first member of his group who married a Chinese American. She offered no information about the marital preferences of the Chinese-American female.

In summary, Wong (1988) indicates that the story of the Chinese family in America is that of change and adaptation. Although there are recent signs of disorganization, including indications of crime and delinquency, the process is one that has been ongoing for the past century and will continue to occur in the future. The safest generalization is that the present day Chinese family is much different from the Chinese families in the past.

SCHOOL EXPERIENCES

Most teachers comment on the delightful qualities of Chinese children. Liu (1950) compared teachers' perceptions of Caucasian and Chinese children and found that teachers remarked on the better behavior, obedience, and self-reliance of Chinese American youngsters. The Chinese—like their Asian counterparts, the Japanese—have done very well in the American educational system and rank as one of the most highly educated minority groups.

Conflict may arise when Chinese youngsters perceive the different styles of their Caucasian peers. They see the informal and casual relationships that Americans have with their parents and are often apt to wonder whether the American model is more desirable. As with most children of immigrant parents, they see their own hard-working but poor parents, their restricted lifestyles, their frugality, and the limited English in the home. The comparison may cause them to be ashamed of their parents, family, and ethnic group.

McGrath (1983), writing for a national news magazine, concluded that the high Asian scholastic achievement is related to the Confucian work ethic. The respect for education coupled with respect for parents results in diligent study habits, few disciplinary problems, high motivation, and high achievement. Asian Americans also stress that education is the only way to achieve upward mobility in an urban, competitive society. The parental push also has its negative aspects. Pressure can lead to mental disturbance, suicide, and the use of drugs. The feeling of letting their parents down can bring about guilt, and the often single-minded dedication to achievement can cause difficulty with non-Asian peer groups.

CHINESE ORGANIZATIONS IN THE UNITED STATES

Hong (1976) writes that the Chinese abroad developed a segmentary system of community organization based on surname, dialect, and ancestral village. Similarities in the three variables formed the basis for important interpersonal and business relationships and was functional in the early days of immigration. However, the segmentary system, which helped to ward off alienation by providing ready access to social and business networks, may be less important for the newer immigration, especially since many of the newcomers are from Taiwan, Hong Kong, and Southeast Asia and do not fit readily into the established organizations.

Organizations such as the Six Companies in San Francisco gained an inordinate amount of power through a variety of means. The restricted opportunities in a racist structure limited the alternatives for most Chinese; the clan

A Chinese celebration in Los Angeles.

and kinship systems ensured a solid membership loyalty. Under these conditions, the Chinese could exploit members of their own group, especially new immigrants with no English or vocational skills, who were highly dependent on ethnic organizations.

New organizations are more apt to reflect the U.S. pattern. Golf clubs and service organizations such as the Chinese Lions Clubs are symptomatic of the influences of acculturation, although their membership is limited to a select group. In spite of these changes, Hsu (1971) feels that the kinship and locality organizations will persist for a very long time; that the American-born Chinese will be slow in initiating or joining cause-oriented organizations, especially of an abstract nature; and finally, in the long run, that newer associations will tend to reflect social and professional interests, although the type, extent, and ethnicity of their membership will be highly dependent on the area of residence and the opportunities available in the dominant culture. Up to now, the Chinese have had no national organization, and their organizations appear to wield little power in the outside community.

RELIGION

Chinese attitudes toward religion reflect the spirit of the culture. Since the Chinese have been nonexpansionist and nondenominational, they have neither sent their missionaries forth to proselytize the world, nor have they been divided by conflicts between sects and denominations. Instead, they have kept a relaxed and polite attitude and have incorporated foreign gods and respected all varieties of supernatural belief. Organized religion, ritualistic attendance, and loyalty to one church have not been the pattern. There are few membership drives, and selective membership, tithing, and the like are not common. Relationships with family and kin tend to have a higher priority than those with gods and temples.

Hsu (1971) feels that roughly one-third of the Chinese in Hawaii are Christian. But their Christianity includes many Chinese ways. For example, except for directly church-sponsored events, very few meetings open or close with a prayer. There is a tendency to reduce rather than to increase the influence of the church.

OTHER PATTERNS IN THE CHINESE COMMUNITY

Friendship patterns in the Chinese community often are secondary to family and kin relationships. Therefore, Chinese individuals are unable to move about as freely as their American counterparts can. They are part of a much larger human network and have less need to go outside it. They do try to bring outsiders into the network; and in this sense, friendships could be labeled "additive," whereas American patterns could be called "replacements."

Several consequences can be deduced from this type of friendship, kinship, and locality network. Helping others within the network is common and includes what could be regarded as intrusion and intervention into family disputes. (Most Americans would be disturbed over this kind of "meddling.") Friendships also tend to be of long duration and are not like the short-lived, "brittle" U.S. kind. Even business relationships, so sacred to the U.S. system, are secondary to the other links; charges of nepotism and reverse discrimination often are hurled at Chinese establishments. Acculturation has changed some Chinese patterns. Many have taken the U.S. business model to heart and give high priority to economic matters but in their social dealings, they may still retain the ethnic network.

PERSONALITY

A study by Sue and Kirk (1972) of Chinese American students at the University of California, Berkeley, tested personality differences of Chinese students and those of other ethnic backgrounds. The test results indicated the following: (1) Chinese students score higher on quantitative sections and lower on verbal sections of ability tests; (2) they are more interested in physical sciences, applied technical fields, and business occupations, and are less interested in social sciences, aesthetic and cultural fields, and verbal and linguistic vocations; (3) they prefer more concrete and tangible approaches to life and are more conforming and less socially extroverted compared to other students.

Sue and Kirk offered several cultural explanations for Chinese American students' lower verbal and higher quantitative scores. First is their bilingual background and insufficient knowledge of English. Second, Chinese American families restrain strong feelings, which inhibits communication. Third, higher quantitative scores could indicate compensatory means of expression. Fourth, quantitative activity emphasizes a "structured, impersonal, and logical approach"—attributes found most desirable to Chinese American students. Finally, early immigrants may have encouraged their children to enter vocations that would maximize economic and social mobility. Vocations in the physical sciences instead of in the social sciences seemed most conducive to this goal, since the latter required skills in written and oral communication and an understanding of Western culture.

Analysis of the family structure further explained the differences in test results. For example, family emphasis on tradition, established rules of behavior, conformity, respect for authority, and submergence of individuality help to explain the discomforts of Chinese American students in new situations and also their tendency to show greater anxiety and less tolerance for ambiguity. Their great emphasis on family loyalty and their distrust of those outside the family contribute to the impression of their lack of concern for the welfare of others. The Chinese tend to "control" behavior through guilt and shame; they worry over the conflict between their culture and the dominant one; and they feel acute discomfort when communicating outside the family. All these factors result in greater emotional distress.

Sue and Kirk warned that these results may be exaggerated because many Chinese Americans are leaving their families and subculture for the first time. To be independent in a new social setting requires a greater degree of adjustment for people who are used to prolonged family dependency and obligation. They concluded that care must be taken in cultural interpretations of traits in terms of values. For example, some Westerners consider being inhibited undesirable because they favor spontaneity. But the Chinese consider the former characteristic to be a sign of self-control and maturity and the latter to be an indication of bad manners. However, Tong (1971) cited a number of limitations in using psychological tests and models on Chinese Americans.

He feels that it is a mistake to judge Chinese Americans by white Anglo-Saxon personality typologies.

CHINATOWNS

The Chinese in the United States represent a compact, urbanized population, with large clusters in Honolulu, San Francisco, Los Angeles, and New York. In these Chinatowns one can hear different languages and music (from atonal Chinese classics to modern rock); taste unusual foods; investigate small shops; choose from a staggering number of restaurants; behold natives, new-comers, old, and young intermingling with the tourists (especially on week-ends); and breathe the odors of barbecued pork, ginger, and soy sauce. Other streets have the quiet, residential air of a typical middle-class community. Yet the temptation to stereotype this diversity is so strong that mention of the word "Chinese" usually elicits images of "opium dens, Tong wars, coolie labor, the yellow peril, highbinders, hatchetmen, laundries, waiters, houseboys, slave wages, unassimilable aliens, and so on" (Sung, 1967:1–2).

These stereotypes survive because of inadequate information. As Sung observed: "From 1909 when Professor Mary Coolidge's book, *Chinese Immi-gration,* was published, to 1960, when Professor Rose Hum Lee's book, *The Chinese in the United States of America,* was imported from Hong Kong, no

A view of New York City's Chinatown, 1946.

serious work about this neglected minority appeared in the United States" (1967:2). The void was filled by Hollywood movies, newspaper articles, and novels that until World War II portrayed the Chinese as variations of Fu Manchu and the Dragon Lady.

Overcrowded Chinatowns are not conducive to good health. The tuberculosis rate among Chinese in San Francisco was 104 per 100,000, compared to 49.6 among the Whites. Tuberculosis is often equated with poverty, poor diet, and unsanitary, overcrowded facilities (Chin, 1965).

Housing for many Chinese is old and poor; crime is on the increase, and employment under sweatshop conditions is not unusual. The Chinese garment shops in San Francisco are notorious for long hours and meager compensation. Upward mobility into supervisorial and administrative positions remains difficult (Chin, 1965).

For a long time Chinatowns, whether in New York, Los Angeles, or San Francisco, were highly dependent on tourism. One consequence was the image of law and order and a safe place to be. But the wave of recent new immigrants has strained the meager resources, so that unemployment, welfare, and other more familiar symptoms of overcrowded ghetto living are becoming visible. There is now a high potential for protest and violence, especially among the younger generations, who are less tolerant of depressed conditions. A high proportion of men can find employment only in Chinese restaurants and an even higher proportion of Chinese women can find work only in the garment industry (Light & Wong, 1975).

Wong (1976) stratified the New York Chinatown into four groups. The leaders are the successful businessmen, generally of the immigrant generation, who have accumulated wealth and are active in family and village associations. The majority of this group is anticommunist and pro-Taiwan, although the establishment of formal relationships between the United States and the People's Republic in 1978 may have an effect. Then there are the more recent immigrants, who consider themselves sophisticated and urbane but who tend to have a lower economic status. The American-born Chinese (Nisei) are often college educated and have professional status. Many from this group do not speak Chinese, and the more successful are apt to move to the suburbs. The fourth group includes illegal aliens, such as sailors who have jumped ship. Therefore, a legitimate question is raised by Chu (1977): "Who speaks for Chinatown?"

As with most immigrant groups, the transfer of power from one generation to another has not been without considerable stress. Because the traditional power elite and the Chinese civic associations have been unwilling to include the younger generations in decision making, many of the younger groups have formed dissident groups independent of the social control of the old community (Lee, 1973).

The new immigrants who are already in their teens face an especially difficult task. Many are trapped in sociocultural conditions that are considered classic in terms of producing problem behavior. They arrive in the country with little knowledge of English and with minimal occupational skills. They face a cultural discontinuity with broken and disorganized families. They live in overcrowded Chinatowns where rates of disease and poor health conditions are high. They face poverty, rejection, discrimination, and unemployment. Their situation is further exacerbated by the relative affluence of those who have achieved professional status but who show little sympathy toward or recognition of the plight of the newcomers. Many feel exploited, both by the larger society and by their own ethnic community. It is no surprise that destructive gang activity and other forms of deviant behavior are occurring in areas like San Francisco's overcrowded Chinatown.

THE CHINESE MODEL

The diversity of the Chinese group is such that a number of models may be necessary to chart their experience. The melting pot is still not taking place; Lyman (1975) found that Chinatowns—whether in the United States, Manila, Bangkok, Calcutta, or Liverpool—have a remarkable similarity. The one common denominator is their resistance to "melting." The Indonesian government questions their loyalty and the Malaysians resent their own poverty and the commercial affluence of the Chinese. In most countries, the Chinese are urged to abandon their exclusiveness and become a part of the community, but a combination of discrimination, institutional racism, and cultural factors appears to reinforce the continued existence of the pluralistic structure.

Lyman (1977) noted that the move to suburbia by the Chinese who have acquired professional status has not melted them into white, middle-class suburbians. Rather, there has been an attempt to constitute a community that may be likened to the suburban Jews in the Chicago area, who also have maintained a sense of community. Rather than assimilation for this highly assimilable group, there has been a continuation of cultural pluralism.

Part of the reason for the continuing pluralistic structure has been the historical occupational and residential segregation that has resulted in effective seclusion from the American mainstream. Very few cross-ethnic or horizontal alliances were established between the Chinese and their non-Chinese counterparts, whether owners, entrepreneurs, or laborers; the Chinese achieved a vertical integration among their own. Antagonism and discrimination reinforced this parallel structure (Hraba, 1979:305).

One possible resolution for the Chinese in the United States is that of bicultural individuals who acculturate to a certain extent. They see the value of learning the American way, especially in the systems of higher education. But they do not wish to assimilate completely because they see the value of retaining much of their ethnic heritage and culture, especially its language and lifestyles. Yet they cannot be completely satisfied in being only "ethnic."

Bicultural adaptation is not totally new, but its being deliberate and voluntary may be. Previously, minorities such as the Chinese were forced into biculturalism through discrimination, living in ethnic ghettos, and a transient's orientation. But now it is legitimate to want to retain one's own culture; the Lau v. Nichols decision in San Francisco supported the teaching and use of the Chinese language in public schools.

The problems of a bicultural adaptation are familiar. Immigrants have always had this problem, but it has somehow been given minor attention as a viable model. One group deems it "schizophrenic," and another deems it "un-American" or "Uncle Tom." Language is one of the more prominent features of bicultural adaptation; it also includes a selective preference for social and cultural relationships from both cultures. However, it may be one of the most appropriate models for a multiethnic society such as that of the United States, although the equality of the cultures and their relative power have to be considered.

The other model that seems appropriate for special groups of Chinese is that of a middleman minority. The Chinese small businessman and trader has had such a role in the Philippines, Malaysia, and in the Mississippi Delta. Loewen (1971) studied the delicate accommodations required of the upwardly mobile Chinese in Mississippi who were playing middlemen between the Whites and Blacks of that region. They avoided group conflict, retained the Chinese culture, but also adopted functional white ways, while still serving as grocers and small businessmen to a predominantly black population.

It would be impossible to pin a simple label on the more than one million Chinese Americans who currently live in the United States. The term "model minority" may fit some; others may prefer to be viewed as simply another immigrant group, while others have acculturated to such an extent that they no longer have an ethnic identity. Many remain proud of their ancestral roots and some retain a strong tie with the mother country. Continued immigration contributes to the diversity. Many of the new immigrants settle in areas such as Monterey Park, a suburb of Los Angeles and the proliferation of Chinese restaurants makes it a paradise for those who "love" Chinese food.

But it should be emphasized that although the Chinese are overrepresented in many areas of achievement in U.S. life, they are also overrepresented among the poor in U.S. society. Racial barriers based on visibility remain as barriers to full and equal participation in American society. There remains a Chinese lens, especially for the newcomers, but the lens may include one from Hong Kong, or Southeast Asia, Taiwan, or parts of the mainland. Living in the various Chinatowns provides a source of comfort, identity, and satisfaction, and the popularity of novels written by Chinese Americans—such as the *Joy Luck Club* and *The Woman Warrior*—reinforces a "Chinese" perception of the world.

REFERENCES

ASSOCIATED PRESS (1995). U.S. Asians earning less than whites. *Los Angeles Times*, December 9, p. D2.

CHIN, J. W. (1965). Problems of assimilation and cultural pluralism among Chinese Americans in San Francisco: An exploratory study. Unpublished master's thesis, University of the Pacific.

CHU, E. (1977). The two faces of Chinatown. *The Journal of Philanthropy, 18* (2), 18–26.

COOLIDGE, M. R. (1909). *Chinese immigration.* New York: Henry Holt.

DANIELS, R., & KITANO, H. H. L. (1970). *American racism: Exploration of the nature of prejudice.* Englewood Cliffs, N.J.: Prentice-Hall.

HONG, L. K. (1976). Recent immigrants in the Chinese-American Community; issues of adaptation and impacts. *International Migration Review, X* (4), 509–514.

HRABA, J. (1979). *American ethnicity.* Itasca, Ill.: F. E. Peacock.

HSU, F. L. K. (1971). *The challenge of the American dream: The Chinese in the United States.* Belmont, Calif.: Wadsworth.

HUANG, L. J. (1976). The Chinese American family. In C. Mendel & R. Haberstein (Eds.), *Ethnic families in America,* (pp. 124–145). New York: Elsevier.

ICHIOKA, Y. (1988). *The Issei.* New York: The Free Press.

KITANO, H. H. L., & DANIELS, R. (1988). *Asian Americans.* Englewood Cliffs, N.J.: Prentice-Hall.

LAI, H. M. (1980). Chinese. In S. Thernstrom, A. Orlov, & O. Handlin (Eds.), *Harvard Encyclopedia of American ethnic groups* (pp. 217–234). Cambridge, Mass.: Harvard University Press.

LEE, R. H. (1960). *The Chinese in the United States of America.* Hong Kong: Hong Kong University Press.

LEE, R. (1973). Patterns of community power: Tradition and social change in American Chinatowns. In D. E. Gelfaud & R. L. (Eds.), *Ethnic conflicts and power: A cross national perspective.* New York: John Wiley.

LIGHT, I. & WONG, C. (1975). Protest or work: Dilemmas of the tourist industry in American Chinatowns. *American Journal of Sociology, 80* (6), 134–168.

LIU, C. H. (1950). The influence of the cultural background on the moral judgement of children. Unpublished doctoral dissertation, Columbia University.

LOEWEN, J. (1971). *The Mississippi Chinese between Black and White.* Cambridge, Mass.: Harvard University Press.

LYMAN, S. (1975). Contrasts in the Community Organization of Chinese and Japanese in America. In N. Yetman & C. H. Steele (Eds.), *Majority and minority* (2nd ed.) (pp. 285–296). Boston: Allyn & Bacon.

LYMAN, S. M. (1977). *The Asian in North America.* Santa Barbara, Calif.: Clio Press.

MCGRATH, E. (1983). Confucian work ethic. *Time,* March 28, p. 52.

PURCELL, V. (1965). *The Chinese in Southeast Asia* (2nd ed.)(p. 2). London: Oxford University Press.

SEO, D. (1995). In school, a minority no longer. *Los Angeles Times*, December, p. A1.

SUE, D. & KIRK, B. (1972). Psychological characteristics of Chinese American college students. *Journal of Counseling Psychology, 19*, 471–478.

SUNG, B. L. (1967). *Mountain of gold.* New York: Macmillan.

TONG, B. (1971). The ghetto of the mind: Notes on the historical psychology of Chinese America. *Amerasia Journal, 1* (3), 1–31.

WEISS, M. (1977). The research experience in a Chinese American community, *Journal of Social Issues, 33* (4), 120–132.

WONG, B. (1976). Social stratification, adaptive strategies and the Chinese community of New York. *Urban Life, 5* (1), 33–52.

WONG, M. G. (1988). The Chinese American Family. In C. Mendel, R. Haberstein, & R. Wright, Jr. (Eds.), *Ethnic Families in America* (pp. 230–257). New York: Elsevier.

Chapter 14

Japanese Americans

The Japanese American experience in the United States is unique in that, as a group, they were herded into concentration camps during World War II, and then in 1988, they received a presidential apology and a sum of $20,000 for survivors of that experience.

Kitano (1969) indicates that the outlook for the group at the end of World War II was dismal—they had lost their possessions, faced a hostile public, and most important, had lost faith in the American system. So if Urashima Taro, the Japanese Rip Van Winkle, had gone away in 1945, he would, upon his awakening in the 1990s, expect to find a poor, powerless, "problem" minority. Some, who were forced to return to the land of their ancestors, would be expected to be eking out a living in a defeated, prostrate nation.

Imagine his surprise—Japanese Americans as one of the more "successful" minorities and the Japanese nation as one of the most powerful economies. And in 1995, two Japanese, one in the United States and the other from Japan, came to prominence. Judge Lance Ito presided at the O. J. Simpson trial and achieved celebrity status, while Hideo Nomo from Japan became "rookie of the year" while pitching for the Los Angeles Dodgers.

HISTORICAL BACKGROUND

Although there were a number of early contacts between Japan and the United States, significant immigration began in the latter quarter of the 19th century. The early migration was to the then kingdom of Hawaii where the

Japanese entered into the plantation economy as contract laborers. Migration to the mainland, especially to California, occurred in the 1890s, so that in 1900, the census identified almost 25,000 Japanese on the West Coast. By 1920 there were more than 110,000.

There were a number of similarities between the Chinese and the Japanese immigrants. In common, they came as single males, and employment was at physically difficult, low-prestige, and low-paying jobs. Both suffered incredible hardships and were victims of prejudice, discrimination, and racism (Takaki, 1989; Kitano & Daniels, 1995). The majority came from the working classes; most Americans could not tell them apart, and they were denied entrance into the mainstream because of their race.

There were also a number of important differences. The Japanese came from a nation that was moving towards modernization and an industrial economy, and many of the immigrants had been exposed to compulsory education. The Japanese nation had been victorious in the Russo-Japanese War, and as Gulick (1914) indicates, it was the first time that a "white" nation had been defeated by a nonwhite nation in modern history. China, at this early juncture, was a nation that was weak and growing weaker, so that while the Japanese had the backing of a growing international power, the Chinese were more dependent on local resources.

The Japanese sent for brides so that family life in America began relatively early, while some Chinese left their wives in China, or remained as bachelors, primarily as a result of the Chinese Exclusion Act of 1882 that closed the door to Chinese immigrants. Although both groups went into agriculture, the Chinese did not establish long-lasting farming communities in rural California, while the Japanese did (Lyman, 1986; Chan, 1991).

The birth of American-born children—the Nisei—also meant that the Japanese were faced with issues concerning acculturation and a permanent place in the larger community, whereas this stage was delayed among the first Chinese immigrants because they had so few children. Each of these factors is important in explaining some of the patterns of differential adaptation, and only under the incredible stereotyping of racism do the Chinese and the Japanese appear identical. As with all ethnic groups, the individual differences within the group are so wide that any generalizations have to be carefully limited.

The concept of generations is useful when exploring the background of the Japanese. There are terms used by the group which reflect the generations: *Issei,* or the first-generation immigrant, born in Japan; *Nisei,* the American-born second-generation children of the Issei; and the *Sansei,* or third-generation children of the Nisei. Generational terms for subsequent generations are available (that is, *Yonsei* for the fourth, *Gosei* for the fifth), but have begun to lose their relevance. An overall term, *Nikkei,* is currently used to identify the total group.

The Issei

The first-generation immigrants, known as the *Issei,* were relatively homogeneous: Most were young and had had four to six years of schooling; most were male; and most had come from rural Japan. The Issei came primarily from southern Japan, particularly the prefectures of Hiroshima, Fukuoka, Kumamoto, Wakayama, and Yamaguchi. The bulk of their immigration took place between 1870 and 1924, after which time the United States immigration laws prohibited the permanent immigration of any Japanese nationals (as well as of all Asians). Not even a token quota was assigned to them.

The immigrants found employment as agricultural laborers, in small business, or as service workers, often working with or for other Japanese; they also established small shops of their own. Japanese tend to be interdependent, and segregated housing patterns served to reinforce the existing ethnic network.

Some Issei returned to Japan in those early days, considering themselves "successful" and hoping to lead a more leisurely life in the home country; others returned as "failures." Those who remained in the United States sent to Japan for women in order to marry and raise children. This practice made their communities in the United States more permanent. Men and women were brought together through an exchange of photos, and many young women were called "picture brides."

The Issei brought with them the behavioral orientations of Meiji Japan (1867–1912), although it was probably a tentative, day-by-day reaction rather than a codified set of values to be rigidly memorized. It also should be emphasized that the Issei came from a vertically stratified society, and behaviors were closely linked to rank, status, and position. Very few of the immigrants came from the upper class. Conversely, because of a degree of selectivity by the Japanese immigration officials, the Issei also were not from the bottom of the class structure.

There was an emphasis on deference, especially to those perceived to be in positions of power and authority; on duty and obligation; and on the importance of the family, the community, and larger groups over the individual. Connor (1977) reported that according to a recent survey, most surviving Issei still retain these orientations, although they also had acquired certain American orientations, such as individualism and self-reliance. Connor's sample included three generations of Japanese Americans and a Caucasian sample drawn from Sacramento, California.

The Issei lived their lives segregated from the U.S. mainstream, and their major interactions revolved around their families and their community. Most of them acquired just enough knowledge about the United States in order to function but left the major task of acculturation and a more secure existence to their American-born children.

The Nisei

The majority of the Nisei were born between 1910 and 1940; by the 1990s, most were well into senior citizen status. Although they were influenced by their parents, they became more acculturated to United States than the Issei did. Discrimination and prejudice caused many Nisei to lower their expectations and lifestyles in order to make a living in the United States. One writer called them the "quiet generation" (Hosokawa, 1969), and although there was a minor furor in the ethnic community over the title, it is a reasonable description.

Life was particularly difficult for this group in the 1920s and 1930s because of discrimination, prejudice, and segregation, especially since the majority of Nisei identified with the country and wished to be treated as U.S. citizens. The plight of the Nisei was such that in 1929, the Carnegie Corporation financed a study at Stanford University that was eventually reported by Strong (1934) under the title *The Second Generation Japanese Problem*. Interviews with the Nisei indicated doubts about their employment, concern over their low status in U.S. society, ambivalence about possibly seeking a future in Japan, and overall insecurity and anxiety about their future in the United States. The objective findings of the study indicated that the Nisei were as bright as the Caucasian as measured by IQ tests; their rates of crime and delinquency were very low; and their school achievement was high. Strong's conclusion was that racial prejudice lay at the root of the "Nisei problem."

In common with the history of immigrant groups, the Nisei moved away from the Issei world towards more U.S. models. It was not always a smooth transition; there was "culture conflict," and the specter of nonacceptance into the mainstream, no matter how "Americanized" they were, remained an ongoing reality.

The Sansei and Other Groups

Some Sansei were born in the wartime evacuation centers of World War II; others were born after the war. By the last decade of the twentieth century, most were in their adult years and were sending their children to high schools and colleges. The differences within this generation and their children are perhaps the greatest and reflect the ongoing changes in the U.S. society. Most have benefitted from the Civil Rights struggles and the increased opportunities for people of color so that their occupational and social mobility surpasses those of the previous generations. Yet, there are those who retain some of the values and lifestyles of their conservative Nisei parents, while others have taken on more radical and militant postures.

Each American-born generation has moved further away from the traditional ancestral culture, although their distinctly Asian features have limited their total acceptance into the mainstream.

Differences among Sansei are especially noticeable according to area of settlement; the Midwesterner and the Easterner are more likely to reflect the orientations of those areas, rather than a Japanese community norm. The one

Sansei student attending a high school in Michigan or New Jersey will have very little in common with the Sansei attending McKinley High School in Honolulu, where there is a high proportion of Japanese Americans, except that of physical likeness.

There are other Japanese groups that can be identified; each important in that they reflect a certain way of looking at the world, although there are obviously variations within each cluster. The *Kibei,* born in the United States to Issei parents, were sent to Japan for much of their upbringing and were exposed to the militaristic values of that culture in the 1930s; the Japanese businessmen (*Kaisha*) have temporary tours of duty and have minimal contact with the Japanese Americans and new immigrants who are the new Issei. By 1960, there were also an estimated 25,000 Japanese war brides, an unknown number of student visas, and the ever-present, camera-toting, ubiquitous Japanese tourist. It is only through stereotyped lenses that this diversity is perceived as being the same.

OUTMARRIAGE

One of the most visible changes among Japanese Americans is that of marrying out of the ethnic group. Table 14–1 shows the steady rise, from below 5 percent in the 1920s to over 60 percent in the 1970s, then down to over 50 percent in 1984 (Kitano & Daniels, 1995:180). The drop in percentage for 1984 is somewhat deceiving since there was an actual increase in the number of outmarriages. *Outmarriage* refers to a Japanese individual choosing a non-Japanese mate; *interracial marriage* refers to a Japanese individual choosing a non-Asian mate.

The generational variable is important in explaining the rise in outmarriage rates in Los Angeles County, although other factors—such as the changing role of the family and community, and the lowering of social, legal, and economic barriers of the dominant community—can also be hypothesized (Kitano, H., Fujino, D., and Takahashi, J., forthcoming).

The move toward marital assimilation and the melting pot is occurring at the same time that there is a call for strong ethnic identification and pluralistic models. It may presage an interesting pattern of multiple Japanese American marital choices, which is perhaps a healthier state since it indicates that there are choices and options, and that the dominant community is no longer as discriminatory as it once used to be.

THE WARTIME EVACUATION

Japanese Americans came into negative prominence during World War II. Their evacuation to detention camps has been variously termed as America's "greatest wartime mistake" and "America's day of infamy." It is the main sub-

Table 14–1   Outmarriage Rates of Chinese, Filipino, Japanese, Korean, and Vietnamese, Total and By Gender for 1975, 1977, 1979, 1984, and 1989, Los Angeles County

Ethnicity	Year	Marriages	Outmarriages		Percent of Outmarriage by Gender	
			Number	Percent	Women	Men
Chinese	1989	1,836	622	33.9	63.0	37.0
	1984	1,881	564	30.0	56.6	43.4
	1979	716	295	41.2	56.3	43.7
	1977	650	323	49.7	56.3	43.7
	1975	596	250	44.0	62.2	37.8
Filipino[a]	1989	1,384	565	40.8	74.2	25.8
Japanese	1989	1,134	588	51.9	58.3	41.7
	1984	1,404	719	51.2	60.2	39.8
	1979	764	463	60.6	52.7	47.3
	1977	756	477	63.1	60.6	39.4
	1975	664	364	54.8	53.6	46.4
Korean	1989	1,372	151	11.0	74.8	25.2
	1984	543	47	8.7	78.6	21.4
	1979	334	92	27.6	79.6	20.4
	1977	232	79	34.1	73.4	26.6
	1975	250	65	26.0	63.1	36.9
Vietnamese[b]	1989	555	147	26.5	54.4	45.6
	1984	560	34	6.0	74.7	25.3

[a]Data for the Filipinos is limited to 1989.
[b]Data for the Vietnamese is limited to 1984 and 1989.

Source: Los Angeles County Marriage License Bureau.

ject of books by Daniels (1971), Girdner and Loftis (1969), Myer (1971), Bosworth (1967), Fisher (1965), Spicer and others (Spicer, Hansen, Luomala, & Opler, 1969), Weglyn (1976), and Zeller (1969). Earlier books are by Eaton (1952), Grodzins (1949), Leighton (1945), Okubo (1946), Thomas, Kikuchi, and Sakoda (1952), Thomas and Nishimoto (1946), and Tenbroek and others (Tenbroek, Barnhart, & Matson, 1954). Many government documents and articles and most books on Japanese Americans discuss the subject. More recent writers on the subject have had the advantage of perusing documents available under the Freedom of Information Act (Irons, 1983) and of hearing testimony under a congressional committee (Commission on Wartime Relocation and Internment of Civilians, 1982). Their findings will be discussed later in the chapter.

However, the evacuation has remained relatively obscure to most Americans; practically every non-Japanese the author has ever met has been ignorant of this event, but sympathetic when told about it. "If we only knew," is the usual reply, with its brave but futile implication that things would have been different. But empirical evidence from the wartime years does not present a reassuring picture. For example, Bloom and Reimer (1945) surveyed various student campuses in 1943; 63 percent of those interviewed on the West Coast and 73 percent in the Midwest felt that the handling of the Japanese during this period was correct. Another survey in conjunction with the Japanese American Research Project at UCLA in 1969 (approximately twenty-five years after the evacuation) indicated that over 48 percent of California respondents surveyed felt that the evacuation was justified.

The 1983 recommendation by the Commission on Wartime Relocation and Internment of Civilians for compensation of $20,000 to those who were evacuated has reawakened the anti-Japanese hostility of certain groups and individuals. For example, the author appeared on several radio talk shows in 1983, and although there were several sympathetic phone calls regarding the evacuation and financial redress, there were also some angry, vituperative calls that left little question that anti-Japanese attitudes have not disappeared. But there were also voices of reason. A syndicated columnist titled an article, "Apology Now Due in Full for the Blot of Internment" (Yoder, 1988), and the United States Congress approved a conference report in 1989 making redress an entitlement program. With the signature of President Reagan in 1988, the estimated 60,000 survivors (which has risen to the 80,000 level) of the World War II camps received $20,000 starting in 1990.[1]

Interest in the internment as a topic for research has continued. A conference held in Utah, the site of one of the wartime centers, led to the publication of a volume titled *Japanese Americans: From Relocation to Redress* (Daniels, Taylor, & Kitano, 1986). Another publication focused on the role of selected Japanese American evacuees who were employed as research assistants, and of Dorothy Thomas, who served as the research director of the Japanese American Evacuation and Resettlement Study (Ichioka, 1989).

The payment of redress and a public apology marked the close of one phase of the evacuation, although it would be wise to keep this incident in the minds of the public so that such an event will not happen again.

---

[1]Harry Kitano, Mitchell Maki, and Megan Berthold are working on a book titled *The Impossible Dream: Japanese Americans and Redress* for the University of Illinois Press. Scheduled publication will be in late 1996.

Prejudice, Discrimination, and Segregation

The necessary conditions for placing groups behind barbed wire (or for more severe actions, such as extermination and genocide) are shaped by prior circumstances, especially by prejudice, discrimination, and segregation (Daniels & Kitano, 1970). Prejudice, usually maintained by stereotyping, leads to the avoidance of a group; discrimination and segregation, maintained by laws, customs, and norms, foster disadvantage and isolation. For a group so cut off, stereotypes become the operating reality, since there is no way of effectively correcting the biased information. If certain incidents crystallize the already negative sentiments, more permanent solutions (concentration camps, exile, isolation, and extermination) may be instituted.

For example, before 1954 the Issei could not become United States citizens; therefore, certain basic civil rights had never been a part of their expectations. They were the targets of stereotyping and legal harassment. Issei could neither vote nor own land; nuisance laws prevented them from employing white women, and the price of their California state fishing licenses was set deliberately high. Antimiscegenation laws discouraged the Issei from believing that they were equal to white people. Stereotyped as less than human and placed at the competitive disadvantage by laws and customs, they were limited in their opportunities for any kind of equal-status contact.

The Nisei had been segregated into Little Tokyos and Osakas, usually in the older and less desirable areas of the cities. These Japanese communities were able to maintain effective social control over their members, and there were none of the usual signs of social disorganization, such as high rates of crime and delinquency.

But segregated ethnic groups lack any equal-access contact and are subject to ethnic stereotypes by the dominant group. The problem is not solely with dominant-group perceptions; other minorities may see the stereotypes as the reality, and even members of the target groups may turn on each other—those with the "desired" qualities (who are more acculturated) may reject their peers. As a consequence, target minorities often find themselves stereotyped, isolated, avoided, and fighting among themselves.

The Japanese in the United States at the time of Pearl Harbor were victims of all of the boundary-maintenance mechanisms; the Filipinos, Chinese, and Koreans had turned against them; most of the majority group thought in terms of the stereotype of the "sly, sneaky, tricky Jap"; and politicians and journalists played upon popular anti-Japanese sentiments. The group itself was divided by generation (Issei, Nisei, Kibei) and by U.S. and Japanese loyalties.

The "Trigger" and Its Effects

Action against the Japanese was triggered by the attack on Pearl Harbor. But plans for the "final solution" were never clear. The momentum was established by a series of actions. The cumulative effect of many decisions, past

Reaction to the internment of Japanese Americans.

feelings and actions of prejudice, discrimination, segregation, panic, racism, and the wartime atmosphere all combined to shape the eventual decision to evacuate and incarcerate the entire Japanese population along the West Coast, whether citizen or alien.

Immediately after Pearl Harbor—December 7, 1941—the FBI rounded up selected enemy aliens, including 2,192 Japanese. Even this roundup, which was logical enough at the time, had its ludicrous moments. Among those arrested were individuals who had contributed money to Japan, who had achieved some degree of prominence, or who belonged to certain organizations. The end result was that many who could have exerted leadership in these trying times were removed.

The Pressure Grows

The incarceration of only selected aliens did not satisfy the Hearst press. The cry "Japs Must Go" was echoed by syndicated Hearst columnist Henry McLemore when he wrote on January 29, 1942:

> I am for the immediate removal of every Japanese on the West Coast to a point deep in the interior . . . let 'em be pinched, hurt, and hungry. Personally, I hate Japanese. And that goes for all of them. (Kitano, 1976:70)

Those advocating the removal of the Japanese included individuals such as then California Attorney General Earl Warren, "liberal" columnist Walter Lippmann, and civil-rights fighter Carey McWilliams; the usual patriotic and right-wing organizations; farm and labor groups; the press; local and national

magazines and newspapers. Most organizations usually alert to cases of blatant discrimination remained silent.

In chronological sequence, the following events occurred: On January 29,
1942, United States Attorney General Francis Biddle established security
areas along the Pacific Coast from which all enemy aliens were to be removed.
On February 19, 1942, President Franklin D. Roosevelt signed Executive
Order 9066, which designated restricted military areas and authorized the
building of "relocation camps." The ten camps were scattered over California,
Arizona, Idaho, Wyoming, Colorado, Utah, and Arkansas.

In March 1942 the evacuation of persons of Japanese ancestry, defined
as anyone with as little as one-eighth Japanese blood, began. By November
more than 110,000 West-Coast Japanese, most of them American citizens,
were behind barbed wire. The rapid, smooth, and efficient evacuation was
aided by the cooperation of the Japanese people themselves. They responded
to posted notices to register, voluntarily assembled at designated points, and
marched off to the trains and buses sent to haul them to the camps.

Beneath this accommodating facade lay the disruption of years of effort.
Homes and possessions were abandoned; personal treasures were sold for a
fraction of their value or were stolen; farms and gardens were ruined; families
disintegrated. Few of the Japanese seemed to expect fair play or justice. The
evacuation was justified "for the good of the Japanese themselves." (It is this
kind of thinking that encouraged the United States to bomb villages and ham-
lets in Southeast Asia "for the good of the inhabitants.")

Although there were riots (Kitano, 1976:34), draft-dodging (Daniels,
1971), and other acts of resistance, most Japanese accepted it, or were resigned to it (*shikataganai*). Four cases eventually wound their way to the
Supreme Court. The cases, each from individual Japanese Americans with
different backgrounds and with different motivations, were Endo,
Hirabayashi, Korematsu, and Yasui (Irons, 1983).

In all of its phases, the forced evacuation and incarceration of the Japanese, whether citizens or aliens, was legally sanctioned. The evacuation ended
in 1944 as it started, on a legal note, when the Supreme Court ruling on the
Endo case revoked the West Coast exclusion orders. Effective January 2,
1945, the Japanese were no longer under forcible detention.

Although there were problems in getting some Japanese to leave, by
June 1946 the concentration camps were closed. Some incidents of vandalism
and terrorism against the Japanese occurred when they returned to their
homes on the West Coast, but these soon ended. Some Japanese moved to the
Midwest and to the East Coast, but many returned to California, and by 1980
the majority were again on the West Coast.

Racism

The most reasonable conclusion is that racism was the primary factor in the
removal of the Japanese. The definition of who was Japanese was based on

"blood," and the presumption of guilt by ancestry condemned an entire race to incarceration. As Daniels and Kitano (1970) pointed out, the actions of the Germans were attributed to evil and sick *individuals,* but the actions of the Japanese were attributed to an evil *race.*

If the Japanese were a menace to the West Coast, then they should have been even more of a menace to Hawaii. But there was no mass jailing of Japanese on the much more vulnerable islands, and this fact supports the belief that West-Coast racism was primarily responsible for the concentration camps. Although Hawaii was not free of racial prejudice and discrimination, it was a racial paradise compared to California. Further, the Japanese were vital to Hawaii's economy (resource power); there were many more Japanese in Hawaii (numerical power); and the commander of the area was a much more enlightened man than his counterpart on the West Coast.

Daniels (1971) points out that when the decision to move the Japanese into the interior was planned, the Army called a special meeting of governors of western states in Salt Lake City on April 7, 1942. Milton Eisenhower was asked to present information to the select group, and one of the basic questions was what would happen to the "Japs" after the war. The United States administration wanted to handle the evacuees with some degree of restraint, including ideas of homesteading and the like, but the hostility of the western governors soon quelled any liberal approach. Cries that no state should be a "dumping ground for California's problems" were typical, and there was almost no alternative but to build settlements on the model of concentration camps with barbed-wire fences and armed guards. The paranoia and fear caused by the Japanese stereotype was powerful indeed.

A government that could herd a race of people into concentration camps could probably also exterminate them. For example, if the Japanese had invaded Hawaii and were threatening the West Coast, passions might have run even higher. Or if the Japanese had actually been dropping bombs on United States' cities, the administration might have used the ultimate retaliation against the Japanese Americans behind barbed wire. The extermination of a group, of course, does not necessarily mean only overt violence. Inadequate diets, the separation of sexes, and sterilization all were mentioned as "solutions" for the Japanese at one time by members of the United States Congress.

The important point is that the momentum acquired through prejudice, stereotyping, discrimination, segregation, and the neutralization of the human qualities of the target group ("tricky, sneaky yellow dogs") sets the stage for more dramatic solutions. Other processes then take over. Organizational roles ("I was just doing my duty") can assume such high priority that placing innocent people behind barbed wire is simple.

Colonel Bendetsen, who was in charge of putting the Japanese into the camps, received high commendation for the effectiveness of his operation. There is little question that if orders were given for more drastic solutions, they would have been dispatched with the efficiency and speed of a people proud of their organizational ability and their reputation for following through on "orders."

THE WORLD WAR II SOLDIER

The exploits of Japanese American soldiers during World War II were remarkable, especially taking into account the fact that many of the volunteers came from the concentration camps, so their families were behind barbed wire while they were fighting for the "cause of freedom." Their actions undoubtedly influenced U.S. public opinion toward a more favorable view of the group. The 442nd Combat Team and the 100th Battalion, composed mainly of Nisei (under Caucasian officers) suffered more than 9,000 casualties, had more than 600 killed in action, and became known as the most decorated unit in U.S. military history. Japanese Americans also played a key role in the Pacific, especially in interpreting, translating, and intercepting Japanese codes.

Recent publications have shed more light on the people, the organizations, and the issues involved in the evacuation. A congressional committee—the Commission on Wartime Relocation and Internment of Civilians—was established by an act of Congress in 1980 to review the facts and circumstances of Executive Order 9066, which had evacuated the Japanese from the West Coast. The Commission was also to assess the impact of the evacuation on the Japanese Americans, to review the directives of the military forces pertaining to the relocation, and to recommend appropriate remedies.

The conclusions of the Commission were reported in 1982 and included the following: that Executive Order 9066 was not justified by military necessity, and that the decisions that followed—detention, ending detention, and exclusion—were not required by military necessity. The broad historical causes that shaped the decision to evacuate were race prejudice, war hysteria, and failure of political leadership. Widespread ignorance was another factor, as well as fear and anger at Japan. The Committee reported that "a grave injustice was done to American citizens and resident aliens of Japanese ancestry who, without individual review or any probative evidence against them, were excluded, removed, and detained by the United States during World War II" (Commission on Wartime Relocation, 1982:18).

The Commission also reported that some of the individuals who carried out the exclusion and detention regretted their actions in their memoirs or other statements after the war. Secretary of the Army Henry L. Stimson recognized that the forced evacuation was a personal injustice to loyal citizens, and Attorney General Francis Biddle reiterated that "the program was ill-advised, unnecessary and unnecessarily cruel." Supreme Court Justice William O. Douglas, who joined the majority opinion in the Korematsu case, said that the evacuation was ever on his conscience. Chief Justice Earl Warren, who had urged the evacuation as Attorney General of California, "deeply regretted the removal order and my own testimony advocating it," while Justice Tom C. Clark, who had been liaison between the Justice Department and the West Defense Department, concluded that the evacuation was a big mistake (Committee on Wartime Relocation, 1982:18).

But several individuals who wielded considerable power and influence over the Japanese Americans during this period have defended their actions. John J. McCloy, then Assistant Secretary of War, had primary responsibility for handling the "Japanese-American question." According to Justice Department records, it was McCloy who removed the "contrariety of evidence" in the government's brief to the Supreme Court that would have alerted that body to evidence that ran counter to the Army report of General DeWitt concerning espionage activities among the Japanese. The FBI investigations concluded that there were no such espionage activities implicating the Japanese, but this report was not included. McCloy, who was perhaps the most powerful hardliner for the internment, continued to be unbending in defending his actions and evidently felt no sense of conflict between conscience and sense of duty (Irons, 1983). He defended his action to his dying day.

Colonel Karl Bendetsen, who also defended his role in the evacuation, was the engineer behind the internment and was the director of the staff of the Civil Affairs Division which produced the "Final Report: Japanese Evacuation From The West Coast, 1942" signed by General John DeWitt. It was Bendetsen who approved the Final Report, which, among other generalizations, said that the Japanese constituted "a relatively homogeneous, unassimilated element bearing a close relationship through ties of race, religion, language, custom and indoctrination to the enemy" (Irons, 1983:216).

Irons also discovered that in the four cases brought before the Supreme Court, the government's own lawyers charged that their superiors had suppressed evidence, and that the key military report under General DeWitt's name contained intentional falsehoods. There were also files that disclosed "the alteration and destruction by War Department officials of crucial evidence in these cases. Rather than expose to the Court the contradictions between this evidence and claims made by Justice Department lawyers, military officials literally consigned the offending documents to the bonfire" (Irons, 1983:ix).

Irons concludes that the scandal of the evacuation goes beyond the indictment of individuals. He takes to task the role of government lawyers, various levels of the judicial system, the Army, and those officials whose loyalties to President Roosevelt included acquiescence on major decisions. The American Civil Liberties Union also shared in the blame for the outcome of the Japanese American cases; their loyalty to FDR barred constitutional challenges in subsequent appeals. Also responsible were "old-boy ties" among high governmental officials; racism and ignorance at all levels of government; political realities (namely that the decisions to release the Japanese from the camps came in 1945, after the November 1944 re-election of the President); and the role of the media.

Many of the issues raised by the evacuation are timeless and universal: the role of the government in controlling and manipulating information; the doctrine of military necessity to justify actions; the influence and power of a charismatic leader to elevate loyalty, partisanship, and duty over conscience and constitutional safeguards; the insulation, ignorance, racism, and influence of old-boy networks in decision making; and the priority of such political concerns as re-election. Then there is the vulnerability of an "unpopular minority"—easy to target, easy to scapegoat, and easy to blame. And for the Japanese American during World War II, one of the most powerful safeguards against the unrestrained actions of government, the free press, was of little assistance, since the newspapers were often at the head of the lynch mob.

THE PRESENT

By the 1990s the original Issei population had almost disappeared; the Nisei were either in retirement or thinking about it, so that the main emphasis was on the Sansei and newer generations. In terms of norms, values, and behaviors, the younger generations have gone through a thoroughly American experience so that it would be difficult to distinguish them from their mainstream peers. However, the fact that they still retain the features of their racial group raises questions concerning visibility, ethnic identity, and participation in the mainstream.

Visibility

The Japanese are a physically visible population, although their Asian features are similar to those of the Chinese and the Koreans, at least to the white majority. Their lifestyles are less visible. They live quiet lives, and their dress and consumption patterns do not stand out. Like their Asian neighbors, they do not quite fit into the black or white categories. In South Africa they may be classified for business purposes as "white," but not on a social level; in the South during World War II they were considered White. Obviously, color classification of the Japanese is not an absolute. However, their distinctive oriental features, including their smaller, slanted eyes, their shorter physical stature and straight black hair, make them easily identifiable ethnics.

One of the techniques adopted by many Japanese was to become less visible. The lifestyles of most Japanese did not reflect their social class; they consistently lived below the average non-Japanese individual of a similar class position. Actions that might bring attention to themselves, especially of a negative nature, were discouraged. Loud talking, loud clothes, big cars, and fancy houses were thought to present a negative image and so were generally discouraged as popular models. To be quiet, to conform, to be modest, and to refrain from actions of a deviant nature were strong role prescriptions. This is still true of many Japanese Americans today, although many Sansei of our acquaintance are beginning to react against the conservative style of their parents. They want the most expensive things from the most prestigious stores; they dress to draw attention; and they constantly clash with their parents over consumption patterns.

Visibility in terms of wearing clean and conservative clothes, getting good grades, and belonging to "good" organizations (YMCA, Scouts) was strongly encouraged. Some attempted to "pass" by having eye operations and adopting Anglo names (common compromise regarding names is to combine a very Anglicized first name with an ethnic surname and sometimes an ethnic middle name), but the proportion has been extremely low. Perhaps the model choice for handling the problem of visibility has been *psychological passing*— identifying and acquiring the American culture at such a rapid rate that the Japanese have been termed America's "model minority."

Social Class

Whatever power the Japanese Americans have acquired is due to their educational and occupational achievement. They are one of the best educated groups in the United States, and their school achievement remains consis-

Successful Japanese and American business people.

tently high. Their incomes are among the highest of all ethnic groups; their housing pattern reflects a middle-class status; very few would be considered "poor." Although the first Issei group started on a relatively homogeneous lower-class level, by the 1980s there was sufficient differentiation to support a wider class structure. Included are millionaires (usually land investors), many professionals (such as doctors, lawyers, dentists, optometrists, and pharmacists), and many teachers, nurses, and engineers, as well as the familiar gardeners and farmers who own their land. Many are also civil service employees.

Occupational mobility and educational achievement are closely related. Levine and Montero (1973), in a study analyzing three generations of Japanese, found that the higher the educational level of the Issei, the more likely that their children would be in high-status occupations. They also reported that a large proportion of the Nisei (71 percent) had white-collar jobs. The higher-status Nisei differed from the blue-collar Nisei in that they: (1) intended to live in primarily white neighborhoods; (2) were less adamant about their children marrying within the ethnic group; (3) were less involved in the ethnic community, including the Buddhist church; and (4) were less likely to speak or read Japanese as fluently or as well.

An analysis of the Japanese family will add to our understanding of its acculturation to the United States and help identify some of the variables that may have slowed this process. The power of the ethnic community and ethnic visibility are variables that help explain differing rates of acculturation. For example, the Japanese in Hawaii are much more apt to retain elements of the Japanese culture than are Japanese families living in Connecticut.

Another important factor is the Japanese work ethic. It is such an integral part of their system that one Japanese professor wrote: "Japanese work as if they were addicted to it" (*Japan Times,* 1973:3). The roots of the work orientation can be traced as far back as the teachings of Confucius and Buddha; the familiar Protestant work ethic is a recent borrowing by Europeans of something that has existed in Asia for many centuries. The Issei immigrants brought their work ethic to the United States. For many, hard work and effort were desirable goals in themselves. We know of surviving Issei who remain uncomfortable with many of the modern work-saving appliances because they entail so little time, effort, and expenditure of energy.

Although there are difficulties in assessing the culture that the Japanese brought to the United States, Nakane (1972) presented a framework that is helpful in understanding the Japanese family in Japan. She stressed the importance of situational membership and the role of the *ie,* or traditional family unit, in socializing family members and in providing the major reference group. Marriages were between *ies* rather than between individuals, and "good" *ies* trained their men and women for appropriate roles in the Japanese social system. Group power and group control were paramount in shaping the attitudes and behaviors of individuals. Group needs had a higher priority than individual needs and desires. Relationships within the ethnic community were primarily noncontractual, and children were socialized towards obedience, conformity, and dependency. In general, the Japanese American family has remained relatively intact, with low rates of separation and divorce, although there is impressionistic evidence that rates of divorce are rising. The family structure was primarily vertical, with father and male children on the top.

Influences on Behavior

Situational orientation is an important part of Japanese-American behavior. Learning how to behave towards those above, below, and equal has meant learning appropriate styles. There are elements of a "schizophrenic adaptation" on the part of the Japanese to life in the United States. But most physically identifiable groups are also faced with the same problem—the how-to-behave problem when interacting with the majority and the behaviors when with one's own group. Therefore, within one individual there is often the many personalities—the "Uncle Tom" to the white man, deferential and humble; the "good son" to his parents, dutiful and obedient; and the "swinger" to his peers, wise-cracking, loud, and irreverent. All of these behaviors are real so that none can be said to give a truer picture except in terms of time, place, and situation (Kitano, 1976:106–107).

> The situational approach is intimately related to power. The less powerful have to learn many adaptations; those with power can afford to use one style. Americans expect others to adapt to them; because of their power, they can often command or buy this recognition. Americans even assume that there are social science universals—"the personality" and "the truth"—whereas the search may be more a reflection of a power position than a social scientific reality.

Acculturation has been the most powerful single influence on Japanese behavior, but it has not been a simple linear movement. The variables of power and visibility have shaped differential styles; Japanese Americans in Hawaii will be different in many instances from their peers along the Pacific and Atlantic seaboards. There is a current reawakening of an ethnic identity and a militancy among the Sansei that may slow the trend toward acculturation.

One of the most influential events hastening acculturation was the evacuation of the Japanese during World War II. It broke up the power of the Issei and the ethnic ghettos, altered family life, scattered Japanese throughout the United States through resettlement, sent many males into the armed forces and overseas, and made many renounce everything Japanese.

Another factor affecting behavior is Japanese child-rearing techniques, which involve less direct confrontation than American techniques do. Parents attempt to provide outside stimuli, divert a child's attention, elicit cooperation, and shape a child's behavior through the force of "others." The fear of being ridiculed, being made to look foolish, and bringing shame on the family are primary sanctions in obtaining desired behavior.

Similar behavior characterizes husband-wife interaction, with more indirect communication, inferences, and unstated feelings, and less direct interaction (loud arguments) than among American couples.

It is our interpretation that Japanese normalize interaction through acknowledgment of different power positions. As Nakane (1972) pointed out, the Japanese social system can be seen as a series of parallels. Each individual is in a set position and has to learn how to interact with those above and those below; escape from the structure is extremely limited. It would therefore be difficult to collide head on continually with those within the system, and various techniques have been developed to handle power, dependence, and potential disruptive conflict.

Social class has always been a factor in the Japanese culture, but it is difficult to transcribe into the American scene. The *ies* tried to make appropriate matches, and "good" families were class conscious. Although most of the immigrants started at the bottom of the U.S. class structure, they did not identify with the lifestyles of the lower classes. Rather, they brought with them many of the values associated with the middle class: high educational expectations for their children, respect for those in authority (including the police), desire to own property, emphasis on banking and savings, and a future orientation. They seldom fully adopted a lower-class style, even though their incomes and housing were clearly in the ghetto areas.

The Japanese American community today shows increasing heterogeneity and the development of a more formal social class system (debutantes, professional organizations). With continued differences in education and income, the stratification may soon become much more crystallized.

Finally, it is important to emphasize that there is no one Japanese or Japanese American culture, just as there is no one American culture. Therefore, acculturation means different things to different families, and this variety is reflected in their attitudes and behaviors. Perhaps the most appropriate generalization is that Japanese families in the United States were different to begin with, and that length of time in the United States has been just one of many influences leading to further change. But despite these differences, there appears to be enough of a thread so that it is still possible to talk of a Japanese American subculture.

The Community

In recent years the old ghetto communities have undergone vast changes. Although there are still recognizable Japanese clusters ("J"-towns), they may be much smaller than before and are usually business centers. The acculturated have moved into better housing, but the predicted demise of the ethnic community has not taken place. Instead, attempts to rebuild and uplift the old

Japanese communities continue, often with capital from Japan as well as with federal funds. There are several hypothesized reasons for this rebirth. Part of the motivation comes from business—J-towns are centrally located, are tourist attractions, and do a thriving business. Furthermore, there has been a constant flow of new Japanese immigrants over the past decades, and many of these newcomers feel comfortable in an ethnic community. Then there is the ever-increasing group of businessmen from Japan, as well as Japanese tourists who also enjoy the ethnic communities. Finally, there are many older Issei, especially of limited economic means, who prefer to spend their last years among their own ethnic group.

The Japanese business structure was an important factor in building the Japanese community. Both the Chinese (*hui*) and the Japanese (*tanomoshi*) used a rotating credit system which makes a pool of money available for investment and credit purposes (Light, 1972). It also aided community cohesion.

Further, as Light found, membership in oriental organizations, being ascriptive, provided group identity, enforced ethnic honor and pride, and motivated members toward achievement that they probably would not have sought otherwise. In contrast, Light argues that black organizations draw on a culturally undifferentiated mass, which includes a high proportion of poor people who do not tend to participate in voluntary organizations. However, in terms of my experience with both the Japanese and Korean American communities, the importance of the "credit" organizations seems to be overstated. Instances of absconding with funds, the stress of the monthly payments, and personality clashes are common knowledge. Because there is often a "What's in it for me?" attitude, the organizational elites are forced to spend much of their time working for popular support.

About the Japanese community, one could say generally:

1. It is much more scattered and dispersed than in earlier times. Business rather than residential centers are more common.
2. Many organizations serve the ethnic community and are modeled after American patterns (Boy and Girl Scouts, the Ys, the Lions, and other service clubs), but they reflect a structural pluralism.
3. Many ethnic professionals (doctors, lawyers, pharmacists) are available to the community.
4. The use of majority social service and psychiatric facilities has, until recently, been low due to the availability of ethnic resources within the Japanese community. However, as the ethnic community changes and can no longer provide adequate resources for itself, more Japanese Americans will be dependent on larger community services; or, alternatively, larger-community (including federal) financing may be necessary to support ethnic institutions. For example, there has been a rise in adolescent drug use among Japanese in Los Angeles. The ethnic community was tapped for funds and raised enough to start a self-help drug center.

However, the continuing rise in drug use may force the Japanese to seek help from the larger community.

5. The ethnic family is still more or less dependent on the community. The Japanese are able to rely on themselves in solving most of their problems, but not all.

6. Japanese communities are not problem-free, contrary to the popular stereotype. Aside from problems common to any community, such as communication, economic well-being, and the like, there are acute problems of the aged, parent-child relationships, and drugs.

In summary, the Japanese Americans represent the oldest Asian American group in terms of families and children. The most dramatic event in their lives was the wartime evacuation of World War II, which was a culmination of prejudice, discrimination, segregation, and of "Japan bashing." The effects of that period still remain, and the idea that the United States Government provided redress remains a cause of wonderment among many evacuees who lived through that era of racial hatred. The evacuation remains a strong lens for viewing the world by the survivors. Camp reunions remain popular.

Since Japanese Americans are often confused with the Japanese in Japan, there is a cause of concern because "Japan bashing" again appears to be on the rise. The issue is that of the "invasion" of Japan made goods and capital; Japanese Americans and other Asian Americans may suffer because of the inability of many in the majority group to differentiate between the American born and those who represent the old ancestral homeland. It is a hope that the wartime evacuation has taught us a lesson on how not to handle racial tensions.

REFERENCES

BLOOM, L., & REIMER, R. (1945). Attitudes of college students toward Japanese Americans. *Sociometry, 8* (2), 157–173.

BOSWORTH, A. P. (1967). *America's concentration camps.* New York: W. W. Norton.

CHAN, S. (1991). *Asian Americans: an interpretive history.* Boston: Twayne.

COMMISSON ON WARTIME RELOCATION AND INTERMENT OF CIVILIANS. (1982). *Personal justice denied.* Washington, D.C.: Superintendent of Documents, U.S. Government Printing Office.

CONNOR, J. (1977). *Tradition and changes in three generations of Japanese Americans.* Chicago: Nelson-Hall.

DANIELS, R. (1971). *Concentration camps U.S.A.: Japanese Americans and World War II.* New York: Holt, Rinehart and Winston.

DANIELS, R. & KITANO, H. H. L. (1970). *American racism: Exploration of the nature of prejudice.* Englewood Cliffs, N.J.: Prentice-Hall.

DANIELS, R., TAYLOR, S. C., & KITANO, H. H. L. (Eds.). (1986). *Japanese Americans: From relocation to redress.* Salt Lake City: University of Utah Press.

EATON, E. H. (1952). *Beauty behind barbed wire: The art of the Japanese in our war relocation camps.* New York: Harper & Row.

FISHER, A. R. (1965). *Exile of a race.* Seattle: Ford T. Publishers.

GIRDNER, A., & LOFTIS, A. (1969). *The great betrayal.* New York: Macmillan.

GRODZINS, M. (1949). *Americans betrayed.* Chicago: University of Chicago Press.

GULICK, S. L. (1914). *The American Japanese problem.* New York: Charles Scribner's Sons.

HOSOKAWA, W. (1969). *Nisei: The quiet Americans.* New York: Morrow.

ICHIOKA, Y. (Ed.). (1989) *Views from within: The Japanese American evacuation and resettlement study.* Los Angeles: Resource Development and Publication.

IRONS, P. (1983). *Justice at war.* New York: Oxford University Press. *Japan Times,* 1973, editorial p. 3.

KITANO, H. H. L. (1976). *Japanese American: The evolution of a subculture* (2nd ed.). Englewood Cliffs, N.J.: Prentice-Hall.

KITANO, H. H. L. & DANIELS, R. (1995). *Asian Americans: Evolving Minorities.* 2nd ed. Englewood Cliffs, N.J.: Prentice-Hall.

KITANO, H. H. L., FUJINO, D., TAKAHASHI, J. *Interracial marriages: Where are the Asian Americans and where are they going.* (forthcoming) Handbook of Asian American Psychology. (ed L. Lee & N. Zane) Newbury Park: Sage Press.

LEIGHTON, A. (1945). *The governing of men* (p. 34). Princeton, N.J.: Princeton University Press.

LEVINE, G. & MONTERO, D. M. (1973). Socioeconomic mobility among three generations of Japanese Americans. *Journal of Social Issues, 29* (2), 33–48.

LIGHT, I. (1972). *Ethnic enterprise in American business and welfare among Chinese, Japanese, and Blacks.* Berkeley: University of California Press.

LYMAN, S. M. (1986). *Chinatown and Little Tokyo: Power, Conflict, and Community Among Chinese and Japanese Immigrants in America.* Milwood, N.Y.: Associated Faculty Press.

MYER, D. (1971). *Uprooted Americans.* Tucson: University of Arizona Press.

NAKANE, C. (1972). *Japanese society.* Berkeley: University of California Press.

OKUBO, M. (1946). *Citizen 13660.* New York: Walter Weatherhill.

SPICER, E. H., HANSEN, A. T., LUOMALA, K., & OPLER, M. K. (1969). *Impounded people.* Tucson, Arizona: The University of Arizona Press.

STRONG, E. K. (1934). *The second generation Japanese problem.* Stanford: Stanford University Press.

TAKAKI, R. (1989). *Strangers from a different shore.* Boston: Little, Brown and Company.

TENBROEK, J., BARNHART, E. N., & MATSON, F. W. (1954). *Prejudice, war and the Constitution.* Berkeley: University of California Press.

THOMAS, D. S., KIKUCHI, C., & SAKODA, J. (1952). *The savage.* Berkeley: University of California Press.

THOMAS, D. S., & NISHIMOTO, R. (1946). *The spoilage.* Berkeley: University of California Press.

WEGLYN, M. (1976). *Years of infamy.* New York: Morrow.

YODER, E. M., JR. (1988). Apology now due in full for the blot of internment. *Los Angeles Times,* April 29, part II, p. 7.

ZELLER, W. D. (1969). *An educational drama.* New York: American Press.

Chapter 15

Koreans and Filipinos

It is difficult to place the Koreans and Filipinos in any ethnic stratification system because of the newness of their immigration. The bulk of their migration took place after the passage of the 1965 Immigration Act so that they are groups primarily in transition.

The Koreans and Filipinos (also known as the Pilipinos) are two of the fastest growing Asian American groups, with the increase primarily due to immigration. Although they have already had an important impact on the Asian American communities, writings on these two groups are relatively scarce when compared to the Chinese and the Japanese. Therefore, the groups are combined; the purpose of this chapter is to present material on the Koreans and Filipinos. Much of the material in this chapter is drawn from *Asian Americans* (Kitano & Daniels, 1995).

THE KOREANS

In 1970, there were an estimated 70,000 Korean residents in the United States; the 1980 Census indicated 357,393 and the 1990 Census reported 798,849. The bulk of the population is made up of the first-generation immigrant. However, since it is primarily a family migration, the second-generation American-born children have already arrived on the scene. As a consequence, intergenerational issues and coming to grips with acculturation and interaction with the dominant culture have come to the forefront at a much earlier time than for the Chinese and Japanese. It should be recalled that both the early Chinese and Japanese immigration was comprised primarily of single males and that family life, including generational issues, were not of immediate concern.

The age range in the Korean community includes the young adult to middle-aged married couples, children spanning infancy to young adulthood, and grandparents. They may have all been born in Korea, but the children are for all intents and purposes similar to the American-born "Nisei" of the Japanese, since their primary schooling will have taken place in the United States. There is even a special term, the "knee high", or 1.5 generation, referring to those who arrived in America at a very young age.

A number of factors, other than the current family migration, make the Korean experience relatively unique when compared to other Asian groups. First, their early immigration was short lived (1902 to 1905), and then their country changed hands, so that when the Japanese established hegemony, the early immigrants became a people without a country. Second, many of their immigrants were Christian, so that the church was and continues to be an important part of the community structure. Third, although the early arrivals settled in Hawaii and on the West Coast, the recent arrivals are much more geographically dispersed than the Chinese and Japanese. Finally, Korea (at least South Korea) was never an enemy nation, as were China and Japan, although during the Korean War, it was divided into the enemy (North) and the ally (South).

Background

Modern Korean history has been influenced by three powerful neighbors—China, Japan, and Russia—and by its strategic location between these nations. China dominated the country as a tributary state until 1868 when Meiji Japan began to contest Chinese influence. The Sino-Japanese War (1894–1895) and the defeat of China led to increasing Japanese influence. The aggressive Japanese policies led Korea to a search for other foreign powers who could limit Japanese aggression, which led to relationships with Russia and the United States.

Diplomatic relations with the United States started in 1882 with the Korea-American Treaty at Chemulpo (now Inchon). The treaty called for free traffic between the two countries, including permission for Koreans to rent and to purchase land in the United States, and reciprocal rights for Americans in Korea. Very few Koreans took the opportunity to come to the United States during this period.

The First Wave

Korean immigration was formally acknowledged by the Shufeldt Treaty, which opened Korea to the Western world in 1882. The significant immigration took place between 1903 and 1905 with the arrival of 7,226 Koreans in Hawaii. In common with most immigrations, they were reacting to a number of pushes and pulls. The push was from home conditions: a cholera epidemic, a drought, a locust plague, famine, and generally poor economic conditions. The primary pull was from Hawaiian plantation owners who wished to limit the power of Chinese and Japanese workers through the importation of another national group of workers, and a desire on the part of the Korean government to gain a favorable image and support from the United States for their immigration policies.

Of the 7,226 immigrants who arrived as plantation workers in Hawaii between 1902 and 1905, over 6,000 were male adults. Less than 60 percent remained in Hawaii; some 1,000 returned to Korea, while another 2,000 moved on to the continental United States. An additional 1,033 were reported as immigrants to Mexico in 1905 (Houchins & Houchins, 1976:135).

The Koreans were a heterogeneous group of male laborers, peasants, low-rank government officials, ex-soldiers, students, and political refugees. In 1905 pressure from Korean politicians, American missionaries, and most important, the Japanese government led to the cessation of immigration. Japan had started to exert its hegemony over Korea through the Treaty of Portsmouth at the conclusion of the Russo-Japanese war; by 1905 Korea was already a Japanese colony, although its official colonial status was not declared until 1910.

Most of the Korean emigrants left home with a weak national identification, but Korean identity, solidarity, and nationalism quickly grew in the United States. Although the Koreans were cut off from their homeland and were in danger of losing their national identity under Japanese rule, they maintained their "Koreanness" by politicizing their communities through involvement in the Korean independence movement. For example, between 1905 and 1907, the Koreans in Hawaii established more than twenty organizations that had as a central theme Korean solidarity and resistance to Japanese occupation. Most of them published their own mimeographed language newspapers. Yang (1979) found that there were over fifteen such publications during this period.

Christian churches were also numerous; there were thirty-one congregations serving 2,800 Koreans; there were also a similar number of Christian churches on the mainland. Besides their ministerial functions for the Korean laborers, Korean pastors in Hawaii also served as interpreters, job placement officers, legal aid advisors, mediators, marriage counselors, teachers, and community workers (Yang, 1979). The Koreans who migrated to the mainland were described as more educated and aggressive, and they set the tone for the community during this early era.

The major problems included the uncertainty of employment and the high proportion of unmarried males. One solution to the marital problem was through "picture brides"—marriages arranged on the basis of an exchange of photographs and letters. A total of 1,066 picture brides emigrated to the United States before the 1924 immigration law closed the door to any further Asian immigration (Yang, 1979). But there remained a significant number of unmarried Korean males who eventually lost interest and contact with the fragmented Korean community.

Most of the immigrants had come for economic reasons and had thoughts of returning, but they could not because Korea was then a Japanese colony. A number of young intellectuals had also come to the United States before the Japanese annexation and with a few exceptions decided to remain in the United States and fight for Korean independence. Most prominent in this group were Ahn Chang-ho, who was a Korean community organizer; Syngman Rhee, who was to eventually return to Korea as the first president of the republic after World War II; and Park Yong-man, who created an armed Korean national brigade in Hawaii with the thought of a military reconquest.

The existence of numerous organizations whose leaders advocated a variety of tactics made it difficult to achieve an overall Korean community unity. Even today there is no central organization among Koreans; as Kim stated, "with new immigrants, new organizations are created, like mushrooms after a spring shower" (1977a:65). Much of the energy and finances of the Korean community during the early era were used to support the activities of Korean patriots and various governments in exile.

Life on the Hawaiian plantations was hard and characterized by racial and ethnic segregation, low wages, and minimal contact with other groups. But part of their sustenance came from the "government in exile" model, where emphasis was to maintain patriotic organizations until such time that they could free their country from Japanese rule (Kitano & Daniels, 1988). Ethnic solidarity remained high; only 104 Korean males were reported to have married out of the group from 1912 to 1924 (Adams, 1937). High rates of exogamy were to occur later in the Hawaiian-born generations.

The adaptation of this initial group provides some interesting data. Harvey and Chung (1980), in writing about the eventual demise of the "back to Korea movement," the small numbers and the lack of a cohesive ethnic community, coupled with the "pull" of the Hawaiian melting pot, had interesting results. For example, there developed a high desire to become American, of obtaining an education, and of entering the professions. As a consequence, the children and grandchildren of the initial immigrant group have one of the highest rates of interethnic marriage and have high levels of education and achievement.

But the rapid move towards acculturation and becoming a part of the Hawaiian mainstream has not been without its cost. There have been high rates of separation and divorce, psychological problems, and other dysfunctional symptoms (Harvey & Chung, 1980).

In summary, the immigrant experiences of this first group in Hawaii between 1903 and 1905 can be summarized as follows: political preoccupation with the takeover of their homeland; the importation of brides, birth of a second generation, ethnic dormancy, rapid acculturation and entering the mainstream, rising rates of outmarriage, and attendant problems.

The Second Wave

The second wave of Koreans arrived between 1951 and 1964 and consisted of a heterogeneous group of wives of American servicemen (the Korean War took place in 1950–53), war orphans, and students. The number of war brides who arrived between 1950 and 1975 was 28,205 and the immigration of this group continues. In Gordon's model, they were maritally assimilated, but many were still in the beginning stages of acculturation. Bok-Lim Kim and Margaret Condon (1975) evaluated the adjustment of the Korean wives of American servicemen and noted some of their problems. Many suffered from culture shock, lack of education, isolation, problems of communication, and general alienation. There were high divorce rates and Kim notes that although there were some successful marriages, there were also cases of physical abuse, suicide, and attempted suicide. The females were marginal, both to the ethnic community and to the mainstream and many of the problems were attributed to their marginality.

Hurh and Kim (1984) report that in 1950, there were 24,945 children in Korean orphanages. Of these, 6,293 were adopted in the United States, mostly through the Holt Adoption Agency, between 1955 and 1966. Approximately 46 percent were adopted by white fathers, 13 percent had black fathers, and the rest by full Koreans. The adoption of Korean children continues to the present day.

Dong Sue Kim (1977) conducted a nationwide study of adopted Korean adolescents. Most were placed in white, middle-class Protestant families in rural areas and small, urban communities. Religious and humanitarian concerns were given as motives for adoption and the children were reported to have healthy self-concepts and to have been successfully adopted.

However, in a later study (Kim & Kim, 1985), the problem of racial differences became apparent. Their physical characteristics set them aside from the mainstream so that the adoptees were seen as Asians, yet they were cut off from their native contacts and their ancestral culture. A common problem was that of marginality to both the mainstream and ethnic cultures.

The last group comprising the second wave was an estimated 5,000 students who came to the United States between 1945 and 1965. Very little is known about this group so that questions such as how many remained in the country, their marital and occupational patterns, and their adaptation remain as topics for future research.

The Third Wave

The third and largest wave of Koreans came as one of the results of the Immigration and Naturalization Act of 1965 and the migration still continues. The Korean share of the United States total immigration rose from 0.7 percent in 1969, to 3.8 percent in 1973, and to 6.2 percent in 1985. However, the estimated 542,000 Koreans in the United States in 1985 gives it third rank to the over 1,000,000 Koreans in Manchuria and the over 600,000 residing in Japan.

The third wave migration mostly consists of families with a large proportion of women and children. It is a highly educated group and is drawn from primarily urban areas. It is difficult to assess their current adaptation because of the recency of their arrival and the lack of research data. However, Bok-Lim Kim (Kim & Condon, 1975) indicates that some of their expectations include (1) economic success, (2) retention of aspects of their Korean culture, (3) rapid mobility to the more desirable areas of housing in the suburbs, and (4) the development of ethnic business districts. Other expectations include permanent residence and American citizenship, a good education for their children, and family reunification.

The reasons for the recent immigration include better employment and educational opportunities and a chance to be reunited with family and other relatives (Kim & Condon, 1975). The immigrants arrive with little knowledge of the United States or the language, but with high expectations. They reflect the influence of the 1965 Immigration Act, which gives priority to those applicants with advanced education, training, and skills. For example, half of the Koreans have had a college education; many come from the middle and upper classes. However, former teachers, professors, and administrators are often obliged to settle for lower-status occupations (Kim, 1980).

Major barriers to participation in the mainstream include lack of familiarity with U.S. society and cultural differences, with a special problem of communicating in English. Other problems, typical for immigrant groups, are those differences between the old culture and the new society, including changes in family roles, conflicts in norms and values, and achievement of a healthy identity in a white society. Generational differences are also appearing.

Adaptation

Hurh (1977) constructed a stage-by-stage model for analyzing the adaptation of the newcomer. Initially, there is a feeling of satisfaction, accomplishment, and relief that the immigrant has finally reached the United States. They share a sense of excitement and enjoy the reunion with family, relatives, and friends. The newcomer is especially impressed by the material affluence of the new country. Many can scarcely believe that they are here.

This stage is generally short-lived, and by the end of the first year a feeling of disenchantment sets in. The harsh realities of the language barrier, the difficulty of finding suitable employment, the social isolation, and culture shock lead to doubts about ever adapting to the new country. There are feelings of homesickness and a possible change in expectations of America. Those who have a command of English are generally in much better shape to pass through this stage. Those who do not may remain at this stage for a long time.

The next phase is cultural assimilation: "The immigrant is now employed, his English is now improving, the family income is stable, and he may even own a car" (Hurh, 1977:90). There are signs of material affluence, self-confidence, and a desire to become American. The immigrants may take on American first names and have increased social contact outside the group. They want to validate their Americanism, and rates of naturalization are very high at this stage. Kim (1977b) reported that Korean rates of naturalization are higher than those of other Asian American groups. This may be the final stage of "making it" for some.

For others, there is another stage in which there is the reawakening of an ethnic identity and a desire to know much more about the culture of Korea. This phenomenon is common among most immigrant groups and has sometimes been named the *Hansen effect,* which refers to the rejection of the immigrant culture by the second generation and a reawakening interest by the third generation. There are no available data on the number of Koreans in each of the phases.

The Korean Model

The model of Korean adaptation is different from that of domination and domestic colonialism. The early first-generation Koreans retained their own culture with little attempt to acculturate and integrate, partly because they envisaged a triumphant return to their homeland. When that homeland was annexed by Japan, much of their energy was aimed at fostering and maintaining their lost identity, while developing a number of competing governments in exile. Perhaps the most appropriate title for this type of adaptation would be a *government-in-exile* model, in which groups see themselves as transients until such time that they can reconquer their homeland. The model is fairly prevalent: Latvians in the United States and the Chinese who fled to Taiwan are examples of the government-in-exile orientation that does not fit any of our traditional models.

The second generation of Koreans, without the emotional or structural ties to the "we shall return" orientation, followed a more traditional path toward acculturation and integration, although it should be noted that their primary outmarriage choices were not to the dominant Caucasians but to other subordinated groups. Many arrived in the United States with capital and high educational and skill levels. Some have started at the bottom in the dual-labor economy as seamstresses and in sweat shops, but many others have gone into small business and into positions appropriate to a middleman minority position. By *middleman,* we refer to a group that is above the status of other minorities because of a competitive advantage or high adaptive capacity (Blalock, 1967:79–84), yet remains below the status of the dominant group. Bonacich (1973) and Kitano (1974) wrote about the Chinese and Japanese in the United States as other possible middleman groups.

The middleman model is based on a dominant-subordinate stratification system. There are basically two competing groups (Whites and Blacks), with the middleman minority serving as a mediating influence between the two power groups. Bonacich and Jung (1979), in surveying Korean small-business

Korean arranging salad bar in New York City store. A great majority of fruit and vegetable stores in the city are family run by Korean immigrants.

activity in Los Angeles, found it an appropriate model to explain current Korean adaptation. Based on middleman concepts, they hypothesized the following Korean economic activity: that Koreans would be overrepresented in the small-business sector, particularly in retailing and small shops; that they would be concentrated in a narrow range of economic activities; that they would serve both a Korean clientele and a substantial non-Korean clientele, particularly the poor and other minorities; that ethnicity would be vital to business development, including the generation of capital, circulating business information, and mutual aid; and that there would be a heavy reliance on a hard-working, loyal work force, including unpaid family members. The data on Korean businesses supported their predictions.

Middleman minorities often serve as buffers between dominant and subordinated groups and can become the targets and scapegoats for the stresses of that system (for example, Jews in Germany during the Nazi era). The pertinent question relates to the length of time a group may serve in that position. Will it become a semipermanent role for the Korean minority, or is it a passing phase in their interaction with the dominant and subordinated groups in our society? More or less permanent middleman positions occur because of a combination of external factors, such as systematic, powerful discrimination (denial of citizenship), and internal factors, such as cultural preferences and psychological identifications (feeling inferior to the dominant group but superior to the subordinated groups).

It is perhaps too early to predict, but it is probable that the Koreans may be the Asian group that will integrate most rapidly into the U.S. system. They are still few in number and scattered, but there has been a strong motivation to become American. They are a well-educated group that greatly values education, and they have family solidarity coupled with a high degree of individualism and a hard-work ethic. The barriers of language and of underemployment may be temporary, and although they face the stresses and strains that are a part of all immigrant life, it appears that they have the perseverance to cope and to overcome. The major barrier is anti-Asian prejudice, which is currently not as formidable as it was in a previous era. Since their middleman orientations are probably not permanent, the Koreans may use these positions as steps toward higher mobility and dispersion.

Korean stereotype.   Hurh (1994) indicates that one stereotype is that Koreans are hard working, but ruthless competitors, especially against African and Hispanic Americans. In the area of business, there is more of an unfavorable, rather than a favorable image. He also adds that Koreans are viewed as isolated and difficult to understand. He believes that if the group is to advance and improve their lives in America, they must understand the negative perceptions and become more active socially and politically. It should also be recognized that the population is primarily first generation, so that language and cultural differences remain as barriers.

The Los Angeles April Riot (Yu, 1994) was a symptom of the problems associated with Korean-black relations. More than 2,000 Korean-owned businesses were damaged, looted, or burned so that their losses were almost one-half of the total losses incurred in the riot.

Chang (1994) in analyzing the riot saw the Rodney King verdict as the trigger; there was evidence of increasing conflict between Korean-African Americans, and Latino-African Americans prior to the riot. There was also misrepresentation of the riot by the mass media, which concentrated on the sensational aspects and ignored the attempts by the community to defuse the situation. He suggests that there is not enough effort to educate the ethnic communities about each other.

Tong-He Koh (1994), in studying the 1.5 generation, already notes a weakening of ethnic identity by generation, which is similar to the experiences of other Asian American groups. There is also strong expectations for higher education, and a respect for the authority of teachers so that continued progress in terms of educational mobility will be forthcoming.

In summary, an individual pattern that is typical is presented by Kim (1980). The father, an ex-government administrator, arrives in the United States with his wife and children. His first job is as a gas station attendant, while his wife secures employment (possibly her first paying job) in a garment factory. By working six to seven days per week, they save enough to open a small shop or restaurant. Eventually, they are able to buy a home and to achieve modest financial independence.

An unknown area is the record of those who have become disillusioned with life in America and have returned to Korea. Because of the ease of travel, the numbers may be considerable.

The first-generation lens is primarily Korean, with a strong Korean identity and strong ties to the mother country. The 1.5 generation's ethnic identity is not as strong as in the first generation, but there is a strong Korean community to reinforce an ethnic identity in cities with large concentrations of the group.

For example, in Los Angeles, there are structurally separate Korean churches of various denominations; a vast number of Korean restaurants and an ever-expanding, visible Koreatown. There are Korean language schools, lawyers, doctors, realtors, and social service agencies so that one could remain Korean and find most of the needs available within the ethnic community. But the influence of acculturation is also strong; large numbers of Korean children are enrolled in the public schools, and their entrance into higher education is impressive. The differencs by generation are visible and often are viewed as "culture conflict."

Because the Koreans are lumped together with other Asian American groups, they are considered to be in the middle of the ethnic stratification system. There is little question that given time, they will soon achieve that status, but at the present time, they would appear to be somewhat below the Chinese, Indian, and Japanese populations.

THE FILIPINOS

The Filipino experience is different from the other Asian groups because they were the direct result of American imperialism. Therefore, for a short period of time, they enjoyed a privileged status as American nationals, although as we shall see, their treatment upon arrival was not significantly different from the prejudice and discrimination that was the lot of their Asian peers.

Early History

The Filipino followed the Chinese and Japanese immigration to the United States. It was largely male immigration, and the young men who came essentially filled the niche in the labor force that had been occupied by the Japanese, who by the 1920s were no longer available in significant numbers to work for Caucasian growers. Had Japanese immigration not been cut off, it is probable that the Filipino migration would not have been as large as it was. However, thanks to American imperialism, the Filipino enjoyed a different status from other Asians. Like other Asians, Filipinos were not eligible for naturalization; but since the United States owned the Philippines, they were not aliens, but nationals.

American ownership of the Philippines came about at the end of the Spanish American War with the signing of the Treaty of Paris (1899). Under American rule, the Filipinos had the right to travel on a U.S. passport and could not be excluded from this country. But in 1934 the Tydings-McDuffie Independence Act, which conferred independence on the Islands, also made the Filipinos aliens for immigration purposes (Melendy, 1980). The legislation immediately imposed a rigid quota of fifty immigrants a year, thus ending, for all practical purposes, Filipino immigration.

Ironically, some of the leading anti-Filipino nativists in California were among the chief advocates of Philippine independence, since independence—or to be precise, the promise of independence—was the ultimate form of exclusion.

Most of the early immigration was to Hawaii. Filipino laborers were needed on the plantations, where they lived segregated lives. There was little opportunity for mobility, so becoming a part of the mainstream remained an elusive dream. Their social lives revolved around an ethnic clubhouse where the primary activities were movies, social dancing, and periodic celebrations. In Honolulu, the Filipinos were divided by language groups—the Tagalogs, Visayans, and Ilocanos. There were even separate facilities for each of the groups, so that barbershops, bars, and poolrooms reflected the separation. But all Filipinos shared in the scarcity of Filipino females; in 1910 the male/female ratio was 10 to 1; in 1940 the ratio was still 3.5 to 1 (Melendy, 1980:358).

Discrimination on the mainland and in Hawaii encouraged another type of stratification system, pitting "we" against "they"—friends and compadres against enemies and others. The "we-they" system that evolved in California was based on older Filipino traditions of reciprocity, obligation, loyalty, and unity. Strong bonds existed between compadres, whereas outsiders were viewed with suspicion (Melendy, 1980).

The major thrust of Filipino immigration lasted about ten years. In 1920 there were only 5,000 Filipinos in the whole country (3,000 in California); by the next census the figures had risen to 45,000 nationwide, with about 30,000 in California. Yet this tiny minority raised the hackles of the California exclusionists, who saw the Filipinos as yet another Asian horde about to overwhelm Caucasian California. A Sacramento exclusionist informed a national magazine audience that, since all American Blacks were descended from a small slave nucleus, even this tiny group represented a danger. Ignoring the fact that very few women came from the Philippines, he insisted, with that mindless arithmetic that California exclusionists delighted in, that "Filipinos do not hesitate to have nine children . . . [which means] 720 great-grandchildren as against the white parents' twenty-seven" (Daniels & Kitano, 1970:67).

But the explosive nature of the Filipino problem was caused not by Filipino reproduction, but by Filipino sex. The sex bugaboo, the ravishing of pure white women by lascivious oriental men, had always lurked in the background of antioriental movements in California. It had never become, overtly, at least, a major factor, for the simple reason that sex relations between oriental men and occidental women had been all but nonexistent. (Intercourse between males of the majority race and females of the minority races aroused little opposition; Chinese and Japanese prostitutes had been a titillating feature of West Coast brothels since gold-rush days.) With the Filipinos, however, the sex issue became tangible. The Filipinos enjoyed and sought the companionship of Caucasian girls; and soon, in every major center of Filipino population in the state, special dance halls sprang up that catered exclusively to the Filipino trade, and a lucrative trade it was. The basic charge was ten cents a minute, and the places did a thriving business.

This kind of "free enterprise" was just too much for most Californians. The conservative *Los Angeles Times* railed against two such dance halls located just a few blocks from the newspaper's headquarters. One set of headlines read:

Taxi-Dance Girls Start Filipinos on Wrong Foot

Lonely Islanders' Quest for Woman Companionship Brings Problems of Grave National Moment

Mercenary Women Influence Brown Man's Ego

Minds Made Ripe for Work of Red Organizers (Daniels & Kitano, 1970:67)

Exclusionists suffered a further shock when the courts ruled that the state's miscegenation statute—which forbade marriages of white persons to "Negroes, Mongolians, or mulattoes"—did not apply to the Filipinos, who were considered Malayans. The California legislature quickly amended the law to extend the ban to "members of the Malay race."

Bogardus (1929), in studying early white attitudes toward the Filipino, found that Whites favored their educational ambition, willingness to do menial tasks, and courtesy and politeness while working in hotels and restaurants. But Whites feared their economic competition, their inability to engage in heavy farm work, their propensity to strike and quarrel, and their forwardness with white girls. Filipinos were welcome if they remained in their place. Job discrimination sent them to the bottom of the economic scale, and housing discrimination segregated them into slums. It was inevitable that overt clashes would result. Melendy wrote:

California's first serious riot occurred at a carnival in Exeter on October 24, 1929, when a Filipino stabbed a white man. Prior to the incident, Filipinos had been abused in town, shoved off sidewalks, and molested by white transient workers. At the carnival, whites threw objects at Filipinos, particularly those in the company of white girls. This led to the stabbing. (1967:7)

The most explosive riot occurred in the Watsonville agricultural area in 1930. Anti-Filipino attitudes were set in motion by the Chamber of Commerce, which passed resolutions harassing Filipinos. The mobs followed suit, and for several days armed white hunting parties roamed the streets looking for Filipinos and invading dance halls. The violence reached a climax with the killing of a Filipino, numerous assaults, and the burning of Filipino dwellings.

By World War II, attitudes toward Filipinos had changed. The "brave little brown brothers" who fought and died alongside the whites at Bataan and Corregidor became the new stereotype. Nonetheless, Filipinos were considered to be an invisible minority group that ranked very low in most ethnic classification schemes.

Visibility

Although they are most often classified as Mongolian and are therefore considered "yellow," Filipinos are of Malayan stock. They also often have Spanish surnames and can be mistaken quite easily for Puerto Ricans or Latin Americans.

Groupings

The Filipinos, or Pinoys, can be divided into four main groups:

1. The first generation, composed primarily of males who immigrated in the 1920s. Most went into agricultural labor and retained their native Philippine dialect. Acculturation for them has been slow.
2. The second and third generations, who were born in America and who have very little contact with their native land, language, or culture.
3. The post-World War II arrivals, many of whom are veterans and war victims.
4. The new immigrants, including many professionals who have come under the liberalized immigration laws of 1965.

The first generation.   These various groupings provide a background for some of the problems facing the Filipinos. For example, the first-generation immigrants—mostly male, less educated, but hard working—have now grown old. Most of them have remained single and have no family ties. Long arduous lives as fruit pickers or laborers have not netted them much capital. Their isolation and poverty make them extremely vulnerable to changing conditions, especially as their earning power declines. Their last years are usually spent in dingy hotel rooms in California valley towns such as Stockton or in the blighted areas of San Francisco. The irony of their plight can be appreciated if we recall the one guiding ethic of their life: hard work.

The second generation.   Racist barriers discouraged intermarriage for first-generation males, but many were able to find mates both from majority-group and other minority-group females. There are almost no empirical data on the number of these intermarriages; however, we would predict a relatively high proportion of separation and divorce, especially when compared to the rates for the other Asian populations. These higher rates of separation and divorce may be attributed to job discrimination, social isolation, subordinate status, as well as to cultural differences such as language and life styles.

The second generation and their children face many problems. Like most racial minorities, they share such problems as lack of social acceptance, low income, low educational achievement, and negative self-image. A special problem has been the lack of education, as summarized by Cordova and others (Cordova, Jamero, Ogilvie, Santos, Tangalan, Tangalan, & Tiffany, n.d.):

1. There is an obvious lack of encouragement, either in the home or in the high schools, to go to college and succeed.
2. There is a noticeable absence of proper counseling to help young Filipinos choose between college or training school.
3. Many counselors lack the knowledge, experience, and rapport to deal adequately with Filipino Americans.
4. Neither the colleges nor the high schools provide any courses in Filipino culture or history.
5. The future plans of many young Filipinos extend no further than the next day, the next month, or the next year.
6. The cost of education is beyond the reach of most Filipino families.

Predictably, there are very few Filipino college graduates, but the numbers are growing. For example, only five Filipino Americans graduated from the three major colleges in the Seattle area in 1971. But in 1994, Filipino applications to UCLA totalled 1,082, ranking third among Asian Americans (Chinese, 3,729, and Koreans, 1,528), and well ahead of the Japanese, 534.

As with many of their peers in other ethnic communities, the second- and third-generation youngsters are unfamiliar with their native country. They generally know nothing of Philippine culture, except through the reminiscences of some older Filipinos with whom they might occasionally be in contact.

The post-World War II veteran.   A number of veterans came to the United States after World War II. Many of them had been in the Filipino Scouts; some brought their families and others came by themselves, with the idea of sending for their families after finding jobs. The author remembers working with a large group of these veterans who immigrated to San Francisco in the 1950s. Many of them were middle-aged, generally unskilled (although they brought with them diplomas from unknown technical and vocational colleges in the Philippines), and quite thoroughly army disciplined. They shared a mixture of patriotism, a naive belief of the wonders of the United States, and a hard-work ethic.

Although life was extremely difficult for them during the early months, the need for unskilled laborers was great, and most of them did make an adaptation to the new country. At occasional meetings in the Asian community, the war veteran can still be spotted by his military bearing and his reminiscences of Bataan and Corregidor.

Another group of veterans are the Filipinos who were in the United States Navy. Most of them served as officer's stewards, but in spite of the Navy's attempt to acculturate these sailors, they continue to retain close ties with the Philippines and to live within their own cultural network (Duff & Arthur, 1973).

The Current Wave

As with the bulk of Asian migration, the immigration legislation of 1965 provided the impetus for Filipino entrance into the United States. The new Filipinos not only changed the size of the population, but also were quite different from the immigrants of times past. A large proportion of arrivals after 1965 have been health professionals, especially nurses. There were also many doctors, engineers, and teachers, which reflected the policy of the immigration legislation of bringing highly skilled professional people to the United States. Most are well educated and are fluent in English. Although many are unable to obtain high status jobs, one Filipino said, "My one day earning here is more than my one month salary in Manila, especially when I do a plus eight (overtime)" (Munoz, 1971:29).

Corizon Aquino, Filipina leader.

Munoz studied the transformation of some Filipinos as they perceived the opportunities in the United States. Whereas in the old country they may have been soft, easy going, even parasitic, indolent, and inefficient, in the new country they became work oriented with a vengeance. Many moonlighted by taking on additional jobs in the evenings and weekends and placed a high value on putting money in the bank and eventually returning to the Philippines to retire.

Although Los Angeles has become a major attraction for Filipino immigrants, they have not developed a cohesive, geographically tight community. Rather, they are widely scattered and are not without problems. Morales (1974), a social worker, found that immigrants had problems with education, finances, unemployment, youth, family, and the elderly. Identity also becomes an issue in the context of culture shock and racism. A large number of Filipino professionals—such as doctors, dentists, and pharmacists—also face problems of licensing in the new country.

Generalizations about the group based on variables such as income, occupation, and education are deceptive since they vary widely according to age, sex, time of immigration, and geographic area of settlement. For example, the old-timer is usually a single male who has lived a life of hard work in low-paying jobs. His education, income, and life savings are meager, and he has generally resided in the least desirable parts of the city and in poor rural areas. On the other hand, the new immigrants, both males and females, arrive with a high level of educational achievement and professional backgrounds. One major complaint concerns underemployment.

Other problems include finances, unemployment, child guidance, the role of the elderly, culture shock, credentialing and licensing. There are also internal problems: Immigrants come from different islands with different languages, ideologies and subcultures. It is difficult to form overall Filipino organizations because of the strength of local ties and competing loyalties. Filipino groups tend to multiply rather than to unify (Melendy, 1980).

Azores (1986–87) studied a current generation of Filipino high school seniors and found that a high percentage had aspirations for a college education. The idea that Filipino youngsters were not desirous of attending college was a myth. However, many of them lacked the grades for advancing into high education; Azores suggested three possible reasons for the discrepancy between aspirations and the reality. One was unrealistic expectations, second was the lack of linkage between aspirations and personal commitment, and thirdly, Filipino students did not define a good student through grades.

Cabezas, Shinagawa, and Kawaguchi (1986–87), in analyzing data from the 1980 Census, found that Filipinos in California suffered economic inequality. Filipinos remained in subordinated positions to the white majority, whether they were sailors, professionals, the educated, the uneducated, the skilled, or the unskilled. Many were clustered in the secondary labor market where the pay was low and where mobility was limited.

Min (1986–87) made a comparison of the Filipinos and Koreans in their orientation towards small business. Language difficulties and other disadvantages in the labor market turned many Koreans toward small business, while the Filipinos, who were more familiar with the language and U.S. business practices, were able to bypass the small business model. The Koreans also had the use of family and extended family members as sources of intensive labor; there were also trading possibilities with an industrialized South Korea. In contrast, the English-speaking Filipino with degrees in medicine and nursing could find employment relatively easily outside of the ethnic community.

Both the Koreans and Filipinos face issues that are related to their country of origin. The division of Korea into the North and the South carries over into split loyalties, just as the division between pro- and anti-Marcos supporters creates divisions in the Filipino-American community. Community solidarity is difficult to maintain when there are these divisive issues.

The Filipino Model

As with all of our previously discussed groups, there is no one model that can encompass the diversity within the Filipino population. The Filipinos represent another variation of the dominant-subordinate model. They emigrated from a country that had been under continuous colonial rule for over 400 years, first under the Spanish, then under the Americans, so that they were accustomed to a subordinated position in relation to white dominance. Cordova (1973) noted that one consequence of this type of association is that the natives are trained not to exceed or surpass the pace of their colonial benefactors.

A large group carried their subordinated position into the Navy, where they served their "superiors" with dedication and duty as stewards and attendants. Upward mobility in this hierarchical structure for Filipinos was extremely rare.

Many early immigrants were single, male laborers and, because of the lack of Filipino women, chose "American" wives (amalgamation) or remained single. The laborer was positioned in the lower half of the socioeconomic structure and never participated in the mainstream of the American culture.

The new immigrants, especially those with professional degrees, fill many middleman positions. There are a goodly number of nurses among Filipino females. One would expect to find male doctors serving in less prestigious and less affluent communities. For example, we have noticed a high proportion of foreign-trained doctors (including those with language problems) at the Martin Luther King Hospital in Watts (Los Angeles) and would expect a similar distribution in other cities.

In closing, the Filipinos are a direct product of American colonialism. Very few profited from this relationship; rather, discriminatory legislation controlled and shaped a male-only group with limited opportunities for normal family life. Recently, there has been a new immigration, and it is hoped that they would not replicate the experience of Carlos Bulosan, an early immigrant and writer. In his moving autobiography, *America Is in the Heart,* (1973) he described what it felt like to be a Filipino in California in the 1920s:

> . . . in many ways it was a crime to be a Filipino in California. I came to know that the public streets were not free to my people; we were stopped each time . . . patrolmen saw us driving a car. We were suspect each time we were seen with a white woman. And perhaps it was this narrowing of our life into an island, into a filthy segment of American society, that had driven [many] Filipinos inward, hating everyone and despising all positive urgencies toward freedom.

REFERENCES

ADAMS, R. (1937). *Interracial marriage in Hawaii.* New York: Macmillan.

AZORES, T. (1986–87). Educational attainment and upward mobility: Perspects for Filipino Americans. *Amerasia Journal 13,* (1), 39–52.

BLALOCK, H. JR. (1967). *Toward a theory of minority group relations.* New York: John Wiley.

BOGARDUS, E. (1929). American attitudes toward Filipinos. *Sociology and Social Research, XIV,* 59–69.

BONACICH, E. (1973). A theory of middleman minorities. *American Sociology Review, 38,* 583–594.

BONACICH, E., & JUNG, T. H. (1979). A portrait of Korean small business in Los Angeles, 1977. (Paper presented at the Korean Community Conference, Sponsored by Koryo Research Institute; Los Angeles, March 10.

BULOSAN, C. (1973). *America is in the heart.* Seattle: University of Washington Press.

CABEZAS, A., SHINAGAWA, L. H., & KAWAGUCHI, G. (1986–87). New inquiries into the socioeconomic status of Pilipino Americans in California. *Amerasia Journal, 13* (1), 1–21.

CHANG, E. T. (1994). Los Angeles "riots" and the Korean-American community. In H-Y. Kwon (Ed.), *Korean Americans: Conflict and harmony* (pp. 159–176). Chicago: Covenant Publications.

CORDOVA, F., JANERO, P., OGILVIE, B., SANTOS, R., TANGALAN, S., TANGALAN, A., & TIFFANY, D. (n.d.). Filipino-American Position Paper. Unpublished paper.

CORDOVA, F. (1973). The Filipino-American: There's always an identity crisis. In S. Sue & N. Wagner (Eds.), *Asian Americans* (pp. 136–139). Palo Alto, Calif.: Science and Behavior Books.

DANIELS, R., & KITANO, H. H. L. (1970). *American racism: Exploration of the nature of prejudice.* Englewood Cliffs, N.J.: Prentice-Hall.

DUFF, D., & RANSOM, A. (1973). Between two worlds: Filipinos in the U.S. Navy. In S. Sue & N. Wagner (Eds.), *Asian Americans* (pp. 202–211). Palo Alto, Calif.: Science and Behavior Books.

HARVEY, Y. S., & CHUNG S-H. (1980). The Koreans. In J. McDermott et al. (Eds.), *Peoples and Cultures of Hawaii* (pp. 134–154). Honolulu: University of Hawaii Press.

HOUCHINS, L., & HOUCHINS C-S. (1976). The Korean Experience in America, 1903–1924. In N. Hundley (Ed.), *The Asian American* (pp. 129–156). Santa Barbara, Calif.: Clio Press.

HURH, W-M. (1977). Comparative study of Korean immigrants in the United States: A typology. *Korean Christian Journal, 2* (Special Spring Issue), 60–69.

HURH, W-M., & KIM, K. C. (1984). *Korean Immigrants in America.* Cranberry, N.J.: Fairleigh Dickinson University Press.

HURH, W-M. (1994). Majority Americans' Perception of Koreans in the United States. In H-Y. Kwon (Ed.), *Korean Americans: Conflict and harmony* (pp. 3–22). Chicago: Covenant Publications.

KIM, B-L. C., & CONDON, M. E. (1975). A study of Asian Americans in Chicago: Their socioeconomic characteristics, problems and service needs. *Interim Report to the National Institute of Mental Health.* Washington, D.C.: Department of Health, Education, and Welfare.

KIM, D. S. (1977). How they fared in American homes: A follow-up study of adopted Korean children. *Children Today, 6,* 2–6, 31.

KIM, D. S., & KIM, S. P. (1985). A banana identity: Asian American adult adoptees in America. Paper presented at the annual meeting of the Council on Social Work Education, Washington, D.C., February 17.

KIM, H-C. (1980). Koreans. In S. Thernstrom, A. Orlov, & O. Handlin (Eds.), *Harvard Encyclopedia of American Ethnic Groups* (pp. 601–606). Cambridge, Mass.: Harvard University Press.

KIM, H-C. (1977a). Ethnic enterprises among Korean immigrants in America. In H-C. Kim (Ed.), *The Korean Diaspora* (pp. 85–107). Santa Barbara, Calif.: Clio Press.

KIM, H-C. (1977b). Ethnic enterprises among Korean immigrants in America. In H-C Kim (Ed.), *The Korean Diaspora* (pp. 85–107). Santa Barbara, Calif.: Clio Press.

KITANO, H. H. L. (1974). Japanese Americans: The development of a middleman minority. *Pacific Historical Review, 43* (4), 500–519.

KITANO, H. H. L., & DANIELS, R. (1995). *Asian Americans.* Englewood Cliffs, N.J.: Prentice-Hall. 2nd ed.

KOH, T-H. (1994). Ethnic identity in first, 1.5 and second generation Korean-Americans. In H-Y. Kwon (Ed.), *Korean Americans: Conflict and Harmony* (pp. 43–54). Chicago: Covenant Publications.

MELENDY, H. B. (1967). California's discrimination against Filipinos. In J. Saniel (Ed.), *The Filipino Exclusion Movement, 1927/1935* (pp. 3, 10). Quezon City, Philippines: Institute of Asian Studies, University of the Philippines.

MELENDY, H. B. (1980). Filipinos. In S. Thernstrom, A. Orlov, & O. Handlin (Eds.), *Harvard Encyclopedia of American ethnic groups* (pp. 354–362). Cambridge, Mass.: Harvard University Press.

MIN, P. G. (1986–87). Filipino and Korean immigrants in small business: A comparative analysis. *Amerasia Journal 13* (1), 53–71.

MORALES, R. (1974). *Makibaba.* Los Angeles: Mountain View Publishers.

MUNOZ, A. (1971). *The Filipinos in the United States.* Los Angeles: Mountain View Publishers.

YANG, E-S. (1979). Korean community, 1903–1970: Identity to economic prosperity. Paper presented at Korean Community Conference, sponsored by Koryo Research Institute; Los Angeles, March 10.

YU, E-Y. (1994). Community-based disaster management: The case of Los Angeles Koreatown during the April 29 riots. In H-Y. Kwon (Ed.), *Korean Americans: Conflict and harmony* (pp. 135–138). Chicago: Covenant Publications.

Chapter 16

Southeast Asians and Pacific Islanders

From relative obscurity, Southeast Asians have achieved a degree of prominence. The Pacific Islanders are still somewhat invisible, although the push for autonomy among native Hawaiians has aroused some media interest. But being in the public eye is not always positive; the problems of groups are often featured, which may add to stereotyped images.

The Southeast Asians include the Vietnamese, Laotians, Cambodians (Kampucheans), Hmong, and the ethnic Chinese. For the Pacific Islanders, the major groups are the Hawaiians, Samoans, Tongans, Guamanians, and Fijians. The purpose of this chapter is to present a brief section on the groups. Their relatively small numbers and the recency of their immigration contributes to the lack of research studies and information about them. We expect that with the surge of interest on the Pacific Rim, there will soon be scholars who will study the above groups as they contribute to the American society.

REFUGEES

The passage of time plays tricks with memories, but it seemed only a short time ago (actually 1975) that the TV screens were showing pictures of masses of Vietnamese, scrambling to board the American planes that would take them away from Saigon. As a consequence, the image that is most strongly associated with the Southeast Asians, especially the Vietnamese, is that of refugees.

The question of who is a refugee is important since the acquisition of that status has different meanings for those who wish to come to the United States or to other countries. Basically, a refugee is a person who flees from his or her country for safety in a time of distress and who would be in danger if returned to the country of origin. Therefore, a person leaving for economic reasons is not considered a refugee, nor is a person who may be able to return to the homeland without fear of persecution.

The experience of the refugee is different from that of most other immigrant groups for a number of reasons. The refugee is an involuntary migrant who may formerly have held a satisfactory and often prominent position at home and felt a commitment to that society. The exodus was undertaken out of necessity and fear, with little thought about the consequences of migration. Many harbor the hope that their fears will not be reinforced and that conditions at home will change, so that the flight will be temporary (Stein, 1979).

Refugees are created when a dominant group no longer wishes to have a minority group reside within its boundaries. Under such a mandate, the dominant group expels, exiles, or deports individuals and groups. More severe treatment of unwanted minorities includes extermination and genocide (see model of domination, Chapter 5). Refugees can be defined as people with a well-founded fear of being persecuted for reasons of race, religion, nationality, or political opinion who would return to their country of origin if conditions warranted. The definition covers people escaping civil wars, dictatorships, communist regimes, and natural disasters. Refugees are as old as history, and the movement of unwanted populations continues to the present day. Since the start of the twentieth century, approximately 100 million people have been uprooted from their homelands and forced to look for new places to live.

By definition, a refugee must have crossed an international border to escape persecution. Refugees have often fled from one impoverished country to another, thereby overburdening the capacity of the receiving nation to provide the services and opportunities for economic well-being. There has been a growing resistance on the part of developing countries to providing permanent asylum in already marginal economies.

In extreme cases, countries have resorted to forced repatriation or a closed-door policy. Recent history suggests that the cost of these policies is considerable when measured in terms of human misery and loss of life. The Thai government's forced repatriation of the Khmer refugees into Kampuchea in 1979–1980 resulted in innumerable deaths from starvation or exhaustion or at the hands of border patrols who did not distinguish between guerrillas and noncombatants.

America has similarly avoided the obligations of first asylum by restricting entry of certain groups. The most notable current examples were the interdiction of the Haitian boat people headed for Florida and the steadfast refusal to grant Salvadorans asylum (Stein, 1983).

Refugee Legislation

Through enactment of the Refugee Act of 1980, the United States adopted the United Nations definition of a refugee, which includes the principle of asylum and resettlement assistance for refugees. Prior to 1980, the United States had responded to the refugee problem with ad hoc emergency legislative measures that varied in their determination of refugee eligibility.

The first legislative enactment distinguishing refugees as a special category was the Displaced Persons Act of 1948. The legislation was enacted after World War II and was designed to allow the entrance of forced laborers from conquered German states and individuals fleeing Soviet persecution. Five years later the Refugee Act of 1953 was passed, offering asylum to victims of national calamities and those fleeing communism in Europe and the Middle East. After the Bay of Pigs incident, Congress acted to regularize and make permanent the immigration status of all Cubans who had arrived in this country since January 1, 1959 by granting them refugee eligibility through the Migration and Refugee Assistance Act of 1962.

The amendments to the Immigration and Nationality Act of 1965, with its broad powers of executive parole authority, established a new precedent in American policy. Initially, parole had been designed as an emergency measure for granting asylum on an individual basis. After 1956 the parole authority was extended to include the mass parole of the Hungarian Freedom fighters, the Cuban refugees entering the United States between 1961 and 1971, and over 100,000 refugees from Indochina in 1976.

The conditions facing present-day refugees such as the Cubans and Southeast Asians appear more difficult when compared to earlier refugee groups. In the past, exiled refugees came during periods of economic expansion and could seek opportunities in unsettled territories and open lands. Consequently, host nations were more relaxed in their immigration policies. But the present-day individual, who may arrive with less training and fewer marketable skills, enters the United States at a time of high unemployment and of a rising sentiment against aliens, who are viewed as economic competitors. There is also a rise in nativist sentiment among those who object to dividing scarce federal dollars with the new refugees. The hostility is especially strong against refugees who have turned to public assistance as a stage in their adaptation to the new society.

THE SOUTHEAST ASIANS

Prior to the arrival of the refugees, the number of Vietnamese in the United States was slightly over 20,000, and the number of Cambodians and Laotians was too small to be counted. In 1980 there were 415,238 Indochinese refugees living in the United States; approximately 78 percent were from Vietnam, 16 percent from Cambodia, and 6 percent from Laos. In 1990, the figures had risen to 614,547 Vietnamese, 149,014 Laotians, 147,411 Cambodians, and 90,547 Hmong. The majority of the refugees live in California, followed by Texas and Washington. Although initial attempts were made to scatter the refugees throughout the country, they have tended to migrate from cold weather states to the warmer sunbelt states. By 1990, a significant percentage of these groups was American born. Twenty percent of the Vietnamese were in this category, with a median age of 6.6 years.

Background

Vietnam, Cambodia, and Laos were all part of the old French colonial empire and were lumped together as French Indochina, even though they were ethnically and culturally diverse. Cambodian culture was strongly influenced by India, Siam, and Annam; Laos was closely related to Thailand and Siam; Vietnam was heavily influenced by China (Wright, 1980). There have been deep historical differences between the groups, as well as intragroup divisions.

In 1975, when the collapse of Saigon seemed imminent, President Ford set up a special Interagency Task Force representing twelve federal agencies to coordinate the resettlement of the Vietnamese refugees. Resettlement camps were erected at Camp Pendleton, California; Fort Chaffee, Arkansas; Eglin Air Force Base, Florida; and Fort Indiantown, Pennsylvania with the purpose of facilitating the assimilation of the refugees into the United States as quickly as possible.

Efforts were made to find sponsors and employment in order to minimize the use of public welfare programs. Wright notes that sponsorship involved an unusual amount of effort. Sponsors committed themselves to provide food, clothing, and shelter, to help in finding employment and enrolling children in schools, to accept financial responsibility for medical care, and to give advice and encouragement to the refugees.

One of the problems of sponsorship involved definitions of a family unit. Many sponsors preferred small units of up to five members, whereas traditional Vietnamese household units could hold up to twenty-five members. Another problem was the focus on assertiveness and independence in their resettlement training, which conflicted with the Vietnamese emphasis on respect and submission to parental wishes.

The Vietnamese

The history of Vietnam includes invasions by the Chinese, French, Japanese, and Americans. The Chinese influence was the longest and most pervasive—Chinese immigration to Southeast Asia dates over 2,000 years—yet relationships between the two groups has seldom been positive. The majority of the Chinese lived in their own segregated communities and were subject to numerous repressive measures (Strand & Jones, 1985).

The French entered Vietnam in 1777 during the era of European conquest and colonization. The treaty of 1787 gave the French exclusive trading rights and access to the ports. French troops and French control did not come about until the 1890s. Once the French gained control, the native Vietnamese were subjected to colonialism, which meant the cessation of civil liberties, such as freedom of speech, participation in the political process, and travel.

There were continuous rebellions against French rule. The most significant was the Revolutionary Youth Movement, founded by Ho Chi Minh in 1925. In 1930 this movement became the Vietnamese Communist Party.

The Japanese moved into Vietnam in 1940, and for the most part, tolerated and cooperated with the existing French colonial institutions, so that Asian colonialism took the place of European colonialism. The defeat of Japan in 1945 left a power vacuum that was partially filled by the Viet Minh, lead by Ho Chi Minh, who had resisted the Japanese and would again resist the French, and then the Americans—Ho's point of view was that they were all foreign intruders.

The French, with American assistance, reoccupied Vietnam after World War II, but their defeat by the Viet Minh at Dienbienphu hastened their departure from the country. An international conference at Geneva, Switzerland

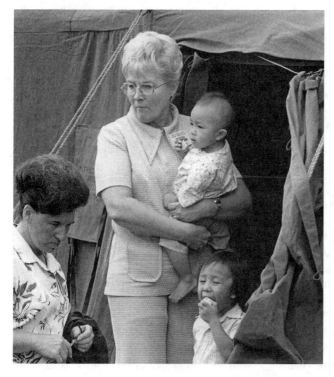

Volunteer worker at a Vietnamese refugee center in Florida, 1975.

in 1954 resulted in France conceding the independence of Vietnam and the neighboring countries of Laos and Cambodia.

Free elections were to be held in all of Vietnam in 1956, but they never took place. Instead, two rival regimes, the Republic of Viet Nam (South Vietnam), and the Democratic Republic of Viet Nam (North Vietnam) evolved under the leadership of Ngo Diem Diem in the South, and Ho in the north.

The United States entered this conflict through a variety of actions. The Truman Administration (1945–1949) gave aid to the French and by the end of the Eisenhower Administration, in January 1961, there were approximately 600 military advisers in Vietnam.

When President Kennedy was assassinated in November 1963, there were more than 16,000 American soldiers in Vietnam and they were beyond the mere advising stage. Under President Johnson, the number of American soldiers grew to almost 475,000 at the end of 1967, not counting another 60,000 men in the offshore fleet, and another 30,000 stationed in Thailand. The war eventually extended into Laos and Cambodia; counting the costs of the conflict in human terms only, more than 50,000 Americans were killed and between two to three million Vietnamese lost their lives. In addition, the war created millions of refugees; one estimate was that between 1965 and 1968, there were three million Vietnamese refugees. Many were housed in refugee camps with primitive facilities, while others fled to Saigon. The mass movement drastically altered the residential patterns; by 1969, South Vietnam changed from a 15 percent urban population to one that had grown to 50 percent urban (Strand & Jones, 1985).

Immigration

It was this background that led to the immigration of large numbers of Southeast Asians. Two waves of refugees can be identified. Many of the first wave were military personnel, civil servants, teachers, farmers, fishermen, employees of the Americans, and Catholics. They were primarily of the middle and upper classes so that life under a communist regime would no doubt have entailed reprisals and personal harm. Nearly half of the heads of households were born in North Vietnam and had fled to the south after the French defeat at Dienbienphu in 1954. Many came in family groups, although there was also a sizable number of single males. There were extremes in wealth: Some had substantial sums of money while others fled with scarcely more than the clothes on their back (Liu, 1979).

The second wave came to the United States after 1975. They were generally less educated, younger, Buddhist, and less prepared for life in the United States than the earlier arrivals. By 1984, more than 700,000 refugees from Southeast Asia had been admitted to the United States. But it should also be noted that other countries were also involved in the refugee issue: China had taken in more than a quarter of a million; France and Canada had over

80,000 each; while Australia, West Germany, and Great Britain had also participated with smaller numbers (Herring, 1986).

The road from Vietnam to the final country of asylum was not an easy one. Rose (1982) described one path—from Vietnam to a first asylum camp in Thailand, to Malaysia and the Philippines. Papers were then checked and information transmitted to New York. If the candidate survived this step, then a search began for possible sponsors. If a match was made, medical clearances came next, followed by a move to a transit center in the United States. Then came the final trip to a prearranged residence.

Other roads included a stay at Refugee Processing Centers in Indonesia or in the Philippines. Refugees were assigned to "cultural orientation classes," while awaiting a move to their final destination. Then there were those refugees known as the "boat people"—escapees from Vietnam, desperately trying to reach Thailand, Malaysia, or other countries by sea. Many suffered unbelievable hardships, including rape, pillaging, and brutal attacks by pirates. An estimated 80 percent of boat people were apparently attacked at least once (Kitano & Daniels, 1988: 141).

Cambodians

The background of the Cambodians, also known as the Kampucheans, includes influences by the Thais, Vietnamese, Chinese, and the Burmese. Western influences include the Spanish, Portuguese, French, and Americans. Cambodia at one time was one of the great civilizations of Southeast Asia. The empire lasted from 802 to 1432 when it became part of the Vietnamese and Siamese kingdoms. It remained a vassal state until the French took control in 1863. Although there were rebellions against the French, the French retained control until 1944 when Prince Sihanouk declared independence, even though the Japanese were then in nominal control. In 1946 it was declared an autonomous state within the French union. In 1955 Sihanouk defeated a French-backed candidate and remained as prime minister. However, problems with the United States led to an increased dependence on Russian and Chinese aid and increased cooperation with North Vietnam in the Vietnam War.

The border area became a sanctuary for the communist forces against air attacks by the South Vietnamese and the Americans. Cambodia was caught between China and North Vietnam on one side and the United States and South Vietnam on the other. When Cambodia came under formal control of the Provisional Revolutionary Government in 1969, the American response was to start intense bombing and a program to defoliate the rubber trees. Between 1970 and 1975, American bombers dropped over a half million tons of bombs on Cambodia.

In 1970, General Lon Nol, with the approval of the United States, overthrew Prince Sihanouk's government and broke off relations with North Vietnam and the Viet Minh.

In 1975, just prior to the American exodus from Vietnam, the Khmer Rouge, under Pol Pot, overthrew General Nol's government. The shift of power from the rightist government of Lon Nol to the communist leadership of Pol Pot was followed by a reign of terror with the murder of at least one million Cambodians by other Cambodians and the forced relocation of others. More than 150,000 fled to Vietnam and at least 33,000 to Thailand. Pol Pot's primary targets were intellectuals, government officials, and urban dwellers, although all classes suffered.

In 1978, Vietnam, now under communist control and aided by the Soviet Union, sought to limit Pol Pot and Chinese influence over the area and therefore invaded Cambodia and installed its own puppet government. This invasion was followed by another mass exodus of an estimated 100,000 who fled primarily from Cambodia to Thailand. The traditional enmity between the Khmer and the Vietnamese, as well as a continued famine, provided the major push out of the country.

Laotians (Hmong)

Refugees from Laos were primarily the Hmong, a people indigenous to China who spread southward into the hills of Laos early in the nineteenth century. Chinese history refers to them as a race living in the mountains, speaking a particular language, and subsisting on an economy based on the cultivation of upland rice, maize, and poppy as cash crops. Their culture shares many elements with the Chinese, and the Hmong are sometimes considered to have been among the first inhabitants of China (Tapp, 1985).

The escalation of the war in Vietnam affected Laos; the country was used as a major supply line for North Vietnam—the Ho Chi Minh trail ran the length of eastern Laos. Massive American bombing of Laos led to the involvement of the Hmong. The Hmong, in cooperation with the Central Intelligence Agency (CIA), became a counterguerilla force, whose assignments included collecting intelligence on North Vietnamese troop movements and rescuing American personnel, including downed American pilots. An estimated 15,000 Hmong died in combat; they were known as courageous and knowledgeable jungle fighters (King & Holley, 1985).

The fall of Vietnam and the withdrawal of American forces led to thousands of Laotians—primarily the Hmong—fleeing their homeland. They fled to a variety of countries, including the United States, France, and French Guiana, although a large number ended up in Thai refugee camps. Tapp (1985), in a visit to the camps in Thailand, indicates a number of problems: disputes between different clans and different political factions; disagreements between those who favored emigration and those who wished to remain in the camps, and those who wished to be resettled in China against those who felt China was the communist enemy. A major dispute was the desire of the Hmongs to foster high birth rates so that they could help each other and regain their lands, as against the desires of the Thais, who ran the camps, to minimize the number of new children.

Camp life was—and continues to be—especially destructive to males. Women had their daily chores, but for the men, there were no fields to cultivate or wars to fight so that the time was spent in idleness, watching cock fights, quarreling, and talking endlessly about the events that got them there. There were instances of deep depression and the appearance of revival movements, led by charismatic leaders (Tapp, 1985).

The experiences of the Hmong in transit were similar to those of the other Southeast Asian groups—sponsorship, clearance, and resettlement. There was an attempt to scatter them throughout the United States, but most have voluntarily resettled in the warm weather areas.

Adaptation of the Southeast Asians

In many ways the adaptation of the various groups that make up the Southeast Asian population is no different from the experiences of other immigrant groups. There are the priorities of everyday living—decent housing, finding a job, and making a living. Then there is the clash of cultures wherein American-born and American-educated children perceive the world differently from their immigrant parents.

On the one hand, they entered the United States when the most visible vestiges of anti-Asian discrimination had undergone change. They could be naturalized, own land, and marry whomever they pleased. But they also arrived at a period when most of the public wished to forget about Vietnam and when most Americans had placed a higher priority on self-fulfillment than on reaching out to help the less fortunate.

There were a variety of instances of conflict between the refugees and the host society. American fishermen have been upset over the fishing tactics of the Vietnamese; Blacks and Chicanos have complained about the special assistance given to refugees which in turn has decreased the resources available to their own struggling communities. The feeling that refugees are getting a special handout is strong and that the American taxpayers have paid for the progress or the non-progress remains a source of resentment (Kitano & Daniels, 1988:154).

Lipset and Raab (1969) identified several groups who would be the most threatened by the influx of refugees. They included the "once hads," often labeled as nativists who would be against any influx of foreigners, and the "never hads," comprised of the disadvantaged, including minority groups who see a double standard in funding priorities and competition for jobs and other scarce resources.

The overall picture of the refugee groups indicates their disadvantage in comparison to other Asian American groups. This is not surprising, given not only the recency of their entrance into the country but also because of the circumstances leading to their migration. They were pushed out of their homelands in panic, with no time for planning; they were herded into overcrowded evacuation camps; there was the search for sponsors, of transit to an unsure welcome, and of entering a modern industrial society with inadequate preparation. Even under these conditions there have already been cases of achievement—one young refugee girl won a national spelling contest.

An undated pamphlet published by the Southeast Asian Community Center provides a look at some of the problems such as survivor guilt and repressed anger or rage at those who have contributed to their plight. Although there were differences in each of the different refugee groups, the Community Center pamphlet included information for those interested in understanding the refugees. Many had lost some or all of their family members and some had come as unaccompanied minors. They had suffered economic and social deprivation in their native countries. Refugee parents were often not in a position to give advice and guidance, since they were torn between their own culture and Western ways. Roles have changed and so have expectations. As the youth become more "American," the gap between parent and child will increase and so will potential sources of conflict. The educational system may not adequately meet the needs of the youth, and the presence of gangs and illegal substances provides fertile opportunities for those who are less integrated into the norms of the community.

Emmons and Reyes (1989), writing about the results of a survey (400 respondents) of Orange County's approximately 100,000 Vietnamese residents, see gangs and crime as the worst problem (that is, extortion and gang behavior from Vietnamese gangs with the local community its primary victims), and assistance in learning English as the greatest need. Nearly two-thirds perceived at least some anti-Vietnamese prejudice, but the majority (54 percent) said that their lives were going "very well," and another 42 percent indicated that things were going "somewhat well." The picture was of a somewhat insular Vietnamese community where the Vietnamese language was the main source of communication in 83 percent of the households; where 76 percent still had contacts and friends in Vietnam and where 61 percent spent their money mainly in Vietnamese stores and restaurants.

Efron (1989) writes about the development of violent, defiant Vietnamese female gangs. Normal adolescent identity problems are exacerbated among the refugees because of cultural and social dislocation, the undermining of their family structure, their lives in the refugees camps, and the immigration experience. Profiles of gang members include orphans, those living with one parent, or those living with foster parents. In many cases, the parental role is taken by poorly educated adults who do not speak English and who have to depend on their children to communicate for them, which contributes to the undermining of parental authority. Problems are especially acute for those teenagers who cannot achieve well in school.

Hein (1995) writes that antipathy towards the Indo-Chinese results more from traditional racism and urban competition rather than resentment from the Vietnamese War. Incidents against them rose from 1975 to 1990; the refugees have used the courts to combat discrimination. The model that appears most appropriate at the present time is that of ethnic resilience, with a high retention of an ethnic identity. Identity is reinforced by racism from the outside and the development of ethnic communities, such as Westminster near Los Angeles.

The establishment of formal relations with Vietnam has changed the course of events for many Vietnamese. Some mistrust the communist regime while others view it as an opportunity to revisit their former homes and to establish business relationships. Perhaps for the majority, making a living in America is the highest priority.

Several summary statements concerning the various refugee groups include:

1. They are a diverse group, with different histories, different levels of "westernization," and different patterns of adaptation.
2. Some have a desire to return to their home country, while others have opted for a permanent life in the United States.
3. The attempts to scatter them throughout the country have generally failed. Most have chosen to migrate to the warm weather states, especially California.
4. The recency of their immigration limits the amount of information available.
5. Many of the issues and problems are similar to the experiences of other immigrant groups. However, their tragic background experiences are an additional element to be considered.
6. At the present time, they are at the bottom of the ethnic stratification model, but it appears that with the American-born generation, there will be upward mobility.

THE PACIFIC ISLANDERS

Possibly the least known group falling under the rubric of Asian Americans are the Pacific Islanders. It was only in the United States Census of 1980 that they were listed (see Table 16–1); prior to that time, they belonged in the "other" category.

The most numerous are the native Hawaiians, who make up 85 percent of the total, followed by the Samoans, Guamanians, and Tongans. The purpose of this section is to provide information on the Samoans, Guamanians, and the Hawaiians. Their inclusion as Asian Americans has more to do with geography than with culture, and even their geographic proximity seems far fetched.

TABLE 16–1   Pacific Islander Population, 1980 and 1990

Group	1980	1990
Polynesian		
Hawaiian	220,278	205,501
Samoan	39,520	57,679
Tongan	6,226	16,707
All other	2,186	3,998
Micronesian		
Guamanian	30,695	47,754
All other	4,813	7,216
Malanesian		
Fijian	2,834	
All other	477	7,218
Pacific Islander, not specified	469	4,519
Total	259,566	350,592

Source: U.S. Census.

Samoans

The Samoan Islands are located in the South Pacific, about 2,300 miles southwest of Hawaii and 1,600 miles northeast of New Zealand. The nine major islands are divided into two political entities, American Samoa and Western Samoa. There were over 27,000 living in American Samoa in 1970 and over 131,000 in Western Samoa in the same year. The islands are described as hot and humid, with high rainfall and a tropical climate (Shu, 1985).

Great Britain, Germany, and the United States were the primary foreign influences over the islands. In 1899, Western Samoa became a colony of Germany; after the defeat of Germany in World War I, it came under the mandate of the League of Nations and was administered by New Zealand. The United States acquired its part of Samoa in 1899, used it primarily as a naval base for the next fifty years, and still maintains sovereignty.

The first modern migration from Samoa occurred in the 1920s to Hawaii. Samoans were brought over to help build the Hawaiian Mormon Temple at Laie, about 35 miles from Honolulu. This initial group was motivated primarily by a religious orientation and most stayed in Laie, in contrast to subsequent groups who tended to move on to Honolulu and other areas where there were better economic opportunities (Pierce, 1956).

The second significant migration occurred after the U.S. Navy transferred administration of the islands to the Department of the Interior in 1950. Many Samoans followed the Navy to Hawaii and to other mainland port cities, such as San Francisco, Los Angeles, and San Diego. The major pulls were for better jobs, a better education, and to join relatives. Samoans from the American territory are able to travel to the United States without passports or visas.

The immigration from a small, peaceful island, surrounded by friends and kin, to an urban area like Los Angeles with its freeways and scattered families creates problems. One Samoan indicated that life was certainly different in Los Angeles. In Samoa and in Hawaii, she never felt that she was a minority, but in California, she definitely was a minority. She relates that in the home islands, distances were short, she was constantly surrounded by family and kin, skin color and language were not a mark of difference, and there was an easy familiarity. The term *faasamoa* denoted common customs, culture, values, and traditions (Milford, 1986).

But in America, the Samoans are invisible, and generally ignored by the dominant community. Their small numbers and the relative insignificance of their home islands in international affairs means little recognition and little power. An additional handicap faced by all Pacific Islanders is their placement as "Asian Americans," so that they are often deemed not qualified for programs designed to help disadvantaged minorities. Major disadvantages include language difficulties, lack of educational and occupational skills, and low income.

Most Samoans live in family and extended family units, as do other Pacific Islanders, and expect to have other relatives join them in a chain migration. Their median age of 16.8 years is well below the national median of 28.8 years; they have an even sex ratio and they tend to marry within the group (Shu & Satele, 1977).

The current adaptation of the first generation of Samoans reflects a bicultural lifestyle. At work, the male may dress and act like his American peers, but at home, he may take off his shoes, put on a *lava lava* (a wraparound skirt), sit on the floor, and speak in Samoan. He may expect his family to behave in a Samoan fashion, where adolescents help in everything from preparing meals to taking care of the younger children (Kotchek, 1980). The effects of exposure to the American culture, especially among the younger generation who are attending American schools, will no doubt have an effect on the old lifestyles.

One special area that differentiates Samoans from other Asian Americans is their athletic ability and large body size. Samoans from Hawaii have achieved a measure of fame by engaging in *sumo,* the Japanese-style wrestling contest, where large body size is a mandatory requirement. Other Samoans have been prominent in American football, both at the college and professional levels.

Guamanians

In many ways the Guamanians and Tongans, as well as other Pacific Islanders, are similar to the Samoans. Guam, Saipan, Tinian, and Rota are territories of the United States and constitute the commonwealth of the Northern Marianas. The islands are located about 1,500 miles east of Manila, 1,500 miles south of Tokyo, and 6,000 miles west of Los Angeles.

Guam was first "discovered" by Magellan on his first trip around the world in 1521 and remained under Spanish rule until the defeat of Spain in the Spanish American War, when it became a United States possession. Japan took over the island during World War II; it has since been returned to the United States.

Early Spanish rule was characterized by a missionary zeal and strong resistance by the native Chamorros; one consequence was the virtual elimination by the Spaniards of the native male population. Early accounts placed the number of natives as over 50,000, but in the first recorded census in 1710, only 3,539 had survived.

Eventually, the natives, composed primarily of females, mixed with Filipinos, Mexicans, Anglos, and Japanese so that the present day Chamorro is likely to be a product of a multiracial background (Kitano & Daniels, 1988).

The year 1970 was important for Guam because the "protection" of the United States military was withdrawn so that new immigrants could now enter the island. The opening of Guam meant increased foreign competition, especially from Filipinos, Koreans, and Taiwanese. Natives often lost their jobs, so that there was a push towards immigration (Munoz, 1979).

The problems of the Guamanians are similar to those of most of the islander populations. They are less experienced and sophisticated about the business and technological world. Unlike their Asian counterparts from more business-oriented societies, they have not opened restaurants, grocery stores, and other small business establishments. Very few gain advanced degrees and enter the professions; most jobs are in the unskilled and semiskilled workforce as custodians, cooks, and clerks. The elderly live isolated from the mainstream; they are more familiar with the political activities and occurrences in the home islands than in their present homes. Past island social support networks have proved useful, but are less relevant in the new environment.

Munoz (1979) writes about the relationship between the United States and Guam over the past century. The priority of the United States Navy was primarily in terms of defense, so that the needs and the problems of the native population was secondary. As such, there developed a paternalistic relationship, characterized by dependency, which left many of the Chamorros unprepared for independent living, once they gained their freedom.

The Hawaiians

The history of Hawaii goes back well over 1,500 years when Polynesian voyagers from the Marquesas Islands and Tahiti colonized the islands. Captain James Cook, the famous English explorer, came to Hawaii in 1778, which was then a thriving and highly stratified culture with over 300,000 inhabitants. Early Hawaii was marked by constant conflict so that the eventual bloody re-

A Hawaiian selling leis at a stand.

unification under the control of Kamehameha I left the islands extremely vulnerable to invasion from the outside (Howard, 1980).

The New England Congregationalist missionaries arrived in 1820. They discovered a totally changed population from the natives that Cook had met. For example, Cook described the strength, intelligence, and cleanliness of the natives who farmed, fished, and enjoyed athletic games and dances. But by the 1820s, there were complaints about their laziness, bad health, and apathy (Fuchs, 1961).

The two most important factors involving the change were the openness and hospitality of the Hawaiians and the popularity of trade. Hawaii became a stopover for many traders who introduced alcohol and European diseases such as syphilis, gonorrhea, pneumonia, smallpox, and cholera with which the

Hawaiian genetic system had no experience. There was widespread drunkenness and sexual activity; Hawaiian chiefs opted for fancy clothes, ornaments, and weapons and worked the natives to the ground in their taste for foreign goods. As Fuchs writes, the old social ties disappeared, group respect vanished, and the old Hawaiian way of life was replaced by overwhelming despair.

The Christian missionaries, largely from New England, also participated in social change. They attacked the native way of life and discouraged the use of the language, and looked down upon their dress, dances, art, and all aspects of the native culture.

There are a variety of ways of looking at the Hawaiians. One view is that they were extremely successful in "melting," so that very few "pure" Hawaiians are left. Therefore, when there is an attempt to identify a native, the chances are high that it will include any number of Asian nationalities—Japanese, Chinese, Korean, or Filipino, as well as white (*haole*) bloodlines. The blend has evolved into an island culture that is titled, simply, local.

Another view is to decry the virtual disappearance of some of the values of the native culture. An open, friendly greeting to strangers is rare, although these very values have no doubt contributed to the demise of the culture. There is an attempt to regain the spirit of *aloha,* but as anyone who has visited the islands recently knows, the spirit is tinged with tourism and commercialism.

There has been an attempt by Native Hawaiians for self determination. The position of the Natives is that the Islands were stolen from them, along with their citizenship, their land, and their independence. There is a similarity between the native Hawaiians and the American Indians—both were conquered and both wish to restore historic water, fishing, hunting, and gathering rights.

SUMMARY

In summary, even though each of the islands represents different cultures, they face similar issues. These include:

1. Vast differences between the economic and social skills required for survival in small, rural, isolated island cultures and those economic, educational, and social skills needed in impersonal, industrialized, urban settings.

2. Loss in status, rank, and prestige. Employment has generally been in low-status jobs in construction, as security guards and watchmen, and in maintenance. Women find employment as hotel maids, hospital aides, in nursing homes, and in canneries. Very few find jobs in the white collar and professional sector.

3. Low wages and high expenses. Pacific Islanders generally have large families and lend assistance to extended family and relatives. Most also

contribute regularly to their church. Both husband and wife often work, and holding several jobs is not unusual.

4. **Problems of identity.** Identity has traditionally been strongly local and tied to land, to the Islands, and to local kinship groups and villages. Time and distance from the Islands weakens the old sources of identity. The new society encourages individual identity and confuses Pacific Islanders with Filipinos, or classifies them as Pacific Islanders and Asian Americans.

5. **Unrealistic stereotypes.** Pacific Island stereotypes include the romantic, exotic South Seas image inspired by popular novels, movies, and public entertainers, or of an aggressive image of heavy drinking and barroom brawling (Shore, 1980).

The common problem for small immigrant groups that emigrate from nonurbanized cultures concerns their ability to handle issues such as culture conflict, culture shock, and the retention of family control and identity in an urbanized, technological setting where values, norms, and lifestyles are so different. The question is, Will indoctrination and socialization to the traditional ways of the Islands be functional or dysfunctional?

Shore (1980) reports that there is still a low incidence of outmarriage by the Pacific Islanders. This is not too surprising since their emigration is recent; the group still has strong ties with the home islands; they are relatively isolated; and contact with other groups is limited.

However, other factors lead to a prediction of the acculturation, integration, and assimilation of the Pacific Islanders. They are few in number, both in the United States and in their home islands, with no strong, visible ethnic community. Their cultural ties, including their native languages, are not functional in the context of trade, education, or other benefits and, unless artificially supported, will probably disappear. Further, discrimination against them is not as widespread as against previous Asian immigrants, so that acculturation and integration appear as logical stages. However, much of their initial integration may be with other Asian and subordinated groups.

REFERENCES

EFRON, S. (1989). Violent, defiant Vietnamese form girl gangs. *Los Angeles Times,* December 12, p. A3.

EMMONS, S., & REYES, D. (1989). Gangs, crime top fears of Vietnamese in Orange County. *Los Angeles Times,* February 5, part I, p. 3.

FUCHS, L. (1961). *Hawaiian pono: A social history of Hawaii.* New York: Harcourt, Brace and World.

HEIN, J. (1995). *From Vietnam, Laos, and Cambodia,* N.Y.: Twayne.

HERRING, G. (1986). *America's Longest War* (2nd Ed.). New York: Knopf.

HOWARD, A. (1980). Hawaiians. In S. Thernstrom, A. Orlov, & O. Handlin (Eds.), *Harvard Encyclopedia of American Ethnic Groups* (pp. 449–452). Cambridge, Mass.: Harvard University Press.

KING, P. H., & HOLLEY, D. (1985). Indochinese find haven, pain in the U.S. *Los Angeles Times,* May 1.

KITANO, H. H. L., & DANIELS, R. (1988). *Asian Americans* (p. 141). Englewood Cliffs, N.J.: Prentice-Hall.

KOTCHEK, L. (1980). Of course we respect our old people, but . . . : Aging among Samoan migrants. *California Sociologist, 3* (2), 197–212.

LIPSET, S. M., & RAAB, E. (1969). *The politics of unreason.* New York: Harper and Row.

LIU, W. (1979). *Transition to nowhere.* Nashville, Tenn.: Charter House.

MILFORD, S. (1985). Imperialism and Samoan national identity. *Amerasia Journal, 12* (1), 48–56.

MUNOZ, F. (1979). An exploratory study of Island migration: Chamorros of Guam. Ph.D. dissertation, University of California, Los Angeles.

PIERCE, B. (1956). Acculturation of Samoans in the Mormon village of Laie, Territory of Hawaii. Master's thesis, University of Hawaii.

ROSE, P. I. (1982). Southeast Asian to America: Links in a chain, Part II. *Catholic Mind, March/April,* 11–25.

SHORE, B. (1980). Pacific Islanders. In S. Thernstrom, A. Orlov, & O. Handlin (Eds.), *Harvard Encyclopedia of American Ethnic Groups* (pp. 736–768). Cambridge, Mass.: Harvard University Press.

SHU, R. (1985). Kinship systems and migrant adaptation: Samoans in the United States. *Amerasia Journal, 12* (1), 23–47.

SHU, R., & SATELE, A (1977). *The Samoan community in Southern California: Conditions and needs.* Chicago: Asian American Mental Health Research Center.

STEIN, B. N. (1979). Occupational adjustment of refugees: The Vietnamese in the United States. *International Migration Review, 13* (1), 25–45.

STEIN, B. N. (1983). The commitment to refugee resettlement. *Annals of the American Academy of Political and Social Science, 487* (May), 187–201.

STRAND, P. J., & JONES, W. JR. (1985). *Indochinese refugees in America.* Durham, N.C.: Duke University Press.

TAPP, N. (1985). *The re-creation of culture: Among refugees from Laos.* London: Refugees Study Programme, British Refugee Council.

U.S. BUREAU OF THE CENSUS. 1990. Census of the Population. Asian and Pacific Islanders in the United States, 1990 CP-3-5. Washington, D.C.: U.S. Government Printing Office.

WRIGHT, M. B. (1980). Indochinese. In S. Thernstrom, A. Orlov, & O. Handlin (Eds.), *Harvard Encyclopedia of American Ethnic Groups* (pp. 508–513). Cambridge, Mass.: Harvard University Press.

Chapter 17

Overview

This chapter will summarize important points for each of the major groups. We will also cover ethnic stratification, ethnic identity, and the lens that provides views of the world; changes by acculturation and generation; the importance of understanding the dominant group; goals of the society, and some final words.

THE BLACK POPULATION[1]

The black population is projected to reach 35 million by the year 2000. This figure will represent 12.8 percent of the total projected U.S. population. Eighty-four percent of the growth since 1980 is due to natural increase, while immigration accounted for the other 16 percent.

An increasingly larger proportion of black families are maintained by either males or females without a spouse. The rising trend of single parent families is occurring in both black and white families.

Fewer Blacks were dropping out of school. The annual high school dropout rate for Blacks declined from 11 percent in 1970 to 5 percent in 1993. Corresponding dropout rates for Whites during the same period were from 5 percent to 4 percent.

The unemployment rate for Blacks continues to be higher than for Whites. The civilian unemployment rates for Blacks was twice that of Whites.

[1]This material is taken from Bennett and DeBarros, 1995.

In 1994, black unemployment rates were 11 percent, compared to 5 percent for Whites.

Median earnings of black year-round full-time workers increased as educational achievement increased. The median income of black married-couple families was higher in families with children. In 1993, one-third of all black persons were poor, up from 31 percent in 1979.

THE HISPANICS[2]

The Hispanic population was 22.8 million in 1993, or 8.9 percent of the total population. Nearly two-thirds of the Hispanics were of Mexican origin.

Hispanics were "younger" than the non-Hispanic white population; their median age was 26.7 percent compared to the white median age of 35.5 years.

Their educational attainment was below the rest of the population, despite significant progress. In 1993, Hispanics with less than a 5th grade education was fourteen times greater than non-Hispanic Whites (0.8 percent).

Other generalizations included the following: Hispanics were more likely to be unemployed; they earned less and were more likely to live below the poverty level than non-Hispanic Whites.

THE AMERICAN INDIAN, ESKIMO, AND ALEUT POPULATION[3]

The American Indian population has grown rapidly; in 1970 the number was 827,000; there were 2.2 million in 1994 and it is estimated to reach approximately 4.3 million by 2060. The increase cannot be attributed to natural increase alone; factors explaining the increase include improvement in the way Census Bureau counted people on reservations and trust lands, continued use of self-identification, and improved outreach efforts.

Other generalizations include the following: that nearly one-half of the American Indians lived west of the Mississippi—Oklahoma, California, Arizona, and New Mexico were the most popular. Nearly two-thirds of the families were married-couple families in 1990, compared to 64.5 percent of the National's families. Educational attainment improved; in 1980, 56 percent were high school graduates, while in 1990, it rose to 66 percent. In 1990, 9 percent had completed a bachelor's degree or higher, compared to 20 percent in the total population.

Poverty remained a major problem; in 1989, 31 percent of American Indians lived below the poverty level compared to 13 percent in the nation. The median family income of American Indian families was $21,750 compared to the $35,225 of all families.

[2]Material in this section was taken from del Pinall, 1995.
[3]This information was taken from Paisano, 1995.

The 1990 Census identified 314 reservations and trust lands. There were 218,320 living on ten of the largest reservations. The per capita income in 1989 for Indians living on reservations and trust lands was $4,478 compared to $8,328 for all Indians.

THE ASIAN AND PACIFIC ISLANDERS[4]

There was an estimated 8.8 million Asian and Pacific Islanders in 1994, up from 7.3 million in 1990. Immigration accounted for about 86 percent of the growth. In the year 2000, it is estimated that there will be 12.1 million, representing about 4 percent of the total population.

Other generalizations include the following: Asian and Pacific Islanders live primarily in the West and in metropolitan areas; they continue to have high educational attainment; they have larger families that non-Hispanic Whites and are comparable to non-Hispanic Whites in income. In 1993, their median family income was $44,460 compared to $41,110 for non-Hispanic Whites. Poverty rates varied; as we have indicated, lumping together all of the groups obscures the differences. However, it provides an overall view that is valuable if read with utmost care.

SAT SCORES

Figure 17–1 shows the 1994 SAT score averages by ethnic group and gender in 1994 reported by the *Daily Bruin* (1996). Asian Americans scored the highest, followed by Caucasians, Native Americans, Latins, Mexicans, Puerto Ricans, and African Americans. Asian Americans do especially well on the Math section; if admission criteria rely heavily on SAT scores, the makeup of college classes will continue to heavily favor the two top groups—which is already a reality—unless there is some form of affirmative action.

SOME PERCEPTIONS

A common perceptual error—especially when viewing objects from a distance—is the blurring of differences so that there is an assumption of homogeneity. Even hills and mountains when viewed from afar have a tendency to become indistinct. Similarly, ethnic groups when perceived from a distance fade into homogeneity. For example, among Asians, the Chinese, Japanese, and Koreans are often mistaken for each other and generalizations concern-

[4]Material in this section was taken from Bennett and Martin, 1995.

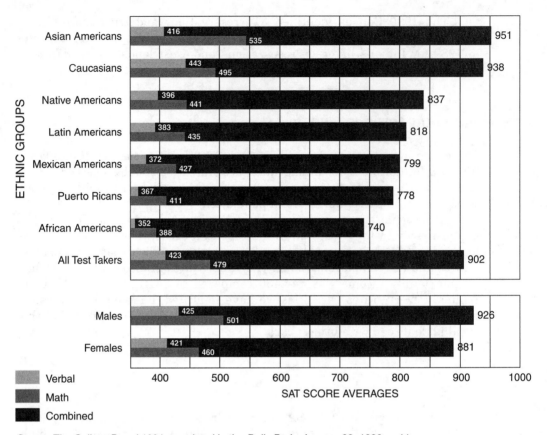

Source: The College Board 1994, as printed in the *Daily Bruin*, January 23, 1996, p. 11.

FIGURE 17–1   1994 SAT score averages by ethnic group and gender.

ing one group are assumed to have validity for them all. But, the closer one gets and the more information one receives, their differences become clearer.

The same generalization can be made concerning the dominant white culture. From afar, there appears to be a great, white monolith, with scores of people who look alike and who seem to hold similar attitudes and values. But the closer one looks, the greater the differentiation. The monolith consists of a variety of religions, of varied social classes, of regional variations, and with roots in a host of different nationalities.

ETHNIC STRATIFICATION

One important, *but not the only,* way of viewing the world is through an ethnic lens. It is obvious that variables such as social class, occupation, age, gender, personality, past experiences and situations are also important in human behavior, but ethnic identity—especially for those groups who are visible and have been treated as ethnics (including racial identity)—is a powerful lens. This is especially true when the issues are framed in terms of race, nationality, and variables that are related to an ethnic identity. As indicated in the opening chapter, the O. J. Simpson trial, when viewed from a variety of frames, illustrated the importance of the racial lens.

Although we recognize the various lenses that are used to view the world, we agree with Omi and Winant (1986) that race is an irreducible element in a person's identity. Race was a key determinant in the Civil Rights Movement, and in the wartime incarceration of the Japanese Americans. It played a major role in the dropping of the atom bomb and continues to play a role in our refugee policy towards the Haitians.

In general, the racial lens is most powerful in groups that have faced a history of racism and discrimination—especially through physical features where in most situations people see the color first, then ethnicity, and finally the person. In most situations, there is initial avoidance so that getting to know the individual behind the color and ethnicity is seldom achieved. In the United States, the groups at the bottom of the ethnic hierarchy are those who are most visible and have been treated most severely in terms of prejudice, discrimination, and racism.

Howell (1995) provides a poignant personal account of what it is to be black. She has to deal with a store clerk who treats her with less courtesy than a white customer; is led to a table in a restaurant close to the kitchen; and plays "tailgate tag" with a Beverly Hills cop because of her skin color. She continues:

> You go to school, work hard, raise a family, move up in your profession. You walk a fine line between your world and theirs holding your breath—waiting. (Waiting and dreading) for the moment when someone looks at you with disdain and mutters an ugly racial epithet, silently or out loud. No matter how well educated you are, no matter how wealthy you are, you know that day will come.

Most members of visible minorities have similar feelings. Insensitive observers accuse minorities of being overly sensitive to racial and ethnic slurs, and wonder why minorities react so negatively to racial stereotypes. Perhaps the old saying of "putting yourself in the other person's moccasins," would be an appropriate rejoinder. It is difficult to ignore one's racial background when one is reminded of it twenty-four hours a day.

In order to develop further understanding, and widening the lens used to deal with racism, an interesting set of questions is posed by Brenda Ness (Ramos, 1995) during a workshop on tolerance and racism. She challenges the audience with the following "Have I" questions:

- Aggressively sought out more information to enhance my own awareness and understanding of racism?

- Spent some time looking at my own racist attitudes and behavior as they contribute to or combat racism around me?
- Re-evaluated my use of terms or phrases that may be perceived by others as degrading or hurtful?
- Openly disagreed with a racist joke or comment among those around me?
- Investigated the curricula of local schools in terms of the treatment of race and racism (also textbooks, assemblies, faculties, staff, and administration)?
- Investigated political candidates at all levels in terms of their stance and activity against racist governmental practices?
- Contributed time, and/or funds to an agency, fund, or program that actively confronts racism?
- Made a personal contract with myself to take a positive stand, even at some possible risk, when the chances arise?
- Complained to those in charge of racist TV and media broadcasts?

There were also a number of other questions that were asked; the basic point was to challenge workshop attendees to focus on their own attempts to deal with racial issues.

It should be noted that the ethnic stratification system is not permanently in place, and that individuals and groups can and do achieve mobility. It is also understood that the stratification is based primarily on income, education, and occupation, and the assumption is that the more minorities act like the dominant group, the higher up in the system they can rise.

Generation and Acculturation

It is important to note that some of the groups—such as the Irish, Italians, Chinese, and Japanese—have been here long enough so that they may be several generations removed from their immigrant parents. As a consequence, they have also been exposed the longest to the U.S. society and are therefore quite "American" in terms of culture and the ability to compete with the natives.

Hansen, in an address in 1937 titled, "The Problem of the Third Generation Immigrant," emphasized the importance of ethnicity and generation. Kivisto and Blanck (1990) in a conference analyzing the contribution of Hansen, edited a volume of essays dealing with the third generation immigrant.

Kivisto writes:

Taken together, these essays amply indicate that a half-century after Hansen's speech, ethnicity in America remains a perplexing, enigmatic topic. They also indicate that Hansen's "problem" not only evokes considerable discussion and debate, but also provides a starting point for treating generations in history and the history of generations. (p. 6–7)

Hansen's thesis describes a sociopsychological process that takes place between parents and children. The immigrant wants to adapt to a society that demands acculturation, but also wants to retain a connection with his or her own church, language and culture. The second generation faces a different world from the first generation—they are more concerned with their adolescent peer group, are intolerant of any deviance, and are more conforming to societal norms. The third generation, more at ease with the society, is much more comfortable in exploring its past and its heritage (Glazer, 1990:105). Each generation is located within a time period, and forces outside of the immigrant family and generations—what is happening in the world outside, including growing up, attending school, entering into the job market, getting married—also enter into the model.

It is important to note that Hansen never intended to create a rigid, mechanistic model and that the importance lies in the process that occurs when immigrant groups enter into a society.

Dysfunctional Effects of Ethnic Stratification

Tumin (1953:393) has provided a number of reasons why a racial stratification system fostering inequality is dysfunctional for the country.

- Racial stratification systems limit the development of the full range of talent available in a society. There is unequal access, unequal opportunity, unequal training and education, and unequal channels of recruitment, all of which tend to affect the motivation of the racial group.
- By limiting the range of available talent, racial stratification systems limit the possibility of expanding the productive resources of a society.
- Racial stratification systems provide the dominant group with the power to shape the acceptance of an ideology that rationalizes the social status quo and labels those who disagree as dissidents, deviants, traitors, or worse.
- Racial stratification systems distribute favorable self-concepts unequally throughout the system. Minority groups are apt to develop negative self-concepts that tend to limit the development of their full potential.
- Status, prestige, and power will also be unequally distributed, so that racist systems limit the sense of belonging and of participating in the decisions of the community.
- The inequalities will also tend to foster alienation, hostility, suspicion, and apathy.

Whether one agrees or disagrees with the stratification and its effects, it is important to recognize that it exists.

THE ENGLISH: WHY ARE THEY IMPORTANT?

The English migration that started in the seventeenth century was, as pointed out by Feagin (1989), colonizing because it involved the invasion and the subordination of a native population. Those groups who came after the English also would have been colonists if they had conquered the English who were already here and placed them in a subordinate position. But, as history tells us, later groups came as immigrants and played subordinate roles—some temporary, others almost permanent—as they attempted to deal with what the English colonists had developed.

It is no wonder that early America had the British stamp; the English were the original settlers and had a numerical superiority for the first several decades. It should also be noted that the single largest group in the seventeenth and eighteenth centuries in the South were the blacks from Africa, but because they came as slaves, they were virtually powerless in determining their own fate.

Feagin (1989) indicates that it was the English, and later, other white Anglo-Saxon groups—which included the Scots, the Welsh, the Scandinavians, and the Germans—that influenced the development and maintenance of the core culture. The political, legal, economic, and social welfare systems were based on familiar English models. The English language, religious values, the work ethic, and the emerging capitalistic system (for the pursuit of profit), as well as music and art were linked to the English tradition. The melody of our national anthem was based on an old English drinking song. American political and legal institutions were shaped by the English and British heritage.

The Declaration of Independence was signed by fifty-six European males: thirty-eight had English backgrounds, while most of the others were Scottish, Scotch Irish, Irish, and Welsh (Ford, 1915:491). It is clear that there was British dominance in all areas of beginning American culture and that ever since their migration, the colonists and their descendants have been the major players in key social, economic, and political positions. They were later joined in their dominant position by other white Protestant groups, so that the study of assimilation starts with the English and other Protestant groups.

The dominance of the English-based culture held sway throughout the 1700s and 1800s, but was modified by the large scale immigration of the late 1800s and early 1900s. These waves brought in religious groups such as the Catholics and Jews; the dominant theme at that time was to melt and merge into the melting pot, and its major effect was to broaden the base of the U.S. culture.

The end of World War II and the Immigration Act of 1965 brought a new immigration: the majority were not of WASP or European background. There also were the civil rights struggles of the Blacks and other disadvantaged minorities who had been systematically denied entrance into the U.S. mainstream. Questions and challenges were mounted concerning the model of assimilation and amalgamation—Was it necessary to become a part of the mainstream in order to be an American?

Although there are current challenges and a possible erosion of WASP influence, of changing goals (Chapter 2), or an emphasis on pluralism, and the development of alternative resources and bases of power, it is still important to note that it is the WASPs who remain in control of corporate offices, board rooms, banks, and foundations (Schrag, 1971). And wealth and power are influential in shaping the political and legal agendas.

Hate Groups

It is also important to acknowledge the existence of hate groups in the society. Kleg (1993) indicates that there are no less than 250 such hate groups and mills. A hate mill refers to individuals and groups who are in the business of providing hate literature and in some cases sponsoring meetings and conclaves. Among white supremacists are groups with titles such as skinheads, Neo-Nazis, Ku Klux Klan, Posse Comitatus, and the Aryan Nations.

Their targets include Blacks, Jews, Asians, and Hispanics. They also tend to be anti-Catholic, anti-homosexual, anti-communist, and in some cases anti-federal government. It is difficult to assess their actual numbers, but it is important to acknowledge the existence of such groups and their ability to disrupt attempts to better intergroup relations.

GOALS OF SOCIETY

On the one hand, it appears relatively easy to achieve a consensus on some of the goals regarding race relations. It would be difficult to argue against the notions that everybody is human and that all individuals should be treated as human beings, and that all Americans should have an equal chance regardless of race, creed, religion, or color. The ideal envisages a colorblind society, where such factors as achievement and motivation are the major factors in evaluation.

But if we gather some of the sentiments that are commonly expressed, we can see the variety of goals as "solutions" to our race-related problems. "Why don't they work hard and become more like us, then they'll be accepted?" "We only want an equal chance, nothing more, nothing less." "Why don't they go back to where they came from?" "Let each group develop its own culture and leave us alone." "Let them prove themselves." "If they act like animals, let them be treated like animals." "Get rid of the hyphenated Americans and we'll see a real America."

These and countless other expressions reflect the lack of consensus and the difficulty in establishing any kind of rational program with much support. Perhaps this multiplicity of goals is one reason why the search for solutions has instead concentrated on the means and processes of human relations. By means and processes we refer to programs such as human relations workshops, group encounters, therapy, and the like, which are geared to treating people as individuals, observing and dealing with racial sensitivities and stereotypes, and feeling good about individual and racial differences. Many of these programs have been effective in achieving their limited goals, but very few have succeeded in addressing the social conditions behind the problem.

The current issues in race relations are different from those of a previous era, when the goal of forming a melting pot was reasonably clear, but the access to the goal was blocked. The barriers to members of a racial minority— that is, those not White, Anglo-Saxon, and Protestant—were so formidable that achieving the goal was not possible. The basic strategies in this era included Americanization (quite successful for certain groups) and discarding the immigrant culture. The problems of prejudice, discrimination, and segregation, however, were not directly addressed, and we ended up with a dominant-dominated stratification system.

When we talk about current goals and the means for achieving them, at least three major points of view should be considered. One perception is that of the dominant white majority. Although there are many viewpoints within this body, majority-group values and majority-group culture have long been equated with being "American" and have been primary in shaping the country's race relations. After the dominant group conquered, overwhelmed, outfought, and outdealt the natives for this land, they forced some nonwhites to join them as slaves and invited others to work as cheap labor. For these people of color, almost impassable barriers to any degree of upward mobility were erected, and the means of becoming like the dominant group were denied.

The white majority holds the power in our society; therefore it is imperative that its definitions of success and its expectations in regard to race relations be considered a significant factor. Their major lens for viewing race relations appears to be on an individualistic level. Individual motivation and achievement are cited and government intervention (i.e., affirmative action, minority set-asides) are viewed as unnecssary.

The second perception is that of the dominated ethnics, and here, too, there are varied opinions. They are the victims of racism, and they lack the resources and the power of the majority group. Their goals, their expectations, and their solutions have been ignored too long. They have suffered under prejudice, discrimination, and segregation; they have felt the effects of incarceration, concentration camps, and genocide; and most are no longer content to remain victims of the social system. Unless the majority group desires to erect new barriers or to use its power to eliminate the minorities, there is no alternative but to begin discussions with ethnics about goals and means. It is hypothesized that individuals and groups who have achieved a degree of upward mobility are more likely to discard the ethnic lens than those who feel trapped by the system. One plausible goal is "relational pluralism," where groups can interact, although the goal of equal status interaction remains a distant reality.

The third perspective—which draws from various sectors, but primarily from the dominant group—includes scholars, professionals, and those in a position to shape government policy. The major tasks for this heterogeneous group include theory and model building, continued research, the formulation of policy, and the implementation of programs.

The task is complicated by the interdisciplinary nature of the problem, for as Van den Berghe (1967) emphasized, race and racism are empirical data that can be used by all the behavioral sciences. To the physical anthropologist, race in the genetic sense may be a subspecification of *homo sapiens;* to the social psychologist, it may be a special instance of prejudice; to the political scientist, a special kind of political ideology; to the sociologist, a form of stratification; to the historian, a byproduct of slavery and colonial expansion; and to the economist, a nonrational factor influencing economic behavior.

One of the problems in academia is similar to one of the problems in race relations—that of framing the issue and of the lens that is used. Academics enculturate according to academic discipline, which provides the frame and the lens to view society. As one consequence, we have a variety of views, with stronger disciplines providing powerful, but more often a narrower lens. Interdepartmental programs are constantly discussed but seldom achieved. Similarly, one of the attempts to provide a variety of frames and of a broader lens in race relations is difficult to achieve, since racism provides such a powerful lens, both for the perpetrator and the victim.

Yet, it would seem that one of the ways of achieving better intergroup relations is to frame issues in broader terms and to provide a wider lens for viewing problems.

OVERALL MODEL

In describing the various racial minorities, our presentation has emphasized the following factors:

1. Reasons for and conditions of migration
2. Background, culture, and power of the minority group
3. Initial contact and reception by the dominant culture
4. Goals—as shaped by the dominant group, the minority group, and their interaction

5. Placement of the group in the stratification system, and the various models for explaining their historical and current status
6. Effects of acculturation and generation
7. Effects of prejudice, discrimination, and segregation
8. Minority-group adaptation
9. Development and maintenance of an ethnic identity

Our overall generalization was that the racial minorities started out in, and continue to remain in, the subordinated sector of the stratification system. Therefore, the most important single issue facing minority groups is that of *inequality*. The various models and goals of society, ranging from pluralism to amalgamation, are all defensible, given equality; but all turn out to be less than ideal under conditions of inequality.

The most common American model has been that of acculturation, integration, and assimilation. But as Hraba (1979:356) noted, under conditions of inequality, the acculturation can be to a "culture of poverty" that has been handed down from generation to generation, or it can be to a subordinated position in the stratification system. One can learn to be an "inferior" as readily as one can learn to be an "equal" or a "superior."

Feagin (1989) also commented on the weakness of acculturation models to deal with the notion that the process can occur at the lower end of the stratification system. The acculturation-integration-assimilation sequence assumes an open system whereby individuals and groups can find their appropriate levels, but it does not take into account the presence of discrimination and other barriers that interrupt the process. It also minimizes the possibility that the dominant group may consciously want to retain subordinated groups at the bottom of the system as an adequate source of labor to fill the less desirable and unwanted jobs in the system.

Greeley (1974) used the term *ethnogenesis* to amplify the meaning of acculturation. He rejected the notion that acculturation inevitably leads to Anglo conformity. Rather, he saw at least three parts to acculturation: One part is Anglo conformity, or conformity to whatever part of the host society one is supposed to become acculturated (including the unequal part of the system); another part is the immigrant or "root" culture; the third and most important part is the "unique adaptive culture," which is the result of the interaction of the first two factors. It is this interaction that makes for the hyphenated American—whether black, Asian, or of Spanish surname—and why they are both different and similar to their brethren who have remained in the homeland. This interaction explains why the Japanese or Chinese scholar from Asia or the Black from an African country sees a certain familiarity among Chinese, Japanese, and black Americans, and yet finds it difficult to fully understand them. This interaction also helps to explain why Ogawa (1978) claimed that the Japanese in Hawaii were different from those from the mainland, and why Kitano (1976) wrote of the differences among Japanese Americans growing up in various sections of the country.

Multiracial Populations

An issue that is the result of increased marriages across racial and ethnic lines is that of "multiracial" populations. Gross (1996) estimates that by the U.S. Census of 2000, there will be between one and two million people of mixed-race descent. California, with its large Latino and Asian population, has already blurred racial and ethnic lines. The problem for the Census is to devise categories to reflect the diversity.

Ideally, people of mixed descent can be bridge builders, bridging the differences between races and cultures, but they can also become marginal to both groups. There is very little research on multiracial populations.

HAVE WE PROGRESSED?

A favorite pastime, as we near the end of the twentieth century, is to speculate whether we are better off today concerning issues of race and racism than we were at the beginning of the 1900s. A review of some of the more widely held beliefs shows us that in some ways there has been progress, and in other ways there has not.

For example, ideas of genetic inferiority have little credibility today, although there remain a number of highly publicized hate groups who hold onto this position. The social Darwinist perspective, quite popular in the early part of the century, has lost ground. The idea that racism was primarily associated with "sick" personalities has also been modified, so that an analysis of broader societal variables, such as structural conditions and inequality have come to the forefront.

Given our immigration history, worldwide factors concerning economic conditions, the need for cheap labor, and migration have also broadened our understanding. But it appears that victims of racism remain as the primary targets for change. Rather than genetic inferiority, there is cultural inferiority—that the solution to our racial problems lies in changing the "culture" of those who are not successful. The idea of cultural inferiority is not new; it was also tied with genetic inferiority so that the term unassimilable meant that certain groups, especially those from Asia, should not be allowed to immigrate because they could not become "American" because of vast differences in race and culture.

The cultural deficit model is used by some to point out that there are some minority groups who have faced discrimination and racism, and yet have managed to become "successful." Sowell (1981) writes that the Chinese and Japanese have confronted color and racial prejudice, but these only served as temporary impediments to their progress. The human capital model, which emphasizes the education and training of the individual, relies heavily on the cultural context. Minorities who are well educated and well trained, with strong families, and high motivation—what Steinberg (1989) refers to as the "right stuff"—supposedly overcome all obstacles posed by race and class to reach the economic pinnacle. Conversely, other groups, conditioned by cultural defects, lag behind in economic competition. The cultural deficit model, just as the genetic inferiority model, justifies existing inequalities. It blames the victims, as though they were the ones responsible for developing the unequal structures and opportunities; as though they were the ones who have created the existing inequalities.

One of the current terms to describe those individuals and groups who are "out of sync" with the rest of the society is the underclass. The underclass generally includes some of the following: high school dropouts, unemployed, welfare recipients, and female-headed households. They also participate in socially negative behavior and reside in the urban ghettoes. A large proportion are Black and Hispanic.

Steinberg (1989:282) criticizes the concept because it has the trappings of objective social science, yet hides the historical and structural sources that have produced and maintained this group. His argument is as follows:

1. The term accepts the established order and ignores the structures of inequality that produce the underclass. The individual becomes the focal point of change and it is too easy to isolate, blame, and attempt to change the victim's antisocial behavior. The presumption is that the underclass can be eliminated by developing programs and policies aimed at changing individual behavior.

2. It denies the historical and group character of the underclass and obscures the role of racism. There are different underclasses by origins, social constitution, circumstances, and demographics. Historically, specific factors have produced different underclasses; the role of racism is especially relevant when discussing the black underclass.

3. It blurs the distinction between race, class, and culture. There should be a conceptual distinction on the distinctive roles that each plays in producing the underclass, the explanatory weight assigned to each, and the dynamic relationships among them should be explored.

It is difficult to argue against the notion that our racial problems are intimately tied to both social class and culture, yet each should be analytically distinct. At one stage, there was a close correlation among them—racial minorities were believed to be genetically and culturally inferior and were consigned to the lower classes. But there were exceptions by ethnic group—historical, demographic, and other variables were different so that the adaptations by ethnic group were also different.

Mass oath to become U.S. citizens, Detroit, 1994.

Wilson (1978) writes about the declining significance of race when discussing the Blacks, a point that had also concerned Asian Americans at an earlier time as they became upwardly mobile. Ethnicity, related to race; generation, a reflection of culture; and class (eth-gen-class) were seen as important variables in understanding the Japanese Americans (Kitano, 1976).

Economic independence and economic equality may be unreachable goals, but without them, minority groups cannot discuss their own priorities without depending on the dominant system. Pluralism, no matter how cleverly stated, is not an attractive model when there is inequality. Steady incomes, better education, and decent housing have transformed some of our former pariah groups into "model minorities," and similar predictions may be made for other groups. It does not mean that life will then become problem-free, for all positions in a social structure have their advantages and disadvantages. But for the minorities, the achievement of some degree of control over their daily lives is a dream that has eluded them for so long that any further delay will be critical to their own lives and may even prove fatal to the entire society. And for the majority group, it is in their power to restructure and to provide opportunities and hope to all people, for it is basically in dominant hands to determine whether ethnic groups become "model" or "problem" minorities.

Another major challenge is how we view our new immigrants, even though we acknowledge that we are a nation of immigrants. Attitudes towards the newcomers have differed in the past, and will continue to differ in the future. Some will see them as necessary labor, others will see them as a threat to their own positions. Immigrants can also be viewed as a resource. A poll taken by the *Los Angeles Times* (Skelton, 1990) indicates that most Americans in the sample thought that immigrants took more from the nation than they gave back, even though others argue that they "put in" more than they "take out."

In conclusion, it is apparent that there are no simple solutions nor adequate wisdom to develop policies that will satisfy the diversity that makes up our society. Nor will it be easy to develop a consensus—historically, groups with more power were able to dictate their preferences. Perhaps the most optimistic sign is that past racist policies have undergone an uneven transformation—two steps forward and one and one-half steps back—and that previous "unacceptable" groups have achieved a degree of mobility. But, as we said in our opening chapter, RACISM IS NOT DEAD, although it is not as overt as it was in the past.

REFERENCES

BENNETT, C. E., & DEBARROS, K. A. (1995). The black population. *Population Profile of the United States, Current Population Reports,* P23–189 (pp. 44–45). Bureau of the Census.

BENNETT, C. E., & MARTIN, B. (1995). The Asian and Pacific Islander population. *Population Profile of the United States, Current Population Reports,* (pp. 48–49). P23–189. Bureau of the Census.

DAILY BRUIN. (1996). 1994 SAT score averages by ethnic group and gender. January 23, p. 11.

DEL PINAL, J. (1995). The Hispanic population. *Population Profile of the United States, Current Population Reports,* P23–189 (pp. 46–47).

FEAGIN, J. (1989). *Racial and ethnic relations.* Englewood Cliffs, N.J.: Prentice-Hall.

FORD, H. J. (1915). *The Scotch Irish in America.* Princeton, N.J.: Princeton University Press.

GLAZER, N. (1990). Hansen's hypothesis and the historical experience of generations. In P. Kivisto & D. Blanck (Eds.), *American Immigrants and Their Generations* (pp. 104–112). Urbana: University of Illinois Press.

GREELEY, A. (1974). *Ethnicity in the United States.* New York: John Wiley.

GROSS, J. (1996). UC Berkeley at crux of new multiracial consciousness. *Los Angeles Times,* January 9, p. A1.

HANSEN, M. (1937). The Problem of the Third Generation American Immigrant, a republication of the 1937 address. Rock Island: Swenson Swedish Immigration Research Center and Augustana College Library, 1987.

HOWELL, M. (1995) An ignorant phone caller hits a nerve. *Los Angeles Times,* December 22, p. B9.

HRABA, J. (1979). *American ethnicity.* Itasca, Ill.: F. E. Peacock.

KITANO, H. H. L. (1976). *Japanese Americans.* Englewood Cliffs, N.J.: Prentice-Hall.

KIVISTO, P. (1990). Ethnicity and the problem of generations in American history. In P. Kivisto & D. Blanck (Eds.), *American immigrants and their generations* (pp. 1–10). Urbana: University of Illinois Press.

KLEG, M. (1993). *Hate, prejudice and racism.* New York: State University of New York Press.

OGAWA, D. (1978). *Kodomo no tame ni.* Honolulu: University of Hawaii Press.

PAISANO, E. L. (1995). The American Indian, Eskimo, and Aleut population. *Population Profile of the United States, Current Population Reports,* (pp. 50–51). P23–189.

RAMOS, G. (1995). "Homework" we should tolerate. *Los Angeles Times,* December 11, p. B3.

SCHRAG, P. (1971). *The decline of the WASP.* New York: Simon & Schuster.

SKELTON, G. (1990). Americans give high marks to quality of life. *Los Angeles Times,* January 1, p. A1.

SOWELL, T. (1981). *Ethnic America.* New York: Basic Books.

STEINBERG, S. (1989). *The ethnic myth: Race, ethnicity, and class in America* (2nd ed.). New York: Atheneum.

TUMIN, M. (1953). Some principles of stratification: A critical analysis. *American Sociological Review, 18,* 387–394.

VAN DEN BERGHE, P. (1967). *Race and racism.* New York: John Wiley.

WILSON, W. J. (1978). *The declining significance of race.* Chicago: University of Chicago Press.

Photo Acknowledgments

Page 3: William H. Rau/Library of Congress.   *Page 5:* AP/Wide World Photos.   *Page 22:* Judy S. Gelles/Stock Boston.   *Page 32:* Bill Aron/PhotoEdit. *Page 41:* Stephanie Maze/Woodfin Camp & Associates   *Page 50:* Chrysler Corporation.   *Page 56:* Lewis Hine/Library of Congress.   *Page 63:* Amy C. Etra/PhotoEdit.   *Page 73:* David Rae Morris/Impact Visuals Photo & Graphics, Inc.   *Page 81:* Lionel Delevingne/Stock Boston.   *Page 95:* Ted Soqui/Impact Visuals Photo & Graphics, Inc.   *Page 100:* Richard Ellis/AFP/Corbis-Bettmann.   *Page 107:* Ron Chapple/FPG International.   *Page 115:* Elena Rooraid/PhotoEdit.   *Page 123:* AP/Wide World Photos.   *Page 139:* Gary Hershorn/Reuters/Corbis-Bettmann.   *Page 156:* UPI/Corbis-Bettmann.   *Page 164:* Rene Burri/Mag-num Photo, Inc.   *Page 173:* Lee Snider/The Image Works.   *Page 182:* Alan Diaz/AP/Wide World Photos. *Page 189:* Robert Lindneux, "Trail of Tears", from the original painting in Woolaroc Museum, Bartesville, Oklahoma/Corbis-Bettmann.   *Page 205:* AP/Wide World Photos.   *Page 218:* Corbis-Bettmann.   *Page 223:* Fred Prouser/Reuters/Corbis-Bettmann. *Page 236:* David Young-Wolff/PhotoEdit *Page 239:* UPI/Corbis-Bettmann.   *Page 253:* UPI/Corbis-Bettmann.   *Page 259:* A. Ramey/Woodfin Camp & Associates. *Page 274:* Margot Granitsas/Photo Researchers, Inc.   *Page 281:* Sylvaine Conord/Impact Visuals Photo & Graphics, Inc.   *Page 291:* UPI/Corbis-Bettmann.   *Page 301:* Suzanne L. Murphy/FPG International.   *Page 319:* Jeff Kowalsky/AP/Wide World Photos.

AUTHOR INDEX

SUBJECT INDEX